THE AUTHORITY

UNDER NEW MANAGEMENT

"Outer Dark"

Warren Ellis - writer **Bryan Hitch** - penciler

Paul Neary - inker **Laura DePuy** - colorist

Ryan Cline with Robbie Robbins (for Idea + Design Works) -- letterers

"The Nativity"

Mark Millar - writer **Frank Quitely** - penciler

Trevor Scott

with **Scott Williams and Mark Irwin** - inkers

David Baron - colorist

Ryan Cline with Bill O'Neil - letterers

Cover by Frank Quitely, Trevor Scott and David Baron

Original series editors

Rachelle Brissenden and John Layman

Collected edition editor

John Layman

Collected edition design

Larry Berry

The Authority created by

Warren Ellis and Bryan Hitch

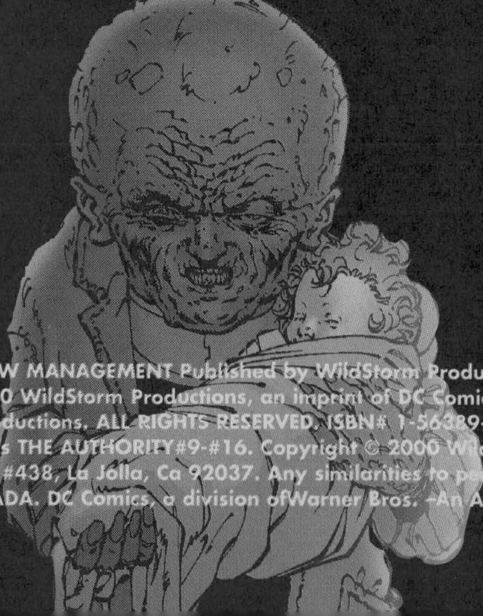

THE AUTHORITY: UNDER NEW MANAGEMENT Published by WildStorm Productions. Second Printing.
THE AUTHORITY is ™ and © 2000 WildStorm Productions, an imprint of DC Comics. Cover, design pages and
compilation © 2000 WildStorm Productions. ALL RIGHTS RESERVED. ISBN# 1-56389-756-3. Originally published in
single magazine form as THE AUTHORITY #9-#16. Copyright © 2000 WildStorm Productions.
Editorial offices: 7910 Ivanhoe St., #438, La Jolla, Ca 92037. Any similarities to persons living or dead are purely
coincidental. PRINTED IN CANADA. DC Comics, a division of Warner Bros. –An AOL Time Warner Company

For Niki and Lili, who put up with me laughing to myself all day as I killed God, and for Mike Heisler, who put me on the route from STORMWATCH to here.

– Warren Ellis

To Paul, Laura and Warren, because this is more than one person's work.

– Bryan Hitch

MARK MILLAR would like to dedicate this collection to Gill and Emily, for loving him, John and Scott, for putting up with him, and to Jim McLaughlin, Randy Lander, Don McPherson, Mike Doran, Beau Yarborough, Dez Skinn, Rich Johnston, Keravin, Wonk, Skyman, Wesman, Tezcat, Negativity, His Majesty and all his pals on the WildStorm Boards for creating a buzz on this book unlike anything he's ever experienced.

– Mark Millar

For Ann Jane, Vin, and Joe.

– Frank Quitely

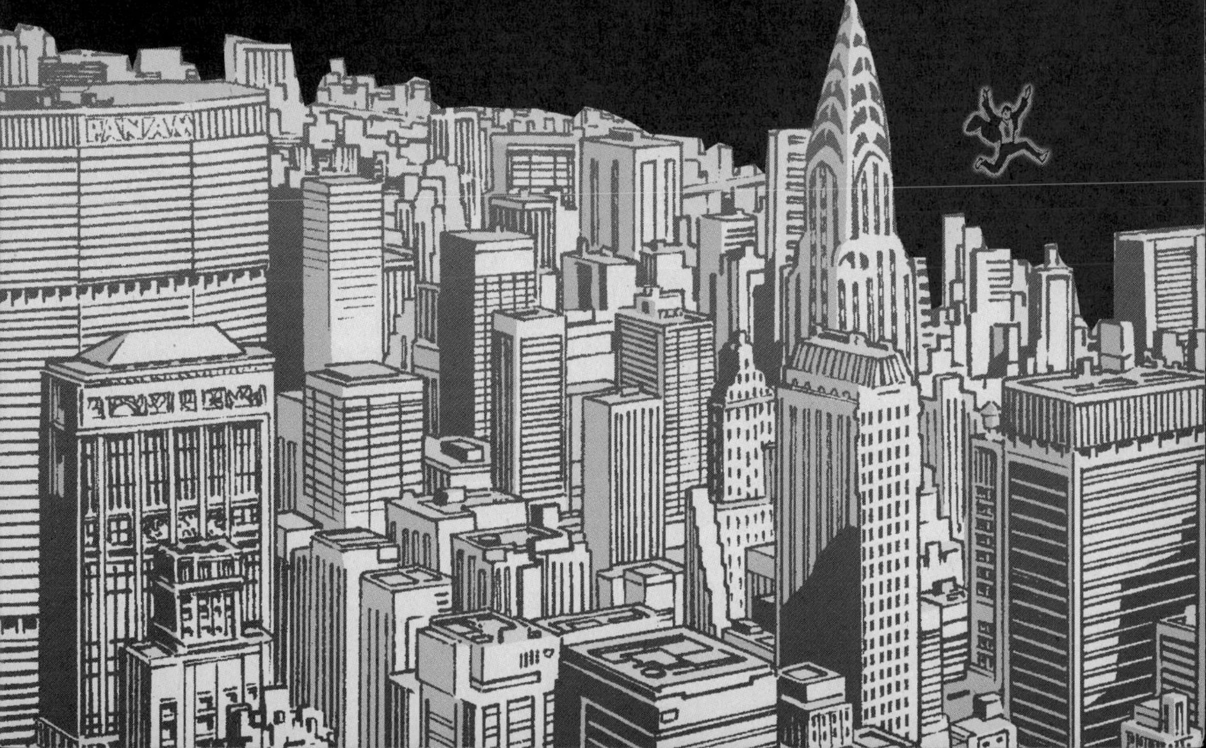
PANAM

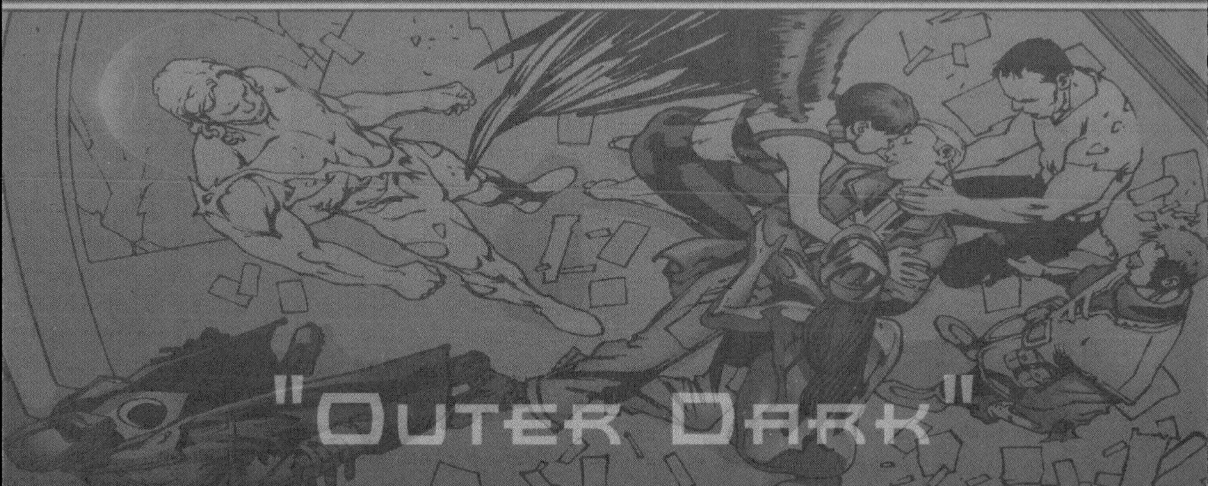
"Outer Dark"

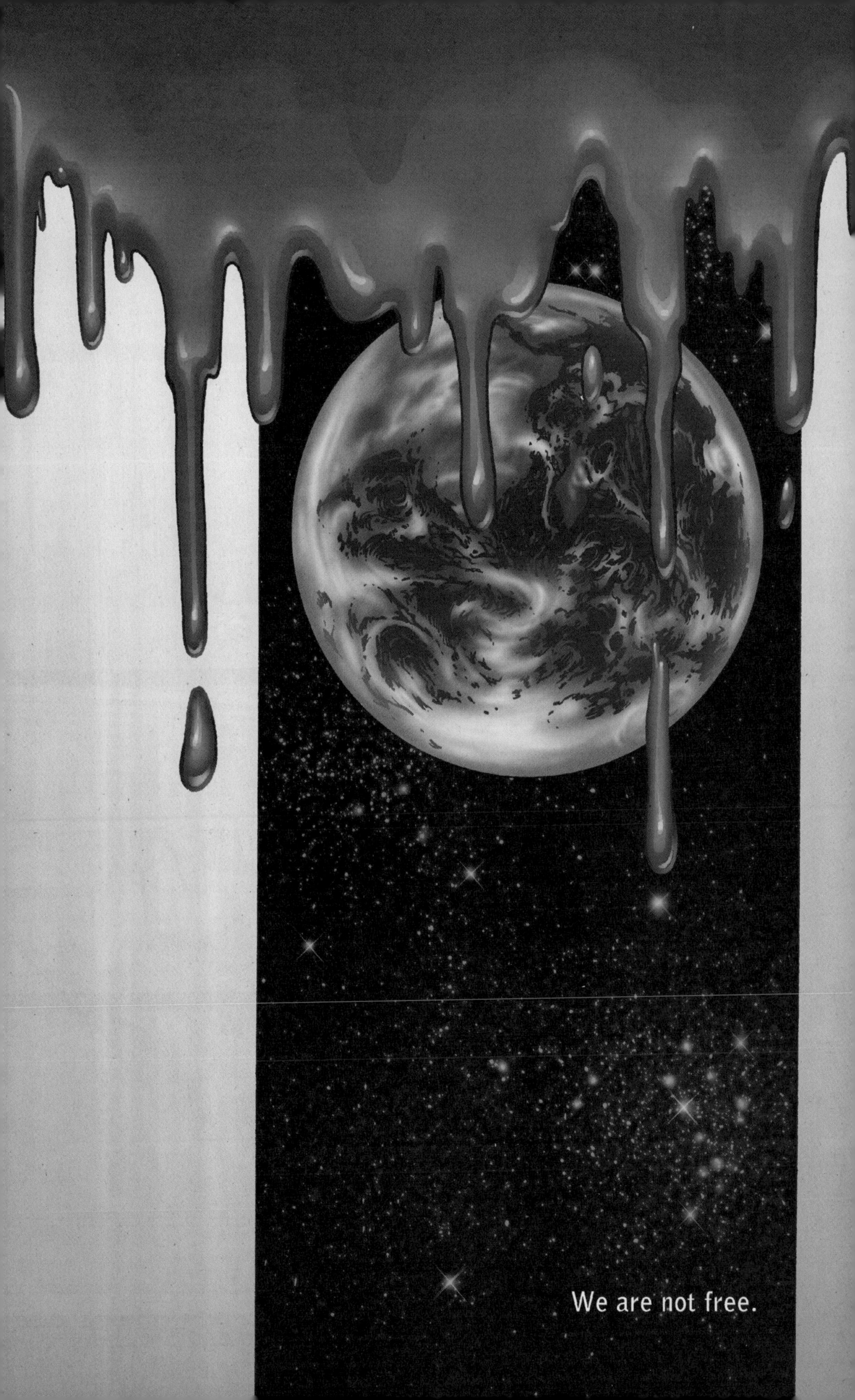
We are not free.

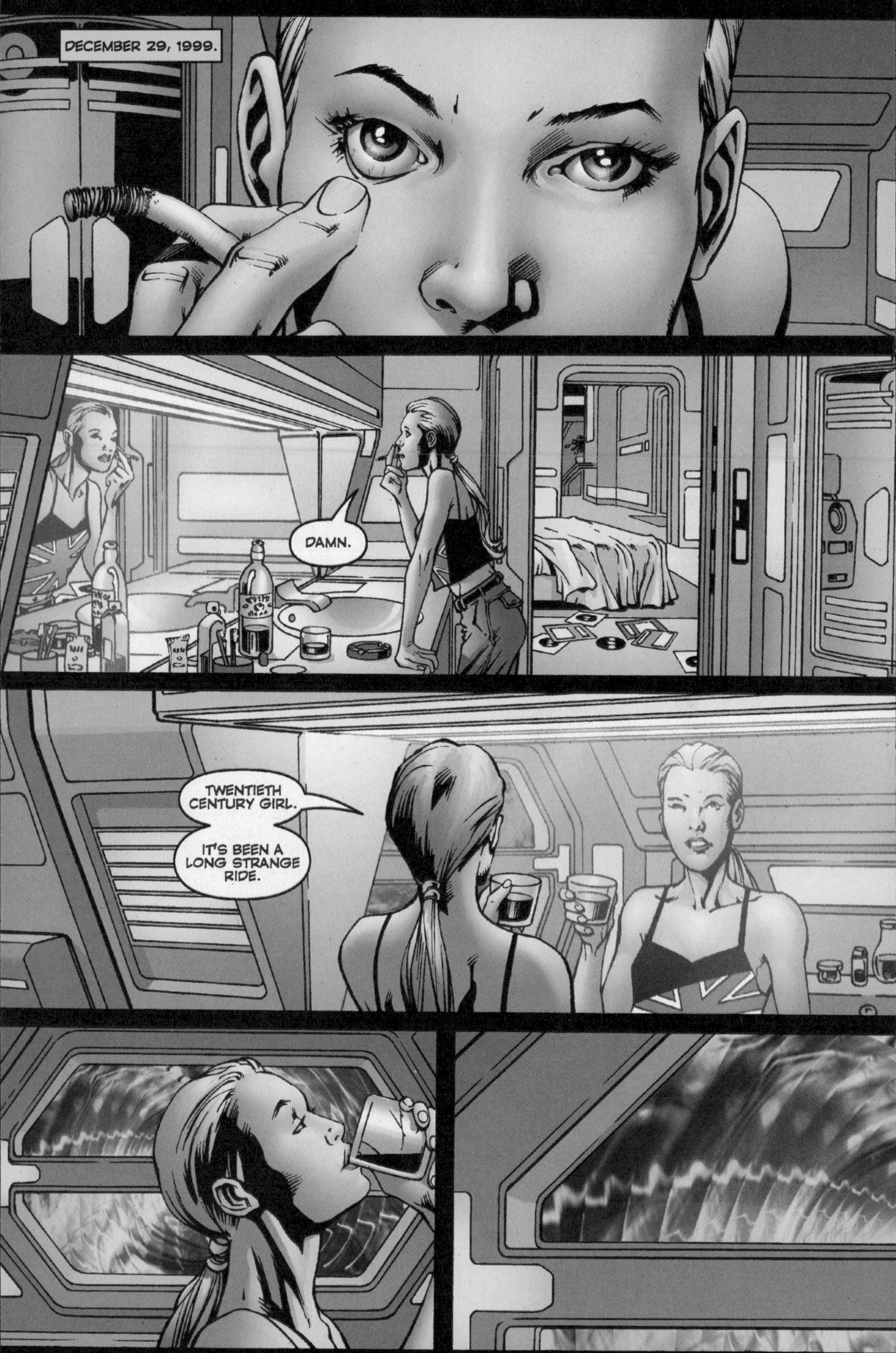
DECEMBER 29, 1999.
DAMN.
TWENTIETH CENTURY GIRL.
IT'S BEEN A LONG STRANGE RIDE.

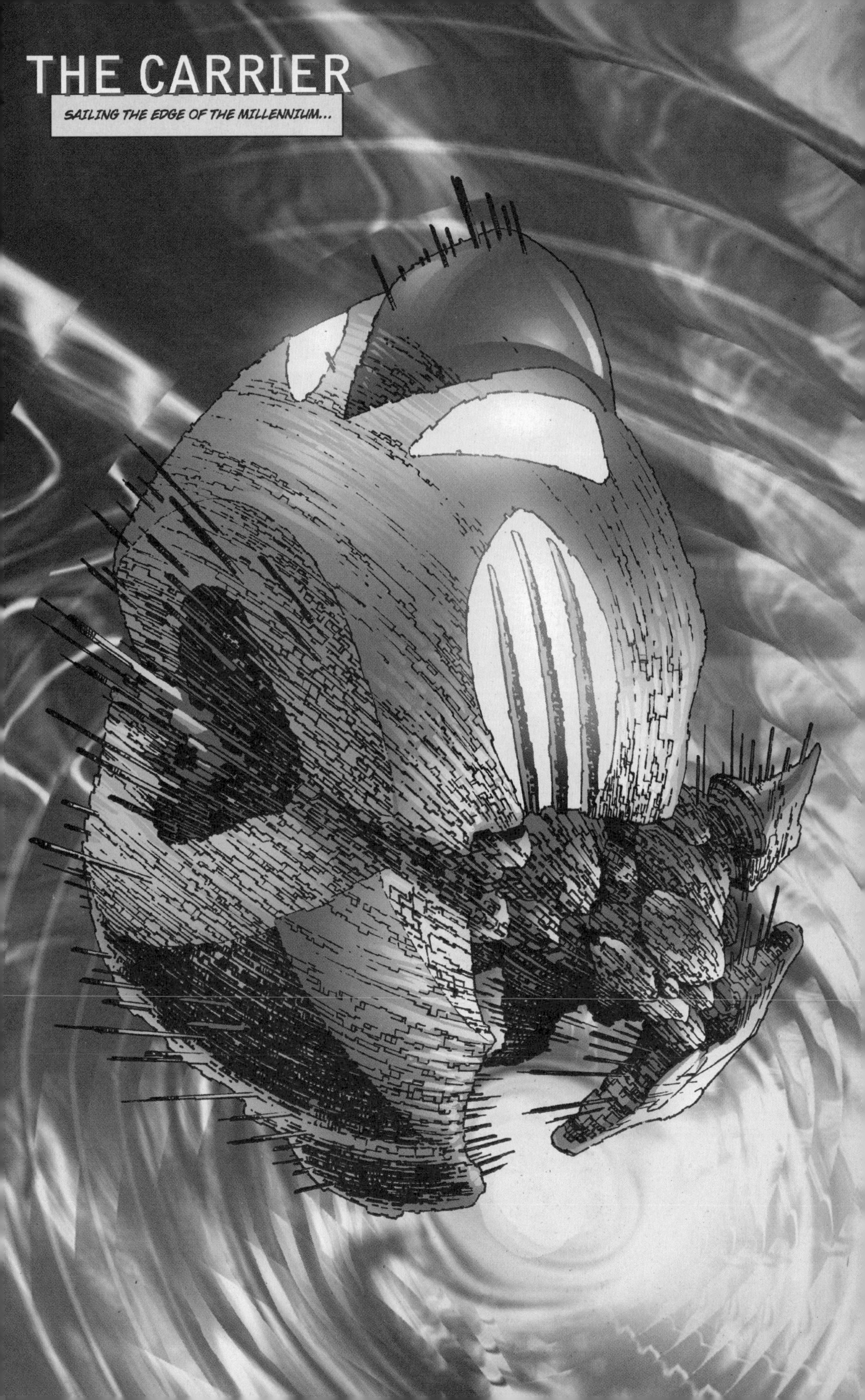
THE CARRIER
SAILING THE EDGE OF THE MILLENNIUM...

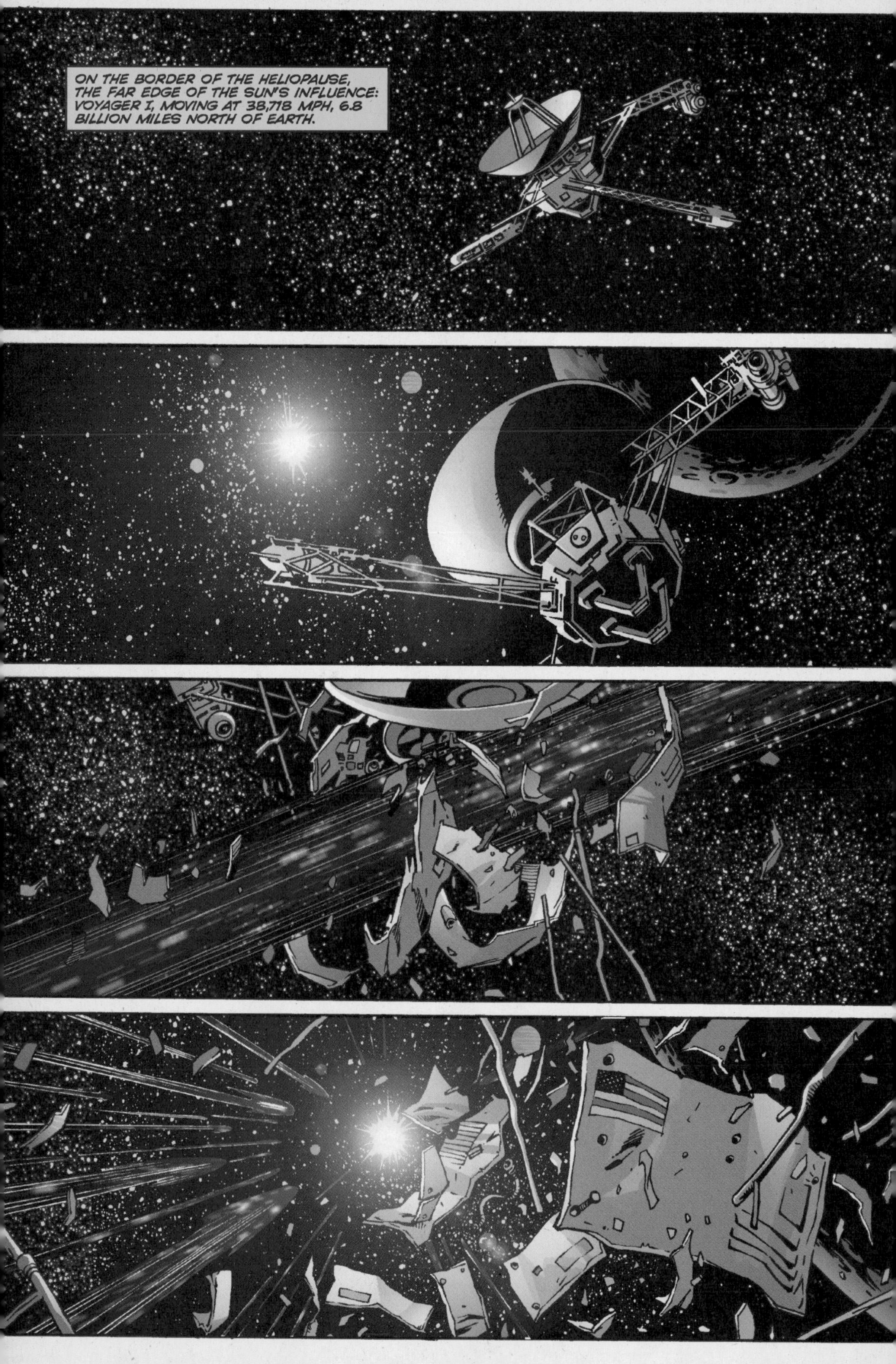
ON THE BORDER OF THE HELIOPAUSE, THE FAR EDGE OF THE SUN'S INFLUENCE: VOYAGER I, MOVING AT 38,718 MPH, 6.8 BILLION MILES NORTH OF EARTH.

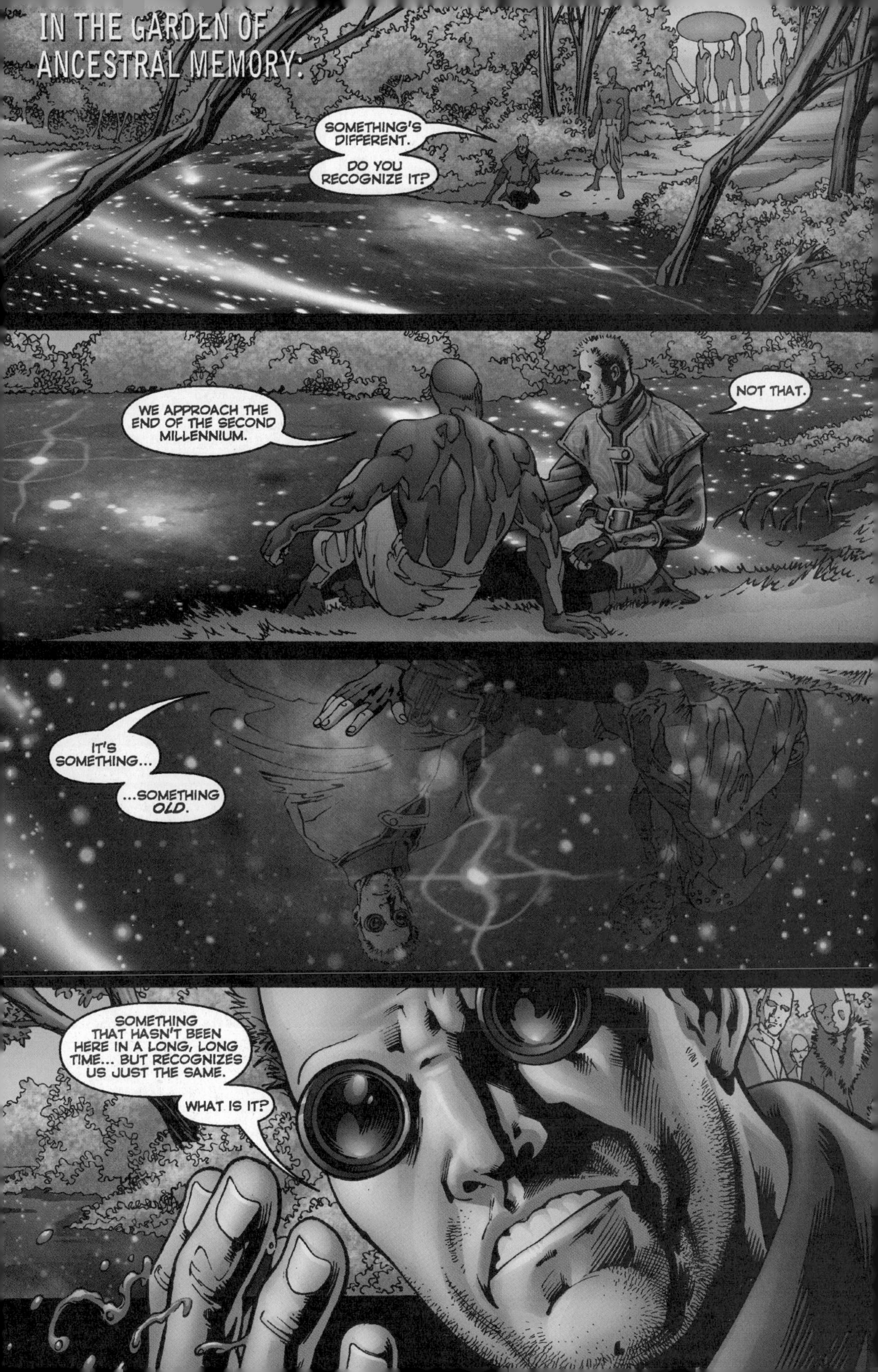
IN THE GARDEN OF ANCESTRAL MEMORY:
SOMETHING'S DIFFERENT.
DO YOU RECOGNIZE IT?
WE APPROACH THE END OF THE SECOND MILLENNIUM.
NOT THAT.
IT'S SOMETHING...
...SOMETHING *OLD*.
SOMETHING THAT HASN'T BEEN HERE IN A LONG, LONG TIME... BUT RECOGNIZES US JUST THE SAME.
WHAT IS IT?

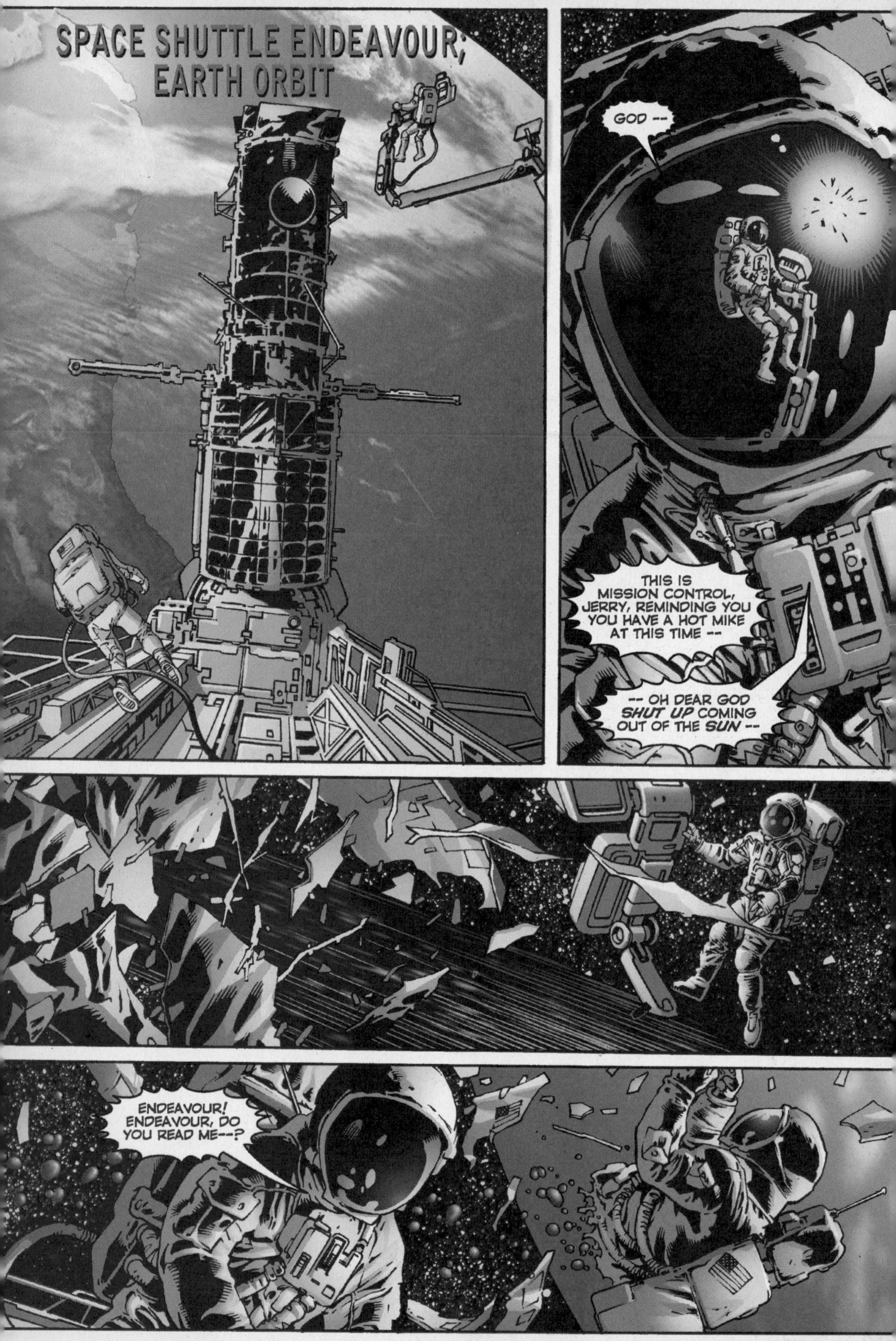
SPACE SHUTTLE ENDEAVOUR; EARTH ORBIT
GOD --
THIS IS MISSION CONTROL, JERRY, REMINDING YOU YOU HAVE A HOT MIKE AT THIS TIME --
-- OH DEAR GOD SHUT UP COMING OUT OF THE SUN --
ENDEAVOUR! ENDEAVOUR, DO YOU READ ME--?

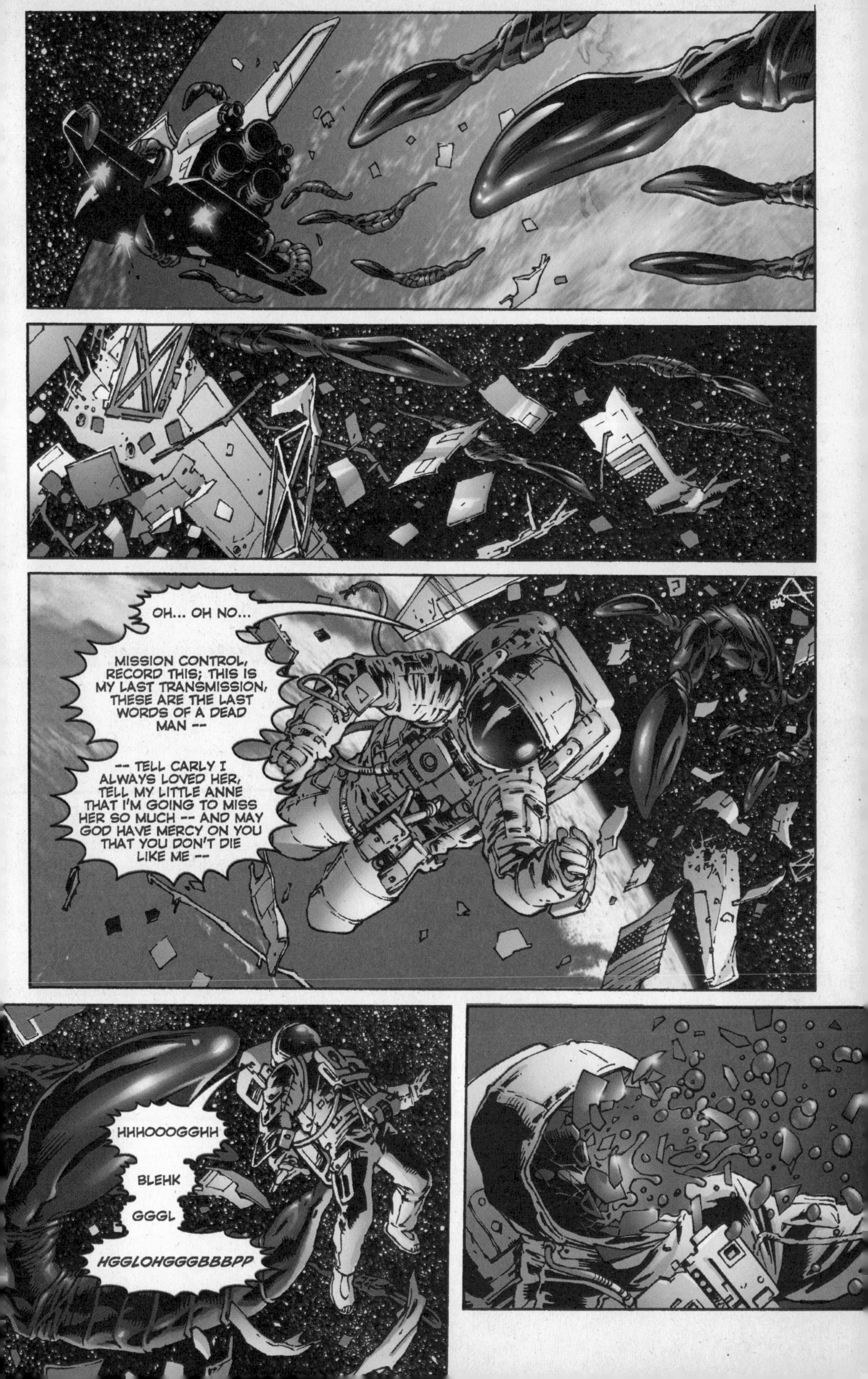
OH... OH NO...
MISSION CONTROL, RECORD THIS; THIS IS MY LAST TRANSMISSION, THESE ARE THE LAST WORDS OF A DEAD MAN --
-- TELL CARLY I ALWAYS LOVED HER, TELL MY LITTLE ANNE THAT I'M GOING TO MISS HER SO MUCH -- AND MAY GOD HAVE MERCY ON YOU THAT YOU DON'T DIE LIKE ME --
HHHOOOGGHH
BLEHK
GGGL
HGGLOHGGGBBBPP

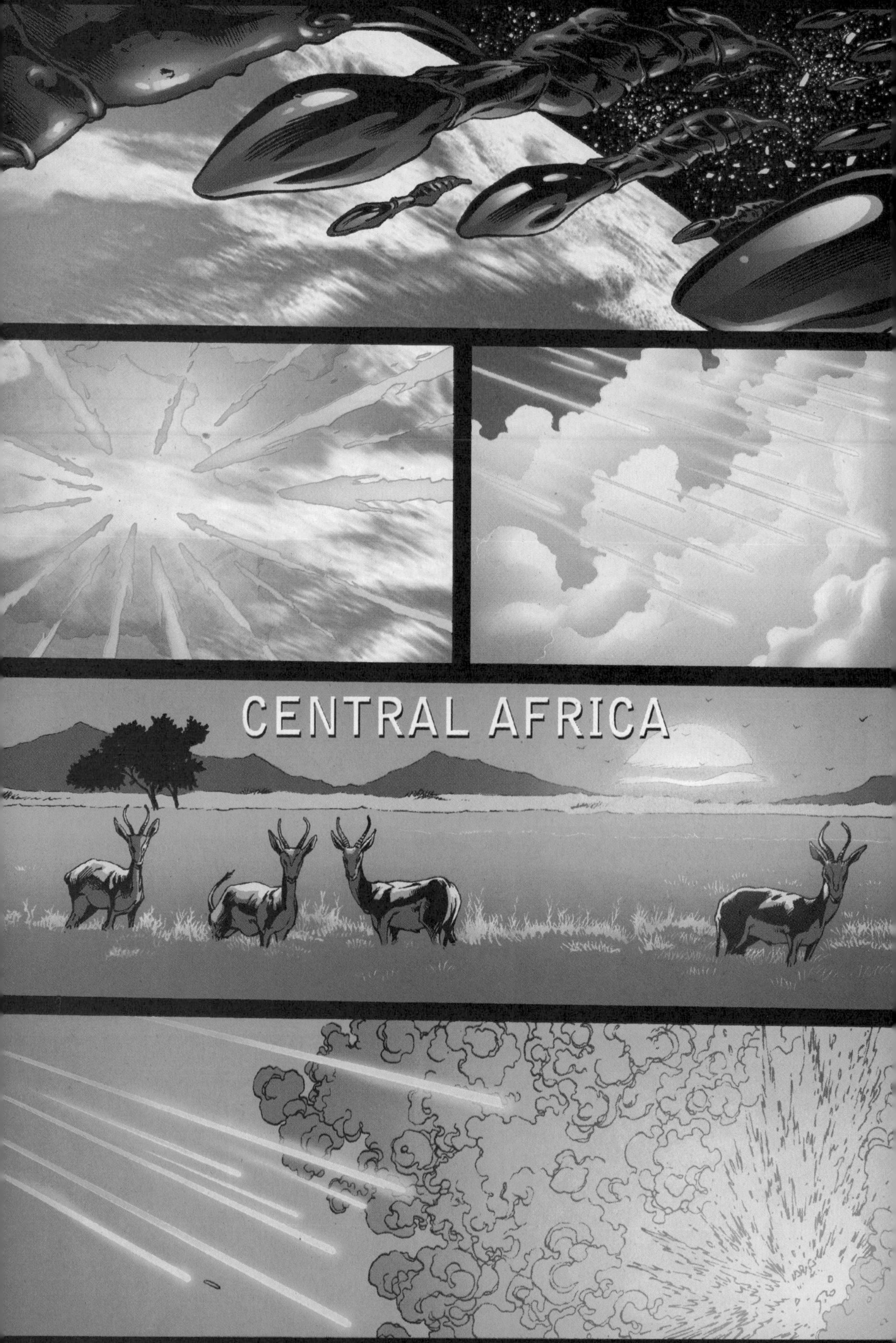
CENTRAL AFRICA

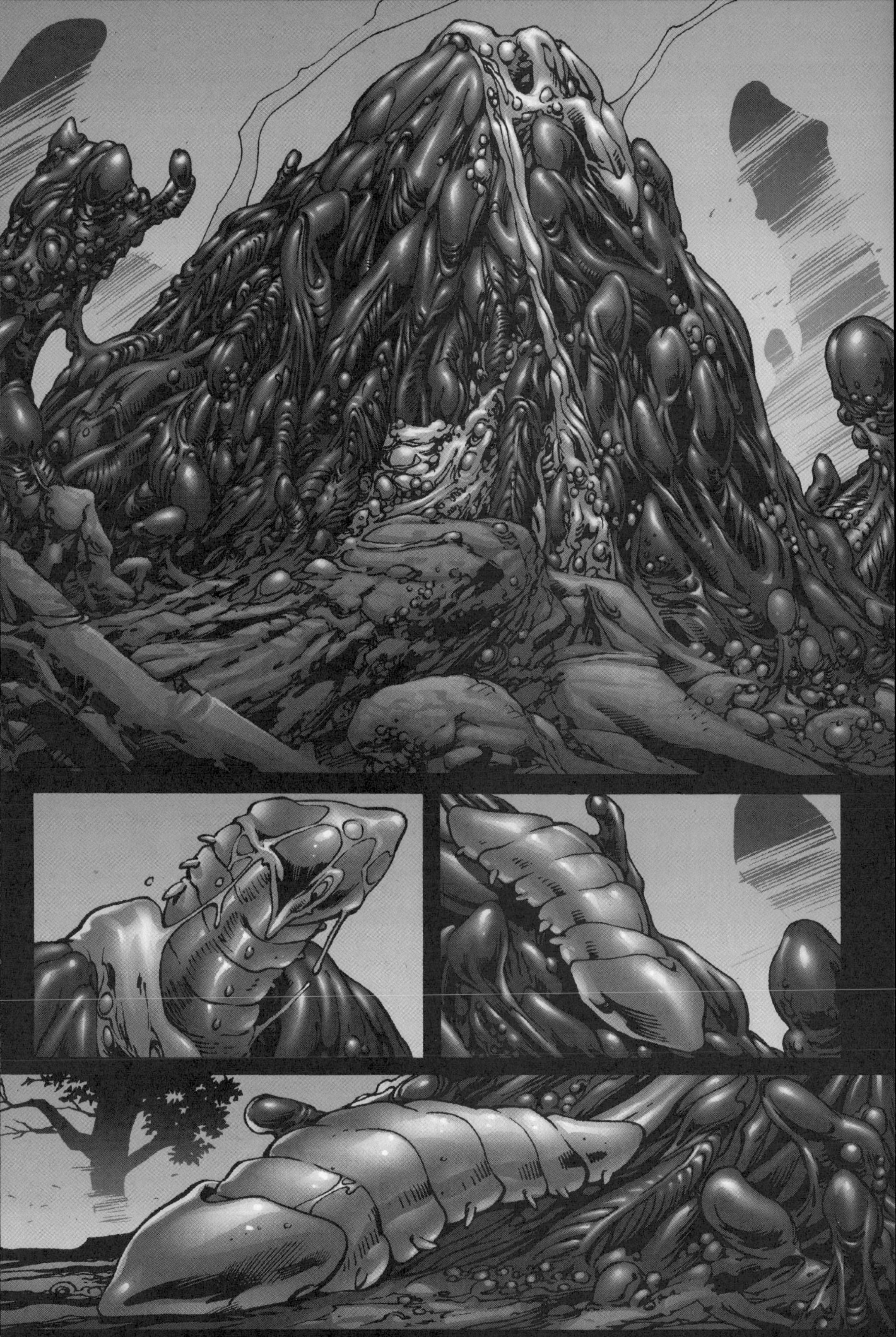

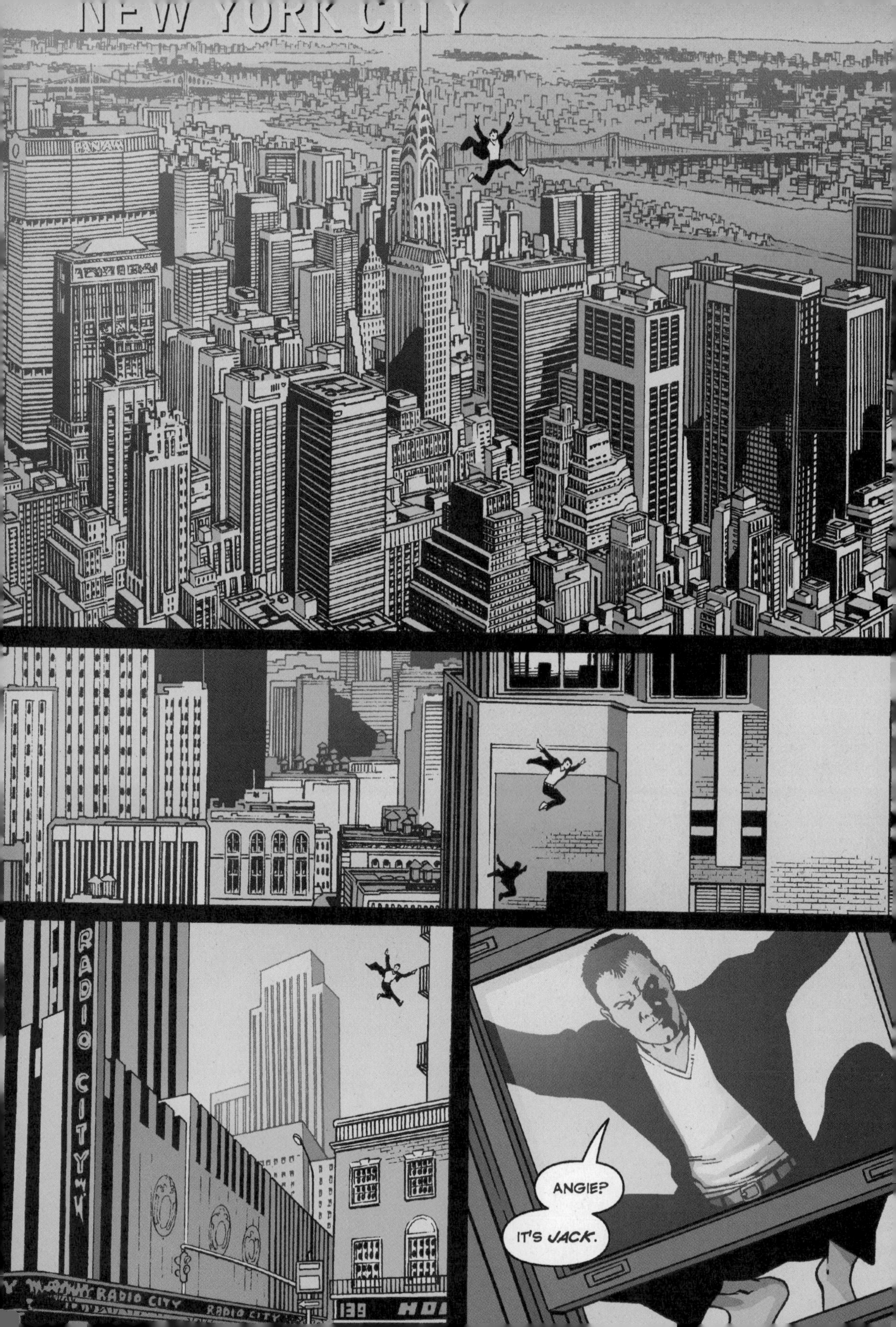
NEW YORK CITY
PANAM
RADIO CITY
RADIO CITY
RADIO CITY
139
ANGIE?
IT'S JACK.

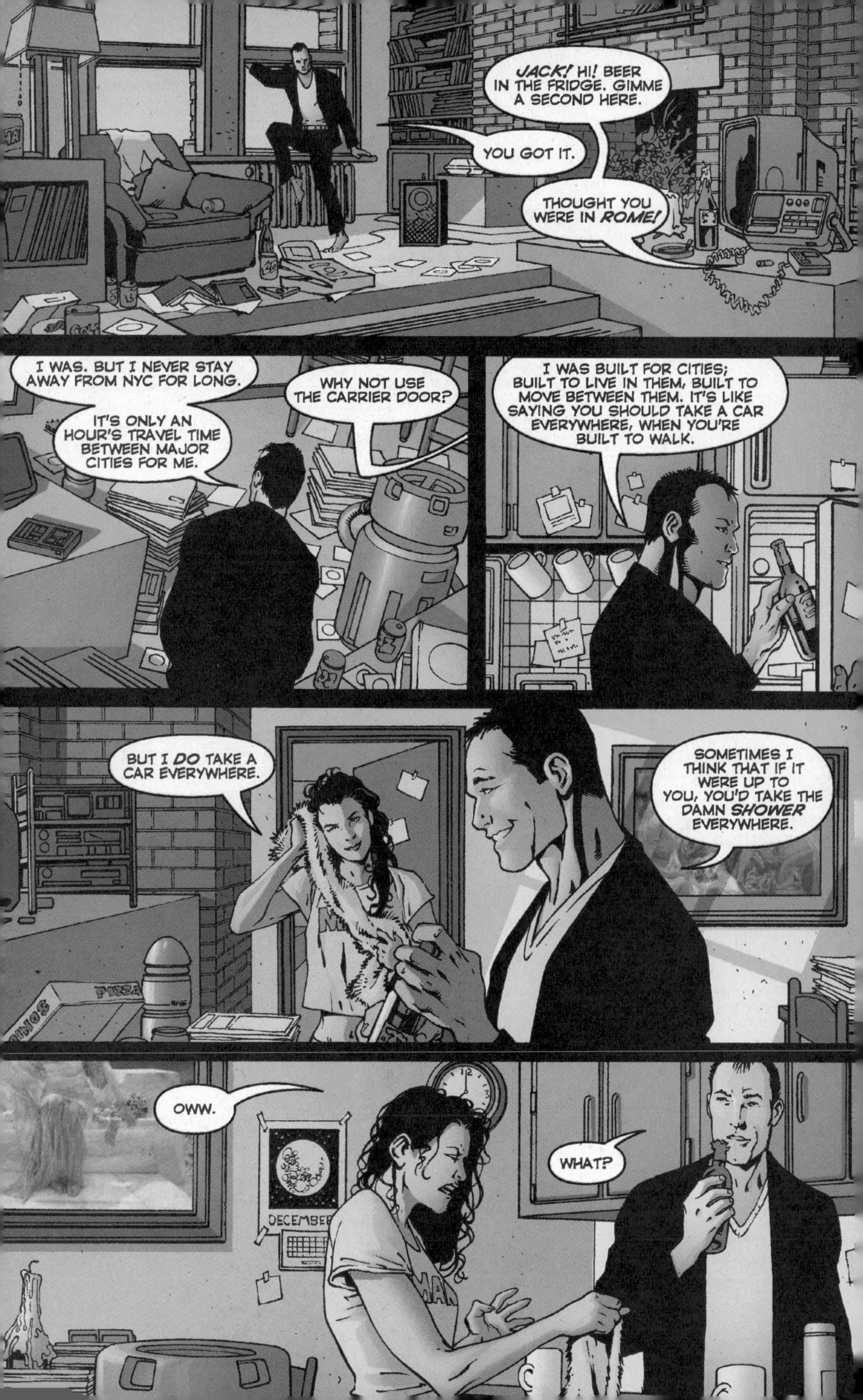
JACK! HI! BEER IN THE FRIDGE. GIMME A SECOND HERE.
YOU GOT IT.
THOUGHT YOU WERE IN ROME!
I WAS. BUT I NEVER STAY AWAY FROM NYC FOR LONG.
IT'S ONLY AN HOUR'S TRAVEL TIME BETWEEN MAJOR CITIES FOR ME.
WHY NOT USE THE CARRIER DOOR?
I WAS BUILT FOR CITIES; BUILT TO LIVE IN THEM, BUILT TO MOVE BETWEEN THEM. IT'S LIKE SAYING YOU SHOULD TAKE A CAR EVERYWHERE, WHEN YOU'RE BUILT TO WALK.
BUT I DO TAKE A CAR EVERYWHERE.
SOMETIMES I THINK THAT IF IT WERE UP TO YOU, YOU'D TAKE THE DAMN SHOWER EVERYWHERE.
OWW.
WHAT?

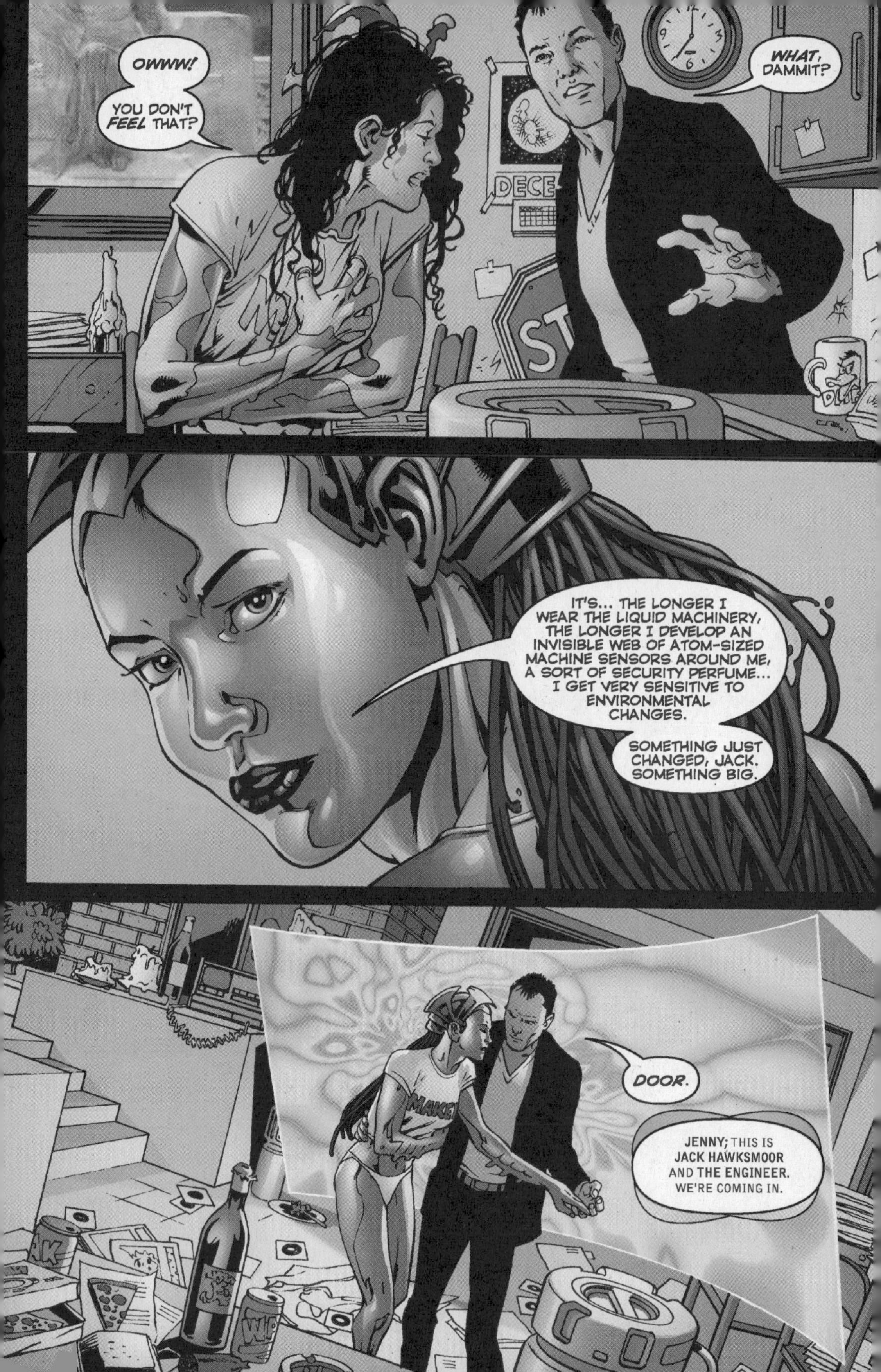
OWWW!
YOU DON'T FEEL THAT?
WHAT, DAMMIT?
DECE
ST
IT'S... THE LONGER I WEAR THE LIQUID MACHINERY, THE LONGER I DEVELOP AN INVISIBLE WEB OF ATOM-SIZED MACHINE SENSORS AROUND ME, A SORT OF SECURITY PERFUME... I GET VERY SENSITIVE TO ENVIRONMENTAL CHANGES.
SOMETHING JUST CHANGED, JACK. SOMETHING BIG.
DOOR.
JENNY; THIS IS JACK HAWKSMOOR AND THE ENGINEER. WE'RE COMING IN.
MAKE

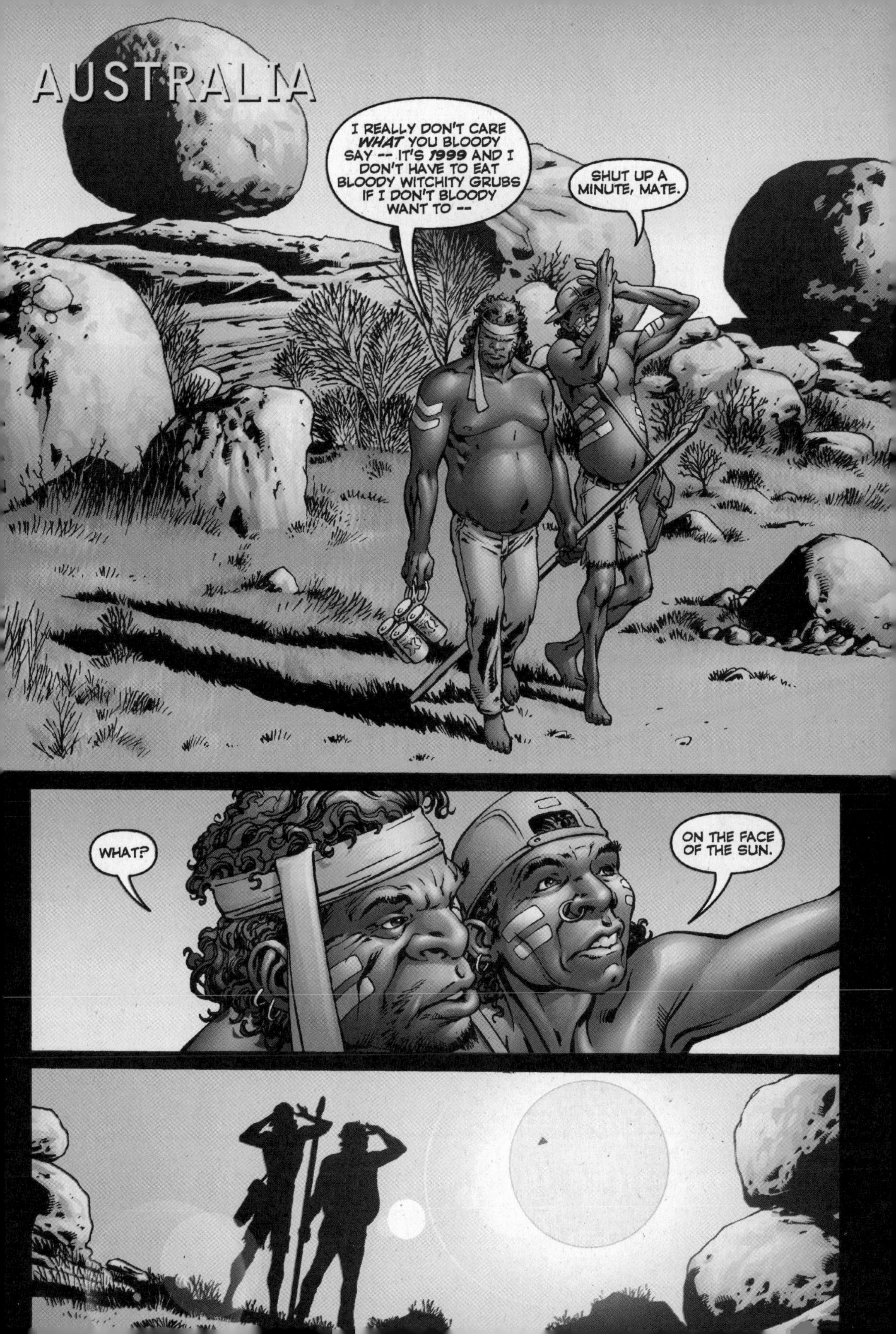
AUSTRALIA
I REALLY DON'T CARE *WHAT* YOU BLOODY SAY -- IT'S *1999* AND I DON'T HAVE TO EAT BLOODY WITCHITY GRUBS IF I DON'T BLOODY WANT TO --
SHUT UP A MINUTE, MATE.
WHAT?
ON THE FACE OF THE SUN.

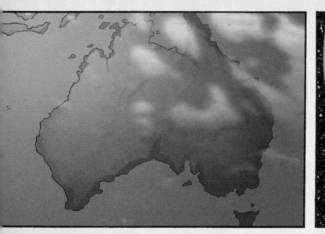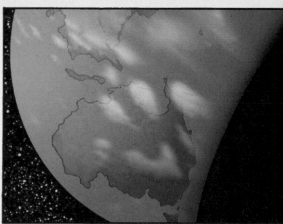

THE MOON

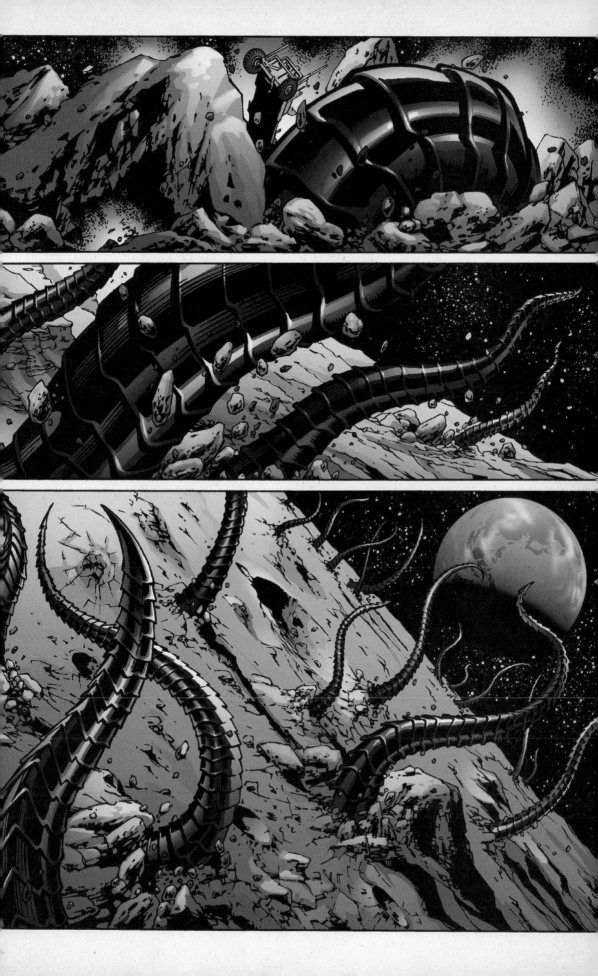

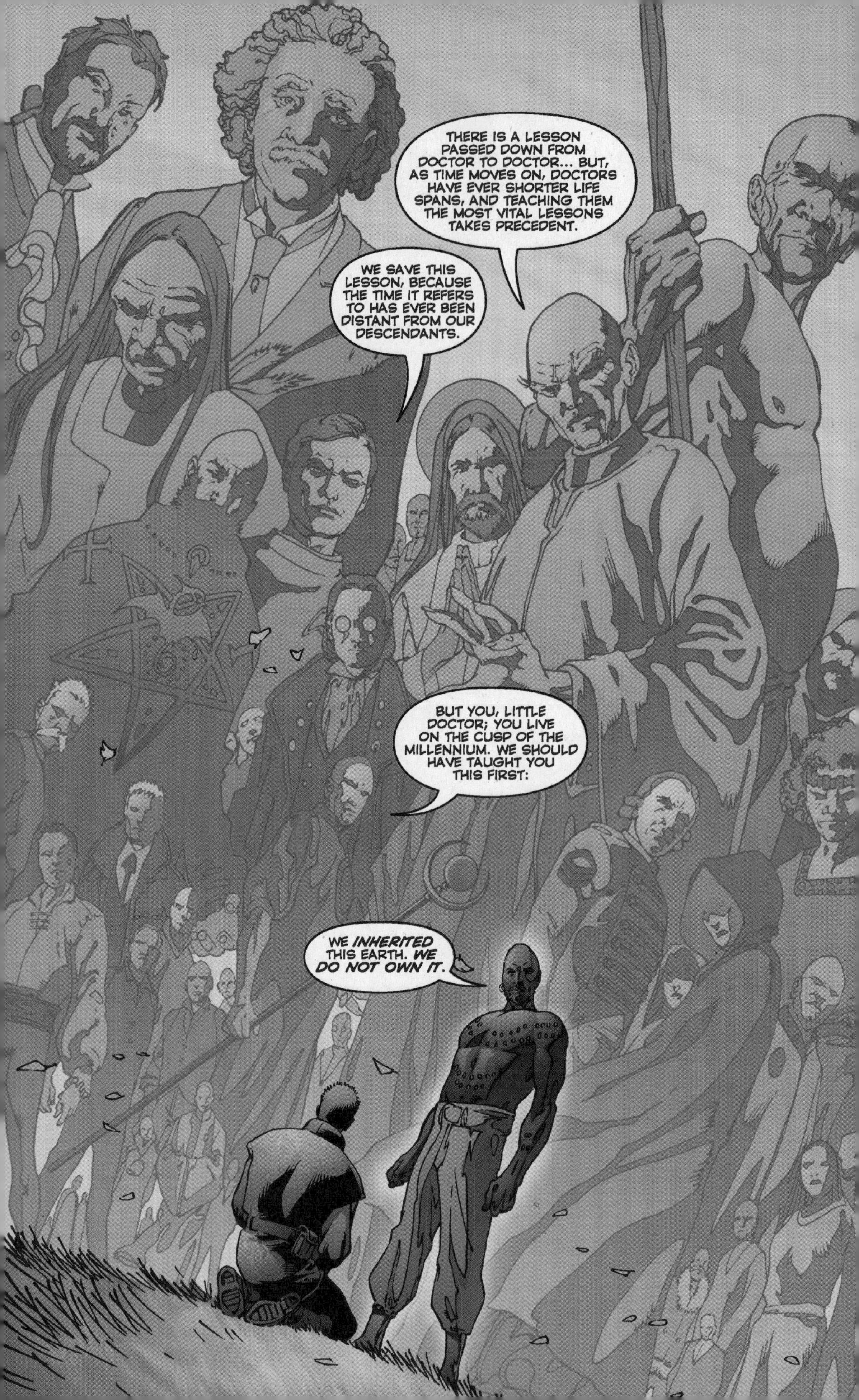
THERE IS A LESSON PASSED DOWN FROM DOCTOR TO DOCTOR... BUT, AS TIME MOVES ON, DOCTORS HAVE EVER SHORTER LIFE SPANS, AND TEACHING THEM THE MOST VITAL LESSONS TAKES PRECEDENT.
WE SAVE THIS LESSON, BECAUSE THE TIME IT REFERS TO HAS EVER BEEN DISTANT FROM OUR DESCENDANTS.
BUT YOU, LITTLE DOCTOR; YOU LIVE ON THE CUSP OF THE MILLENNIUM. WE SHOULD HAVE TAUGHT YOU THIS FIRST:
WE *INHERITED* THIS EARTH. ***WE DO NOT OWN IT.***

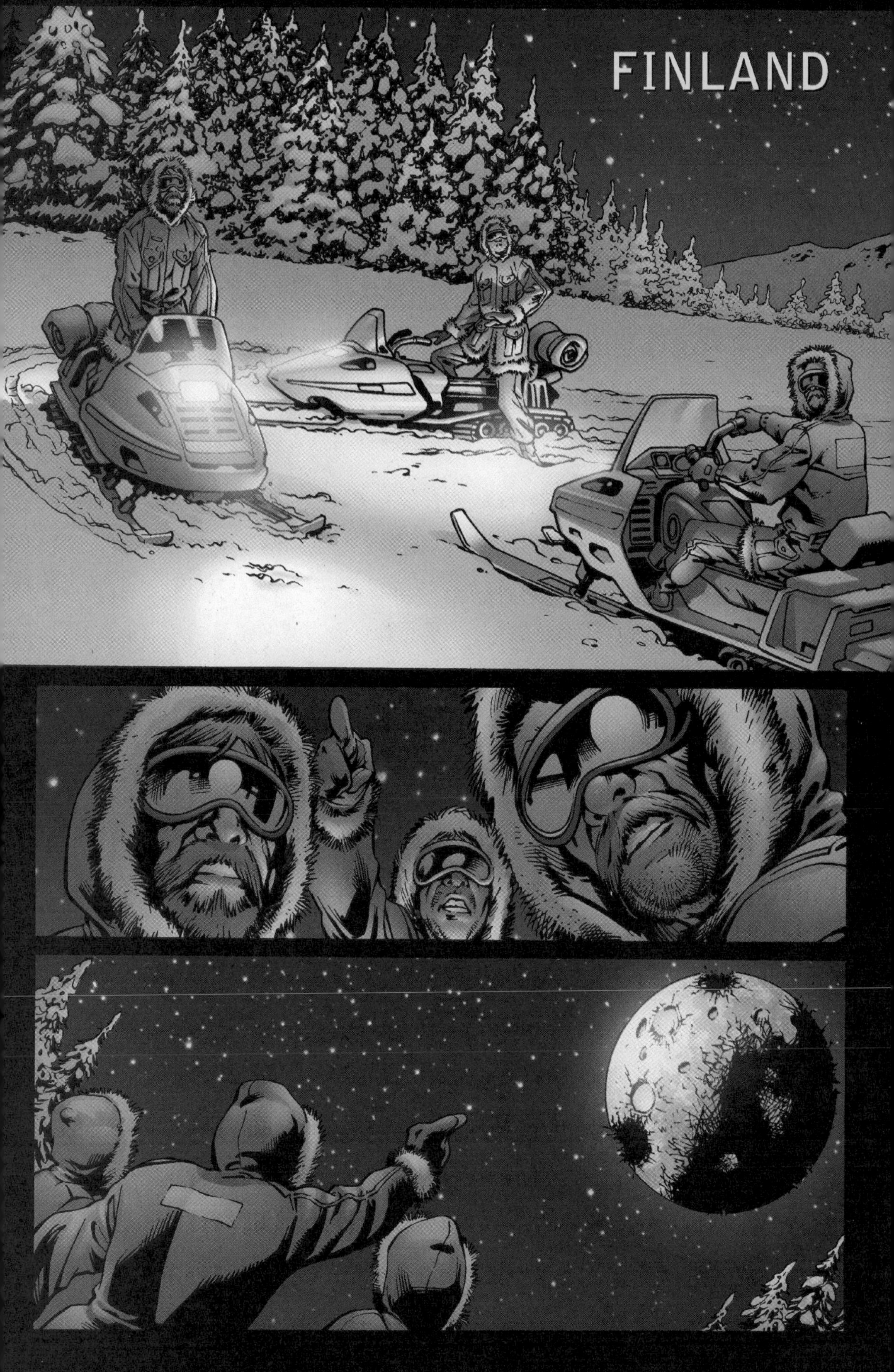
FINLAND

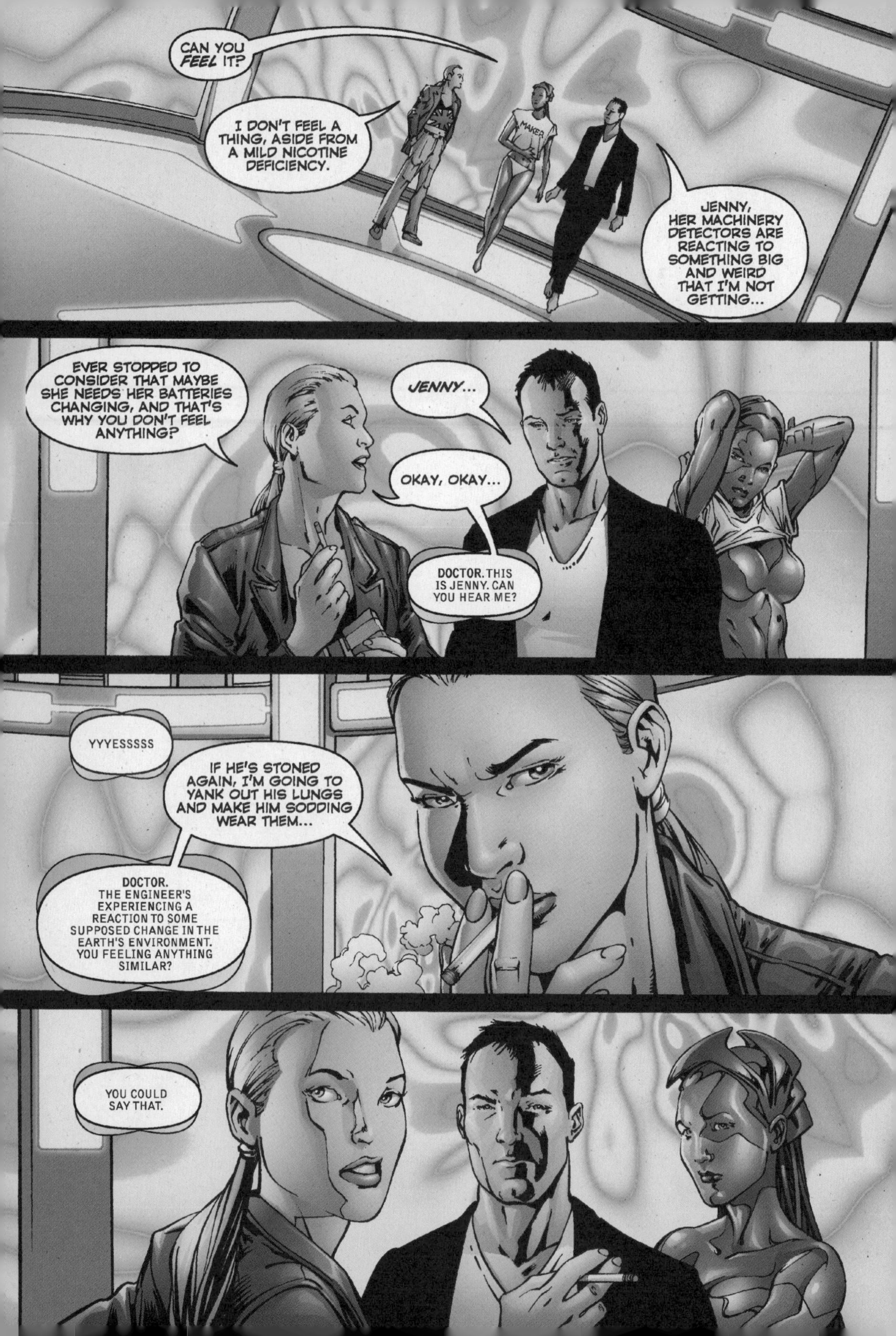
CAN YOU *FEEL* IT?
I DON'T FEEL A THING, ASIDE FROM A MILD NICOTINE DEFICIENCY.
JENNY, HER MACHINERY DETECTORS ARE REACTING TO SOMETHING BIG AND WEIRD THAT I'M NOT GETTING...
MAKER
EVER STOPPED TO CONSIDER THAT MAYBE SHE NEEDS HER BATTERIES CHANGING, AND THAT'S WHY YOU DON'T FEEL ANYTHING?
JENNY...
OKAY, OKAY...
DOCTOR. THIS IS JENNY. CAN YOU HEAR ME?
YYYESSSSS
IF HE'S STONED AGAIN, I'M GOING TO YANK OUT HIS LUNGS AND MAKE HIM SODDING WEAR THEM...
DOCTOR. THE ENGINEER'S EXPERIENCING A REACTION TO SOME SUPPOSED CHANGE IN THE EARTH'S ENVIRONMENT. YOU FEELING ANYTHING SIMILAR?
YOU COULD SAY THAT.

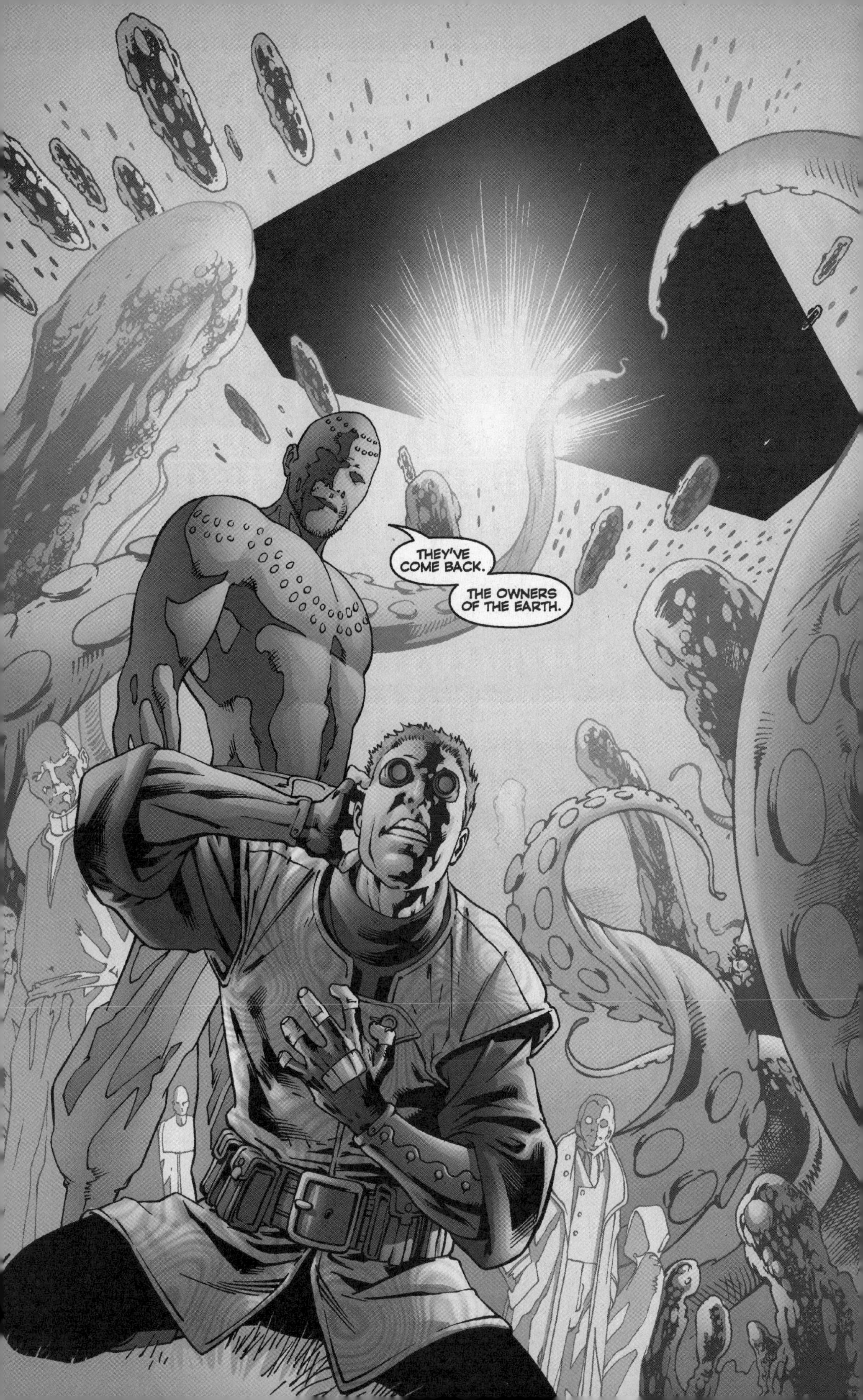
THEY'VE COME BACK.
THE OWNERS OF THE EARTH.

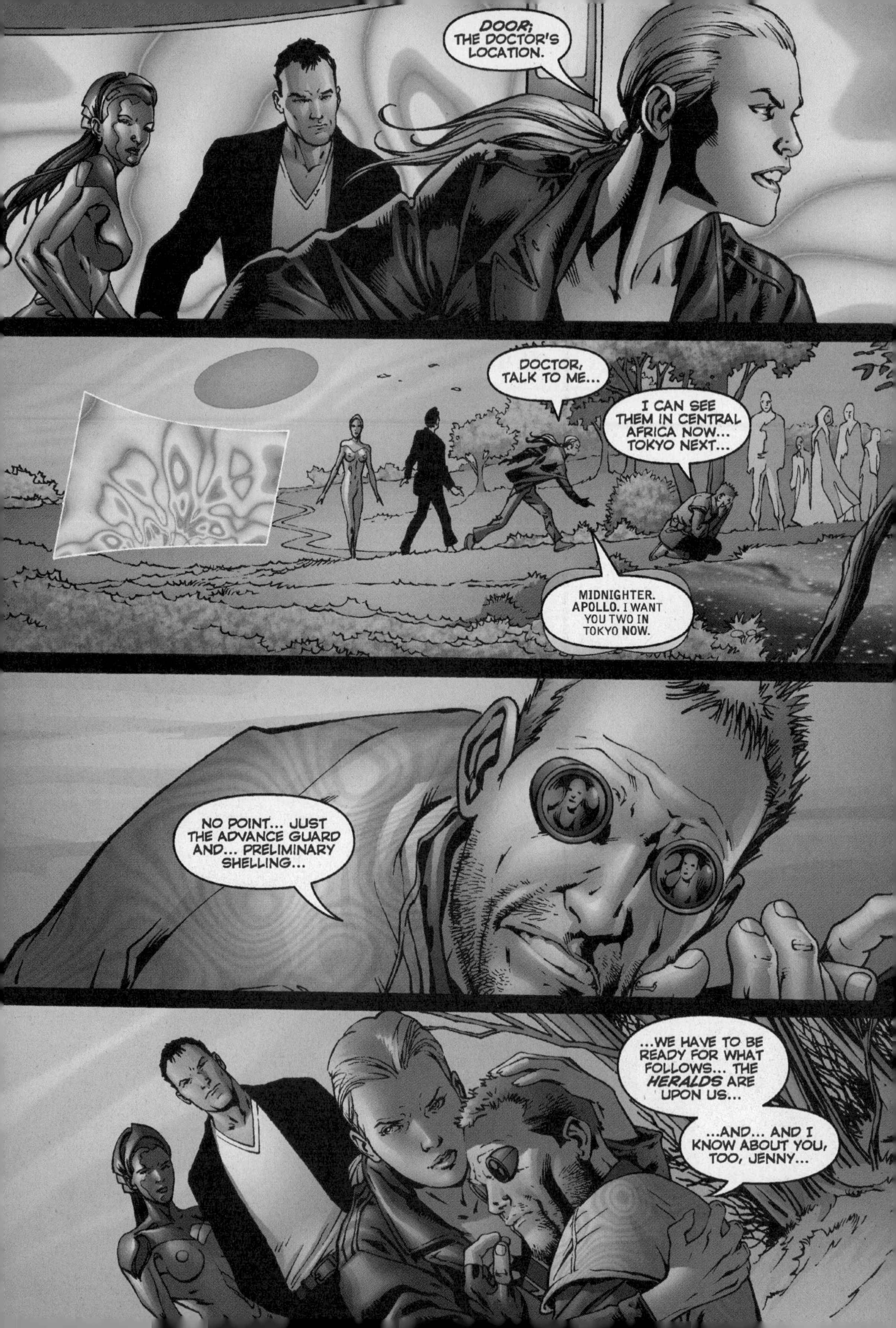
DOOR; THE DOCTOR'S LOCATION.
DOCTOR, TALK TO ME...
I CAN SEE THEM IN CENTRAL AFRICA NOW... TOKYO NEXT...
MIDNIGHTER. APOLLO. I WANT YOU TWO IN TOKYO NOW.
NO POINT... JUST THE ADVANCE GUARD AND... PRELIMINARY SHELLING...
...WE HAVE TO BE READY FOR WHAT FOLLOWS... THE HERALDS ARE UPON US...
...AND... AND I KNOW ABOUT YOU, TOO, JENNY...

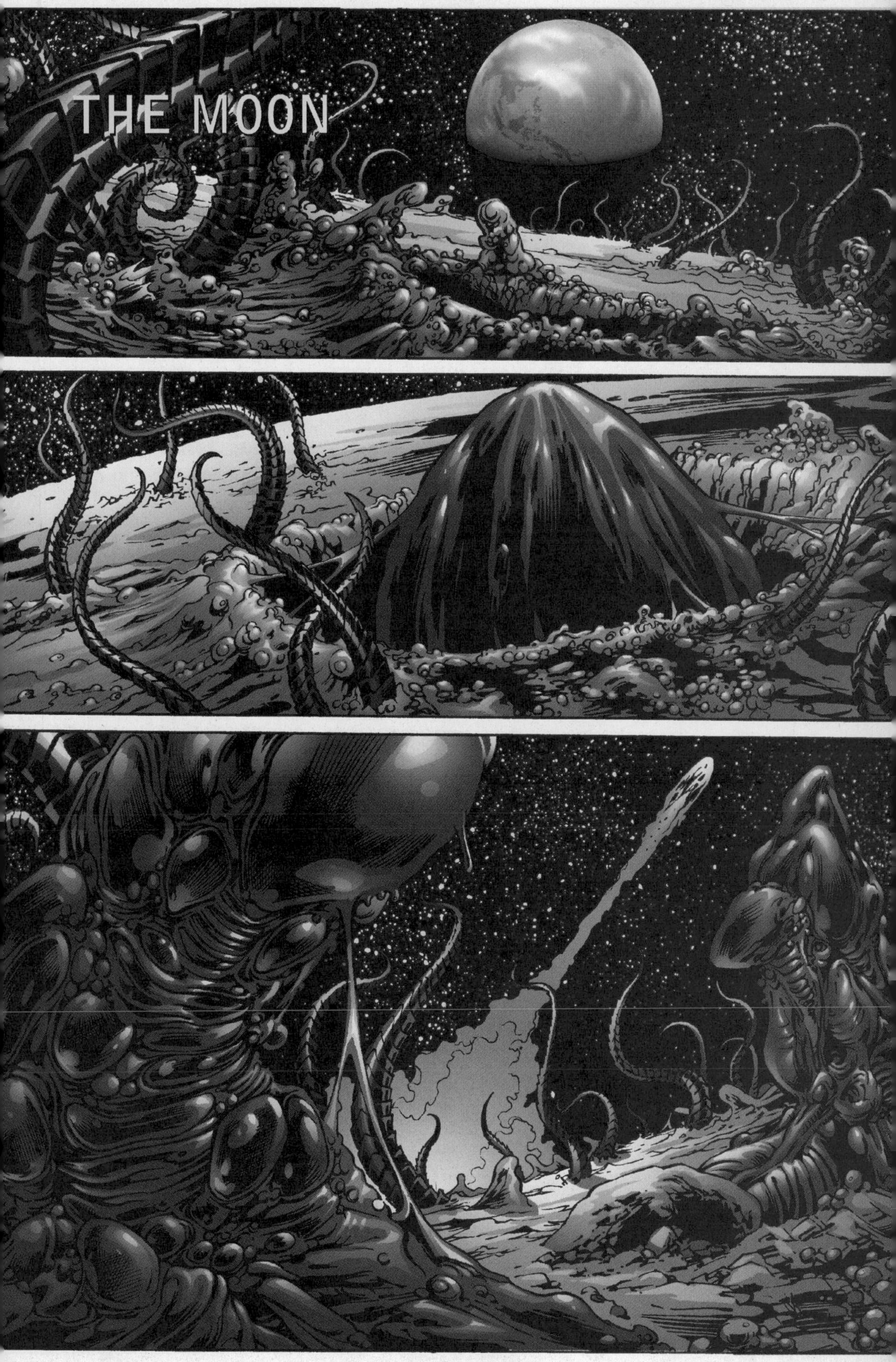
THE MOON

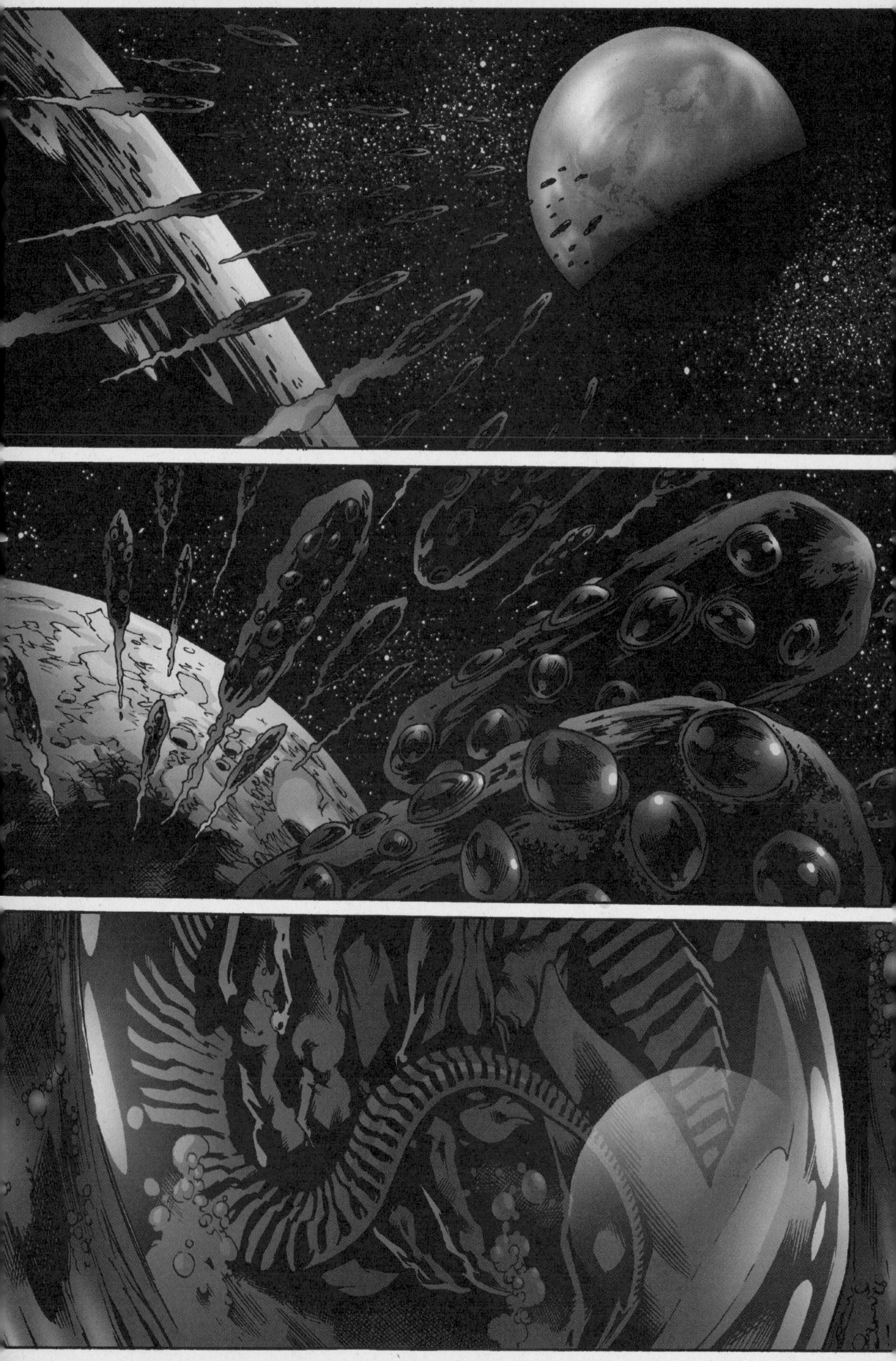

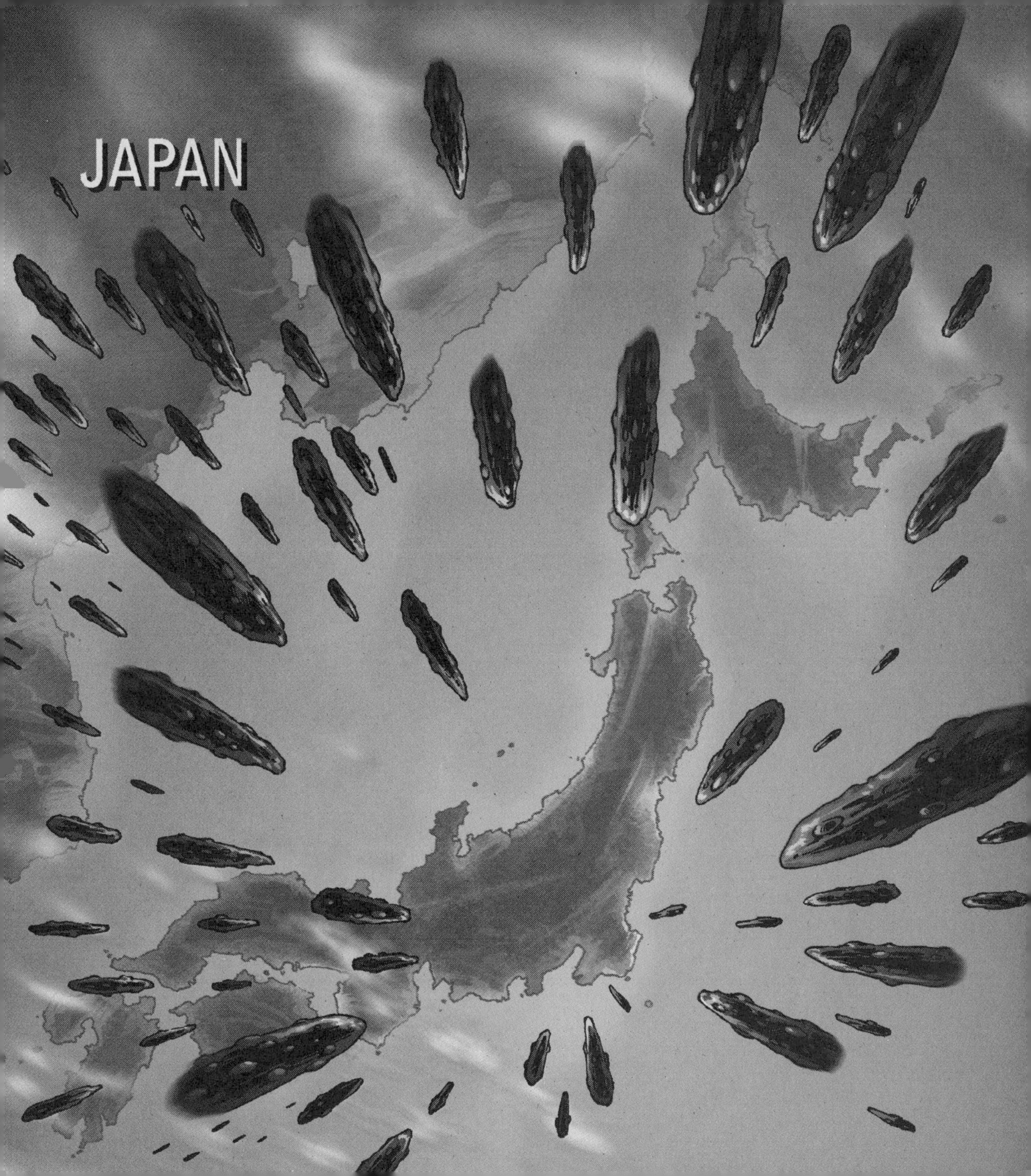
JAPAN

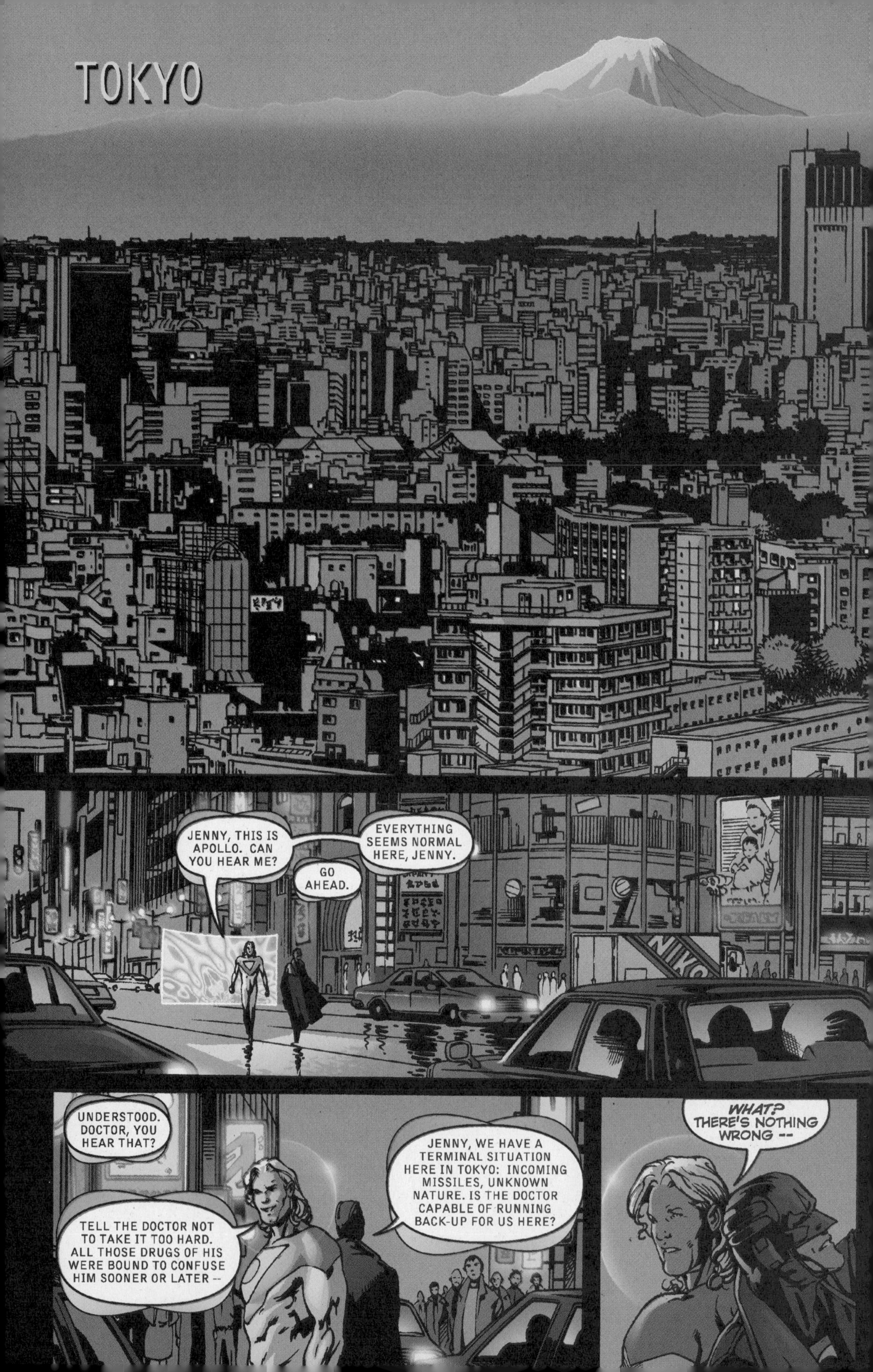
TOKYO
JENNY, THIS IS APOLLO. CAN YOU HEAR ME?
GO AHEAD.
EVERYTHING SEEMS NORMAL HERE, JENNY.
UNDERSTOOD. DOCTOR, YOU HEAR THAT?
TELL THE DOCTOR NOT TO TAKE IT TOO HARD. ALL THOSE DRUGS OF HIS WERE BOUND TO CONFUSE HIM SOONER OR LATER --
JENNY, WE HAVE A TERMINAL SITUATION HERE IN TOKYO: INCOMING MISSILES, UNKNOWN NATURE. IS THE DOCTOR CAPABLE OF RUNNING BACK-UP FOR US HERE?
WHAT? THERE'S NOTHING WRONG --

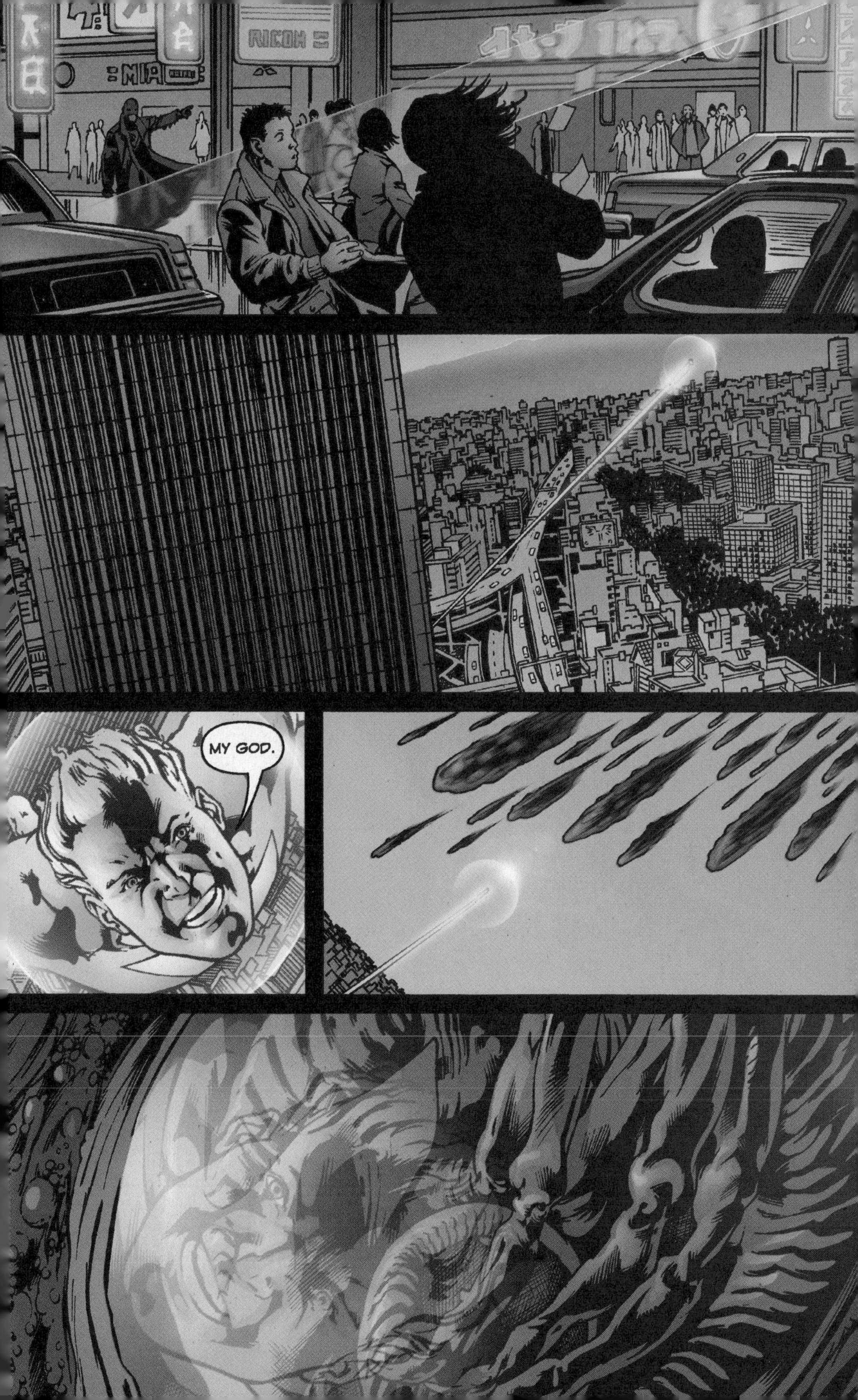
RICOH
MIA
MY GOD.

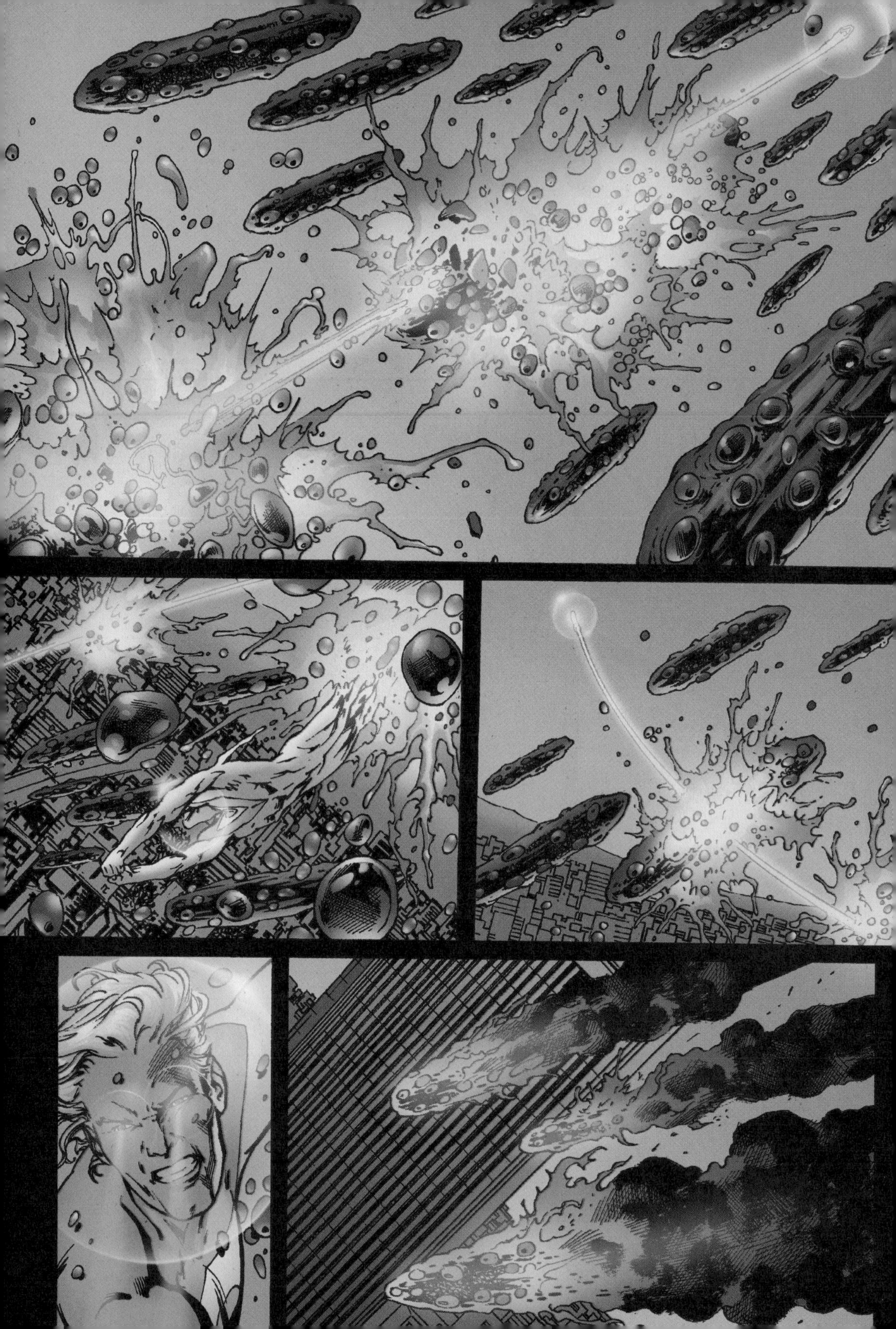

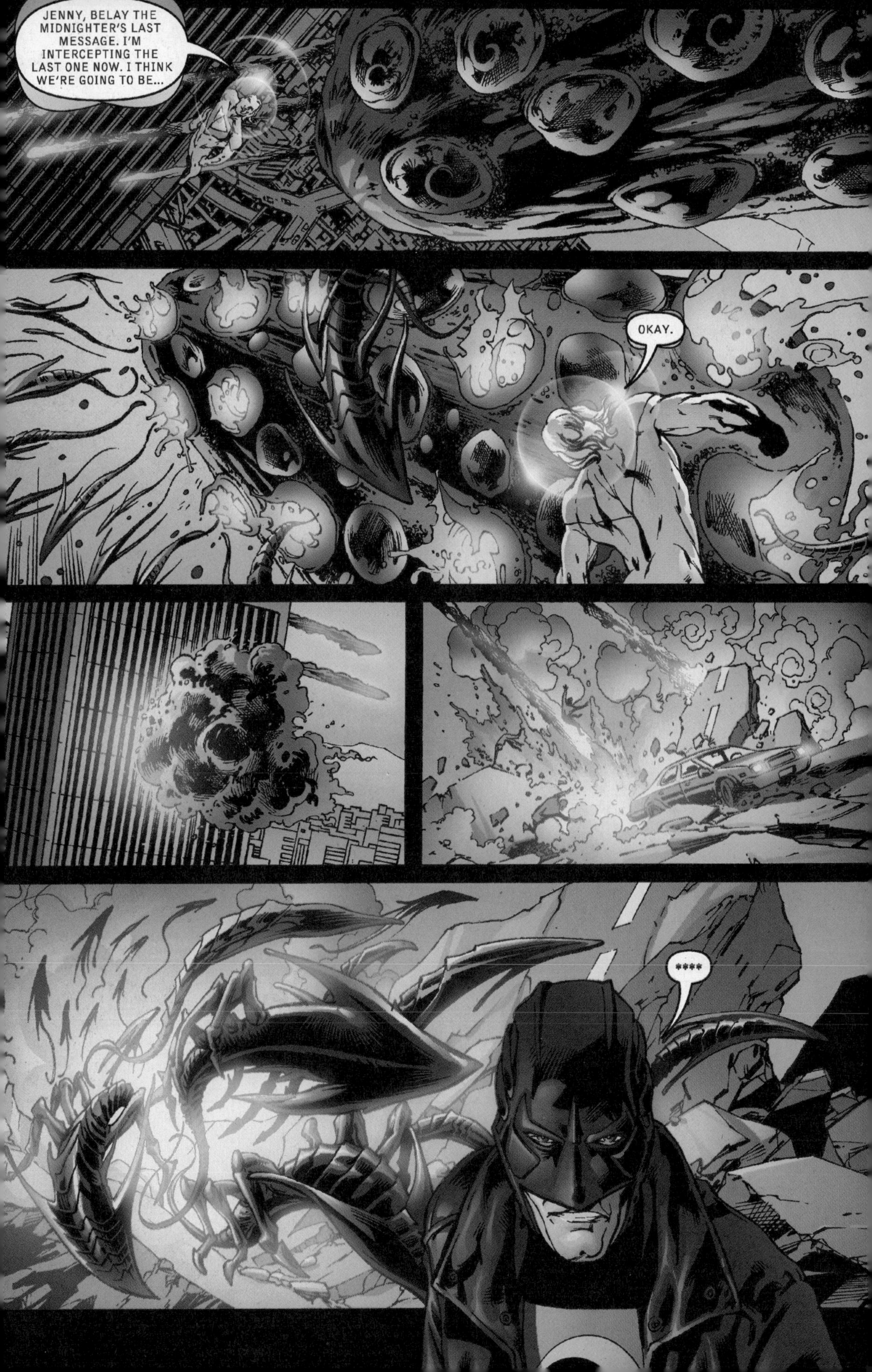
JENNY, BELAY THE MIDNIGHTER'S LAST MESSAGE. I'M INTERCEPTING THE LAST ONE NOW. I THINK WE'RE GOING TO BE...
OKAY.
****

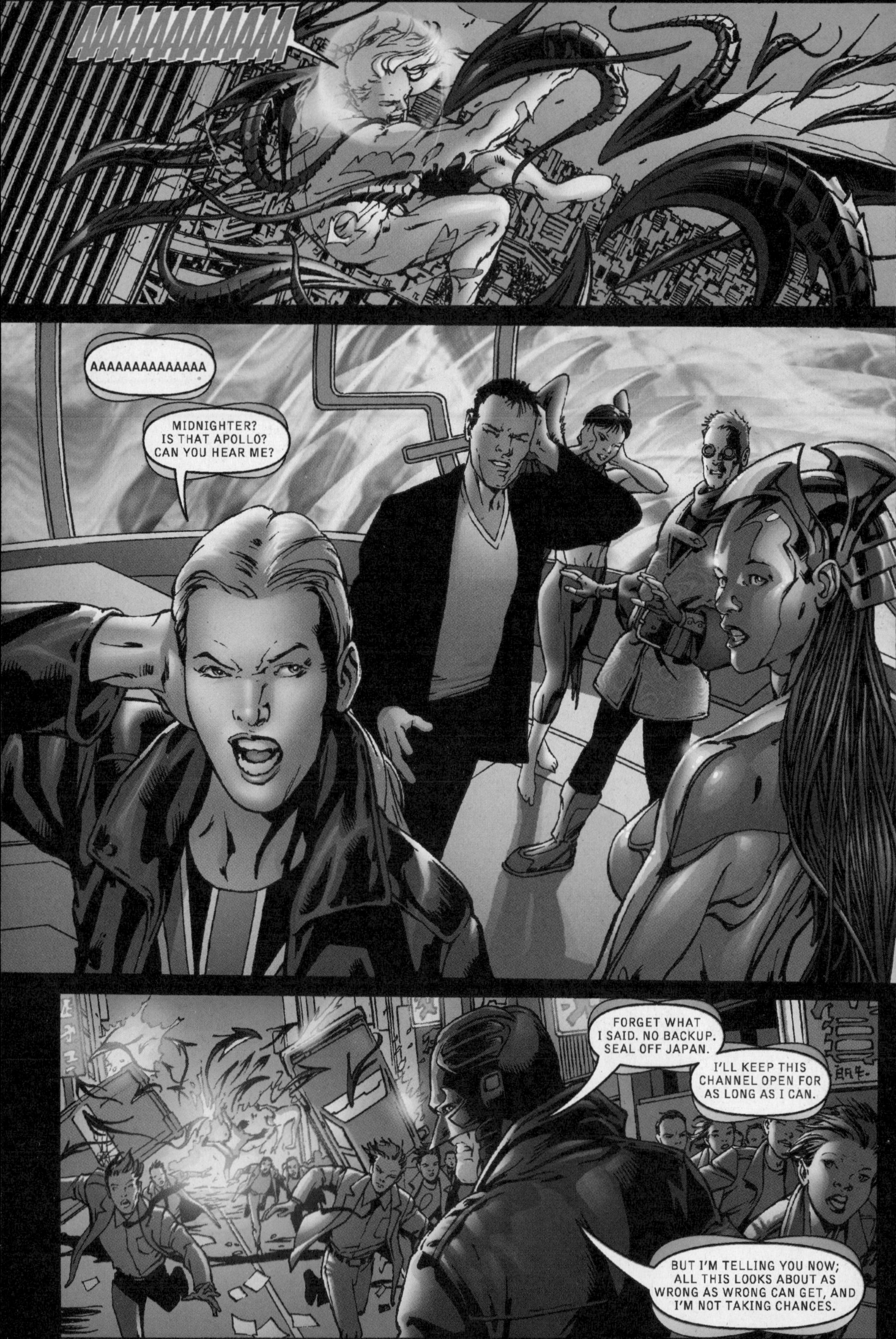
AAAAAAAAAAAA
AAAAAAAAAAAAAA
MIDNIGHTER? IS THAT APOLLO? CAN YOU HEAR ME?
FORGET WHAT I SAID. NO BACKUP. SEAL OFF JAPAN.
I'LL KEEP THIS CHANNEL OPEN FOR AS LONG AS I CAN.
BUT I'M TELLING YOU NOW; ALL THIS LOOKS ABOUT AS WRONG AS WRONG CAN GET, AND I'M NOT TAKING CHANCES.

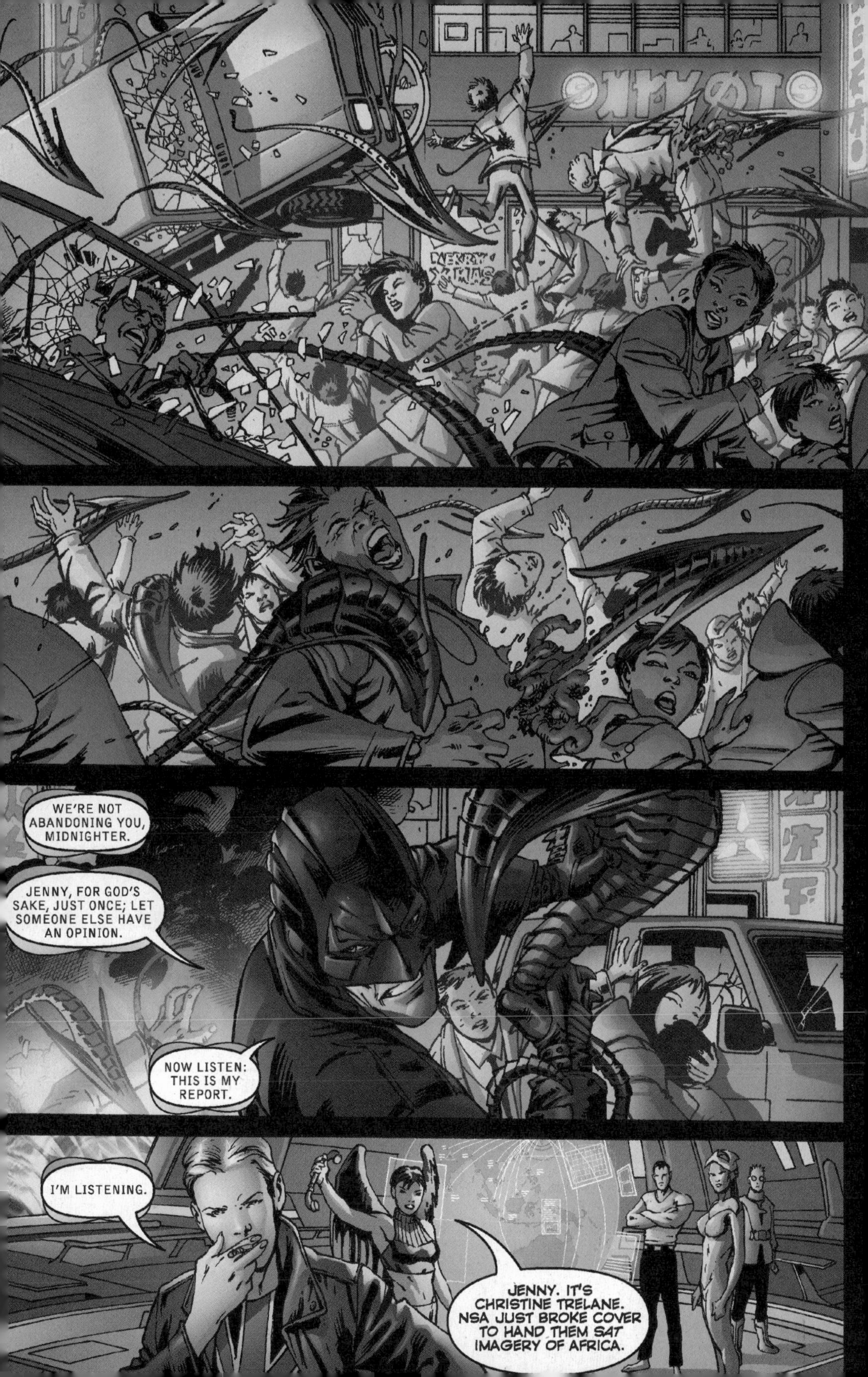
MERRY XMAS
WE'RE NOT ABANDONING YOU, MIDNIGHTER.
JENNY, FOR GOD'S SAKE, JUST ONCE; LET SOMEONE ELSE HAVE AN OPINION.
NOW LISTEN: THIS IS MY REPORT.
I'M LISTENING.
JENNY. IT'S CHRISTINE TRELANE. NSA JUST BROKE COVER TO HAND THEM SAT IMAGERY OF AFRICA.

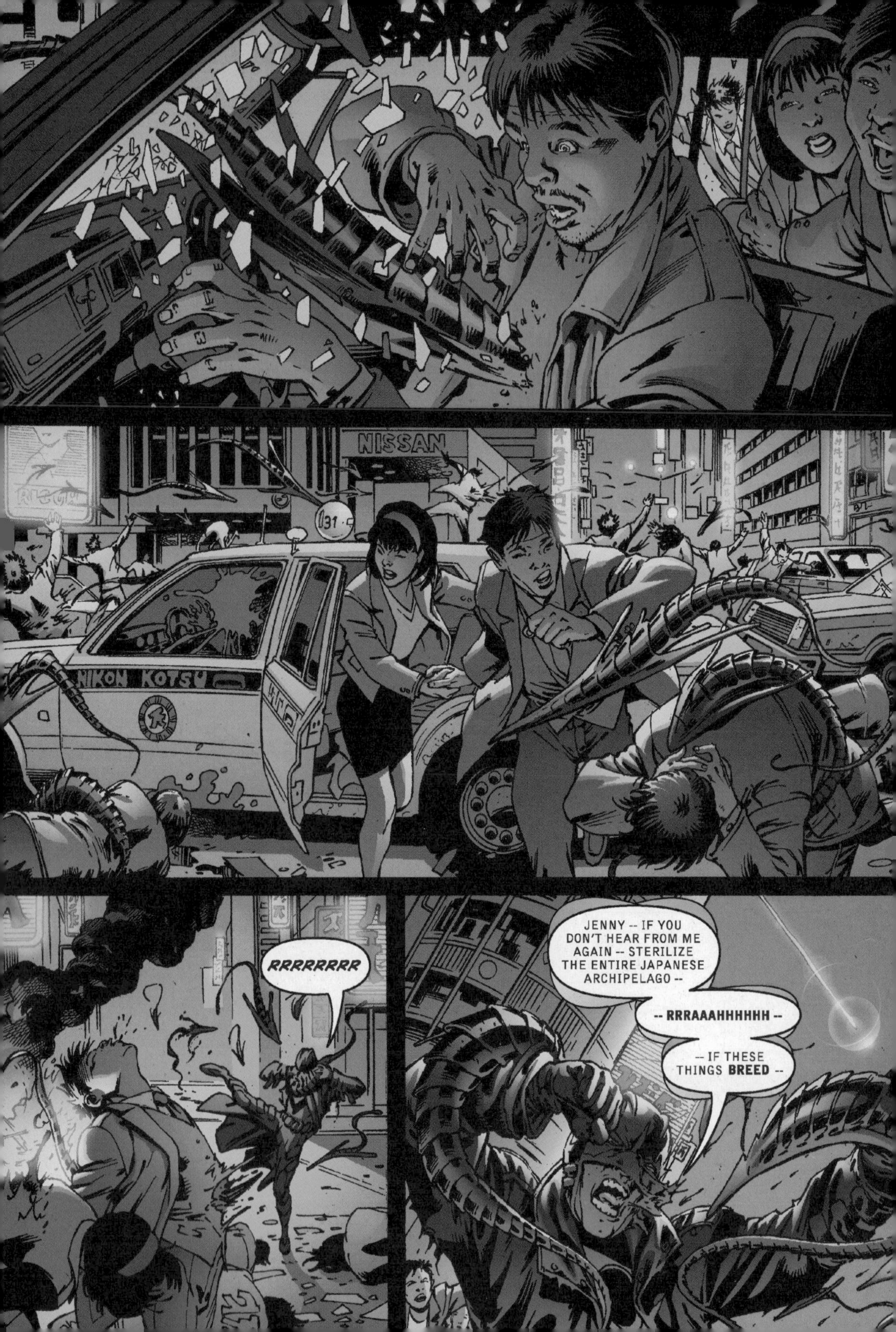
NISSAN
NIKON KOTSU
RRRRRRRR
JENNY -- IF YOU DON'T HEAR FROM ME AGAIN -- STERILIZE THE ENTIRE JAPANESE ARCHIPELAGO --
-- RRRAAAHHHHHH --
-- IF THESE THINGS BREED --

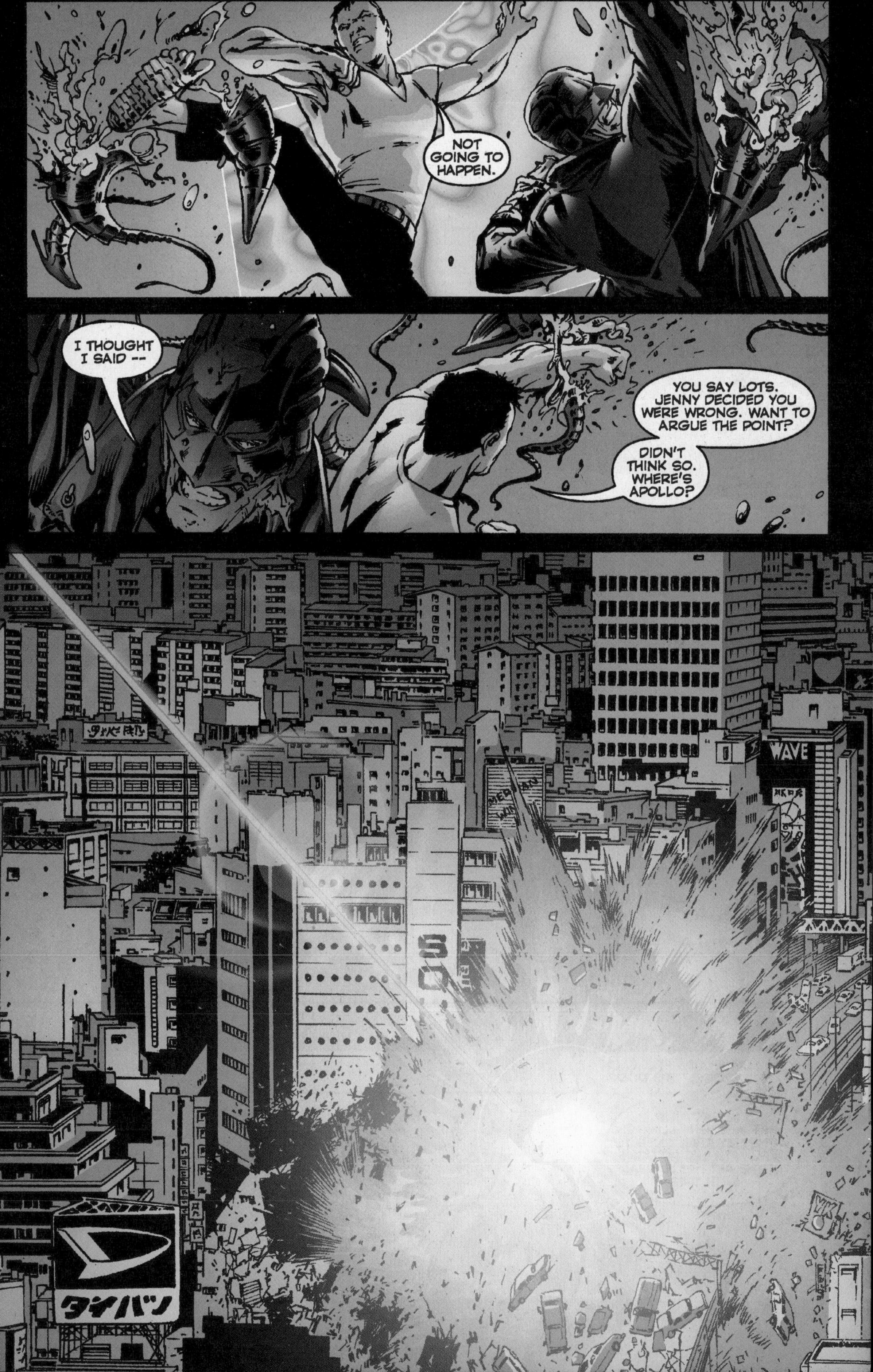
NOT GOING TO HAPPEN.
I THOUGHT I SAID --
YOU SAY LOTS. JENNY DECIDED YOU WERE WRONG. WANT TO ARGUE THE POINT?
DIDN'T THINK SO. WHERE'S APOLLO?
WAVE

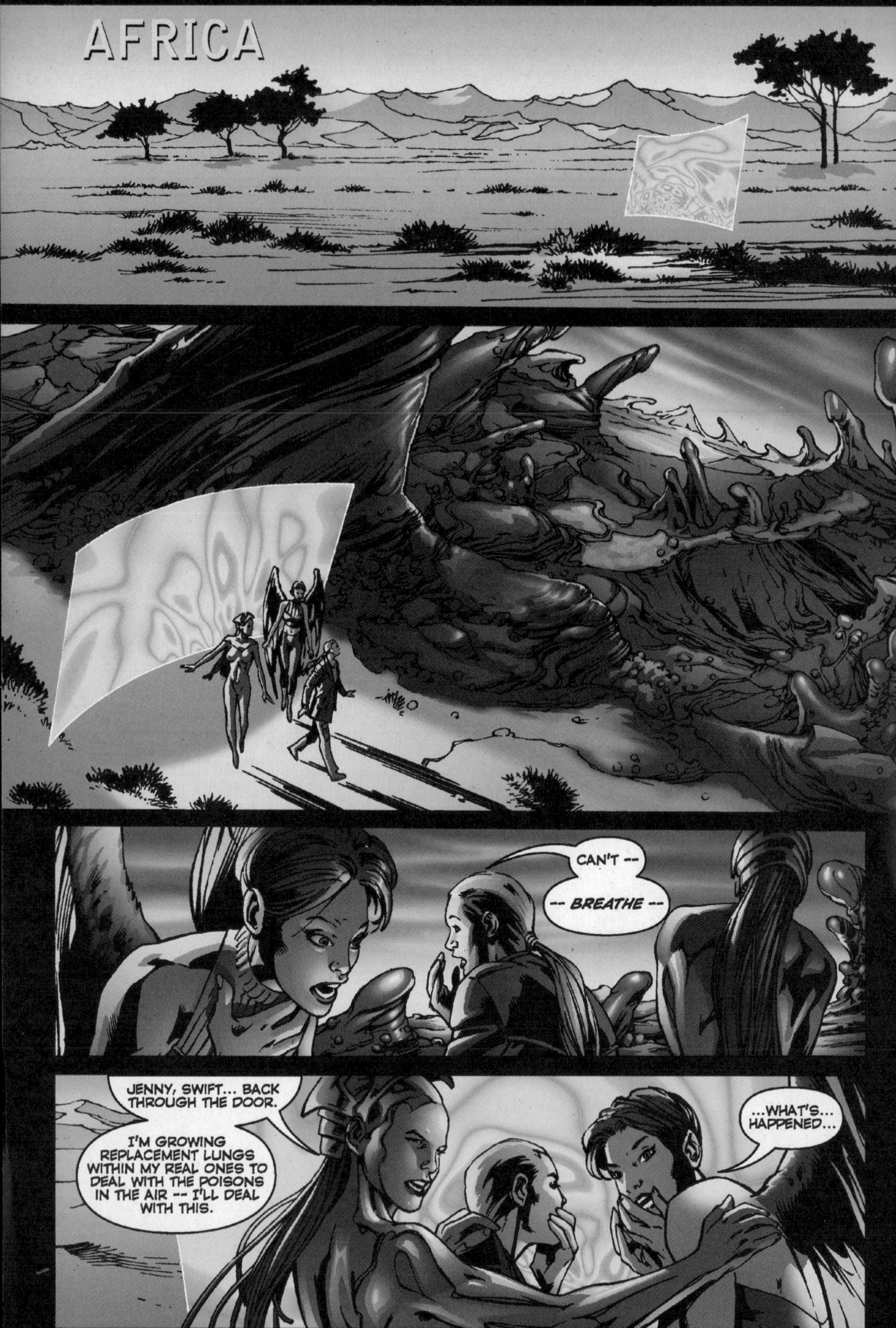
AFRICA
CAN'T --
-- BREATHE --
JENNY, SWIFT... BACK THROUGH THE DOOR.
I'M GROWING REPLACEMENT LUNGS WITHIN MY REAL ONES TO DEAL WITH THE POISONS IN THE AIR -- I'LL DEAL WITH THIS.
...WHAT'S... HAPPENED...

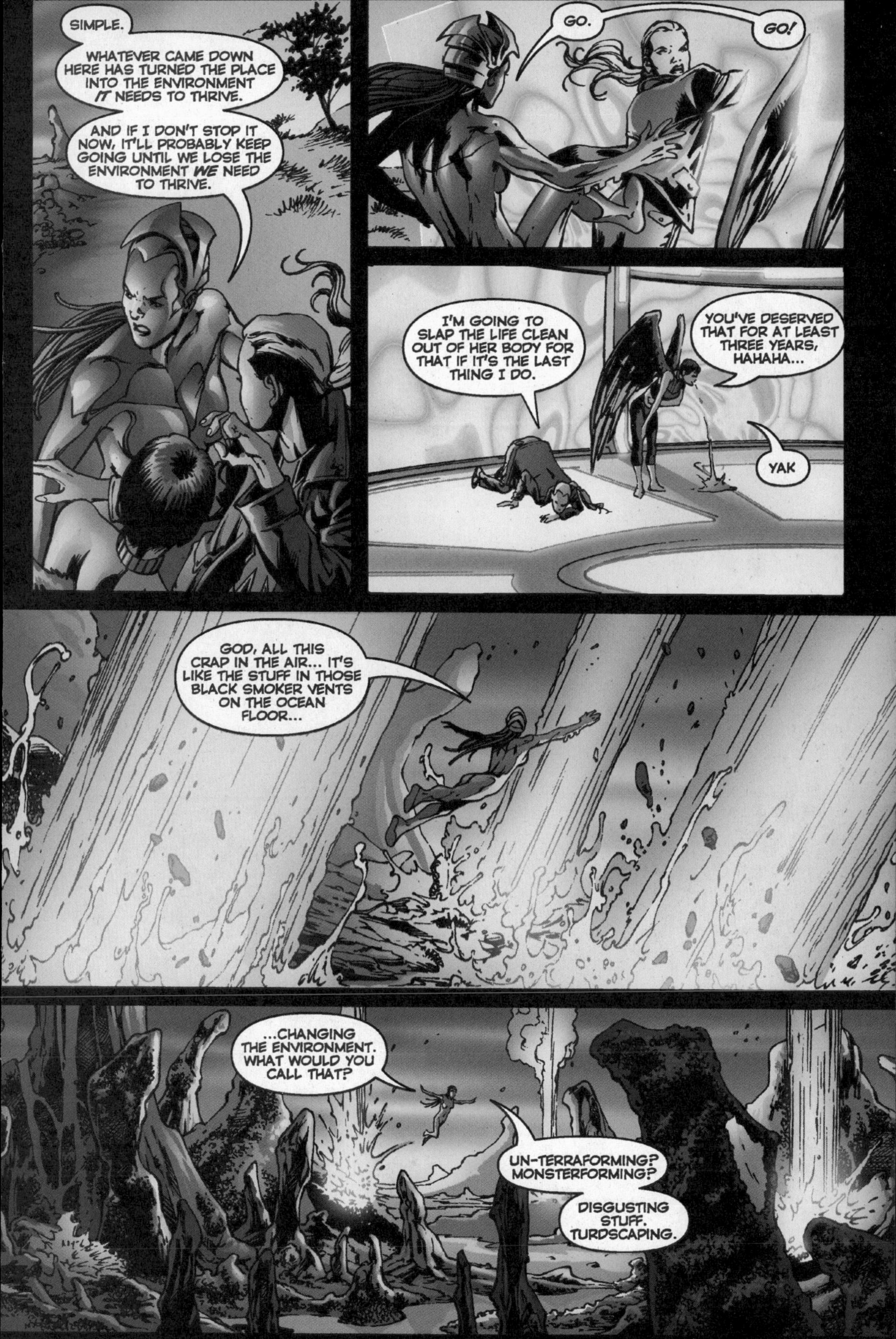
SIMPLE.
WHATEVER CAME DOWN HERE HAS TURNED THE PLACE INTO THE ENVIRONMENT *IT* NEEDS TO THRIVE.
AND IF I DON'T STOP IT NOW, IT'LL PROBABLY KEEP GOING UNTIL WE LOSE THE ENVIRONMENT *WE* NEED TO THRIVE.
GO.
GO!
I'M GOING TO SLAP THE LIFE CLEAN OUT OF HER BODY FOR THAT IF IT'S THE LAST THING I DO.
YOU'VE DESERVED THAT FOR AT LEAST THREE YEARS, HAHAHA...
YAK
GOD, ALL THIS CRAP IN THE AIR... IT'S LIKE THE STUFF IN THOSE BLACK SMOKER VENTS ON THE OCEAN FLOOR...
...CHANGING THE ENVIRONMENT. WHAT WOULD YOU CALL THAT?
UN-TERRAFORMING? MONSTERFORMING?
DISGUSTING STUFF. TURDSCAPING.

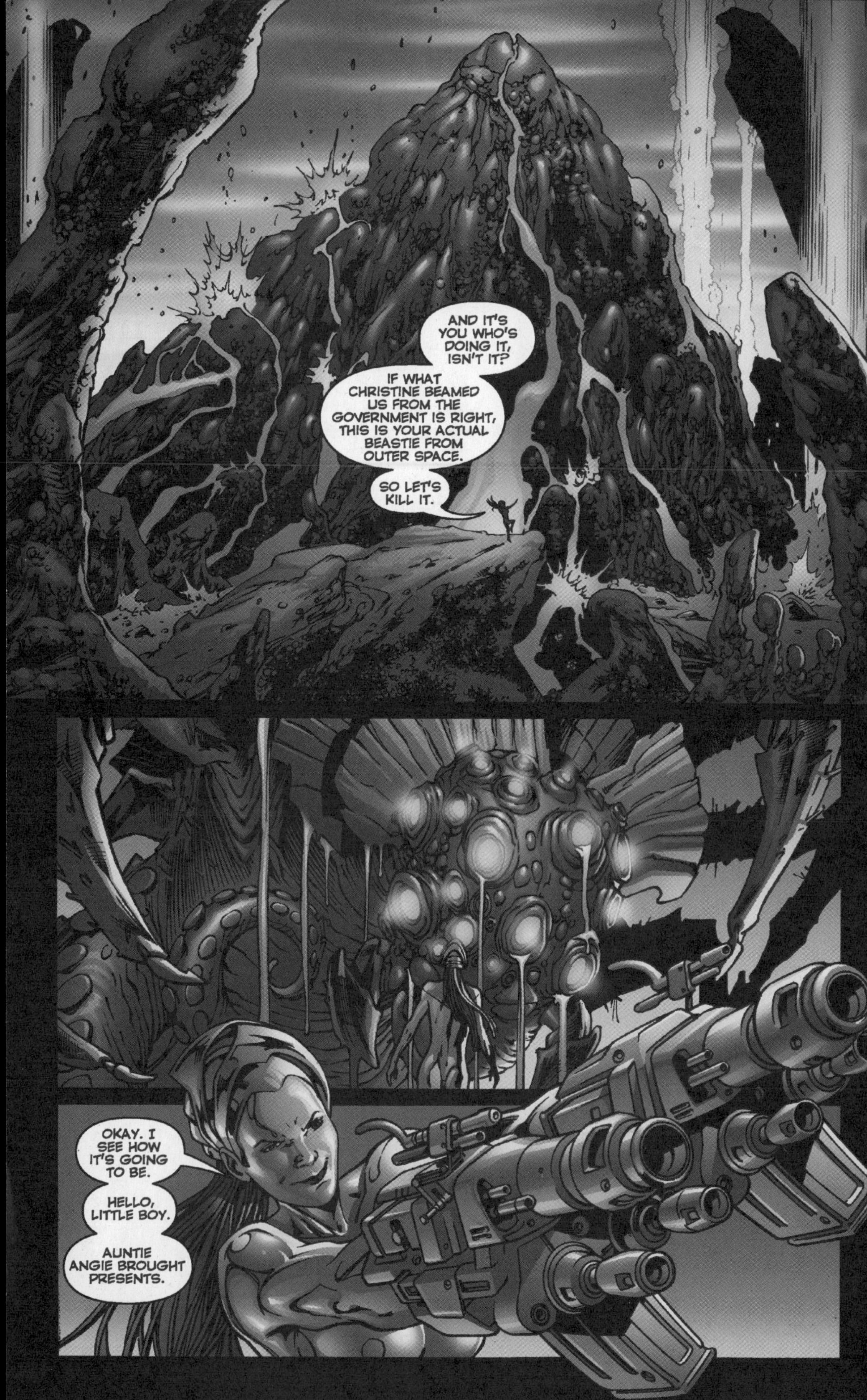
AND IT'S YOU WHO'S DOING IT, ISN'T IT?
IF WHAT CHRISTINE BEAMED US FROM THE GOVERNMENT IS RIGHT, THIS IS YOUR ACTUAL BEASTIE FROM OUTER SPACE.
SO LET'S KILL IT.
OKAY. I SEE HOW IT'S GOING TO BE.
HELLO, LITTLE BOY.
AUNTIE ANGIE BROUGHT PRESENTS.

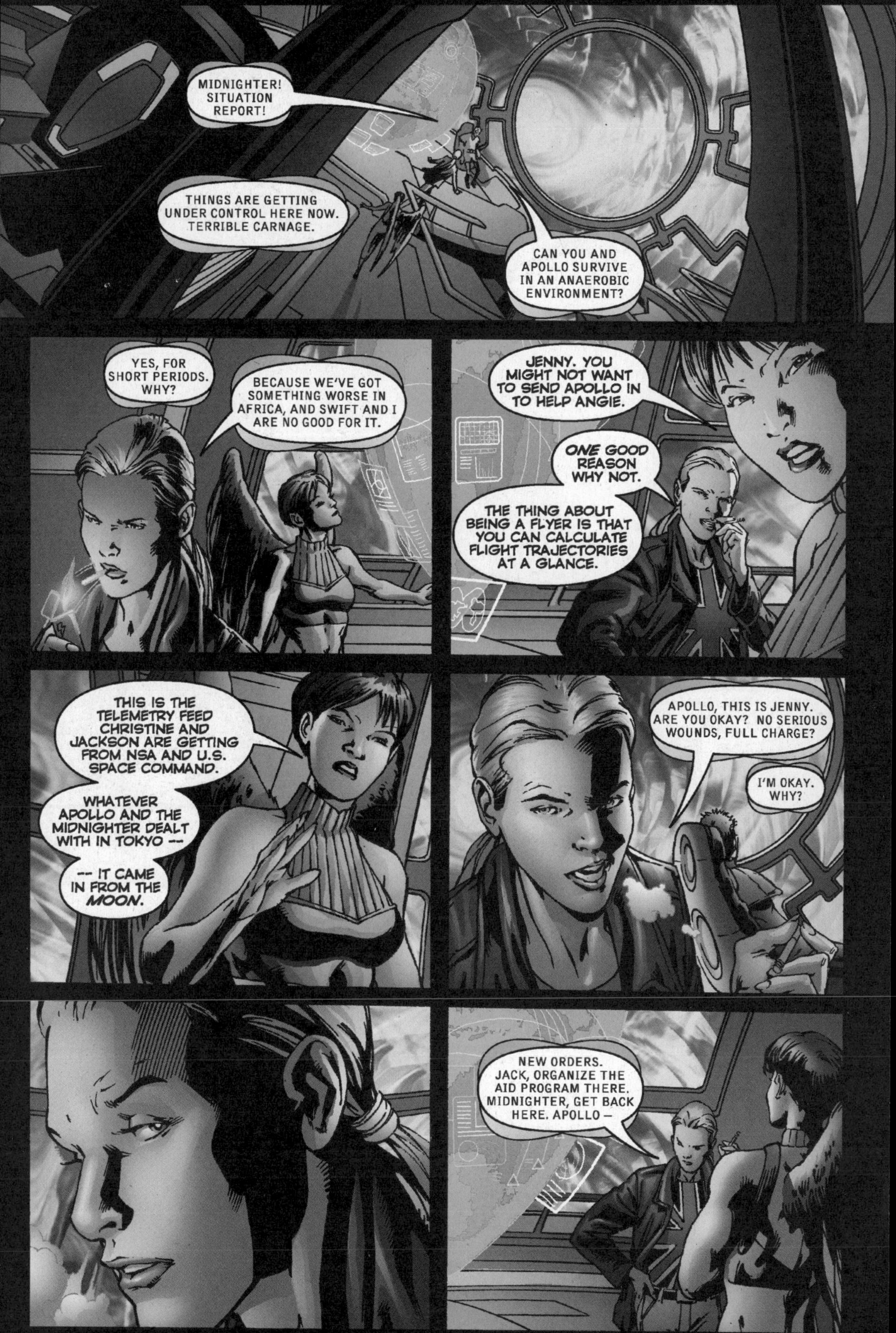
MIDNIGHTER! SITUATION REPORT!
THINGS ARE GETTING UNDER CONTROL HERE NOW. TERRIBLE CARNAGE.
CAN YOU AND APOLLO SURVIVE IN AN ANAEROBIC ENVIRONMENT?
YES, FOR SHORT PERIODS. WHY?
BECAUSE WE'VE GOT SOMETHING WORSE IN AFRICA, AND SWIFT AND I ARE NO GOOD FOR IT.
JENNY. YOU MIGHT NOT WANT TO SEND APOLLO IN TO HELP ANGIE.
ONE GOOD REASON WHY NOT.
THE THING ABOUT BEING A FLYER IS THAT YOU CAN CALCULATE FLIGHT TRAJECTORIES AT A GLANCE.
THIS IS THE TELEMETRY FEED CHRISTINE AND JACKSON ARE GETTING FROM NSA AND U.S. SPACE COMMAND.
WHATEVER APOLLO AND THE MIDNIGHTER DEALT WITH IN TOKYO --
-- IT CAME IN FROM THE MOON.
APOLLO, THIS IS JENNY. ARE YOU OKAY? NO SERIOUS WOUNDS, FULL CHARGE?
I'M OKAY. WHY?
NEW ORDERS. JACK, ORGANIZE THE AID PROGRAM THERE. MIDNIGHTER, GET BACK HERE. APOLLO –

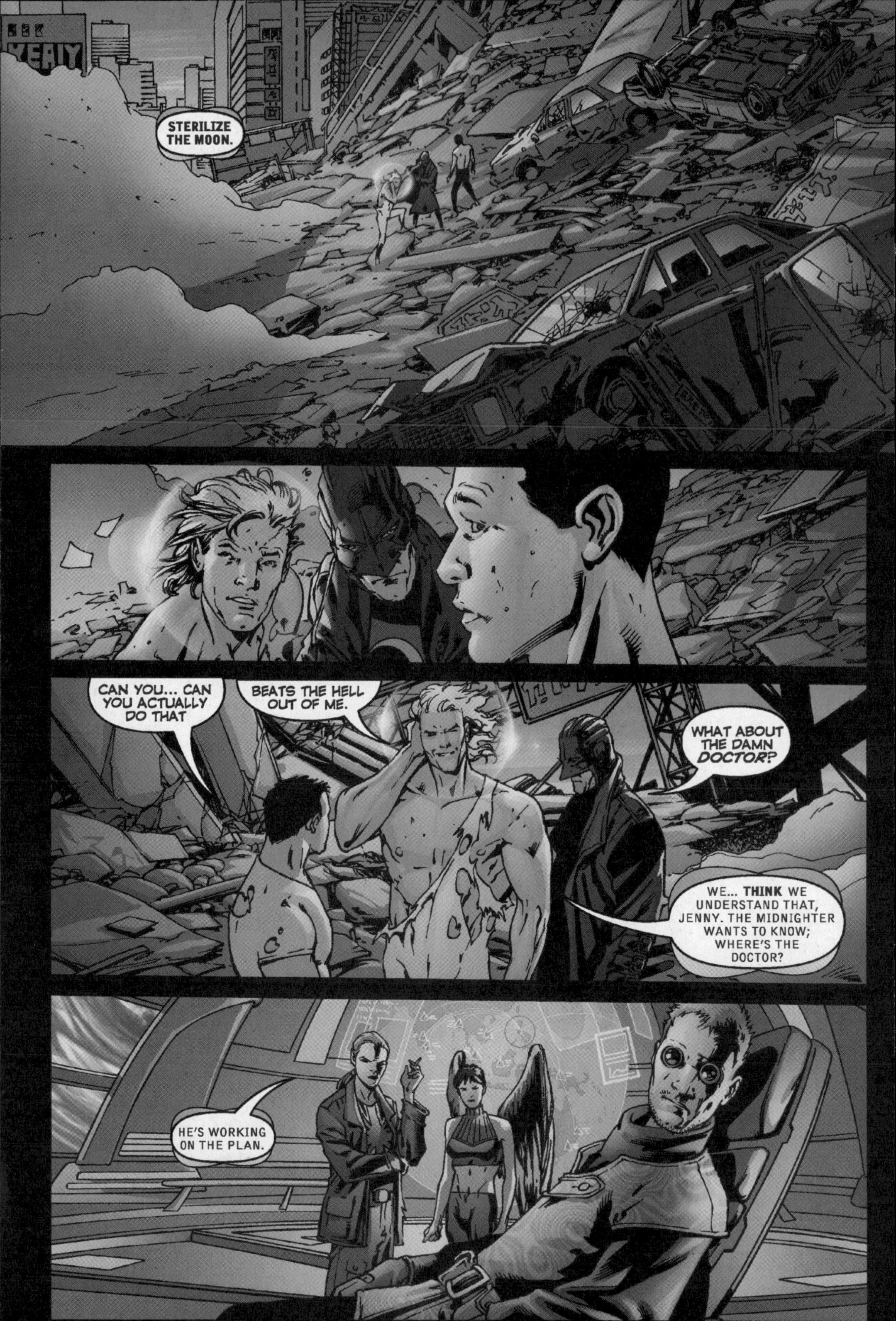

STERILIZE THE MOON.
CAN YOU... CAN YOU ACTUALLY DO THAT
BEATS THE HELL OUT OF ME.
WHAT ABOUT THE DAMN *DOCTOR*?
WE... **THINK** WE UNDERSTAND THAT, JENNY. THE MIDNIGHTER WANTS TO KNOW; WHERE'S THE DOCTOR?
HE'S WORKING ON THE PLAN.

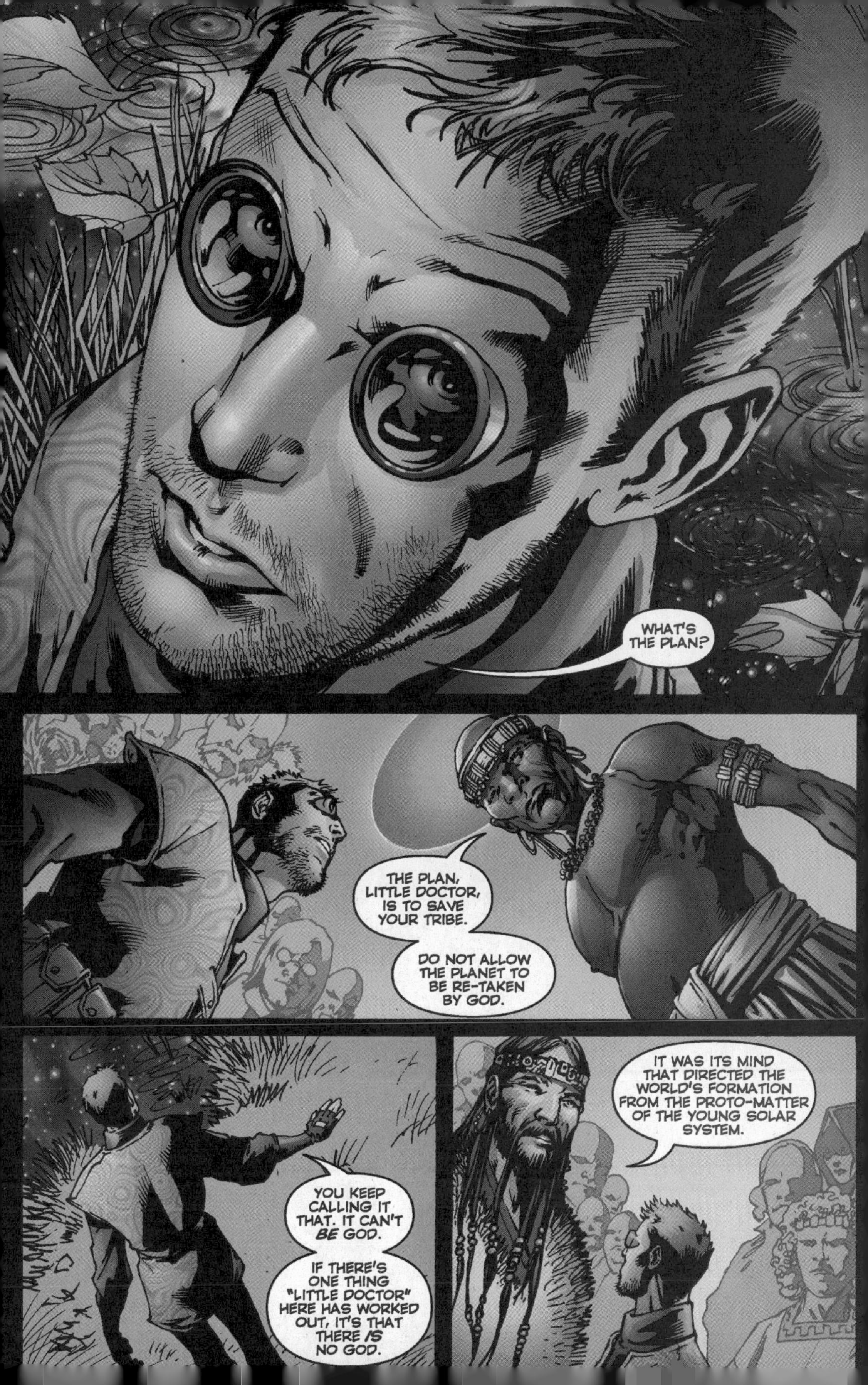
WHAT'S THE PLAN?
THE PLAN, LITTLE DOCTOR, IS TO SAVE YOUR TRIBE.
DO NOT ALLOW THE PLANET TO BE RE-TAKEN BY GOD.
YOU KEEP CALLING IT THAT. IT CAN'T *BE* GOD.
IF THERE'S ONE THING "LITTLE DOCTOR" HERE HAS WORKED OUT, IT'S THAT THERE *IS* NO GOD.
IT WAS ITS MIND THAT DIRECTED THE WORLD'S FORMATION FROM THE PROTO-MATTER OF THE YOUNG SOLAR SYSTEM.

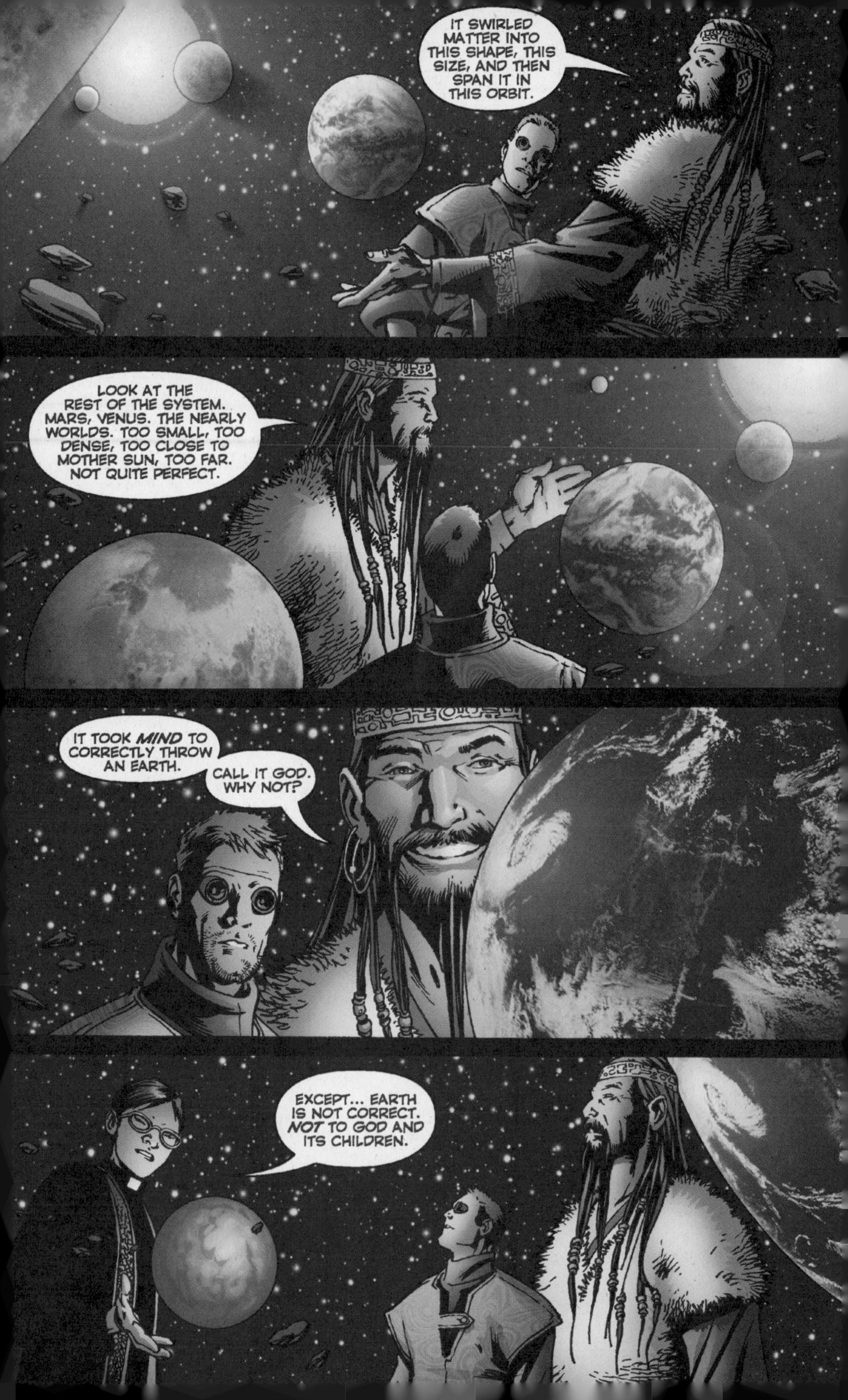
IT SWIRLED MATTER INTO THIS SHAPE, THIS SIZE, AND THEN SPAN IT IN THIS ORBIT.
LOOK AT THE REST OF THE SYSTEM. MARS, VENUS. THE NEARLY WORLDS. TOO SMALL, TOO DENSE, TOO CLOSE TO MOTHER SUN, TOO FAR. NOT QUITE PERFECT.
IT TOOK *MIND* TO CORRECTLY THROW AN EARTH.
CALL IT GOD. WHY NOT?
EXCEPT... EARTH IS NOT CORRECT. *NOT* TO GOD AND ITS CHILDREN.

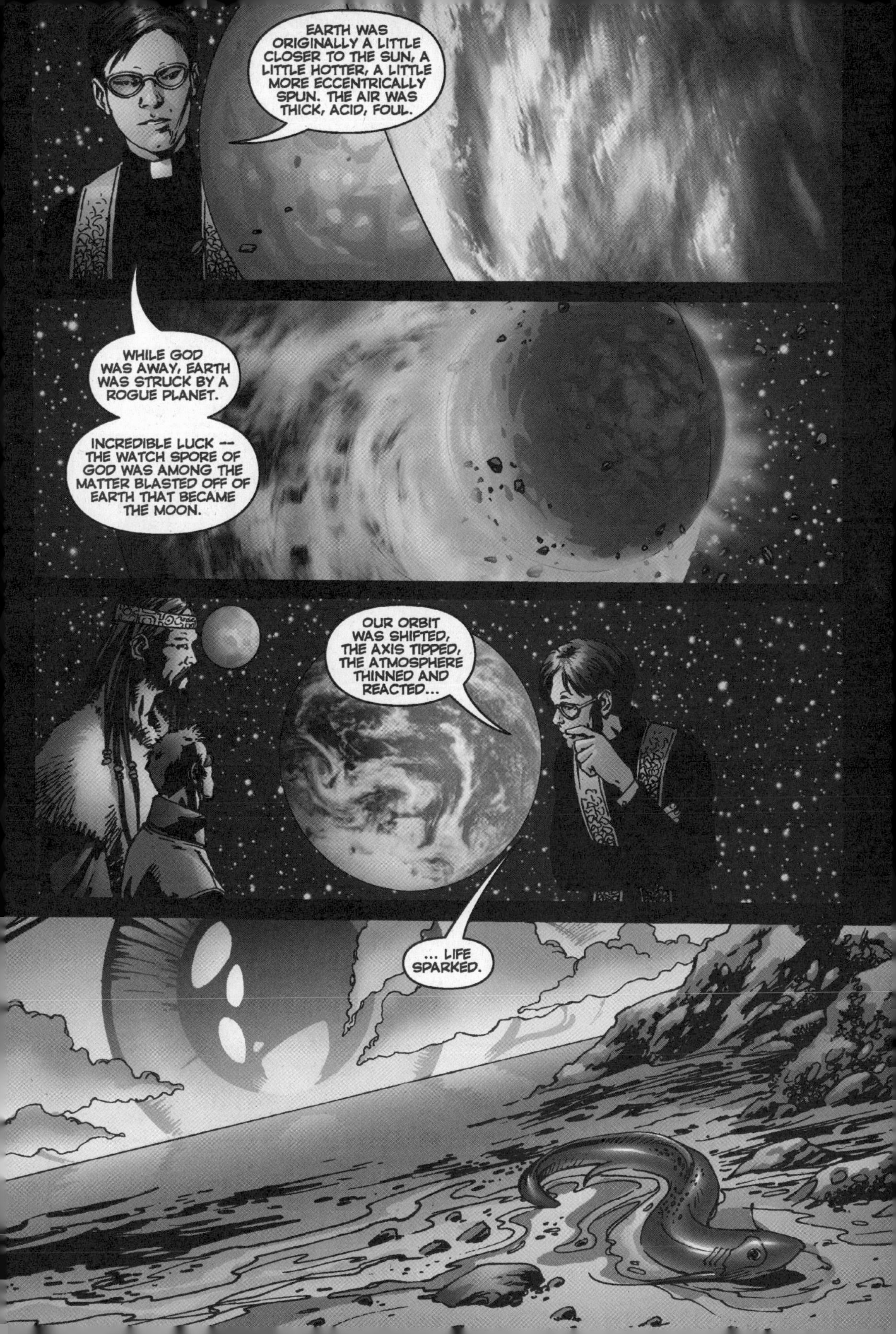
EARTH WAS ORIGINALLY A LITTLE CLOSER TO THE SUN, A LITTLE HOTTER, A LITTLE MORE ECCENTRICALLY SPUN. THE AIR WAS THICK, ACID, FOUL.
WHILE GOD WAS AWAY, EARTH WAS STRUCK BY A ROGUE PLANET.
INCREDIBLE LUCK -- THE WATCH SPORE OF GOD WAS AMONG THE MATTER BLASTED OFF OF EARTH THAT BECAME THE MOON.
OUR ORBIT WAS SHIFTED, THE AXIS TIPPED, THE ATMOSPHERE THINNED AND REACTED...
... LIFE SPARKED.

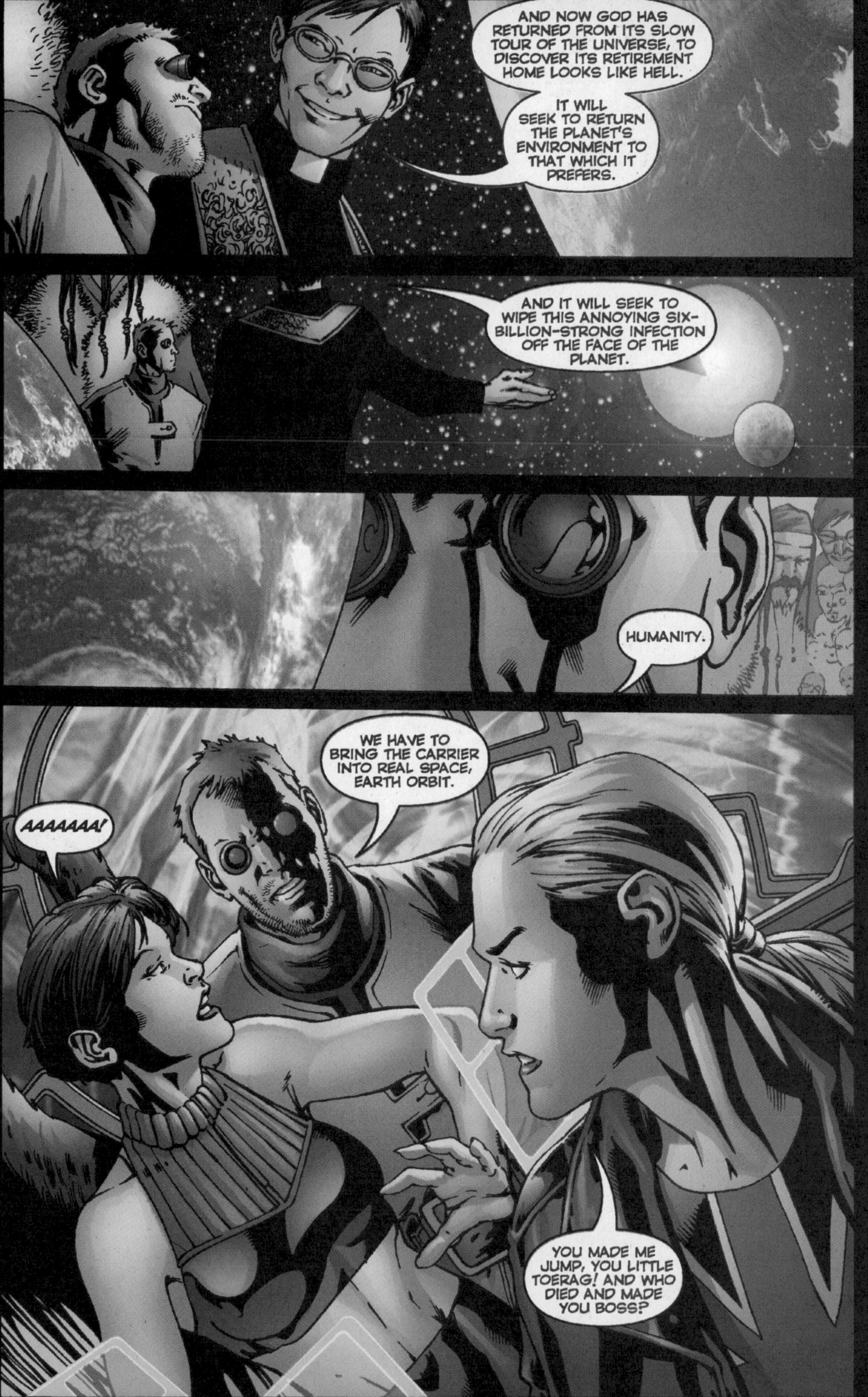
AND NOW GOD HAS RETURNED FROM ITS SLOW TOUR OF THE UNIVERSE, TO DISCOVER ITS RETIREMENT HOME LOOKS LIKE HELL.
IT WILL SEEK TO RETURN THE PLANET'S ENVIRONMENT TO THAT WHICH IT PREFERS.
AND IT WILL SEEK TO WIPE THIS ANNOYING SIX-BILLION-STRONG INFECTION OFF THE FACE OF THE PLANET.
HUMANITY.
WE HAVE TO BRING THE CARRIER INTO REAL SPACE, EARTH ORBIT.
AAAAAAA!
YOU MADE ME JUMP, YOU LITTLE TOERAG! AND WHO DIED AND MADE YOU BOSS?

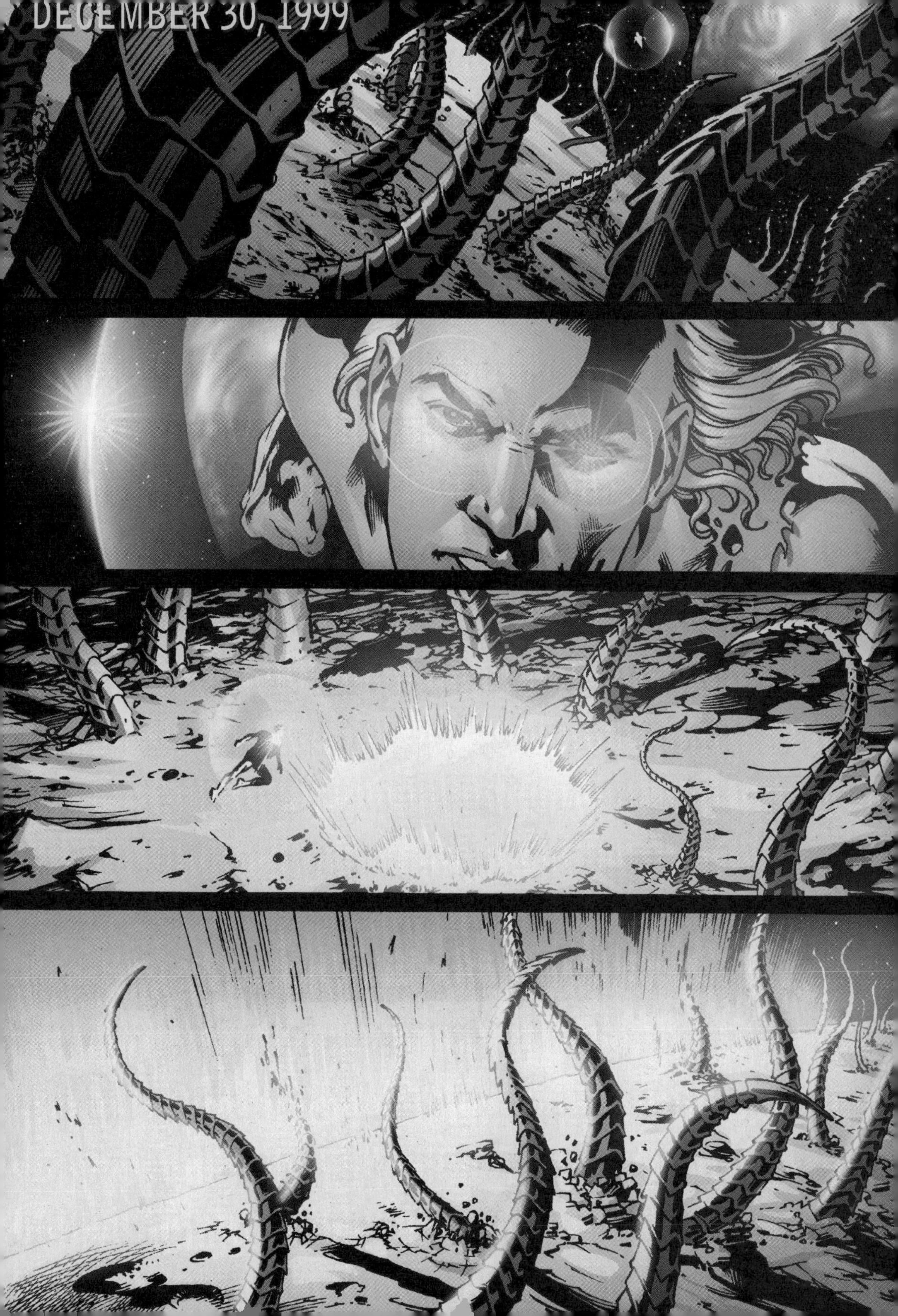
DECEMBER 30, 1999

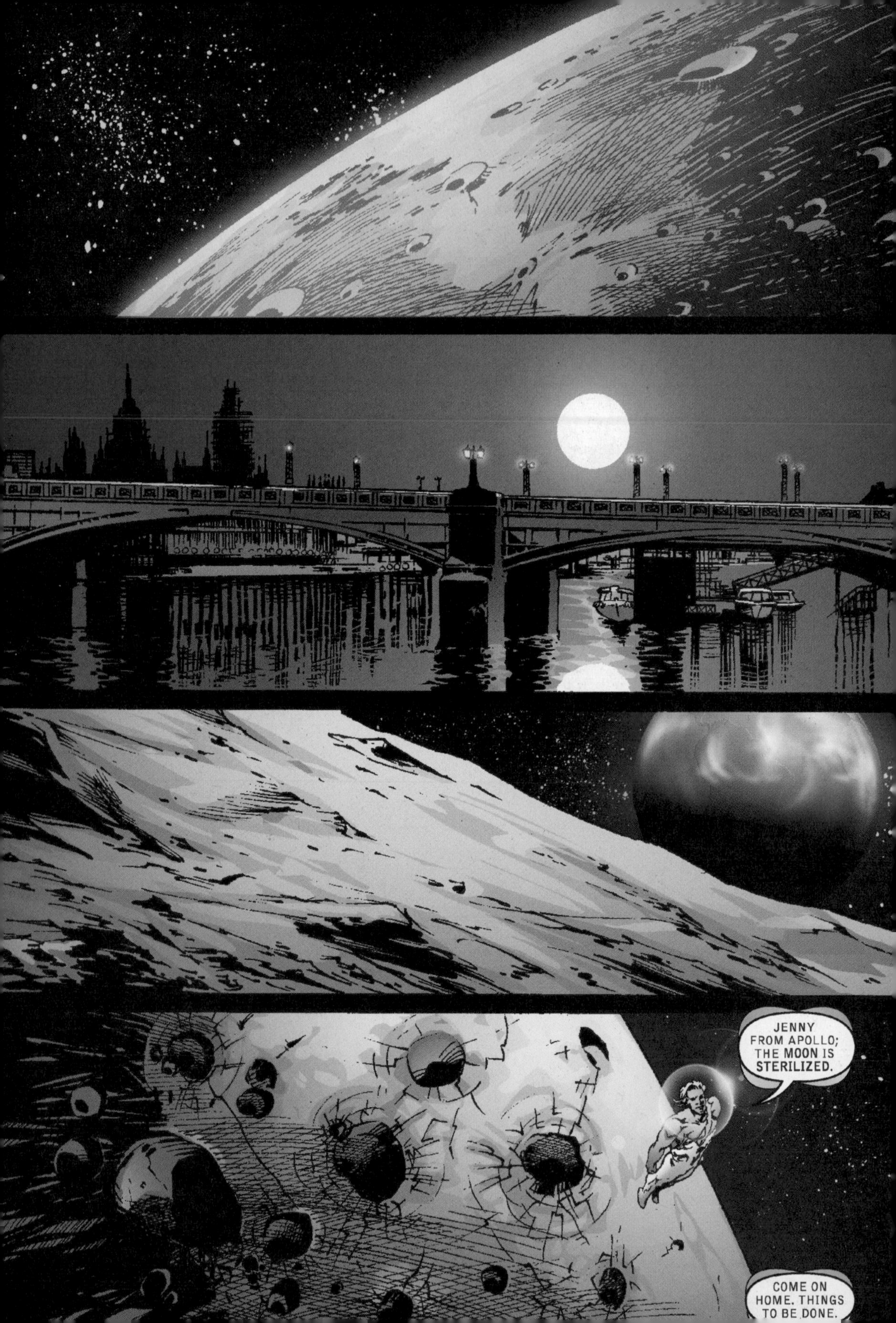
JENNY FROM APOLLO; THE MOON IS STERILIZED.
COME ON HOME. THINGS TO BE DONE.

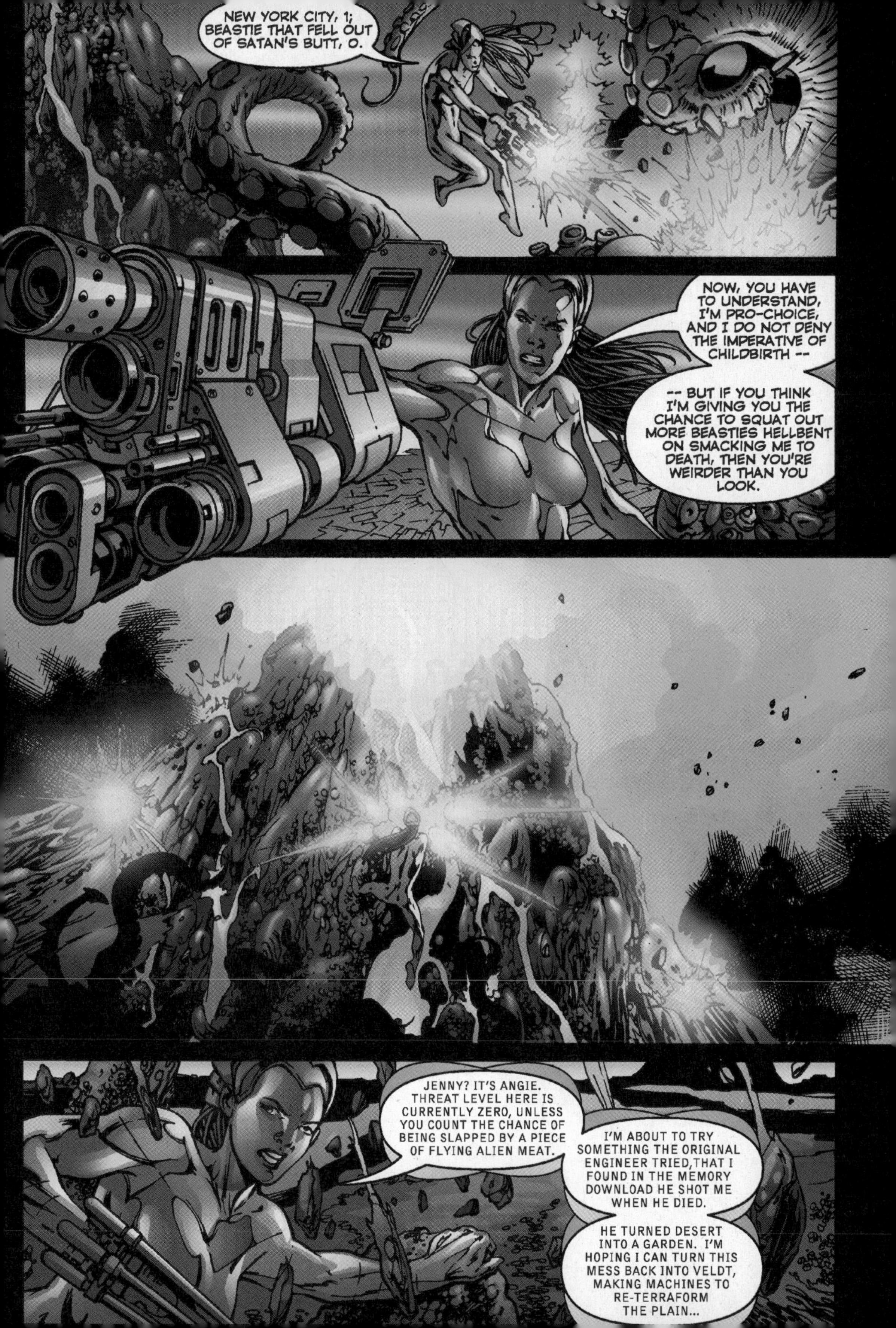

NEW YORK CITY, 1; BEASTIE THAT FELL OUT OF SATAN'S BUTT, 0.
NOW, YOU HAVE TO UNDERSTAND, I'M PRO-CHOICE, AND I DO NOT DENY THE IMPERATIVE OF CHILDBIRTH --
-- BUT IF YOU THINK I'M GIVING YOU THE CHANCE TO SQUAT OUT MORE BEASTIES HELLBENT ON SMACKING ME TO DEATH, THEN YOU'RE WEIRDER THAN YOU LOOK.
JENNY? IT'S ANGIE. THREAT LEVEL HERE IS CURRENTLY ZERO, UNLESS YOU COUNT THE CHANCE OF BEING SLAPPED BY A PIECE OF FLYING ALIEN MEAT.
I'M ABOUT TO TRY SOMETHING THE ORIGINAL ENGINEER TRIED,THAT I FOUND IN THE MEMORY DOWNLOAD HE SHOT ME WHEN HE DIED.
HE TURNED DESERT INTO A GARDEN. I'M HOPING I CAN TURN THIS MESS BACK INTO VELDT, MAKING MACHINES TO RE-TERRAFORM THE PLAIN...

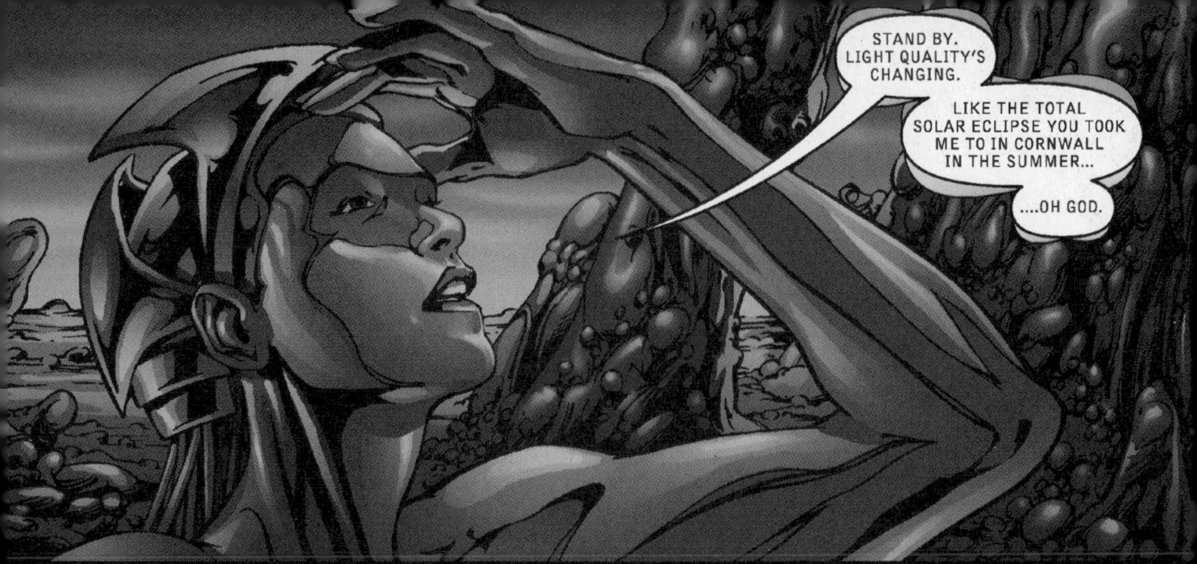
STAND BY. LIGHT QUALITY'S CHANGING.
LIKE THE TOTAL SOLAR ECLIPSE YOU TOOK ME TO IN CORNWALL IN THE SUMMER...
....OH GOD.
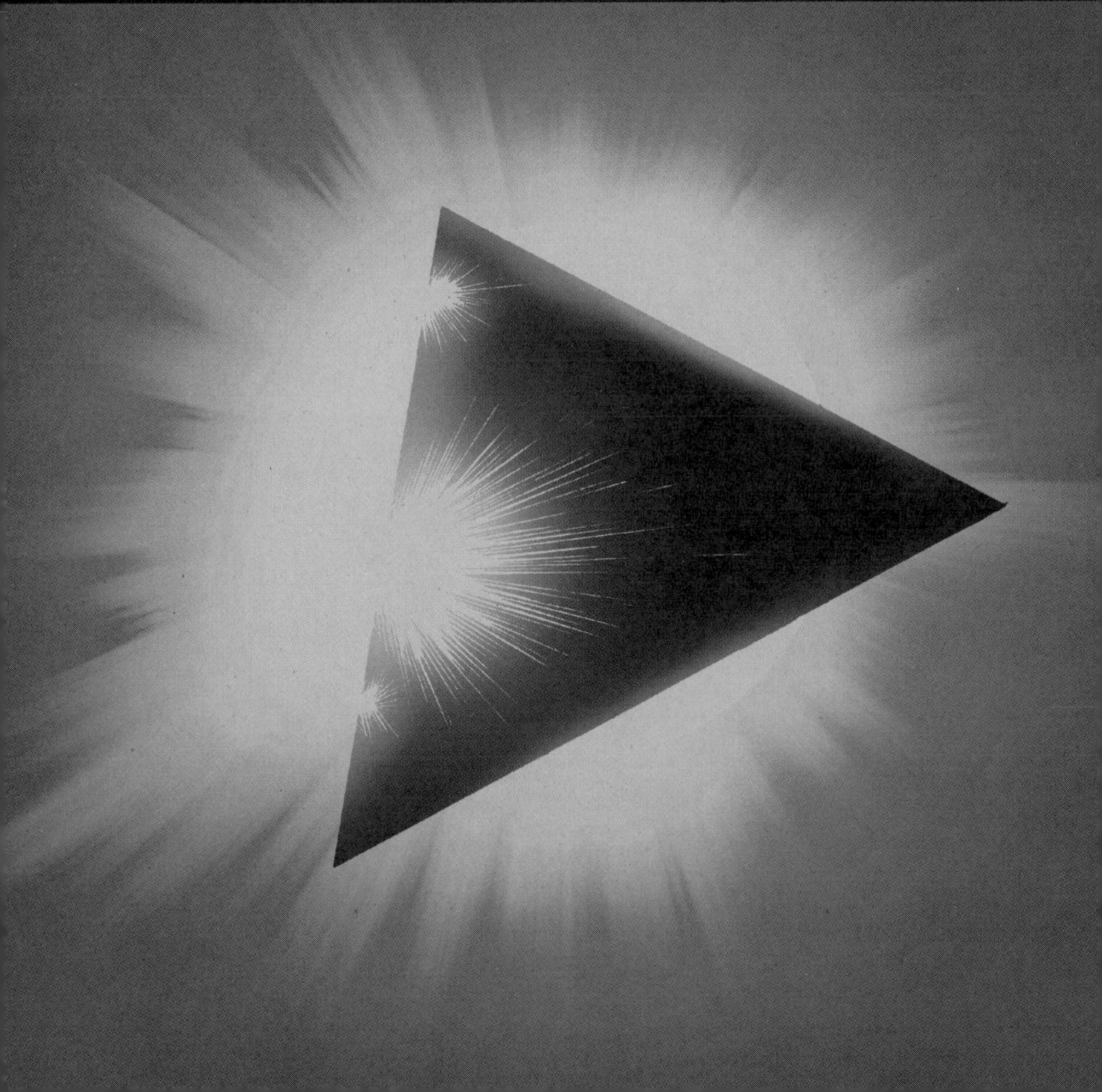

AFRICA

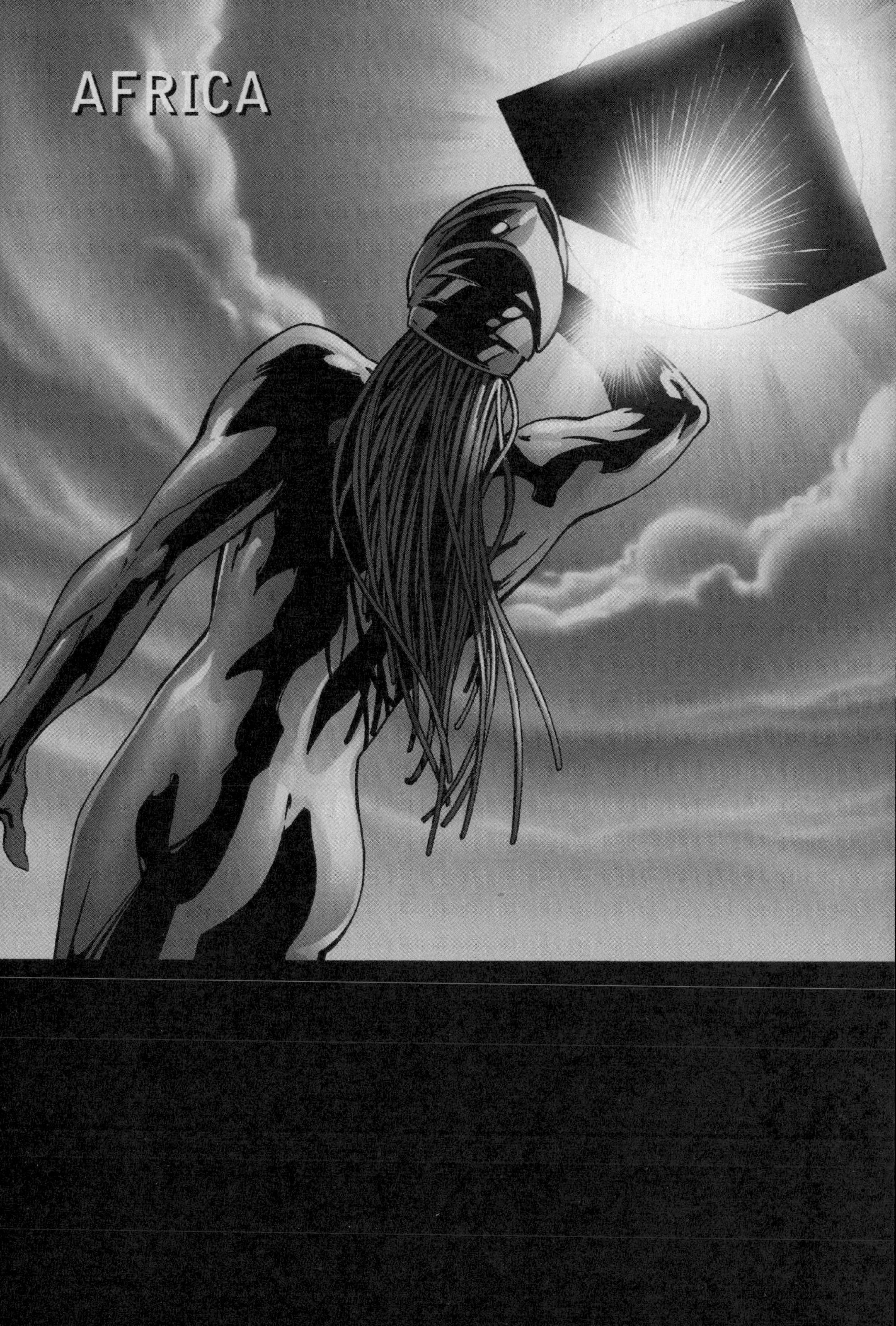

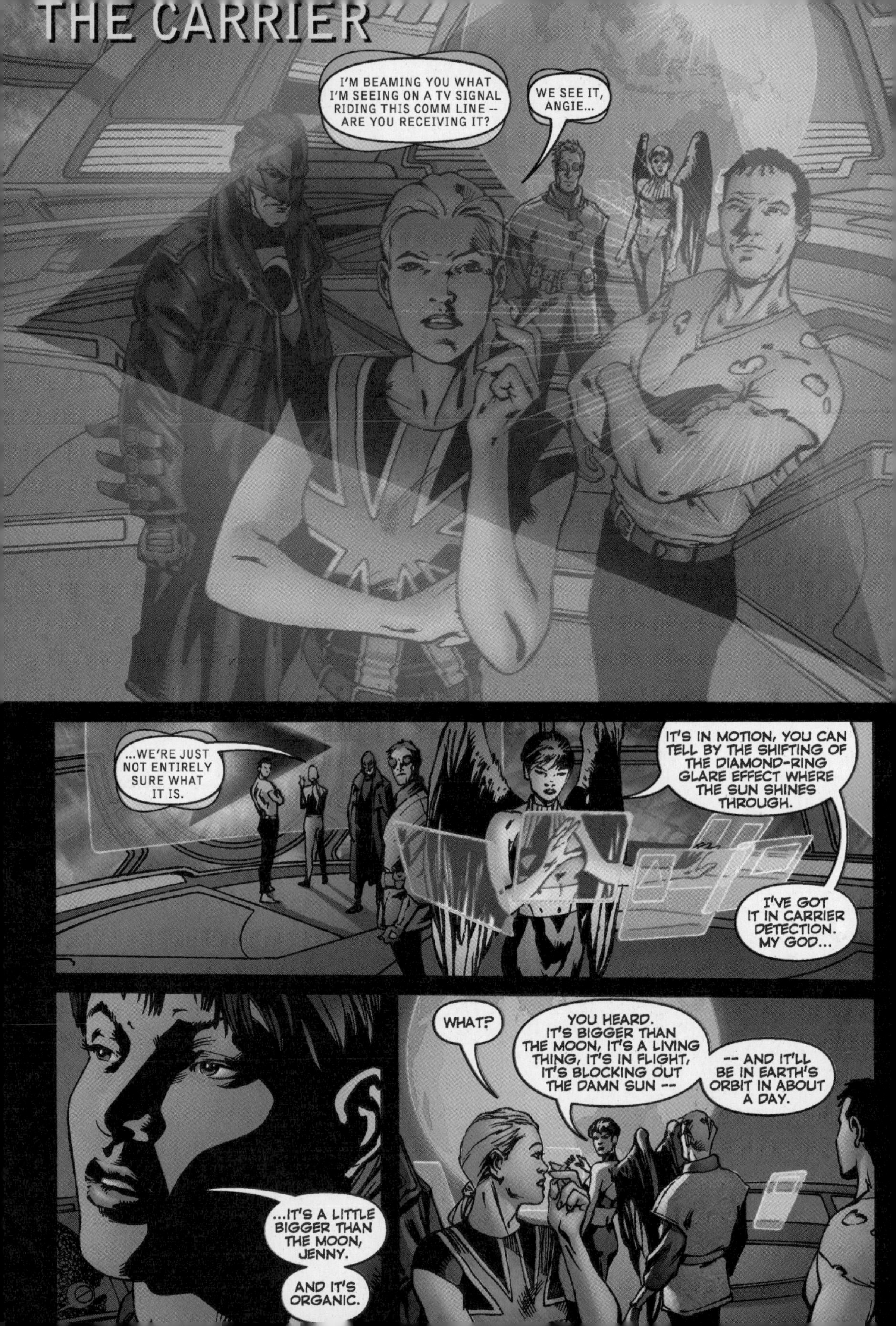
THE CARRIER
I'M BEAMING YOU WHAT I'M SEEING ON A TV SIGNAL RIDING THIS COMM LINE -- ARE YOU RECEIVING IT?
WE SEE IT, ANGIE...
...WE'RE JUST NOT ENTIRELY SURE WHAT IT IS.
IT'S IN MOTION, YOU CAN TELL BY THE SHIFTING OF THE DIAMOND-RING GLARE EFFECT WHERE THE SUN SHINES THROUGH.
I'VE GOT IT IN CARRIER DETECTION. MY GOD...
...IT'S A LITTLE BIGGER THAN THE MOON, JENNY.
AND IT'S ORGANIC.
WHAT?
YOU HEARD. IT'S BIGGER THAN THE MOON, IT'S A LIVING THING, IT'S IN FLIGHT, IT'S BLOCKING OUT THE DAMN SUN --
-- AND IT'LL BE IN EARTH'S ORBIT IN ABOUT A DAY.

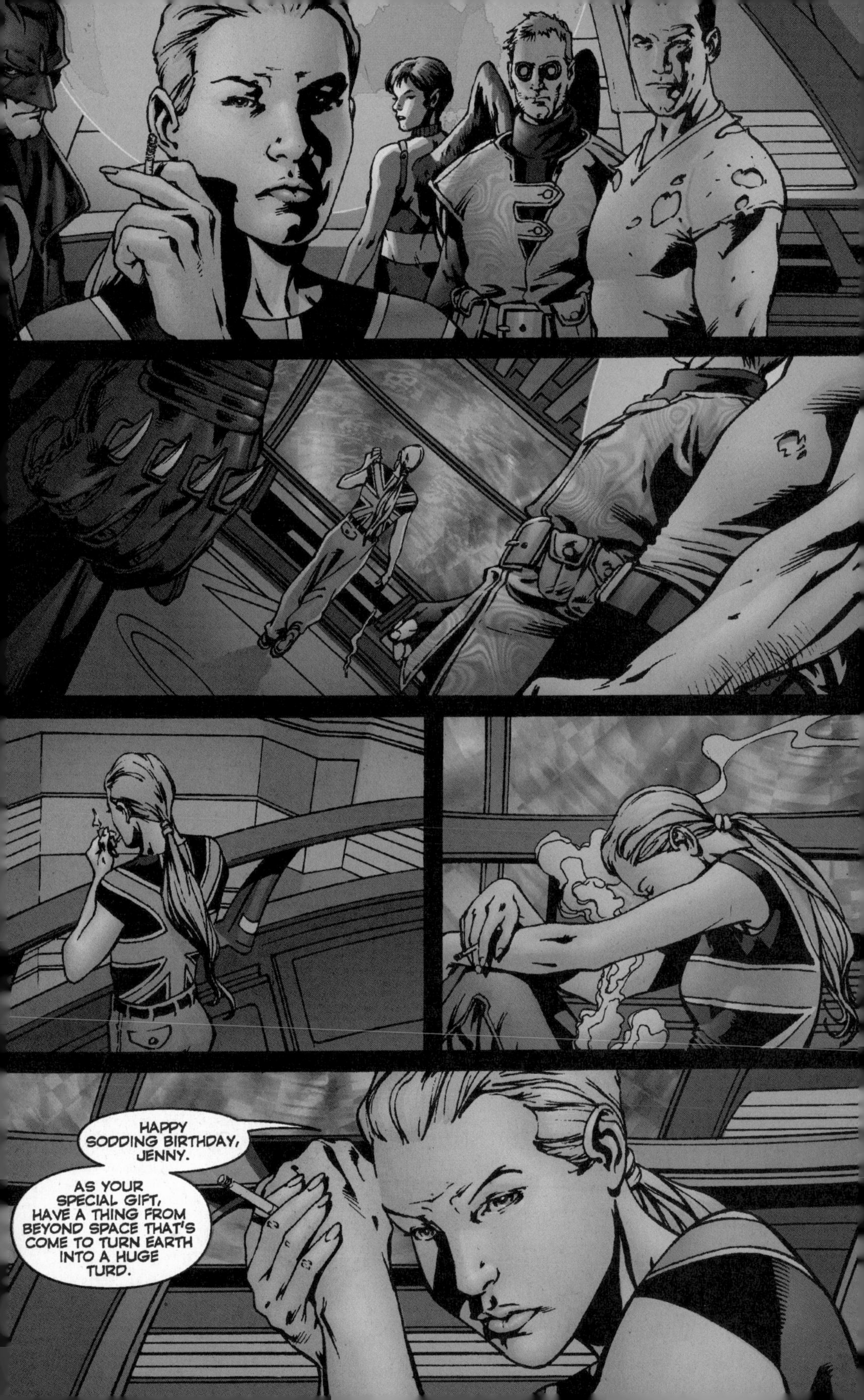
HAPPY SODDING BIRTHDAY, JENNY.
AS YOUR SPECIAL GIFT, HAVE A THING FROM BEYOND SPACE THAT'S COME TO TURN EARTH INTO A HUGE TURD.

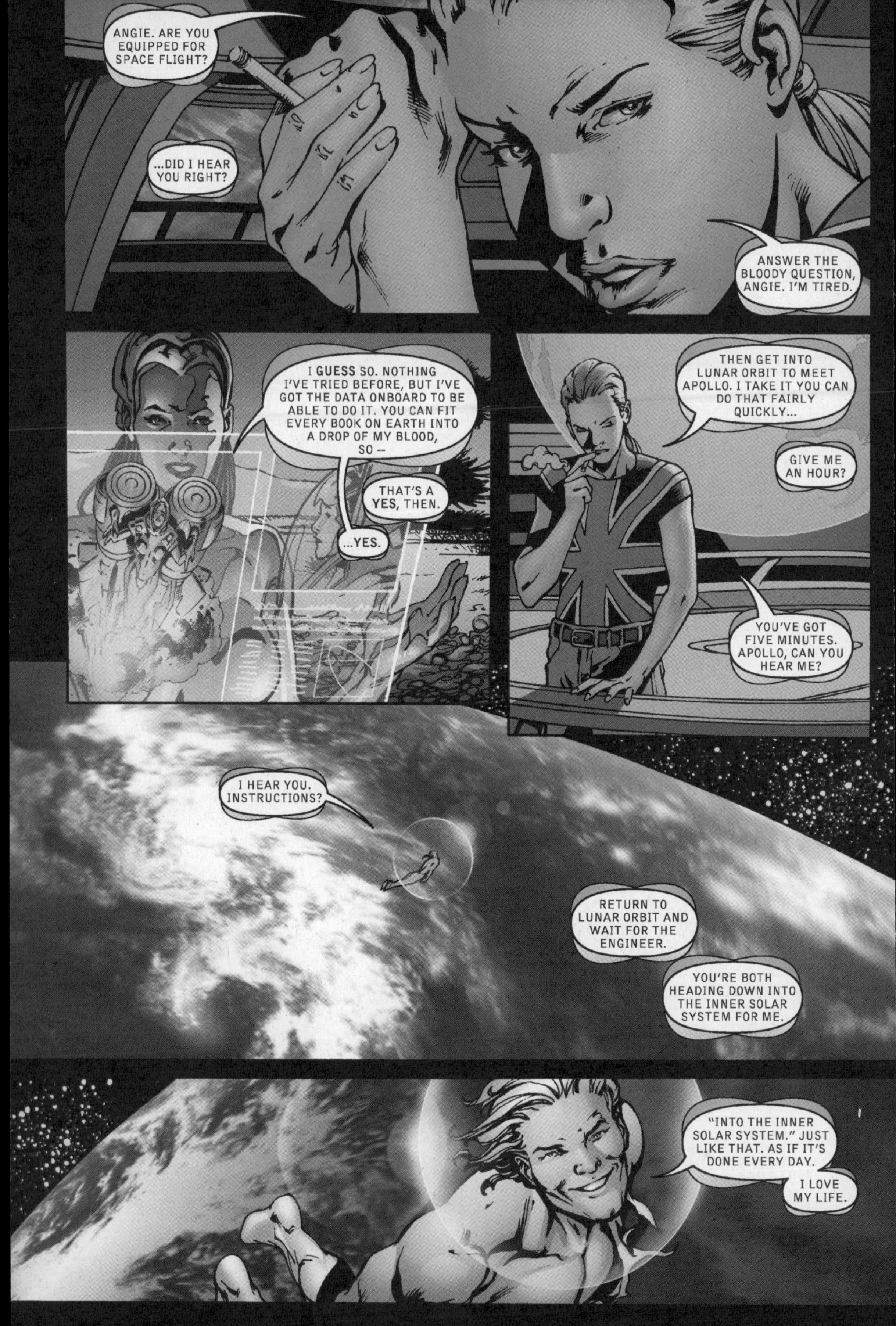
ANGIE. ARE YOU EQUIPPED FOR SPACE FLIGHT?
...DID I HEAR YOU RIGHT?
ANSWER THE BLOODY QUESTION, ANGIE. I'M TIRED.
I GUESS SO. NOTHING I'VE TRIED BEFORE, BUT I'VE GOT THE DATA ONBOARD TO BE ABLE TO DO IT. YOU CAN FIT EVERY BOOK ON EARTH INTO A DROP OF MY BLOOD, SO --
THAT'S A YES, THEN.
...YES.
THEN GET INTO LUNAR ORBIT TO MEET APOLLO. I TAKE IT YOU CAN DO THAT FAIRLY QUICKLY...
GIVE ME AN HOUR?
YOU'VE GOT FIVE MINUTES. APOLLO, CAN YOU HEAR ME?
I HEAR YOU. INSTRUCTIONS?
RETURN TO LUNAR ORBIT AND WAIT FOR THE ENGINEER.
YOU'RE BOTH HEADING DOWN INTO THE INNER SOLAR SYSTEM FOR ME.
"INTO THE INNER SOLAR SYSTEM." JUST LIKE THAT. AS IF IT'S DONE EVERY DAY.
I LOVE MY LIFE.

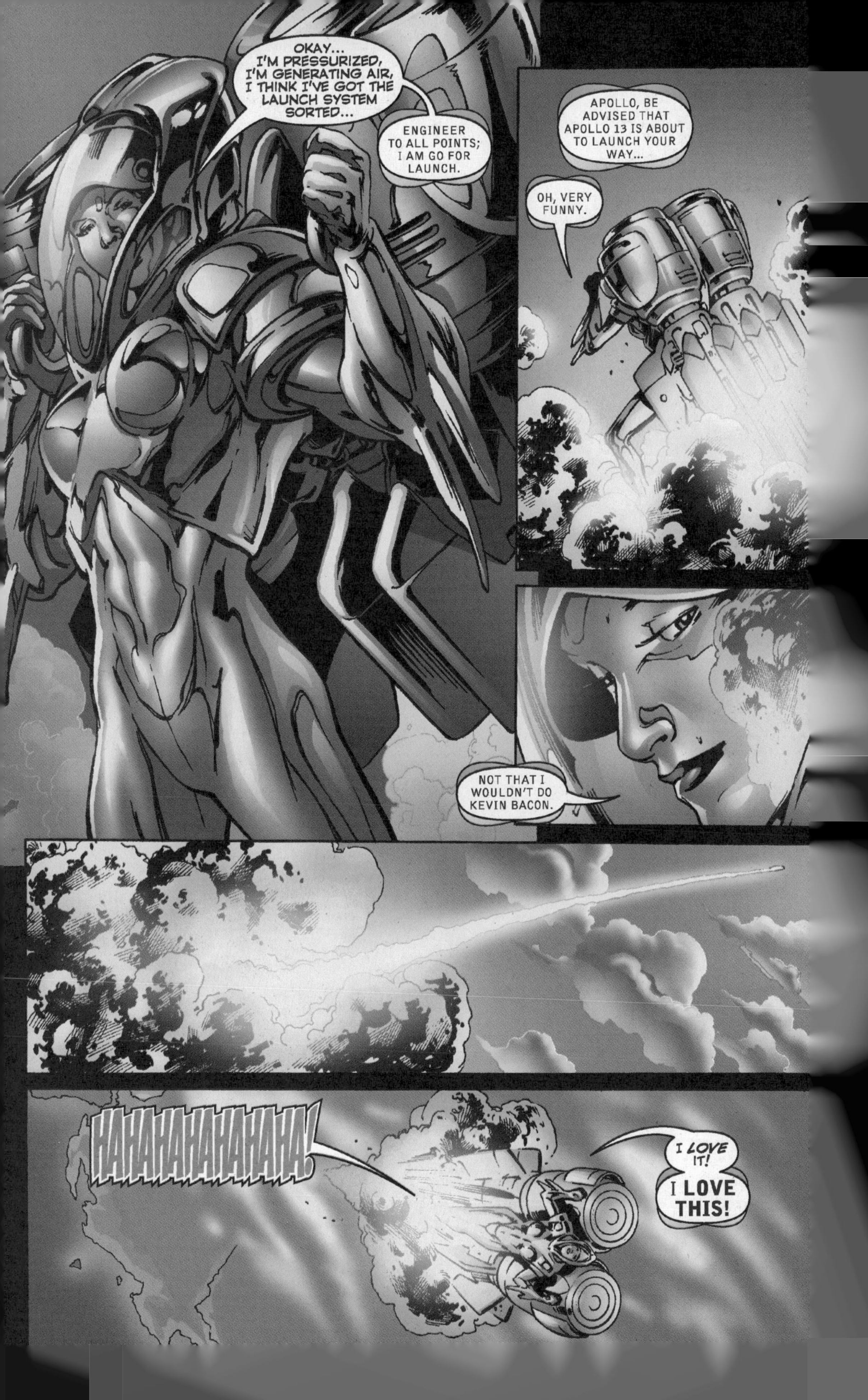
OKAY... I'M PRESSURIZED, I'M GENERATING AIR, I THINK I'VE GOT THE LAUNCH SYSTEM SORTED...
ENGINEER TO ALL POINTS; I AM GO FOR LAUNCH.
APOLLO, BE ADVISED THAT APOLLO 13 IS ABOUT TO LAUNCH YOUR WAY...
OH, VERY FUNNY.
NOT THAT I WOULDN'T DO KEVIN BACON.
HAHAHAHAHAHAHA!
I LOVE IT!
I LOVE THIS!

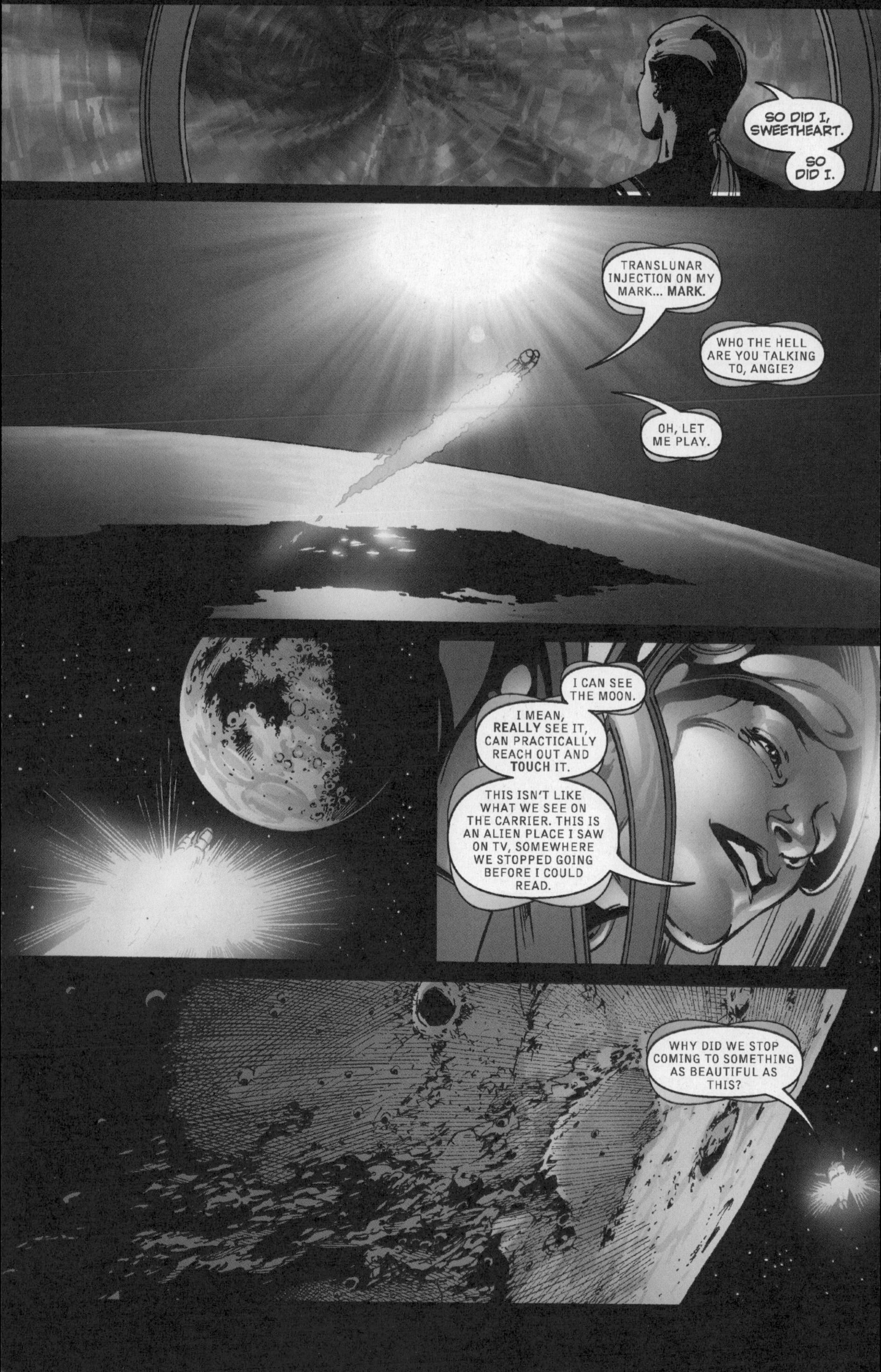
SO DID I, SWEETHEART.
SO DID I.
TRANSLUNAR INJECTION ON MY MARK... MARK.
WHO THE HELL ARE YOU TALKING TO, ANGIE?
OH, LET ME PLAY.
I CAN SEE THE MOON.
I MEAN, REALLY SEE IT, CAN PRACTICALLY REACH OUT AND TOUCH IT.
THIS ISN'T LIKE WHAT WE SEE ON THE CARRIER. THIS IS AN ALIEN PLACE I SAW ON TV, SOMEWHERE WE STOPPED GOING BEFORE I COULD READ.
WHY DID WE STOP COMING TO SOMETHING AS BEAUTIFUL AS THIS?

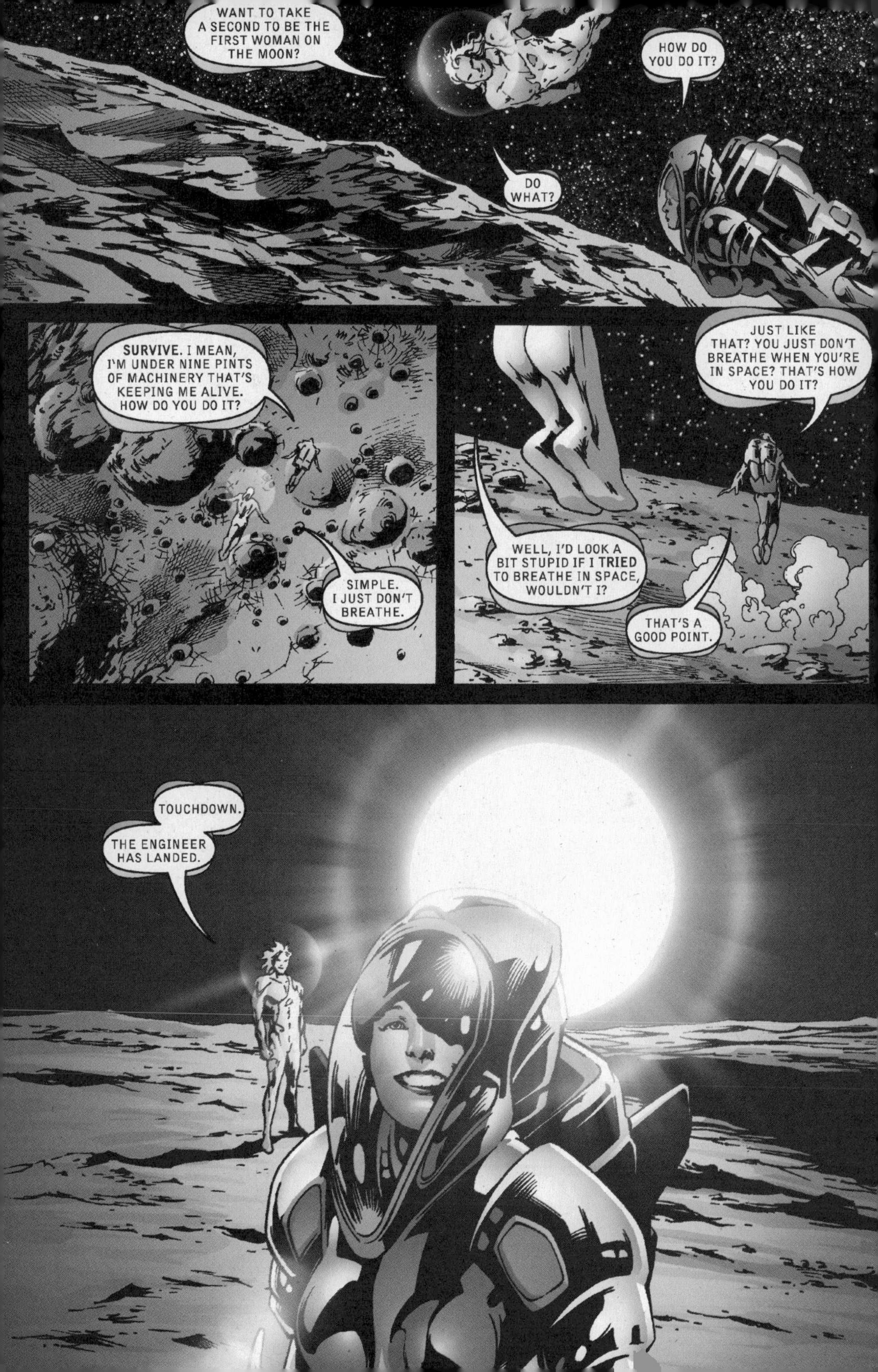

WANT TO TAKE A SECOND TO BE THE FIRST WOMAN ON THE MOON?
HOW DO YOU DO IT?
DO WHAT?
SURVIVE. I MEAN, I'M UNDER NINE PINTS OF MACHINERY THAT'S KEEPING ME ALIVE. HOW DO YOU DO IT?
SIMPLE. I JUST DON'T BREATHE.
JUST LIKE THAT? YOU JUST DON'T BREATHE WHEN YOU'RE IN SPACE? THAT'S HOW YOU DO IT?
WELL, I'D LOOK A BIT STUPID IF I TRIED TO BREATHE IN SPACE, WOULDN'T I?
THAT'S A GOOD POINT.
TOUCHDOWN.
THE ENGINEER HAS LANDED.

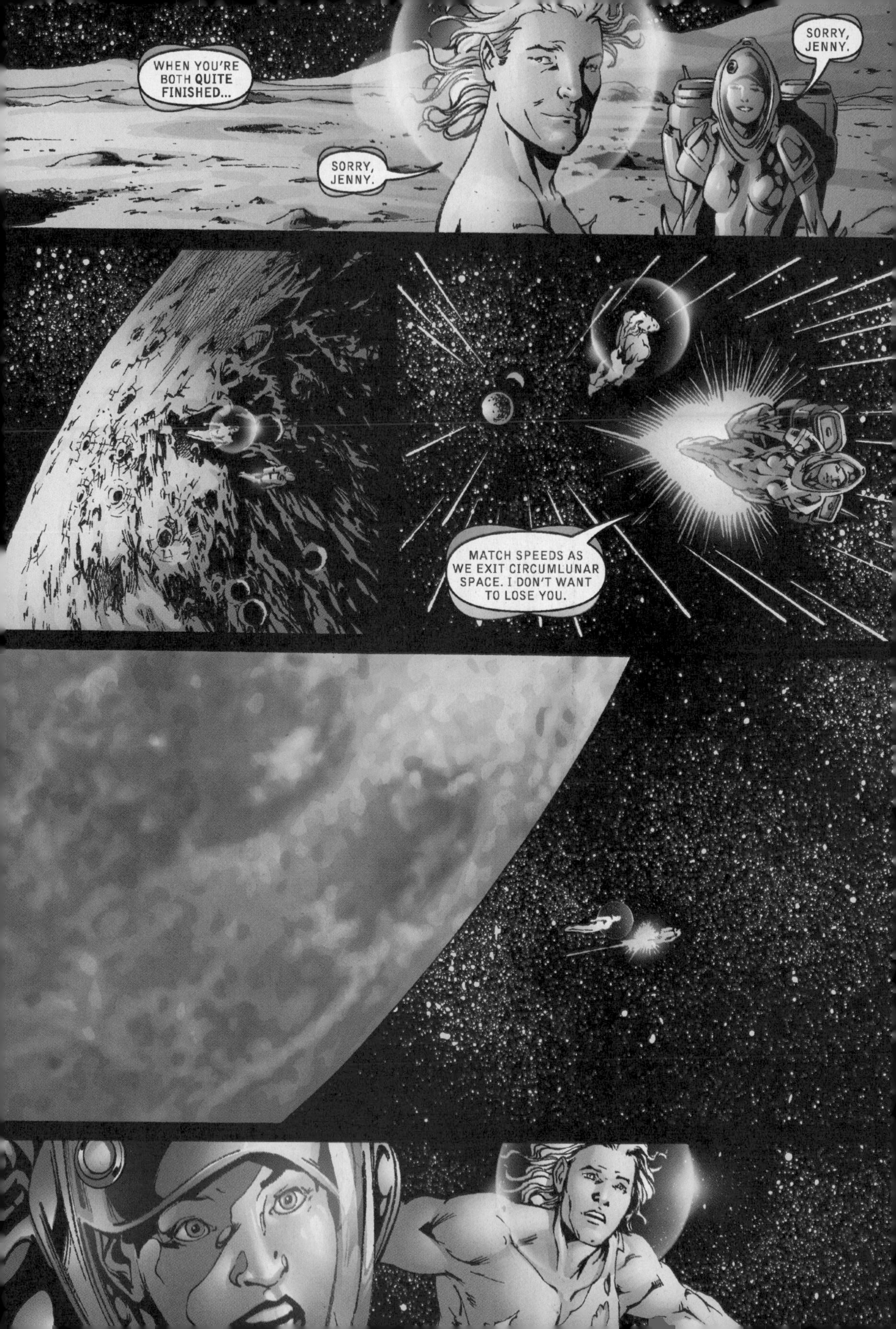
WHEN YOU'RE BOTH QUITE FINISHED...
SORRY, JENNY.
SORRY, JENNY.
MATCH SPEEDS AS WE EXIT CIRCUMLUNAR SPACE. I DON'T WANT TO LOSE YOU.

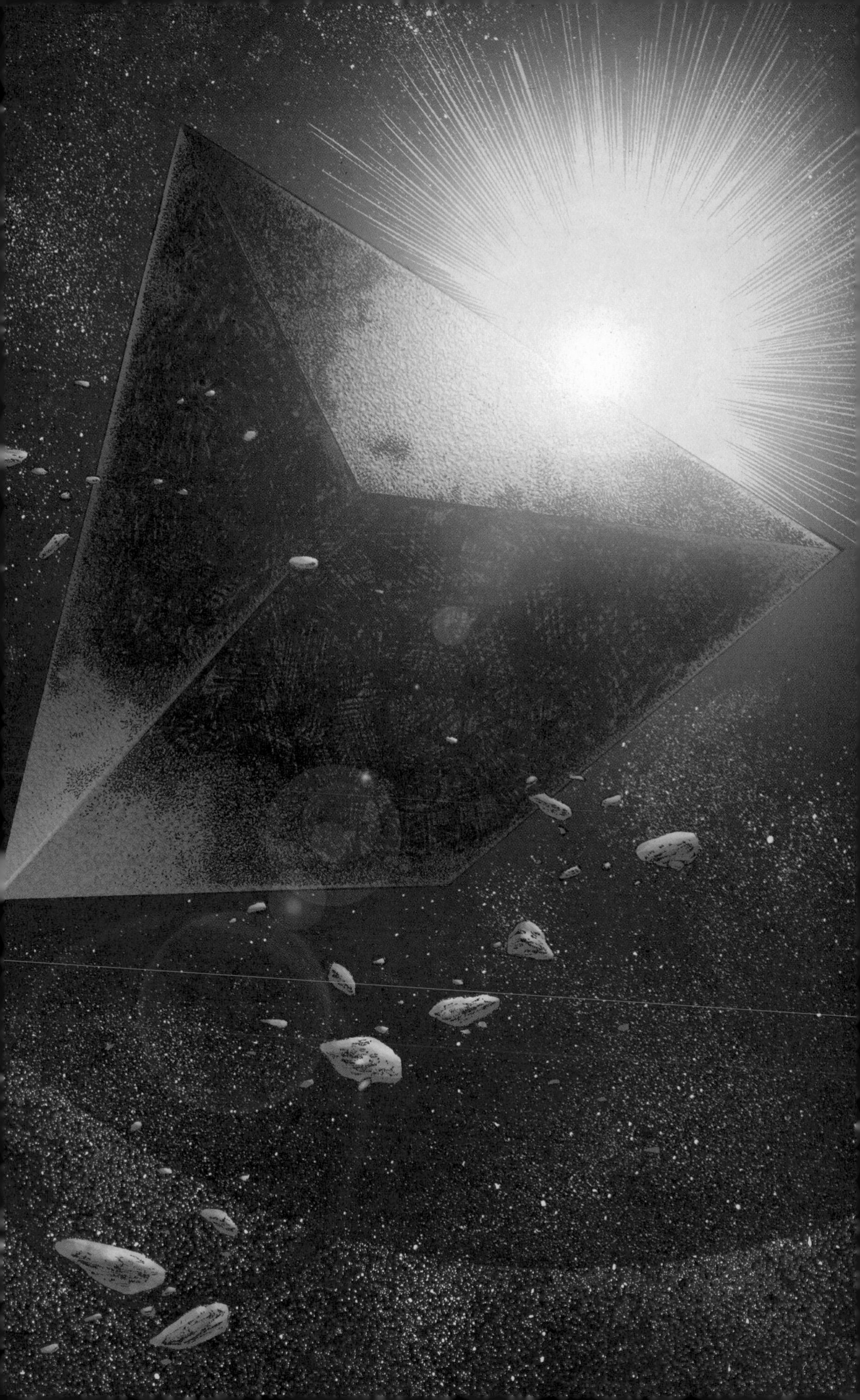

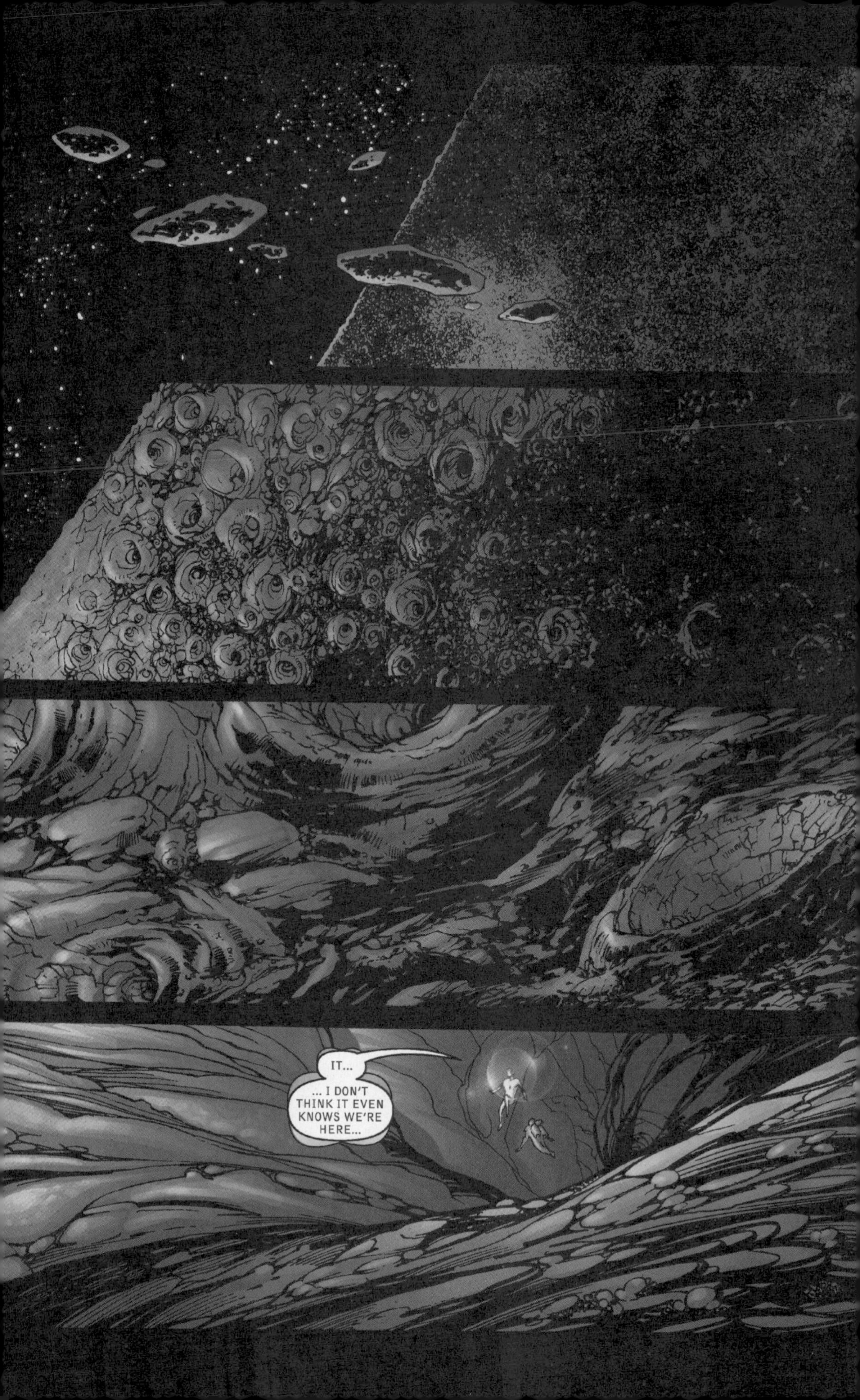
IT...
... I DON'T THINK IT EVEN KNOWS WE'RE HERE...

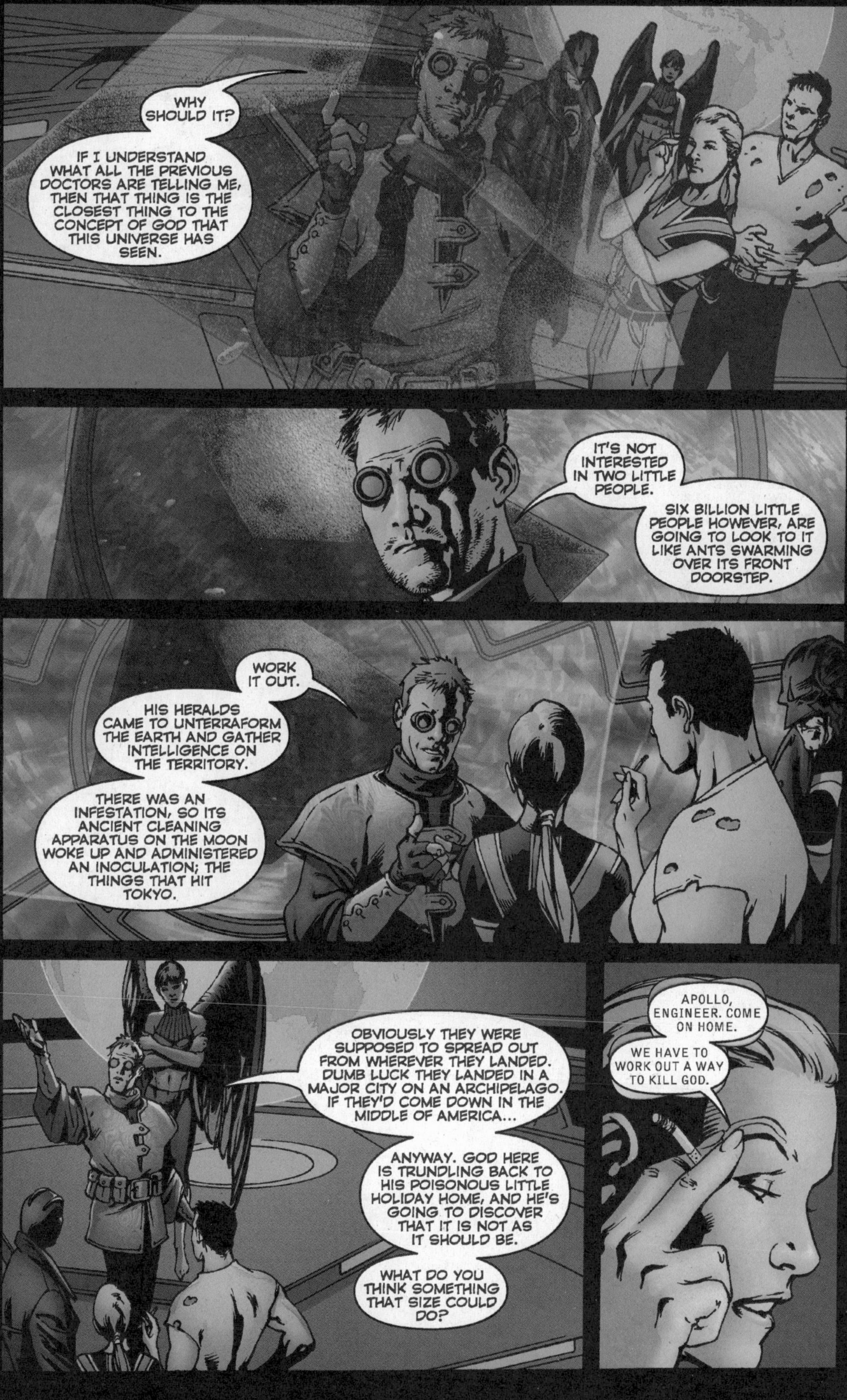
WHY SHOULD IT?
IF I UNDERSTAND WHAT ALL THE PREVIOUS DOCTORS ARE TELLING ME, THEN THAT THING IS THE CLOSEST THING TO THE CONCEPT OF GOD THAT THIS UNIVERSE HAS SEEN.
IT'S NOT INTERESTED IN TWO LITTLE PEOPLE.
SIX BILLION LITTLE PEOPLE HOWEVER, ARE GOING TO LOOK TO IT LIKE ANTS SWARMING OVER ITS FRONT DOORSTEP.
WORK IT OUT.
HIS HERALDS CAME TO UNTERRAFORM THE EARTH AND GATHER INTELLIGENCE ON THE TERRITORY.
THERE WAS AN INFESTATION, SO ITS ANCIENT CLEANING APPARATUS ON THE MOON WOKE UP AND ADMINISTERED AN INOCULATION; THE THINGS THAT HIT TOKYO.
OBVIOUSLY THEY WERE SUPPOSED TO SPREAD OUT FROM WHEREVER THEY LANDED. DUMB LUCK THEY LANDED IN A MAJOR CITY ON AN ARCHIPELAGO. IF THEY'D COME DOWN IN THE MIDDLE OF AMERICA...
ANYWAY. GOD HERE IS TRUNDLING BACK TO HIS POISONOUS LITTLE HOLIDAY HOME, AND HE'S GOING TO DISCOVER THAT IT IS NOT AS IT SHOULD BE.
WHAT DO YOU THINK SOMETHING THAT SIZE COULD DO?
APOLLO, ENGINEER. COME ON HOME.
WE HAVE TO WORK OUT A WAY TO KILL GOD.

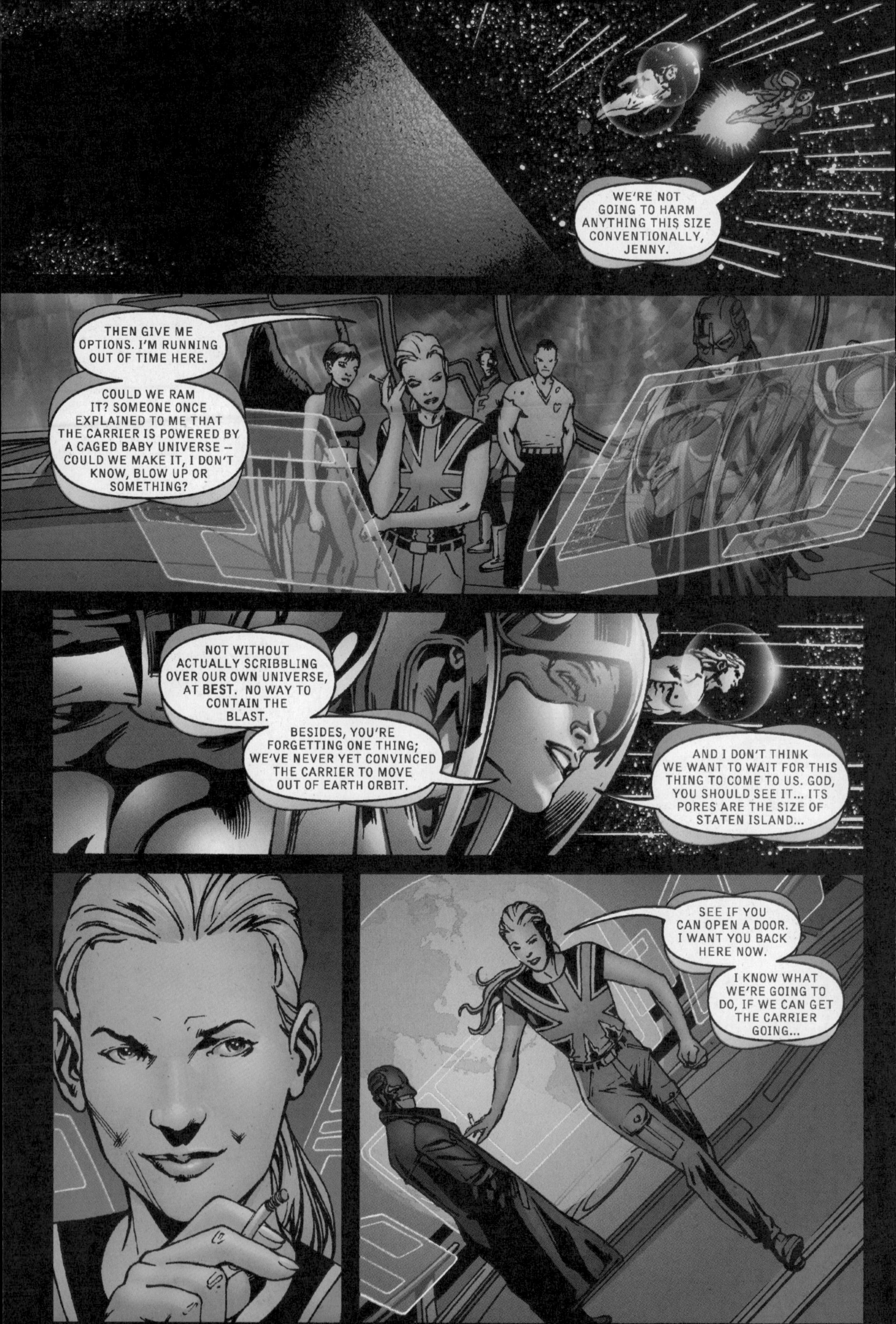
WE'RE NOT GOING TO HARM ANYTHING THIS SIZE CONVENTIONALLY, JENNY.
THEN GIVE ME OPTIONS. I'M RUNNING OUT OF TIME HERE.
COULD WE RAM IT? SOMEONE ONCE EXPLAINED TO ME THAT THE CARRIER IS POWERED BY A CAGED BABY UNIVERSE -- COULD WE MAKE IT, I DON'T KNOW, BLOW UP OR SOMETHING?
NOT WITHOUT ACTUALLY SCRIBBLING OVER OUR OWN UNIVERSE, AT BEST. NO WAY TO CONTAIN THE BLAST.
BESIDES, YOU'RE FORGETTING ONE THING; WE'VE NEVER YET CONVINCED THE CARRIER TO MOVE OUT OF EARTH ORBIT.
AND I DON'T THINK WE WANT TO WAIT FOR THIS THING TO COME TO US. GOD, YOU SHOULD SEE IT... ITS PORES ARE THE SIZE OF STATEN ISLAND...
SEE IF YOU CAN OPEN A DOOR. I WANT YOU BACK HERE NOW.
I KNOW WHAT WE'RE GOING TO DO, IF WE CAN GET THE CARRIER GOING...

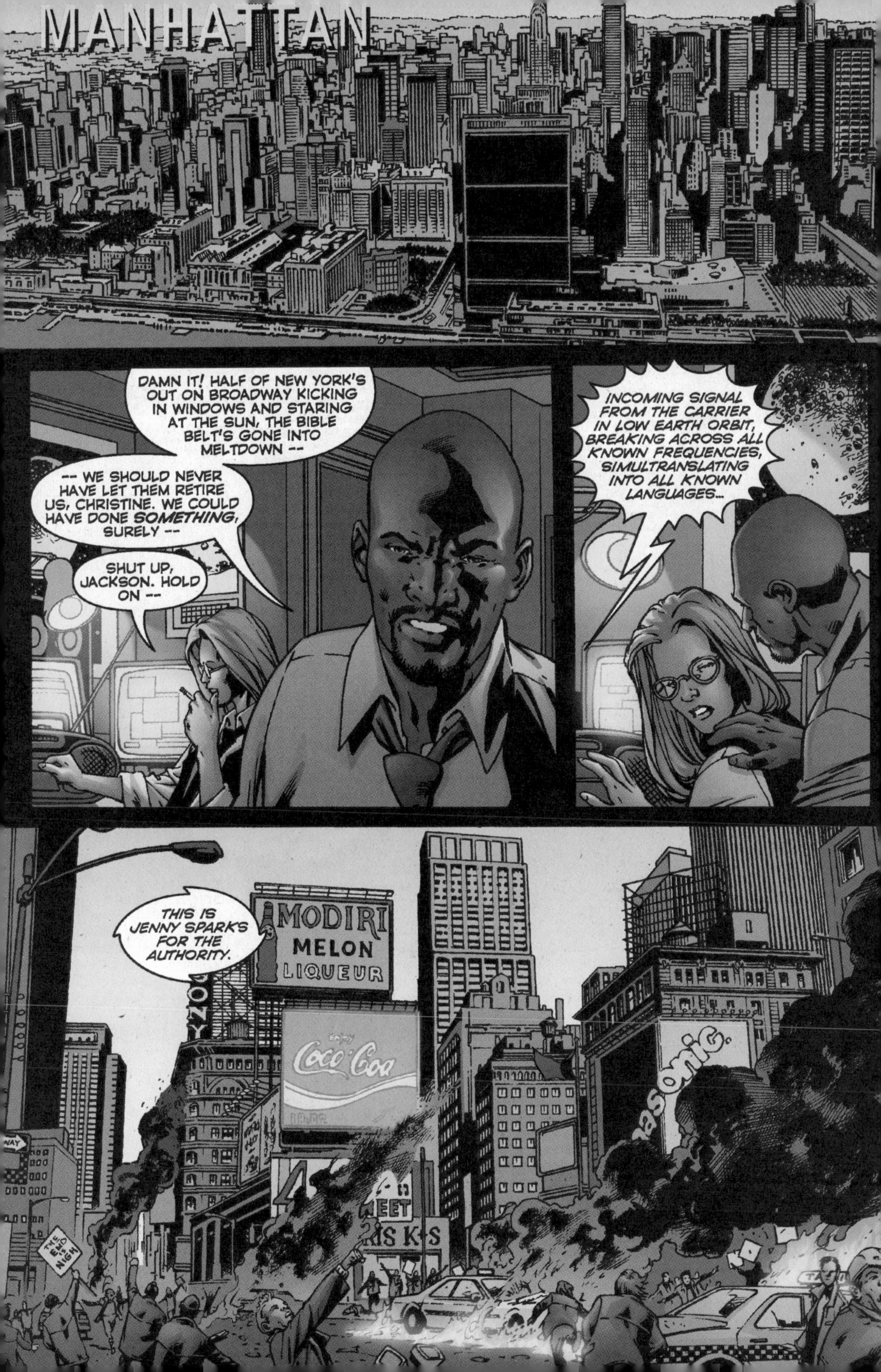
MANHATTAN
DAMN IT! HALF OF NEW YORK'S OUT ON BROADWAY KICKING IN WINDOWS AND STARING AT THE SUN, THE BIBLE BELT'S GONE INTO MELTDOWN --
-- WE SHOULD NEVER HAVE LET THEM RETIRE US, CHRISTINE. WE COULD HAVE DONE *SOMETHING*, SURELY --
SHUT UP, JACKSON. HOLD ON --
INCOMING SIGNAL FROM THE CARRIER IN LOW EARTH ORBIT, BREAKING ACROSS ALL KNOWN FREQUENCIES, SIMULTRANSLATING INTO ALL KNOWN LANGUAGES...
THIS IS JENNY SPARKS FOR THE AUTHORITY.
MODIRI
MELON
LIQUEUR
Coca-Cola
THE END IS NIGH

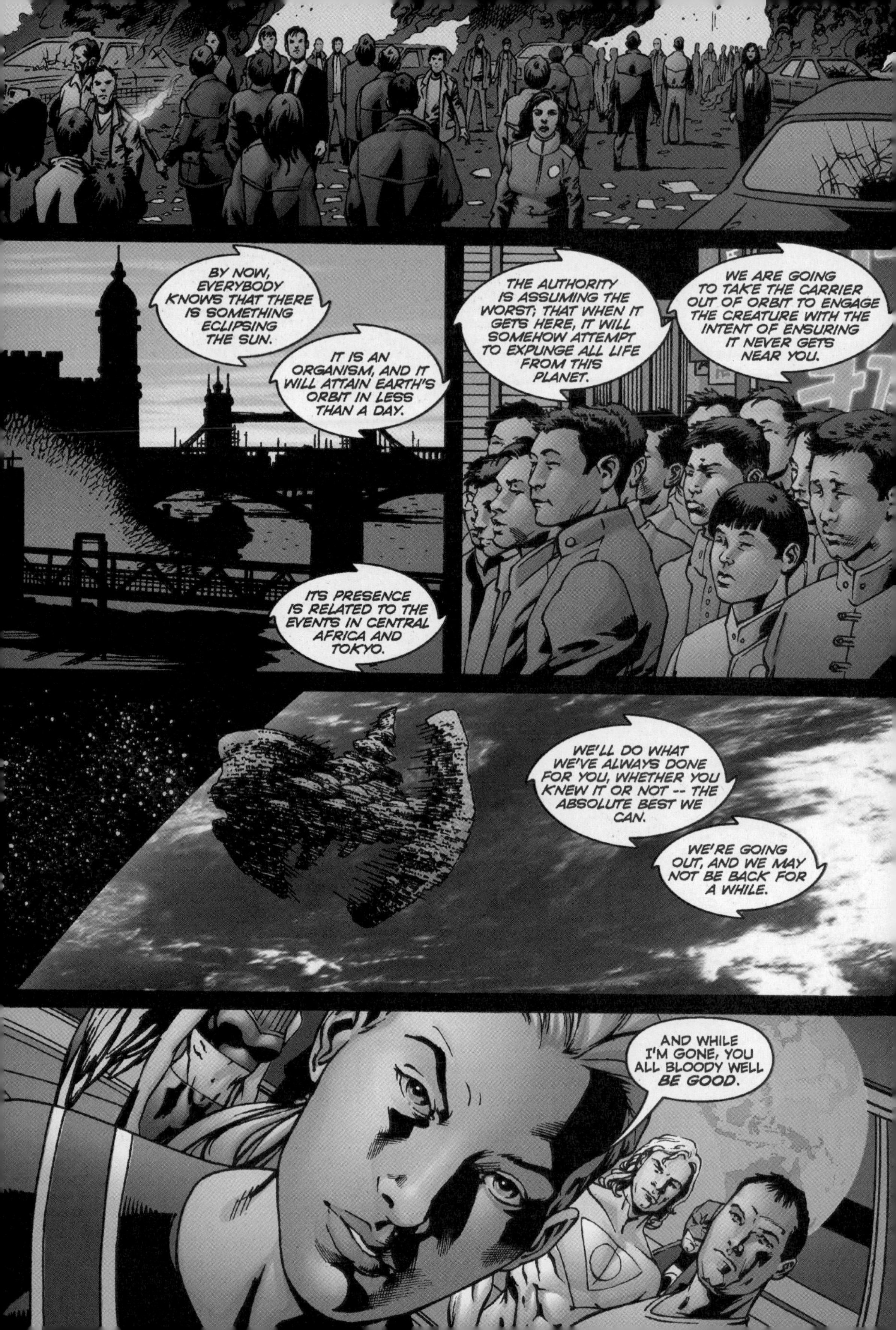
BY NOW, EVERYBODY KNOWS THAT THERE IS SOMETHING ECLIPSING THE SUN.
IT IS AN ORGANISM, AND IT WILL ATTAIN EARTH'S ORBIT IN LESS THAN A DAY.
ITS PRESENCE IS RELATED TO THE EVENTS IN CENTRAL AFRICA AND TOKYO.
THE AUTHORITY IS ASSUMING THE WORST; THAT WHEN IT GETS HERE, IT WILL SOMEHOW ATTEMPT TO EXPUNGE ALL LIFE FROM THIS PLANET.
WE ARE GOING TO TAKE THE CARRIER OUT OF ORBIT TO ENGAGE THE CREATURE WITH THE INTENT OF ENSURING IT NEVER GETS NEAR YOU.
WE'LL DO WHAT WE'VE ALWAYS DONE FOR YOU, WHETHER YOU KNEW IT OR NOT -- THE ABSOLUTE BEST WE CAN.
WE'RE GOING OUT, AND WE MAY NOT BE BACK FOR A WHILE.
AND WHILE I'M GONE, YOU ALL BLOODY WELL BE GOOD.

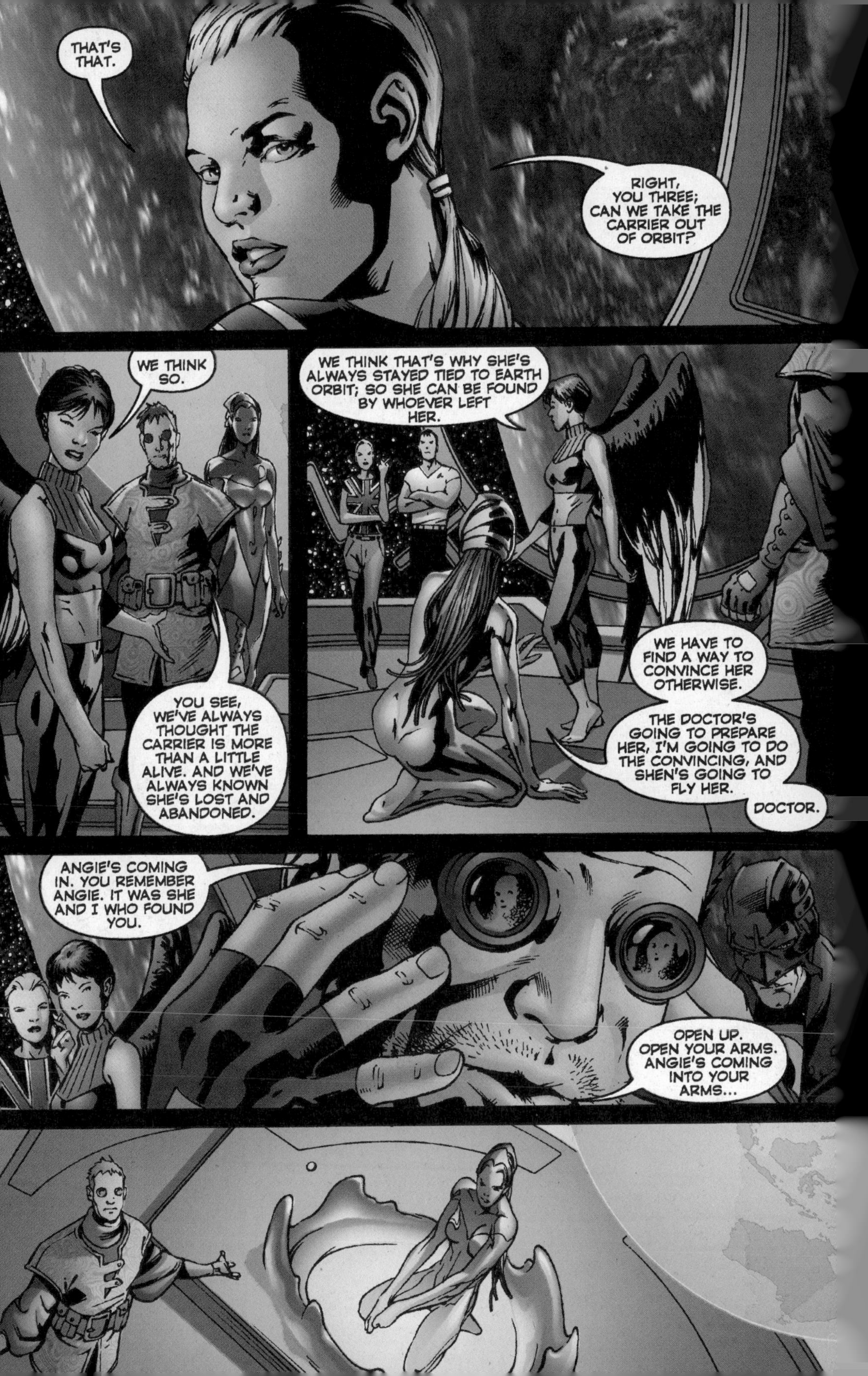
THAT'S THAT.
RIGHT, YOU THREE; CAN WE TAKE THE CARRIER OUT OF ORBIT?
WE THINK SO.
YOU SEE, WE'VE ALWAYS THOUGHT THE CARRIER IS MORE THAN A LITTLE ALIVE. AND WE'VE ALWAYS KNOWN SHE'S LOST AND ABANDONED.
WE THINK THAT'S WHY SHE'S ALWAYS STAYED TIED TO EARTH ORBIT; SO SHE CAN BE FOUND BY WHOEVER LEFT HER.
WE HAVE TO FIND A WAY TO CONVINCE HER OTHERWISE.
THE DOCTOR'S GOING TO PREPARE HER, I'M GOING TO DO THE CONVINCING, AND SHEN'S GOING TO FLY HER.
DOCTOR.
ANGIE'S COMING IN. YOU REMEMBER ANGIE. IT WAS SHE AND I WHO FOUND YOU.
OPEN UP. OPEN YOUR ARMS. ANGIE'S COMING INTO YOUR ARMS...

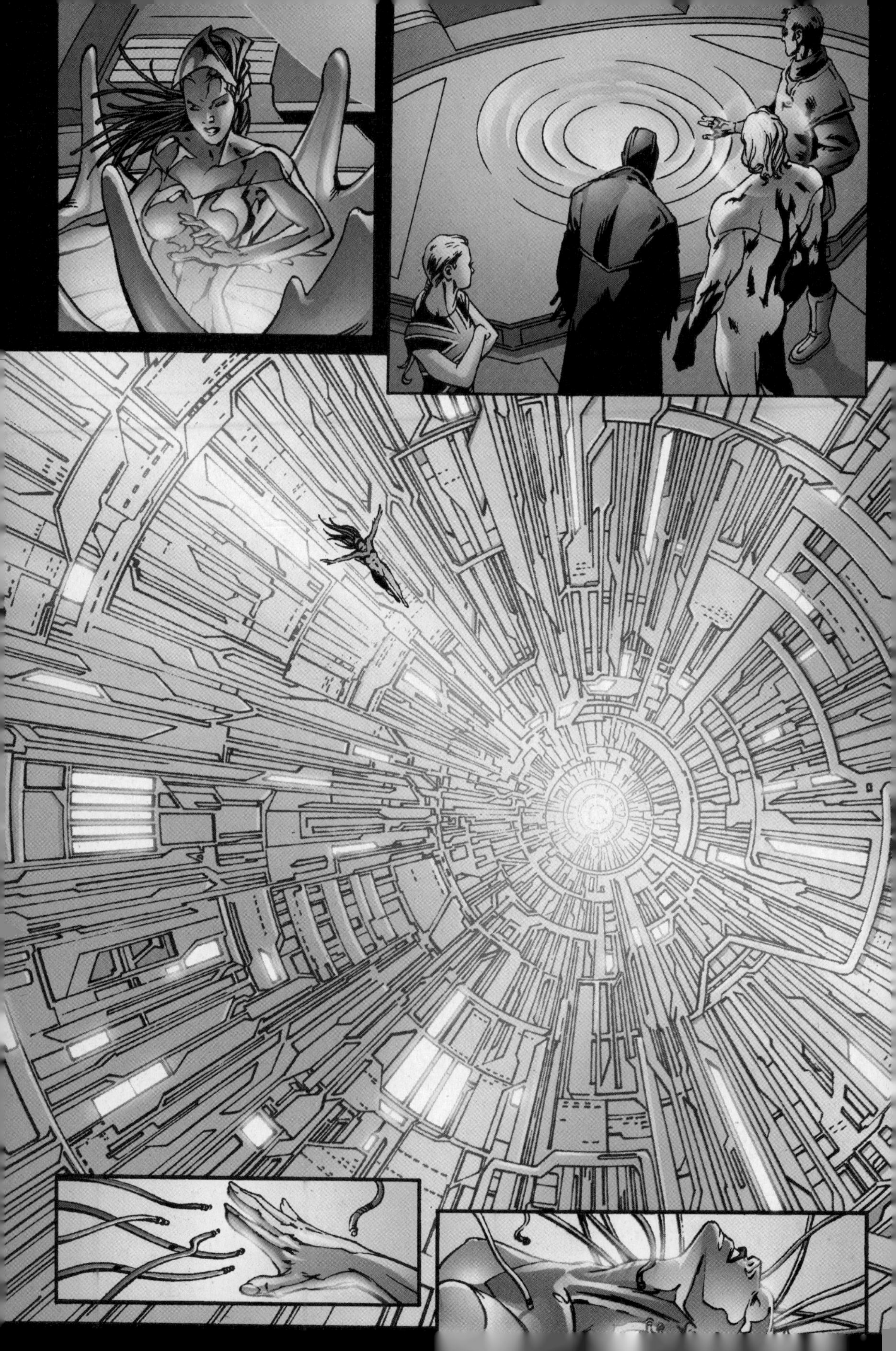

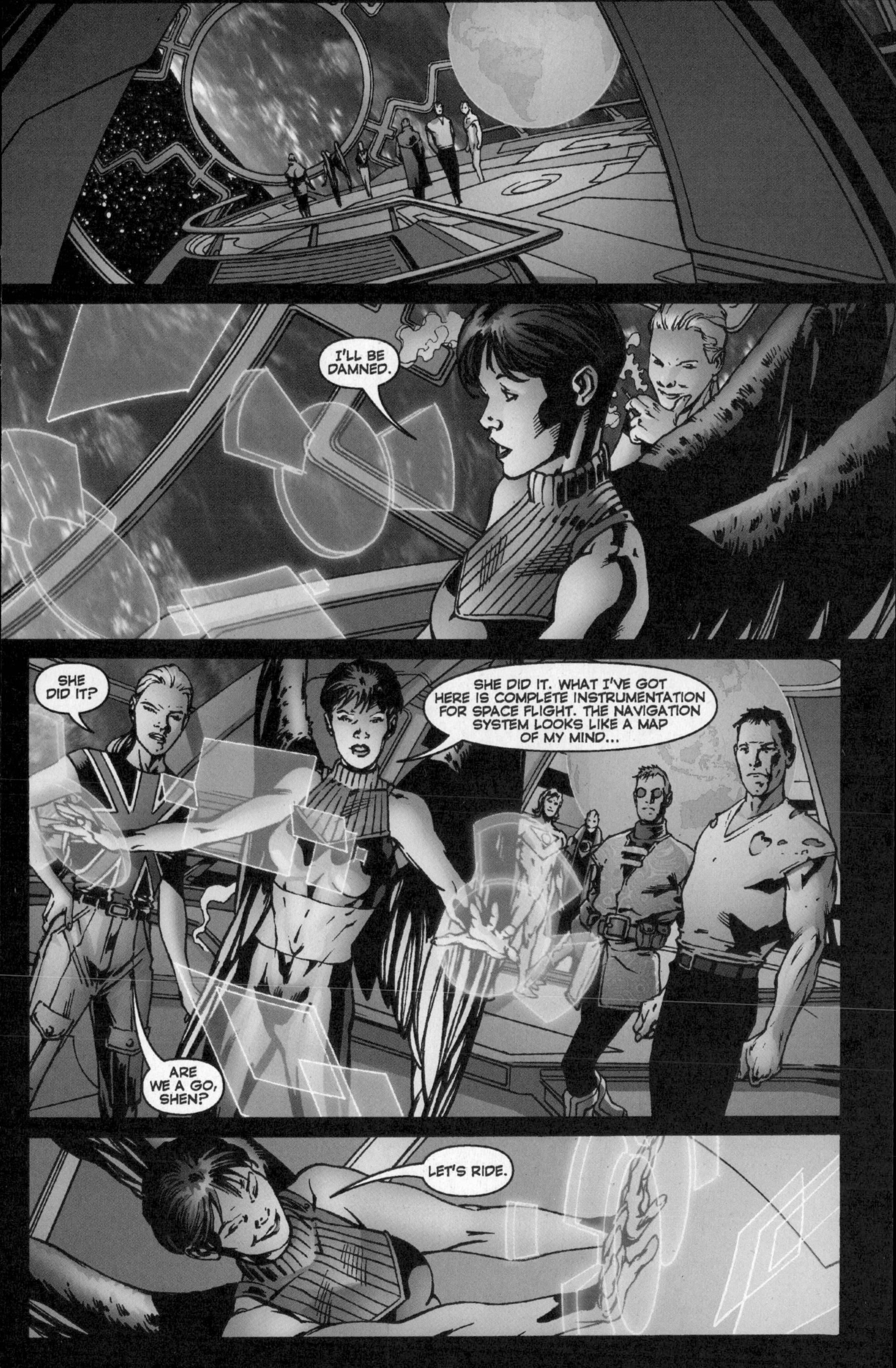
I'LL BE DAMNED.
SHE DID IT?
SHE DID IT. WHAT I'VE GOT HERE IS COMPLETE INSTRUMENTATION FOR SPACE FLIGHT. THE NAVIGATION SYSTEM LOOKS LIKE A MAP OF MY MIND...
ARE WE A GO, SHEN?
LET'S RIDE.

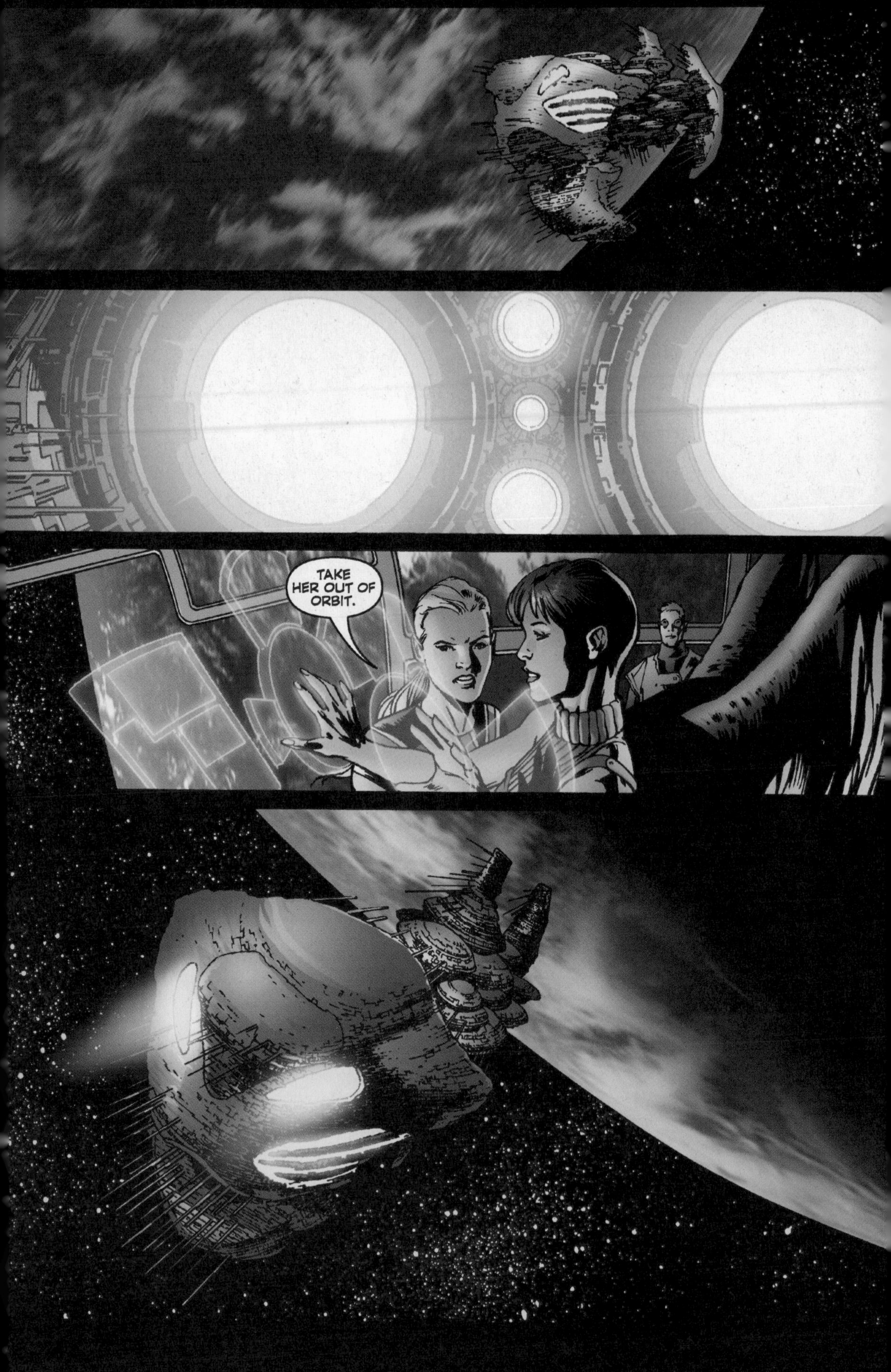
TAKE HER OUT OF ORBIT.

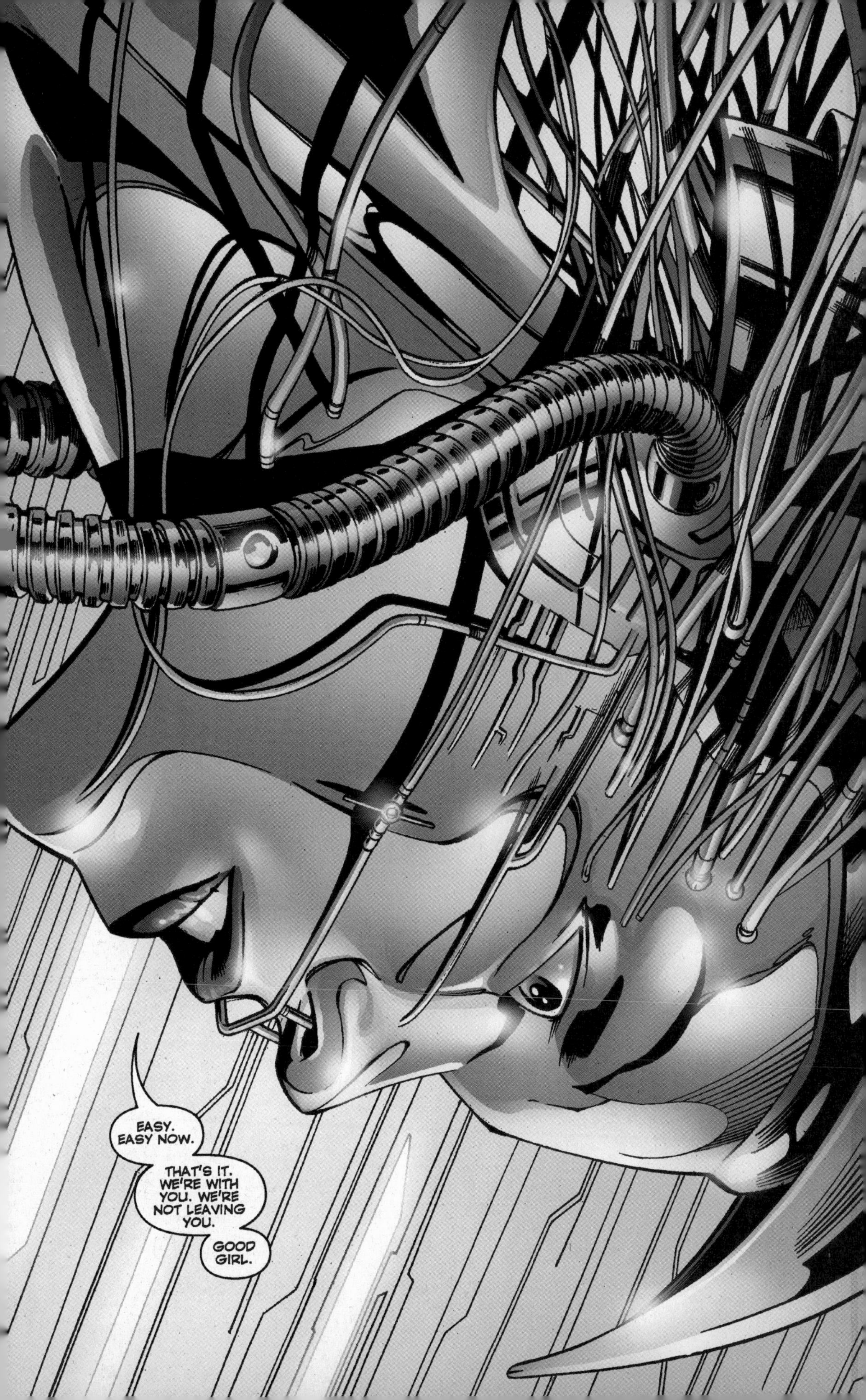
EASY. EASY NOW.
THAT'S IT. WE'RE WITH YOU. WE'RE NOT LEAVING YOU.
GOOD GIRL.

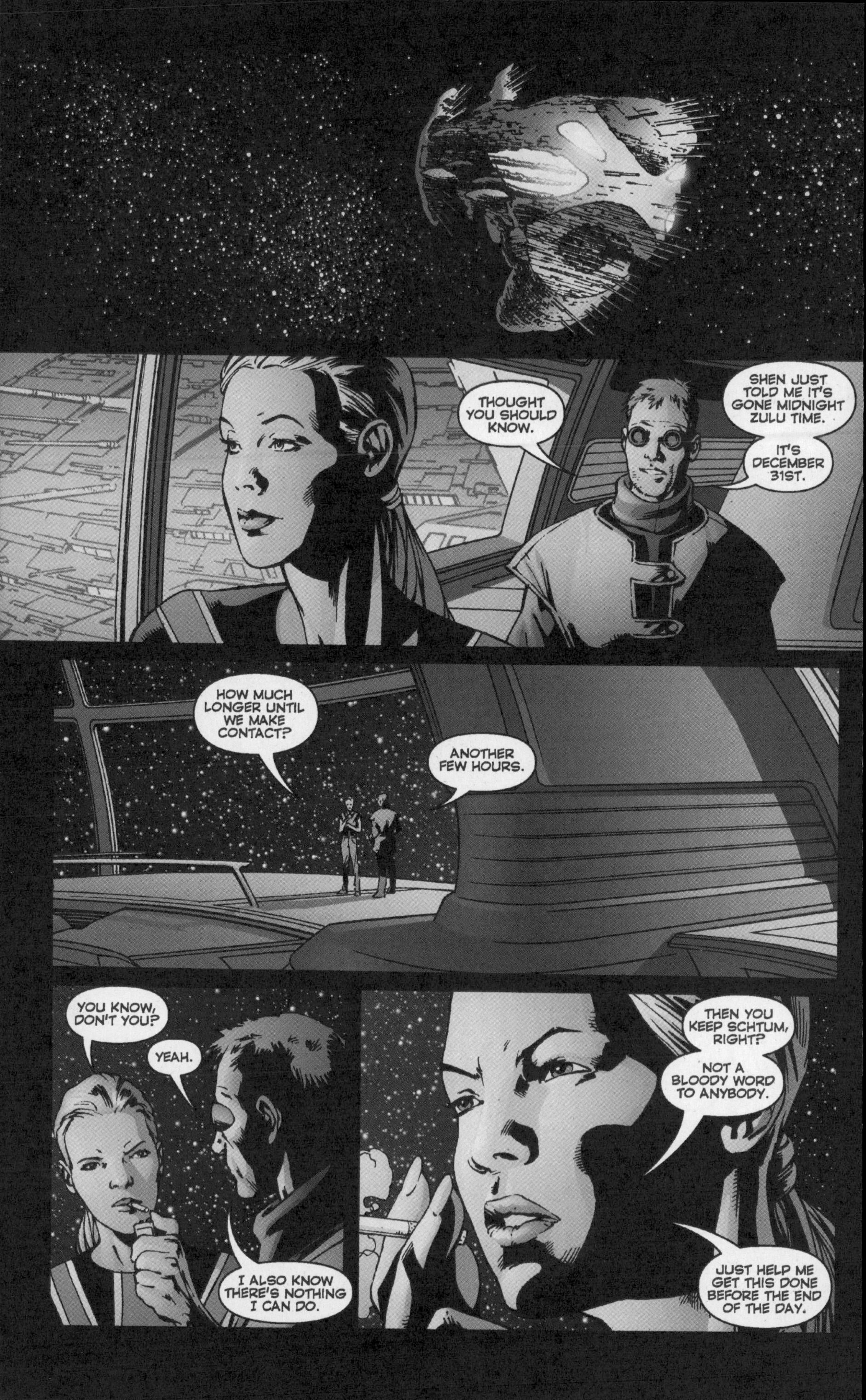
THOUGHT YOU SHOULD KNOW.
SHEN JUST TOLD ME IT'S GONE MIDNIGHT ZULU TIME.
IT'S DECEMBER 31ST.
HOW MUCH LONGER UNTIL WE MAKE CONTACT?
ANOTHER FEW HOURS.
YOU KNOW, DON'T YOU?
YEAH.
I ALSO KNOW THERE'S NOTHING I CAN DO.
THEN YOU KEEP SCHTUM, RIGHT?
NOT A BLOODY WORD TO ANYBODY.
JUST HELP ME GET THIS DONE BEFORE THE END OF THE DAY.

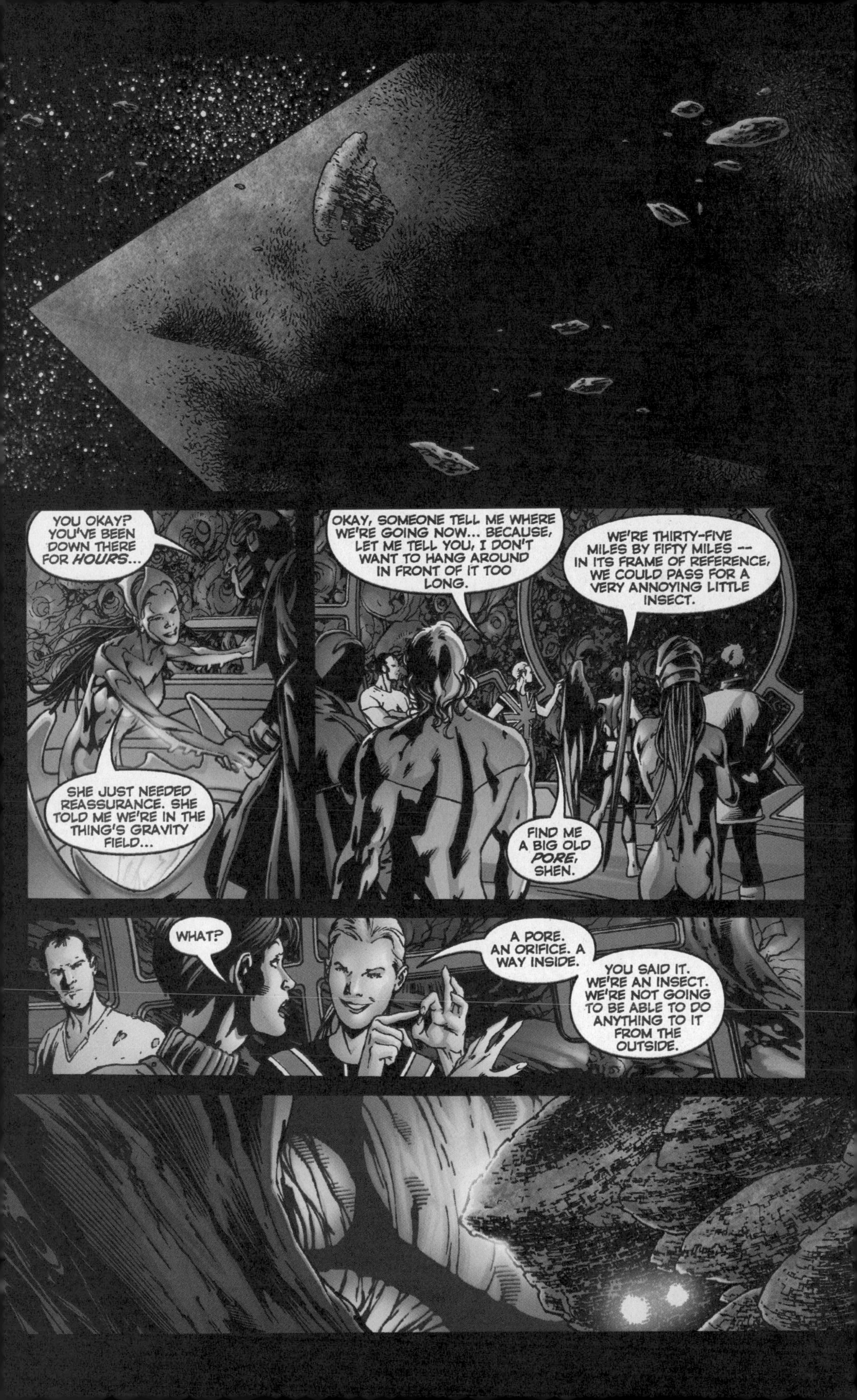

YOU OKAY? YOU'VE BEEN DOWN THERE FOR HOURS...
SHE JUST NEEDED REASSURANCE. SHE TOLD ME WE'RE IN THE THING'S GRAVITY FIELD...
OKAY, SOMEONE TELL ME WHERE WE'RE GOING NOW... BECAUSE, LET ME TELL YOU, I DON'T WANT TO HANG AROUND IN FRONT OF IT TOO LONG.
WE'RE THIRTY-FIVE MILES BY FIFTY MILES -- IN ITS FRAME OF REFERENCE, WE COULD PASS FOR A VERY ANNOYING LITTLE INSECT.
FIND ME A BIG OLD PORE, SHEN.
WHAT?
A PORE. AN ORIFICE. A WAY INSIDE.
YOU SAID IT. WE'RE AN INSECT. WE'RE NOT GOING TO BE ABLE TO DO ANYTHING TO IT FROM THE OUTSIDE.

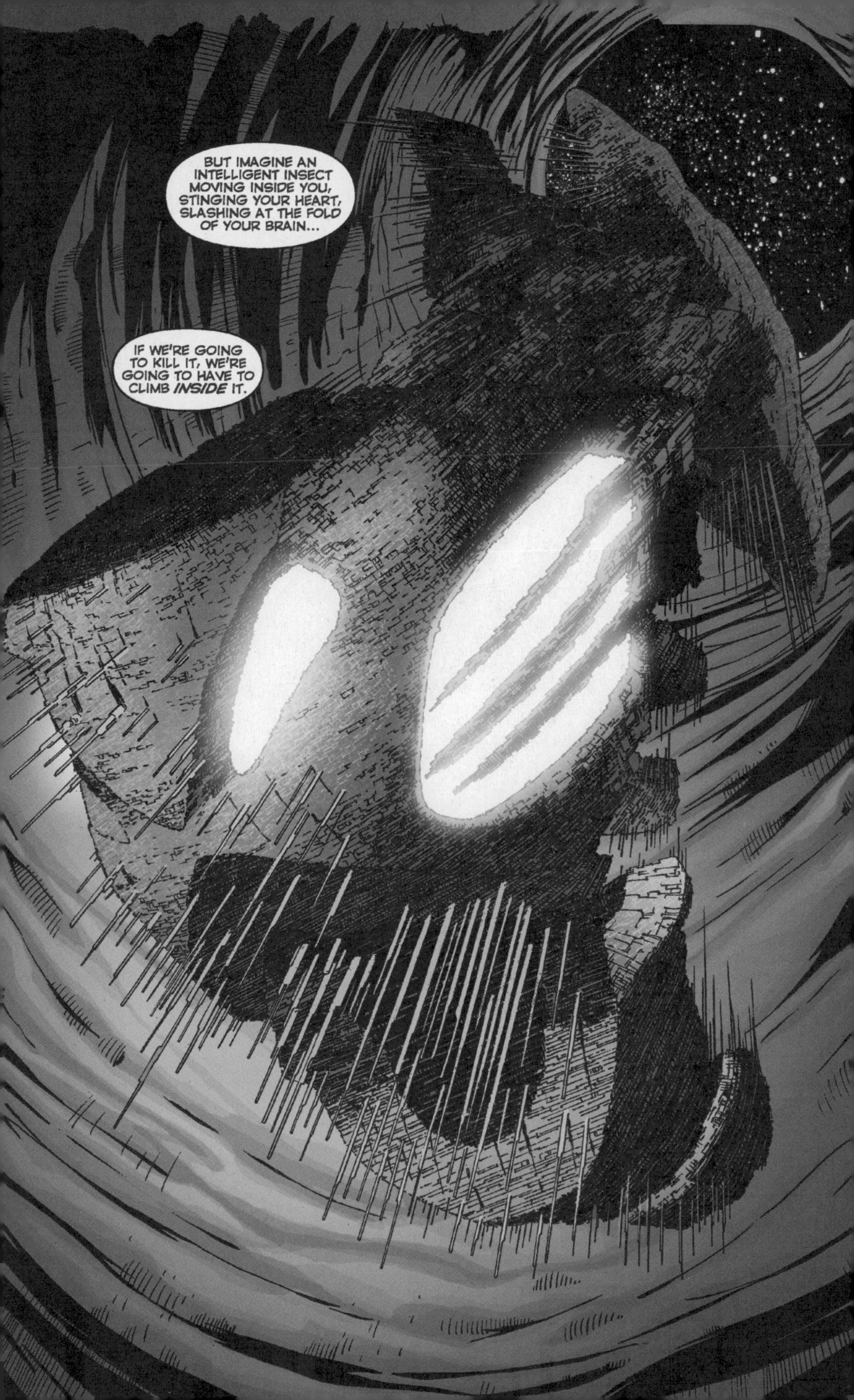
BUT IMAGINE AN INTELLIGENT INSECT MOVING INSIDE YOU, STINGING YOUR HEART, SLASHING AT THE FOLD OF YOUR BRAIN...
IF WE'RE GOING TO KILL IT, WE'RE GOING TO HAVE TO CLIMB *INSIDE* IT.

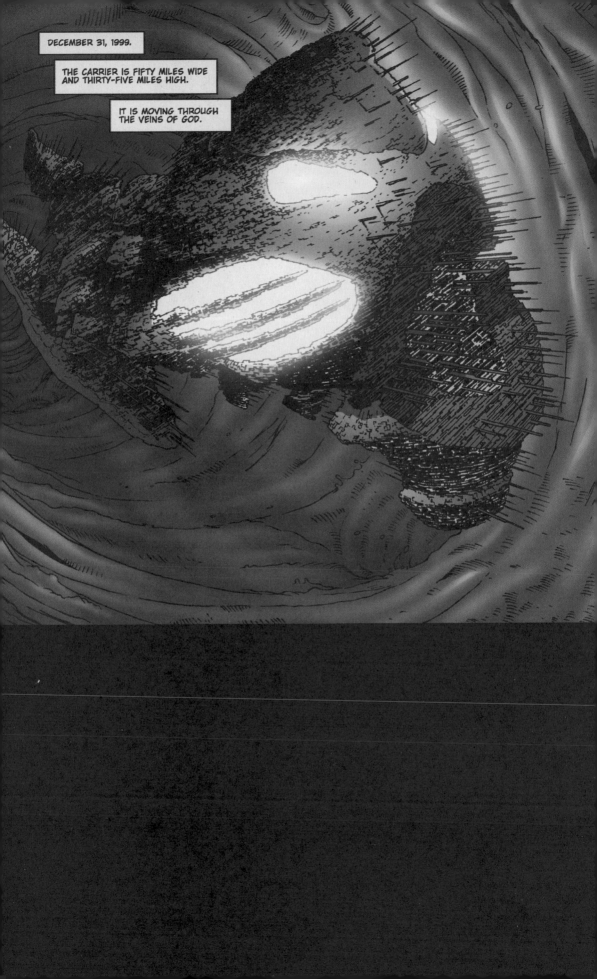

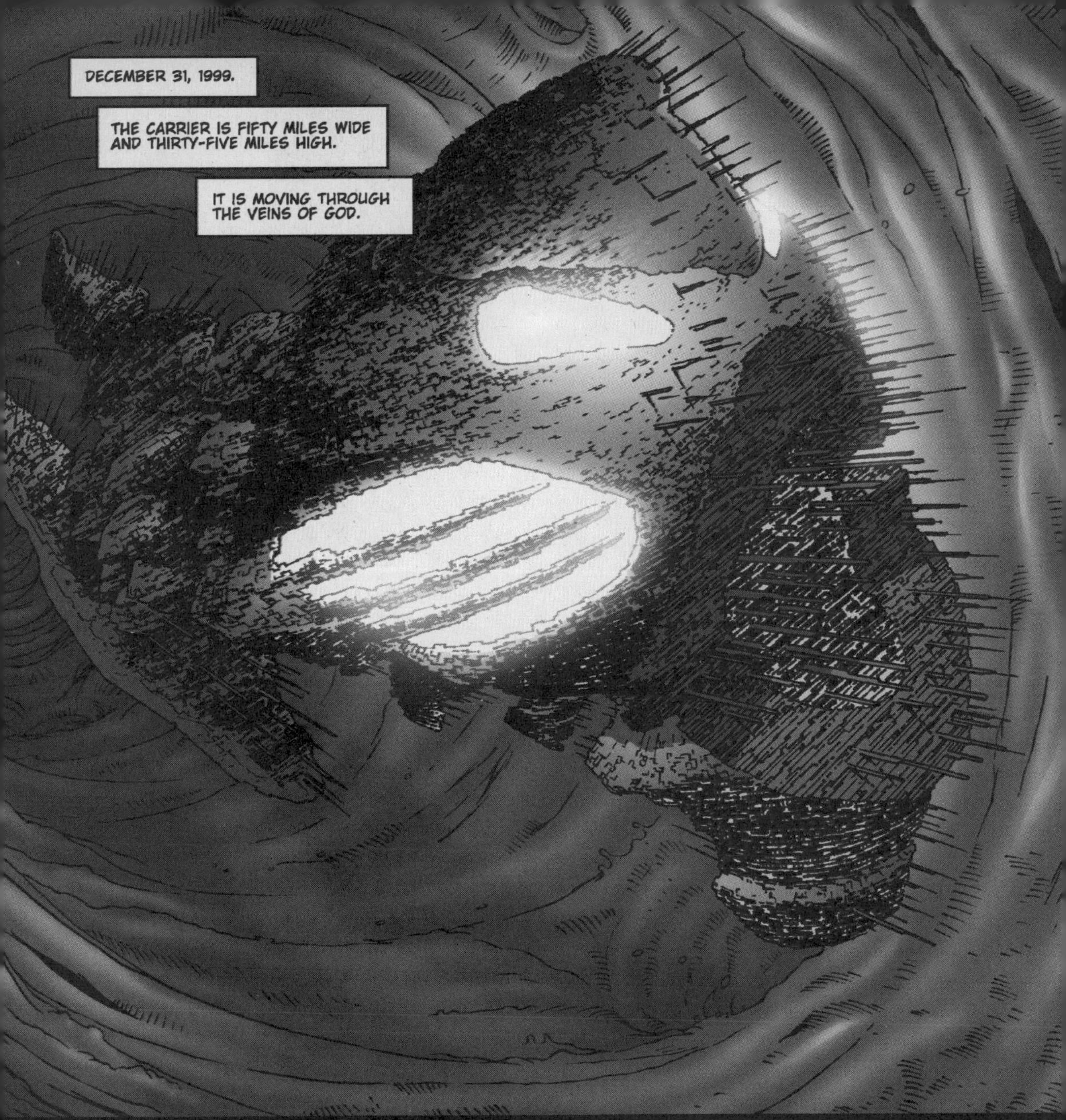
DECEMBER 31, 1999.
THE CARRIER IS FIFTY MILES WIDE AND THIRTY-FIVE MILES HIGH.
IT IS MOVING THROUGH THE VEINS OF GOD.

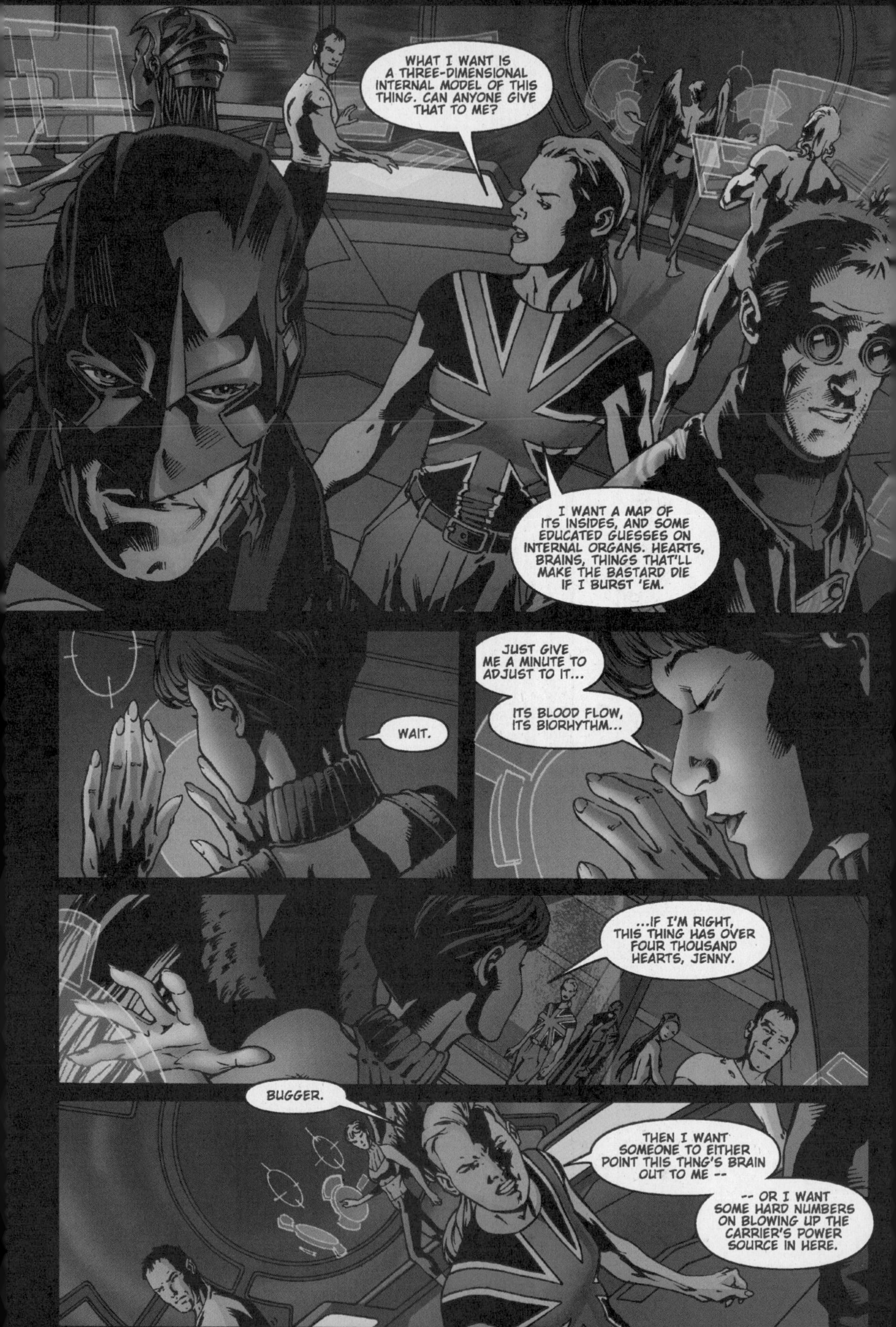
WHAT I WANT IS A THREE-DIMENSIONAL INTERNAL MODEL OF THIS THING. CAN ANYONE GIVE THAT TO ME?
I WANT A MAP OF ITS INSIDES, AND SOME EDUCATED GUESSES ON INTERNAL ORGANS. HEARTS, BRAINS, THINGS THAT'LL MAKE THE BASTARD DIE IF I BURST 'EM.
WAIT.
JUST GIVE ME A MINUTE TO ADJUST TO IT...
ITS BLOOD FLOW, ITS BIORHYTHM...
...IF I'M RIGHT, THIS THING HAS OVER FOUR THOUSAND HEARTS, JENNY.
BUGGER.
THEN I WANT SOMEONE TO EITHER POINT THIS THNG'S BRAIN OUT TO ME --
-- OR I WANT SOME HARD NUMBERS ON BLOWING UP THE CARRIER'S POWER SOURCE IN HERE.

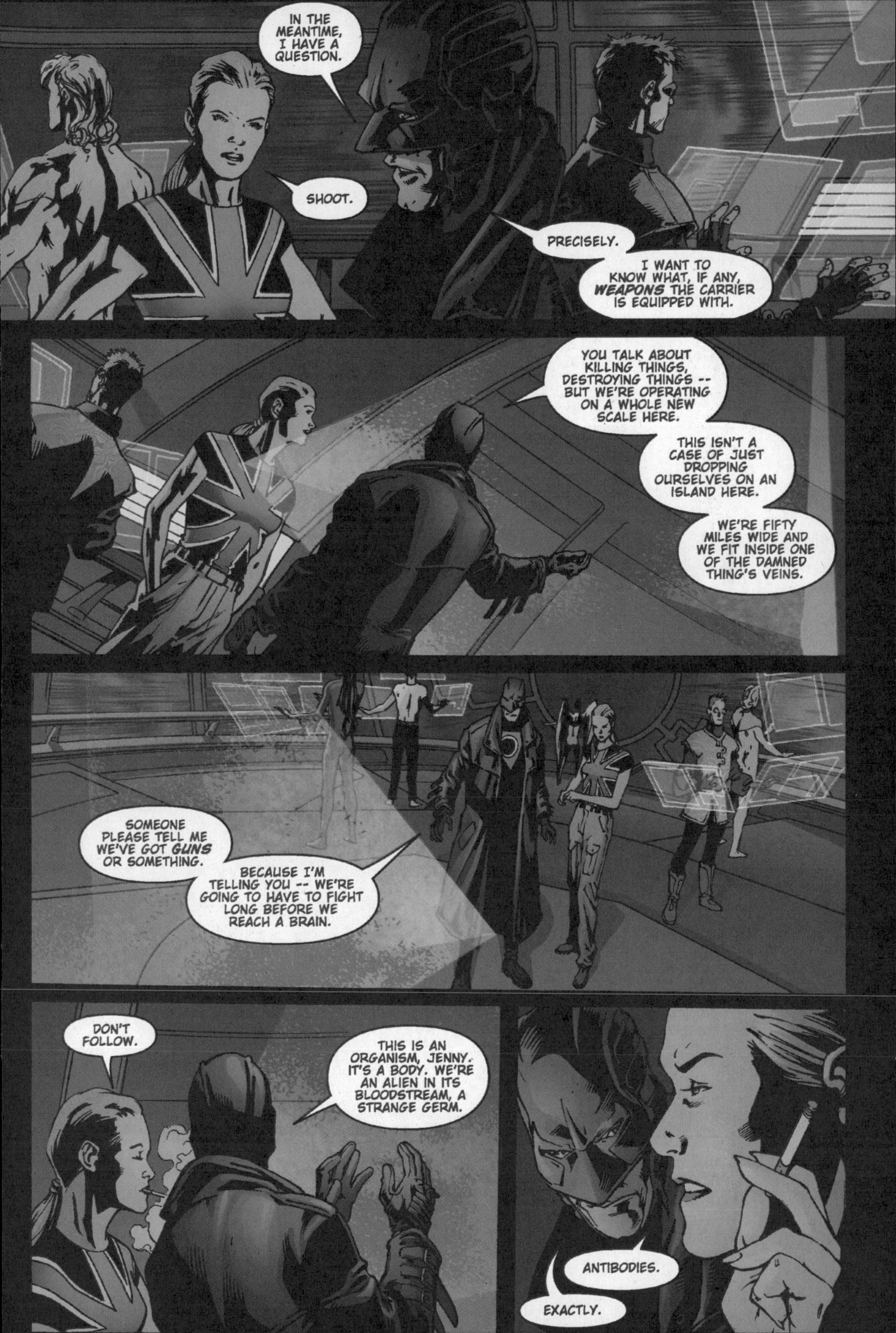
IN THE MEANTIME, I HAVE A QUESTION.
SHOOT.
PRECISELY.
I WANT TO KNOW WHAT, IF ANY, WEAPONS THE CARRIER IS EQUIPPED WITH.
YOU TALK ABOUT KILLING THINGS, DESTROYING THINGS -- BUT WE'RE OPERATING ON A WHOLE NEW SCALE HERE.
THIS ISN'T A CASE OF JUST DROPPING OURSELVES ON AN ISLAND HERE.
WE'RE FIFTY MILES WIDE AND WE FIT INSIDE ONE OF THE DAMNED THING'S VEINS.
SOMEONE PLEASE TELL ME WE'VE GOT GUNS OR SOMETHING.
BECAUSE I'M TELLING YOU -- WE'RE GOING TO HAVE TO FIGHT LONG BEFORE WE REACH A BRAIN.
DON'T FOLLOW.
THIS IS AN ORGANISM, JENNY. IT'S A BODY. WE'RE AN ALIEN IN ITS BLOODSTREAM, A STRANGE GERM.
ANTIBODIES.
EXACTLY.

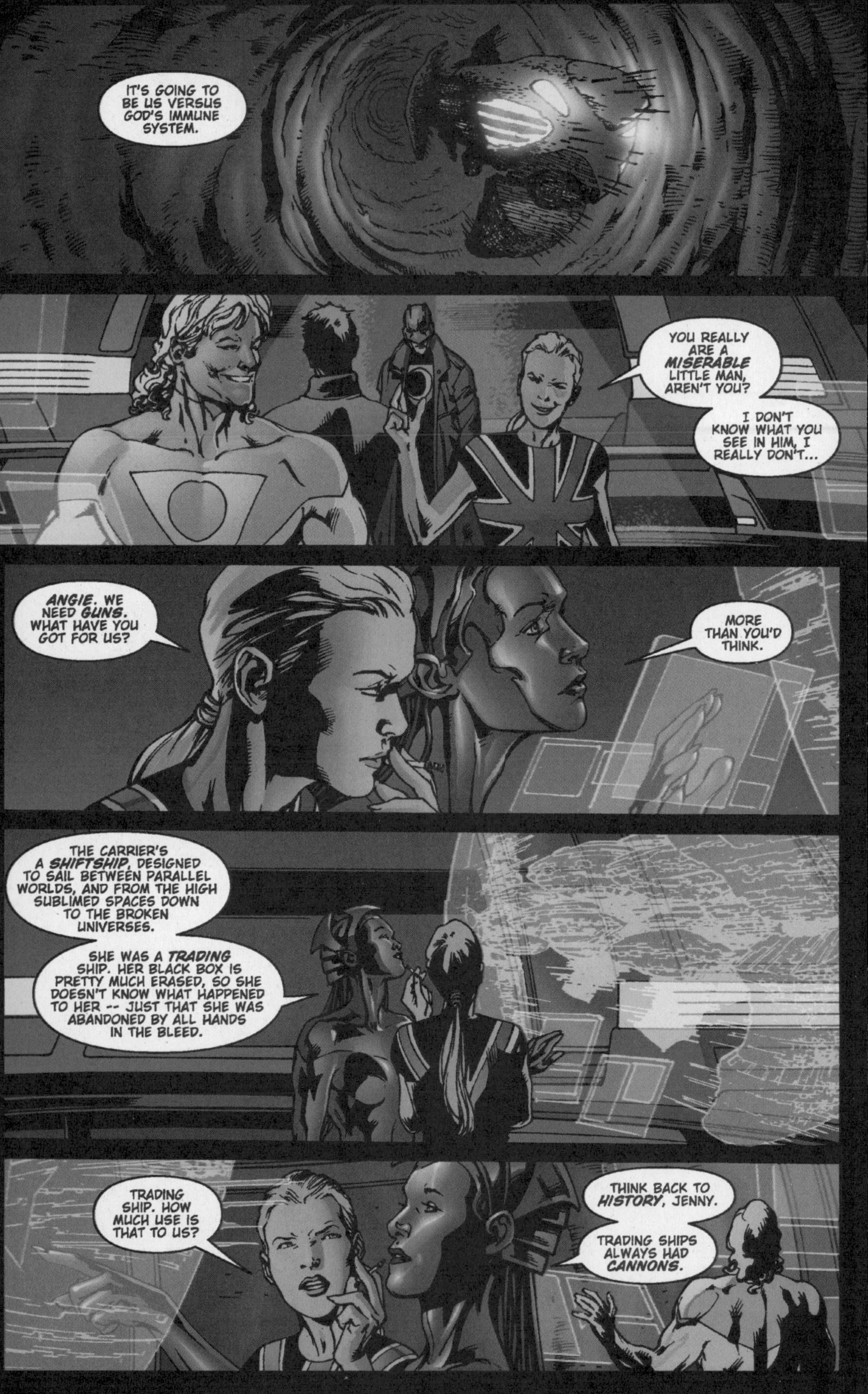
IT'S GOING TO BE US VERSUS GOD'S IMMUNE SYSTEM.
YOU REALLY ARE A MISERABLE LITTLE MAN, AREN'T YOU?
I DON'T KNOW WHAT YOU SEE IN HIM, I REALLY DON'T...
ANGIE. WE NEED GUNS. WHAT HAVE YOU GOT FOR US?
MORE THAN YOU'D THINK.
THE CARRIER'S A SHIFTSHIP, DESIGNED TO SAIL BETWEEN PARALLEL WORLDS, AND FROM THE HIGH SUBLIMED SPACES DOWN TO THE BROKEN UNIVERSES.
SHE WAS A TRADING SHIP. HER BLACK BOX IS PRETTY MUCH ERASED, SO SHE DOESN'T KNOW WHAT HAPPENED TO HER -- JUST THAT SHE WAS ABANDONED BY ALL HANDS IN THE BLEED.
TRADING SHIP. HOW MUCH USE IS THAT TO US?
THINK BACK TO HISTORY, JENNY.
TRADING SHIPS ALWAYS HAD CANNONS.

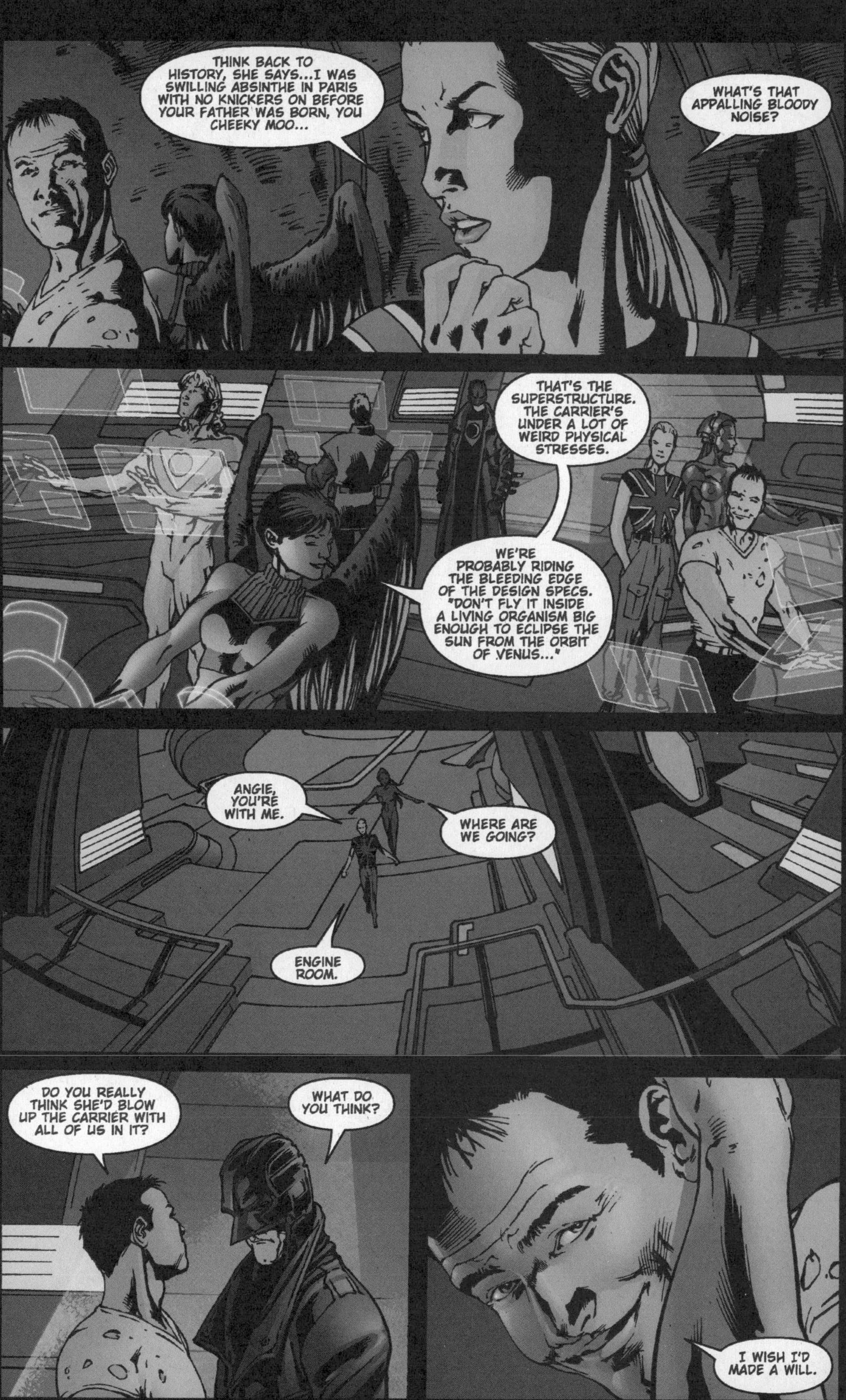
THINK BACK TO HISTORY, SHE SAYS...I WAS SWILLING ABSINTHE IN PARIS WITH NO KNICKERS ON BEFORE YOUR FATHER WAS BORN, YOU CHEEKY MOO...
WHAT'S THAT APPALLING BLOODY NOISE?
THAT'S THE SUPERSTRUCTURE. THE CARRIER'S UNDER A LOT OF WEIRD PHYSICAL STRESSES.
WE'RE PROBABLY RIDING THE BLEEDING EDGE OF THE DESIGN SPECS. "DON'T FLY IT INSIDE A LIVING ORGANISM BIG ENOUGH TO ECLIPSE THE SUN FROM THE ORBIT OF VENUS..."
ANGIE, YOU'RE WITH ME.
WHERE ARE WE GOING?
ENGINE ROOM.
DO YOU REALLY THINK SHE'D BLOW UP THE CARRIER WITH ALL OF US IN IT?
WHAT DO YOU THINK?
I WISH I'D MADE A WILL.

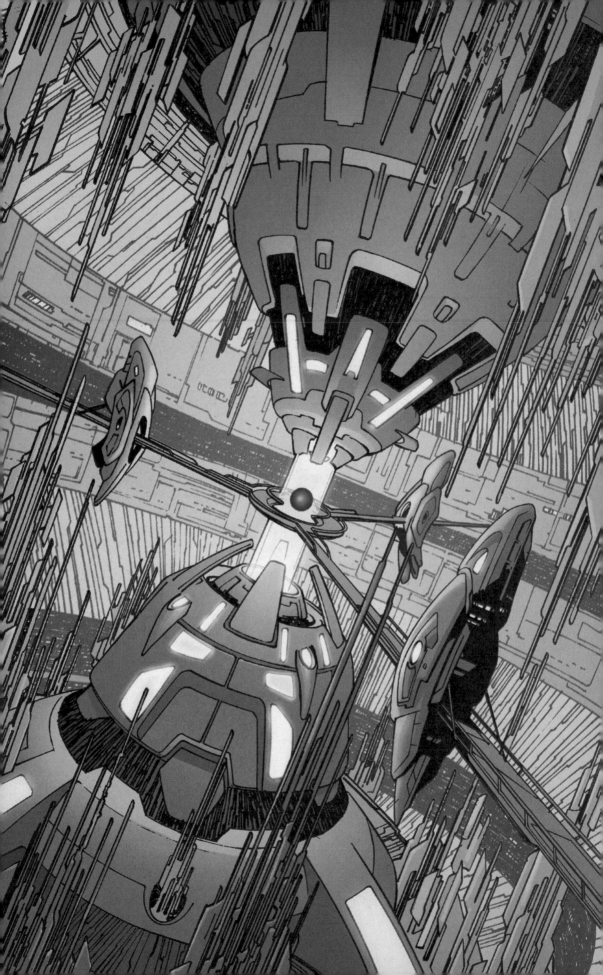

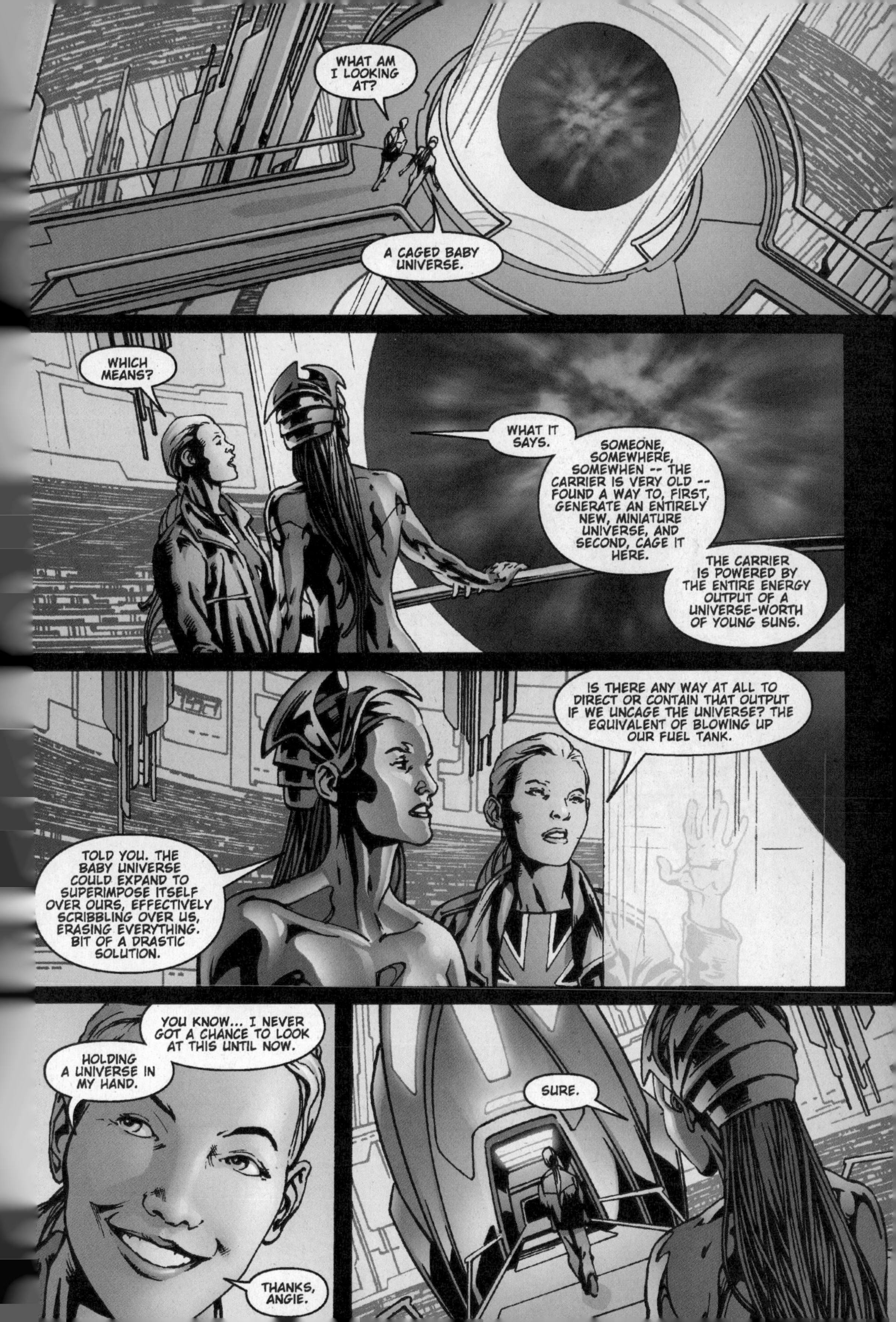

WHAT AM I LOOKING AT?
A CAGED BABY UNIVERSE.
WHICH MEANS?
WHAT IT SAYS.
SOMEONE, SOMEWHERE, SOMEWHEN -- THE CARRIER IS VERY OLD -- FOUND A WAY TO, FIRST, GENERATE AN ENTIRELY NEW, MINIATURE UNIVERSE, AND SECOND, CAGE IT HERE.
THE CARRIER IS POWERED BY THE ENTIRE ENERGY OUTPUT OF A UNIVERSE-WORTH OF YOUNG SUNS.
IS THERE ANY WAY AT ALL TO DIRECT OR CONTAIN THAT OUTPUT IF WE UNCAGE THE UNIVERSE? THE EQUIVALENT OF BLOWING UP OUR FUEL TANK.
TOLD YOU. THE BABY UNIVERSE COULD EXPAND TO SUPERIMPOSE ITSELF OVER OURS, EFFECTIVELY SCRIBBLING OVER US, ERASING EVERYTHING. BIT OF A DRASTIC SOLUTION.
YOU KNOW... I NEVER GOT A CHANCE TO LOOK AT THIS UNTIL NOW.
HOLDING A UNIVERSE IN MY HAND.
THANKS, ANGIE.
SURE.

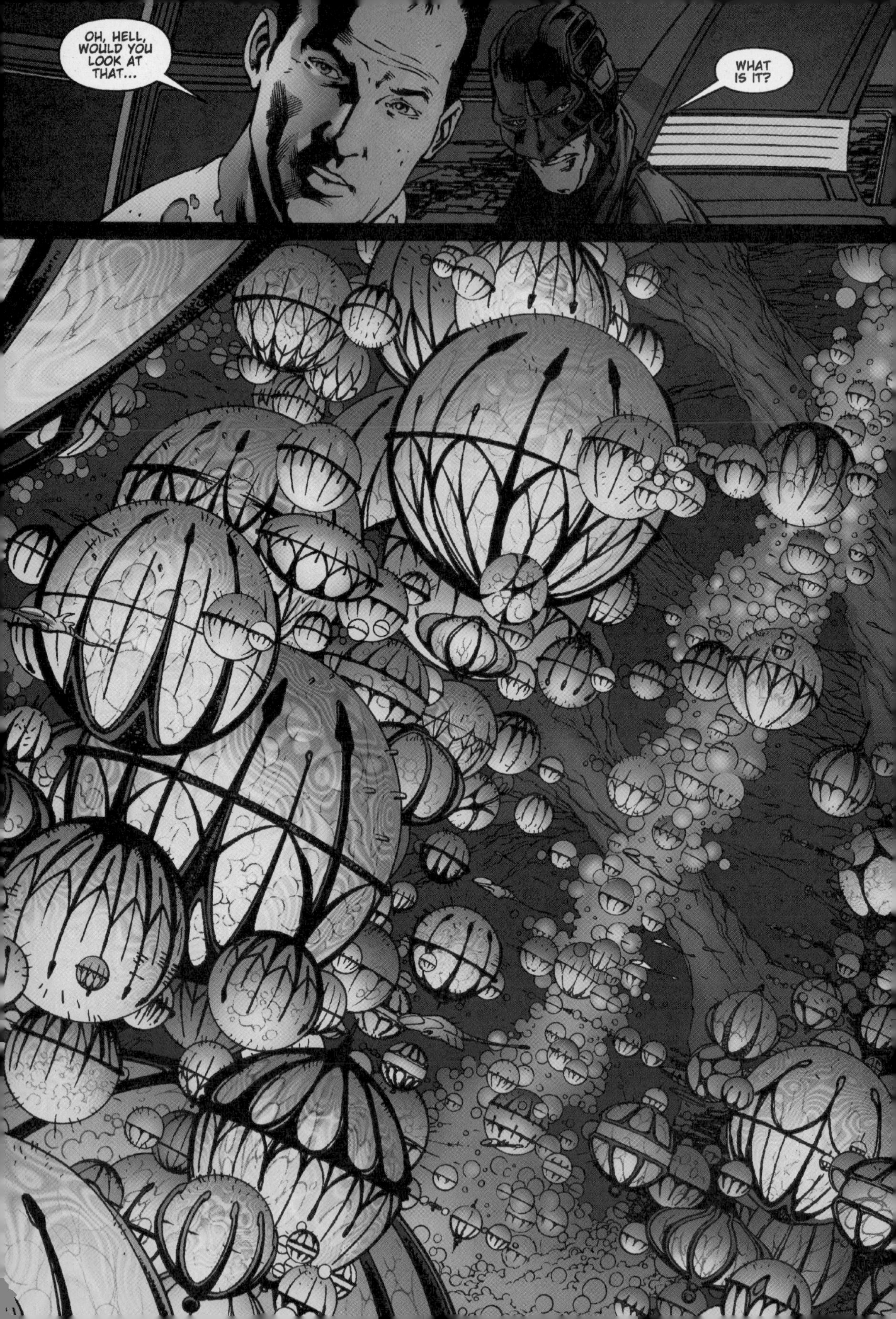

OH, HELL, WOULD YOU LOOK AT THAT...
WHAT IS IT?

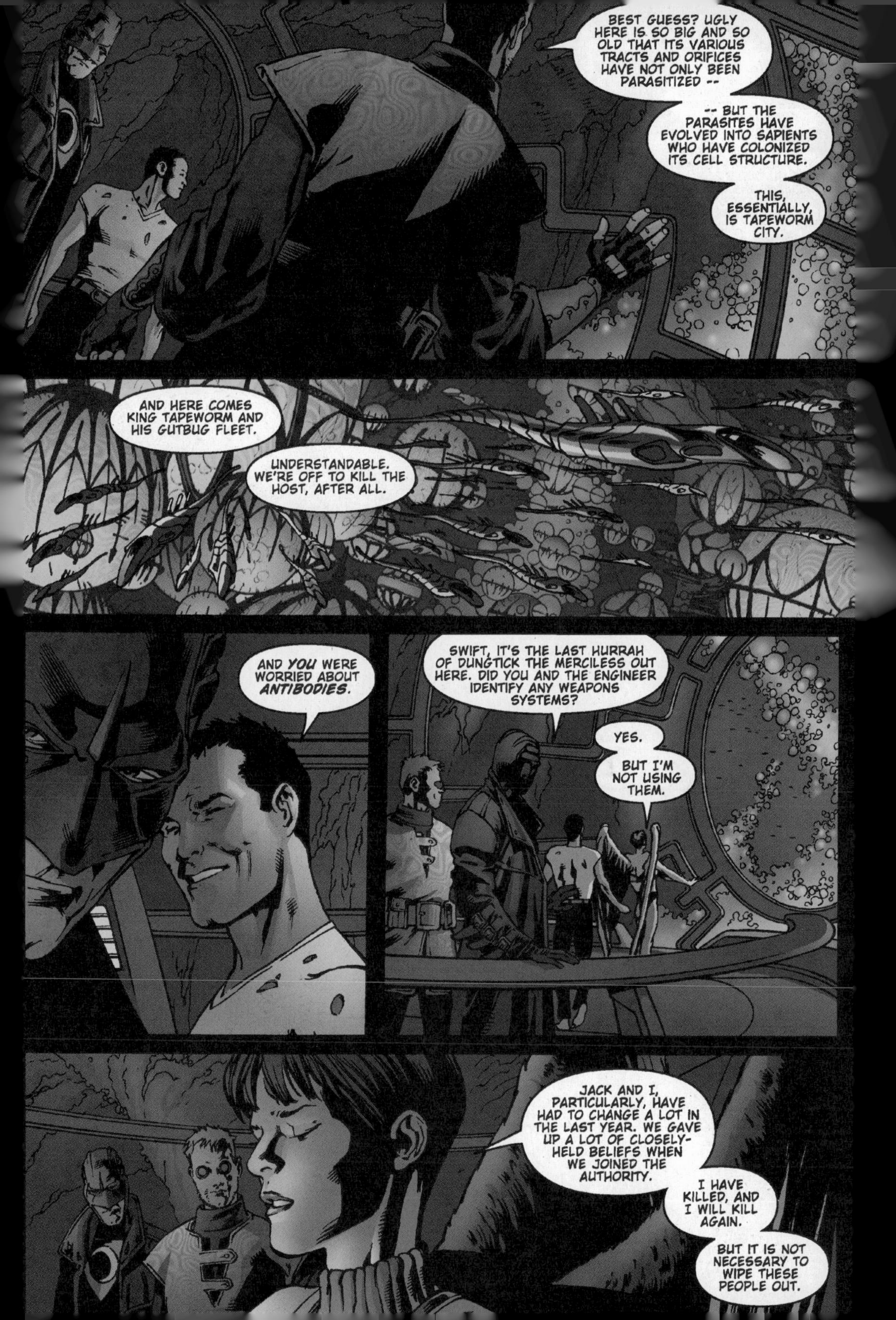
BEST GUESS? UGLY HERE IS SO BIG AND SO OLD THAT ITS VARIOUS TRACTS AND ORIFICES HAVE NOT ONLY BEEN PARASITIZED --
-- BUT THE PARASITES HAVE EVOLVED INTO SAPIENTS WHO HAVE COLONIZED ITS CELL STRUCTURE.
THIS, ESSENTIALLY, IS TAPEWORM CITY.
AND HERE COMES KING TAPEWORM AND HIS GUTBUG FLEET.
UNDERSTANDABLE. WE'RE OFF TO KILL THE HOST, AFTER ALL.
AND *YOU* WERE WORRIED ABOUT *ANTIBODIES*.
SWIFT, IT'S THE LAST HURRAH OF DUNGTICK THE MERCILESS OUT HERE. DID YOU AND THE ENGINEER IDENTIFY ANY WEAPONS SYSTEMS?
YES.
BUT I'M NOT USING THEM.
JACK AND I, PARTICULARLY, HAVE HAD TO CHANGE A LOT IN THE LAST YEAR. WE GAVE UP A LOT OF CLOSELY-HELD BELIEFS WHEN WE JOINED THE AUTHORITY.
I HAVE KILLED, AND I WILL KILL AGAIN.
BUT IT IS NOT NECESSARY TO WIPE THESE PEOPLE OUT.

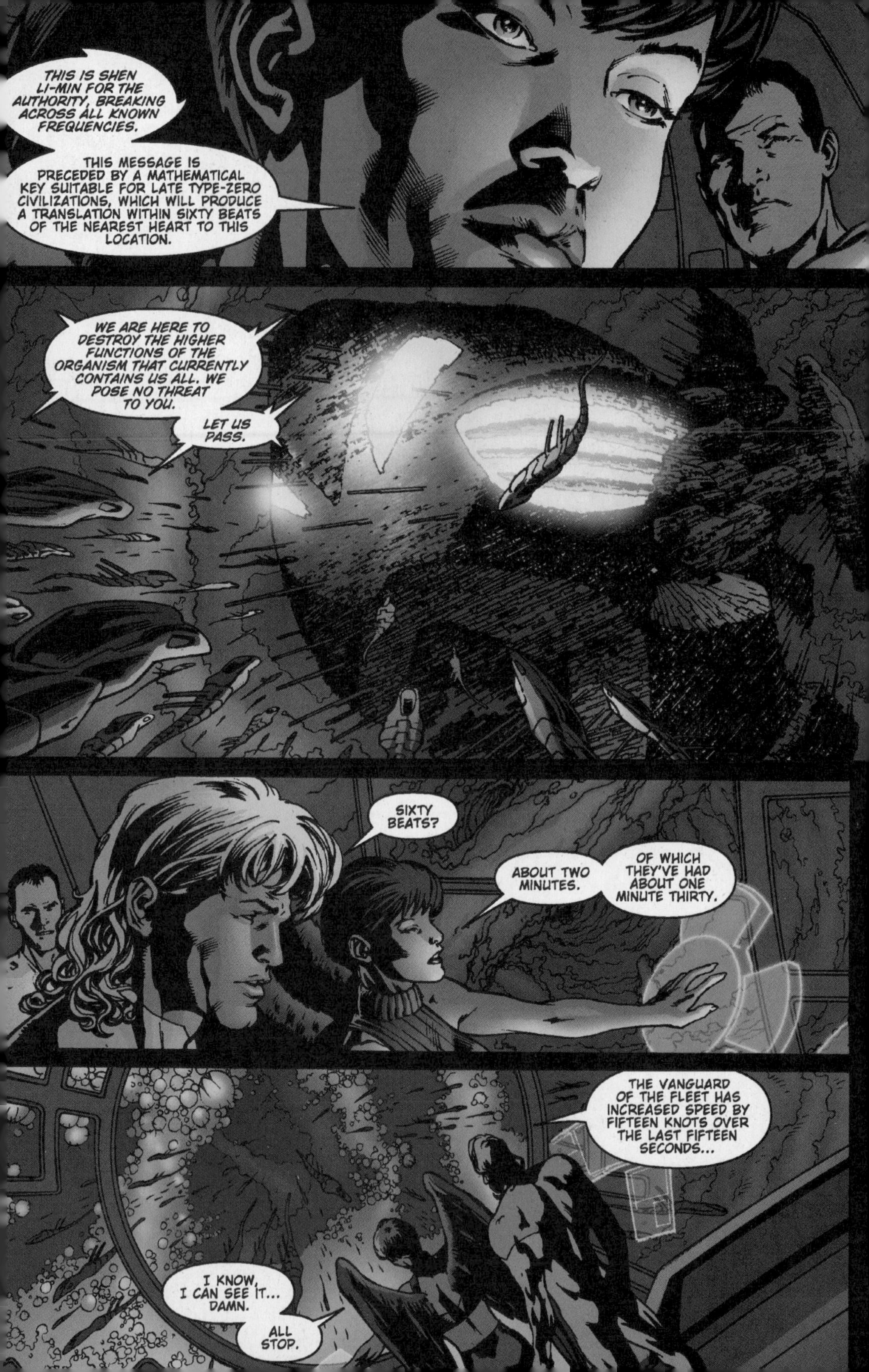
THIS IS SHEN LI-MIN FOR THE AUTHORITY, BREAKING ACROSS ALL KNOWN FREQUENCIES.
THIS MESSAGE IS PRECEDED BY A MATHEMATICAL KEY SUITABLE FOR LATE TYPE-ZERO CIVILIZATIONS, WHICH WILL PRODUCE A TRANSLATION WITHIN SIXTY BEATS OF THE NEAREST HEART TO THIS LOCATION.
WE ARE HERE TO DESTROY THE HIGHER FUNCTIONS OF THE ORGANISM THAT CURRENTLY CONTAINS US ALL. WE POSE NO THREAT TO YOU.
LET US PASS.
SIXTY BEATS?
ABOUT TWO MINUTES.
OF WHICH THEY'VE HAD ABOUT ONE MINUTE THIRTY.
THE VANGUARD OF THE FLEET HAS INCREASED SPEED BY FIFTEEN KNOTS OVER THE LAST FIFTEEN SECONDS...
I KNOW, I CAN SEE IT... DAMN.
ALL STOP.

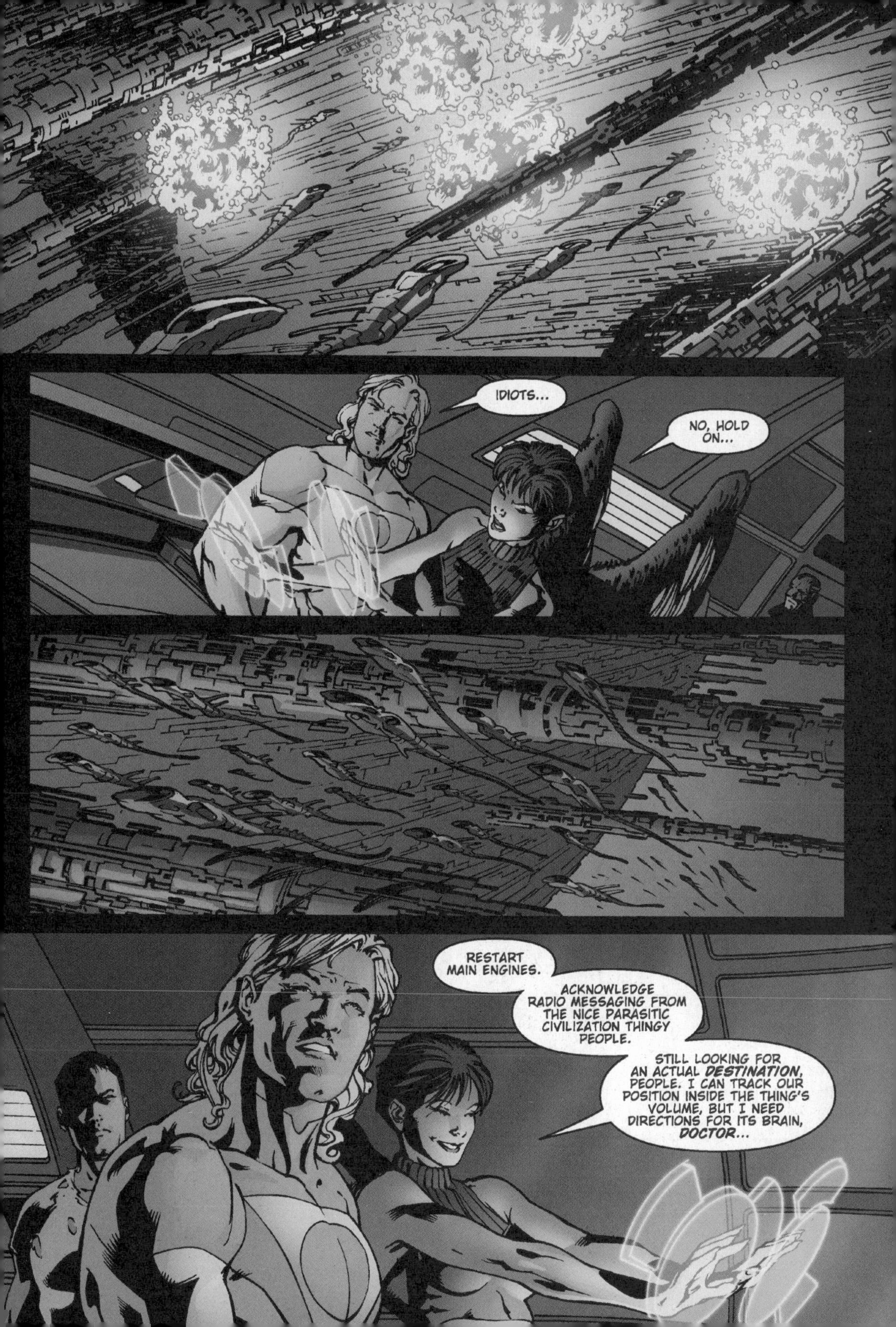
IDIOTS...
NO, HOLD ON...
RESTART MAIN ENGINES.
ACKNOWLEDGE RADIO MESSAGING FROM THE NICE PARASITIC CIVILIZATION THINGY PEOPLE.
STILL LOOKING FOR AN ACTUAL ***DESTINATION***, PEOPLE. I CAN TRACK OUR POSITION INSIDE THE THING'S VOLUME, BUT I NEED DIRECTIONS FOR ITS BRAIN, ***DOCTOR***...

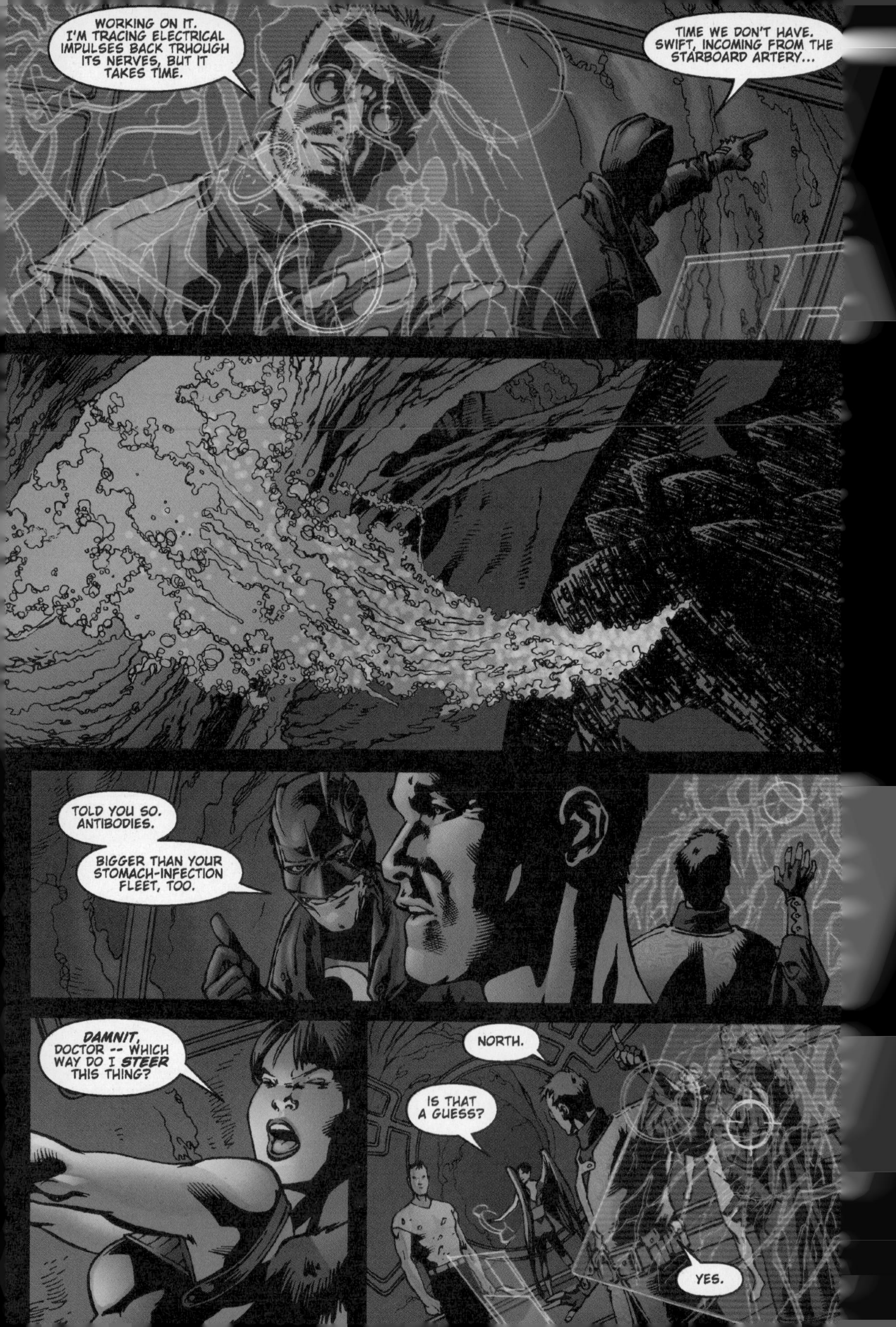
WORKING ON IT. I'M TRACING ELECTRICAL IMPULSES BACK TRHOUGH ITS NERVES, BUT IT TAKES TIME.
TIME WE DON'T HAVE. SWIFT, INCOMING FROM THE STARBOARD ARTERY...
TOLD YOU SO. ANTIBODIES.
BIGGER THAN YOUR STOMACH-INFECTION FLEET, TOO.
DAMNIT, DOCTOR -- WHICH WAY DO I STEER THIS THING?
NORTH.
IS THAT A GUESS?
YES.

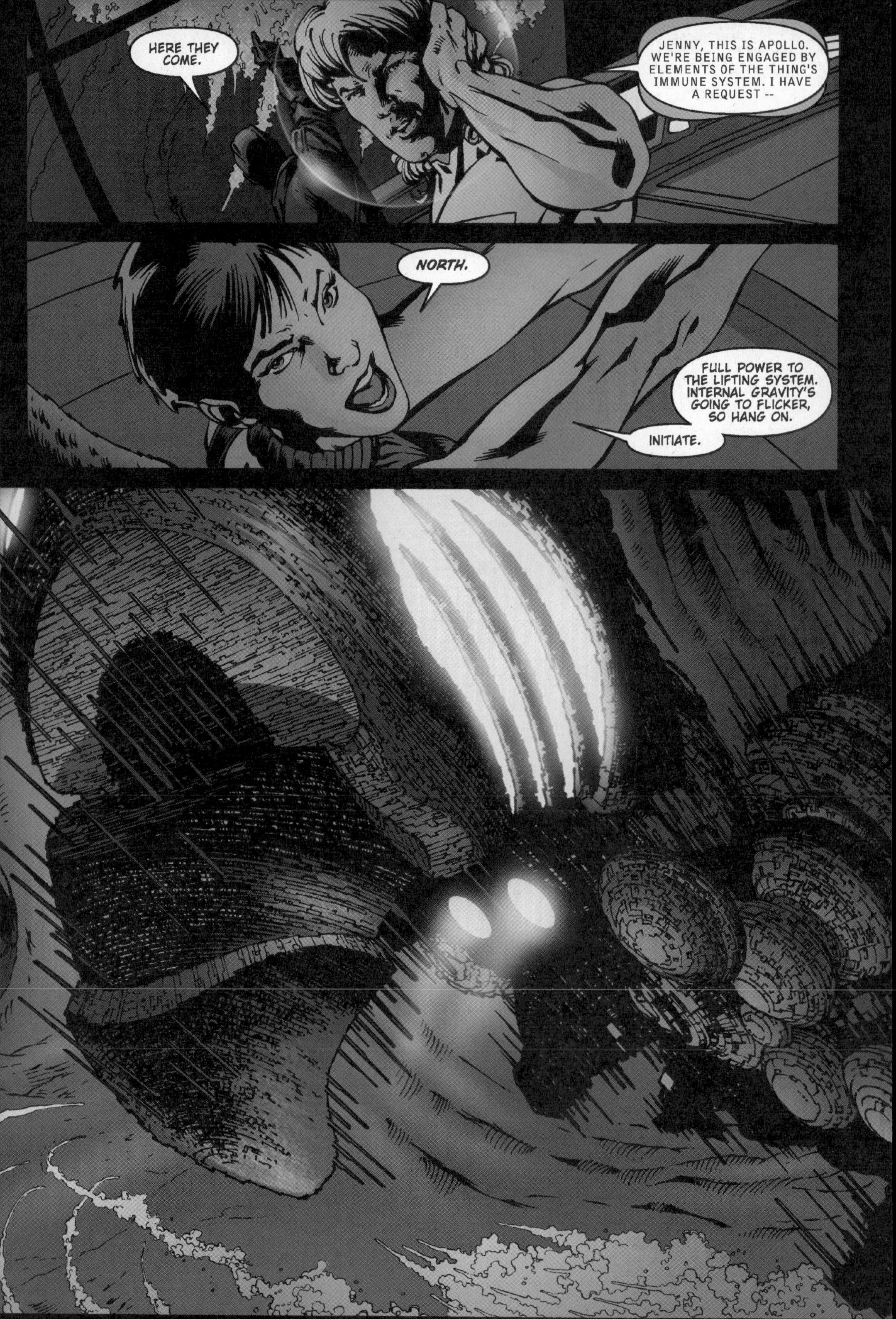
HERE THEY COME.
JENNY, THIS IS APOLLO. WE'RE BEING ENGAGED BY ELEMENTS OF THE THING'S IMMUNE SYSTEM. I HAVE A REQUEST --
NORTH.
FULL POWER TO THE LIFTING SYSTEM. INTERNAL GRAVITY'S GOING TO FLICKER, SO HANG ON.
INITIATE.

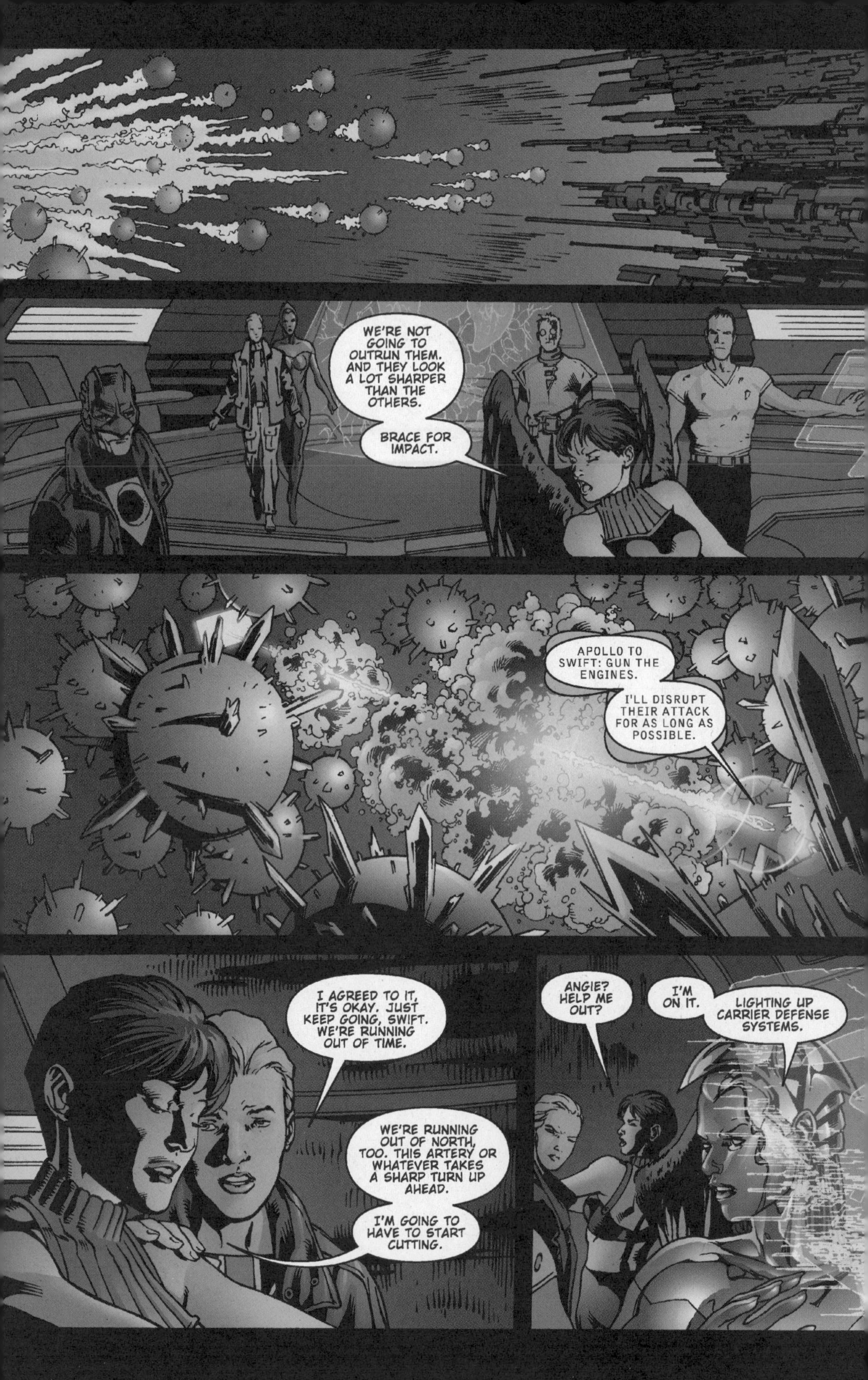
WE'RE NOT GOING TO OUTRUN THEM. AND THEY LOOK A LOT SHARPER THAN THE OTHERS.
BRACE FOR IMPACT.
APOLLO TO SWIFT: GUN THE ENGINES.
I'LL DISRUPT THEIR ATTACK FOR AS LONG AS POSSIBLE.
I AGREED TO IT, IT'S OKAY. JUST KEEP GOING, SWIFT. WE'RE RUNNING OUT OF TIME.
WE'RE RUNNING OUT OF NORTH, TOO. THIS ARTERY OR WHATEVER TAKES A SHARP TURN UP AHEAD.
I'M GOING TO HAVE TO START CUTTING.
ANGIE? HELP ME OUT?
I'M ON IT.
LIGHTING UP CARRIER DEFENSE SYSTEMS.

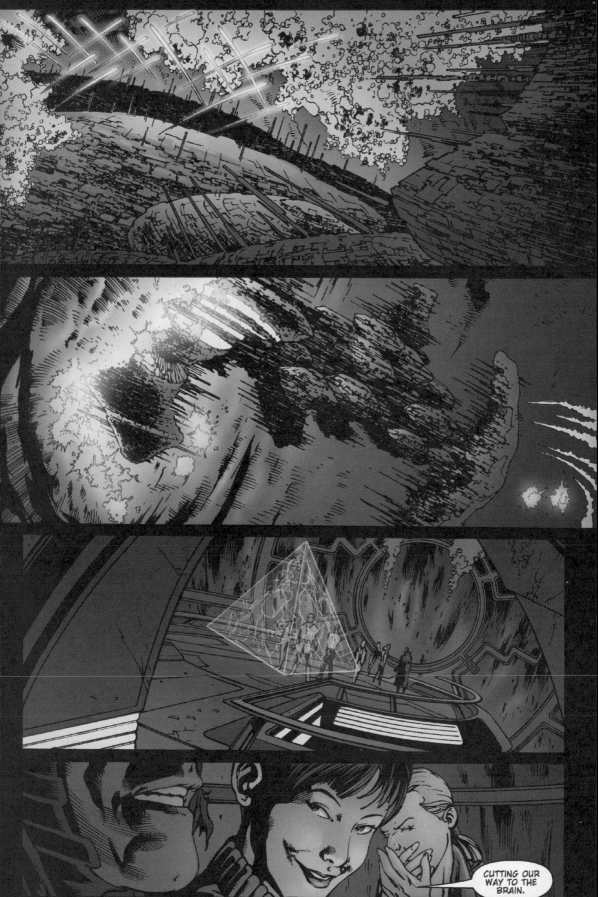

CUTTING OUR WAY TO THE BRAIN.

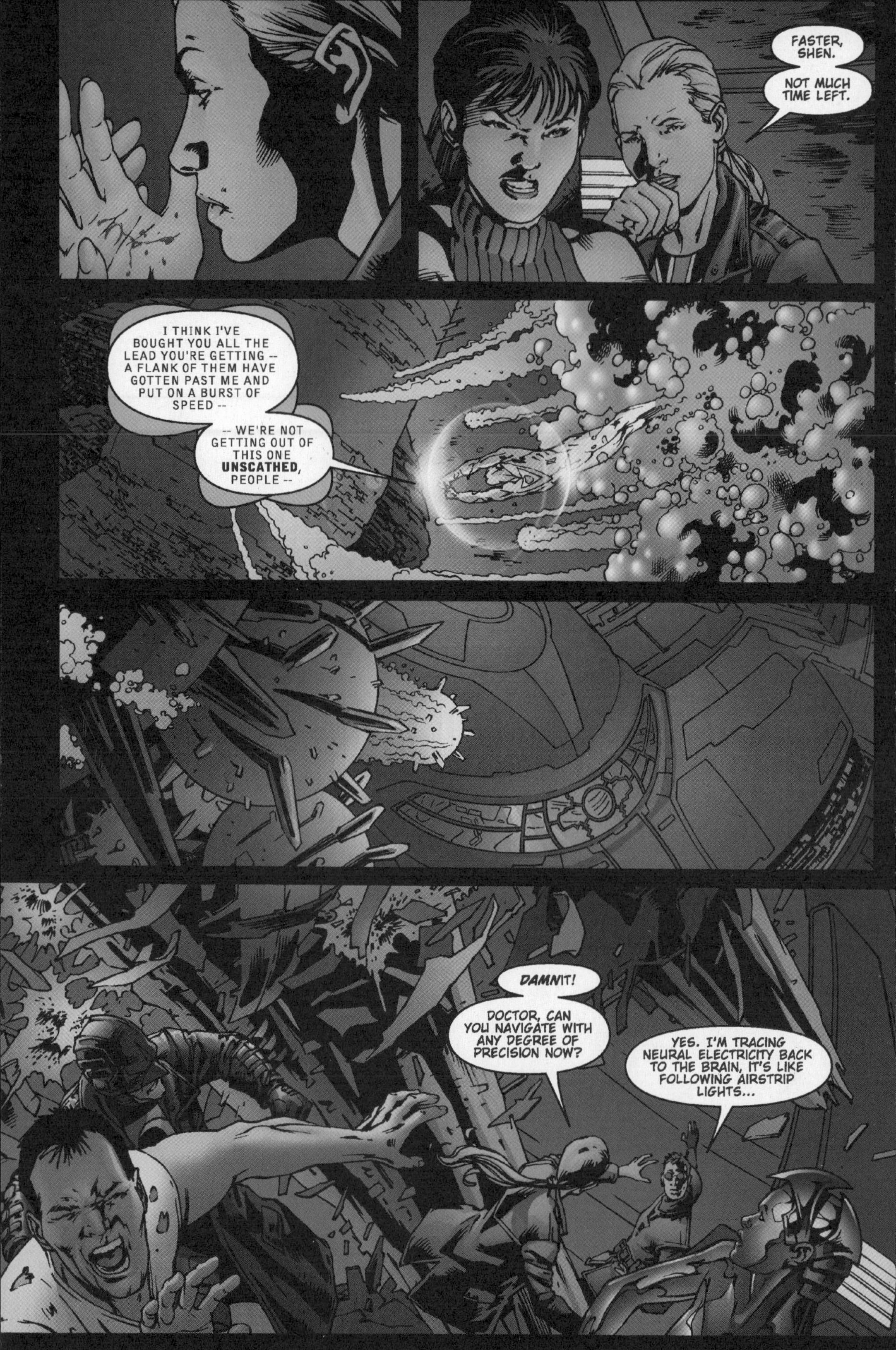
FASTER, SHEN.
NOT MUCH TIME LEFT.
I THINK I'VE BOUGHT YOU ALL THE LEAD YOU'RE GETTING -- A FLANK OF THEM HAVE GOTTEN PAST ME AND PUT ON A BURST OF SPEED --
-- WE'RE NOT GETTING OUT OF THIS ONE **UNSCATHED**, PEOPLE --
*DAMN*IT!
DOCTOR, CAN YOU NAVIGATE WITH ANY DEGREE OF PRECISION NOW?
YES. I'M TRACING NEURAL ELECTRICITY BACK TO THE BRAIN, IT'S LIKE FOLLOWING AIRSTRIP LIGHTS...

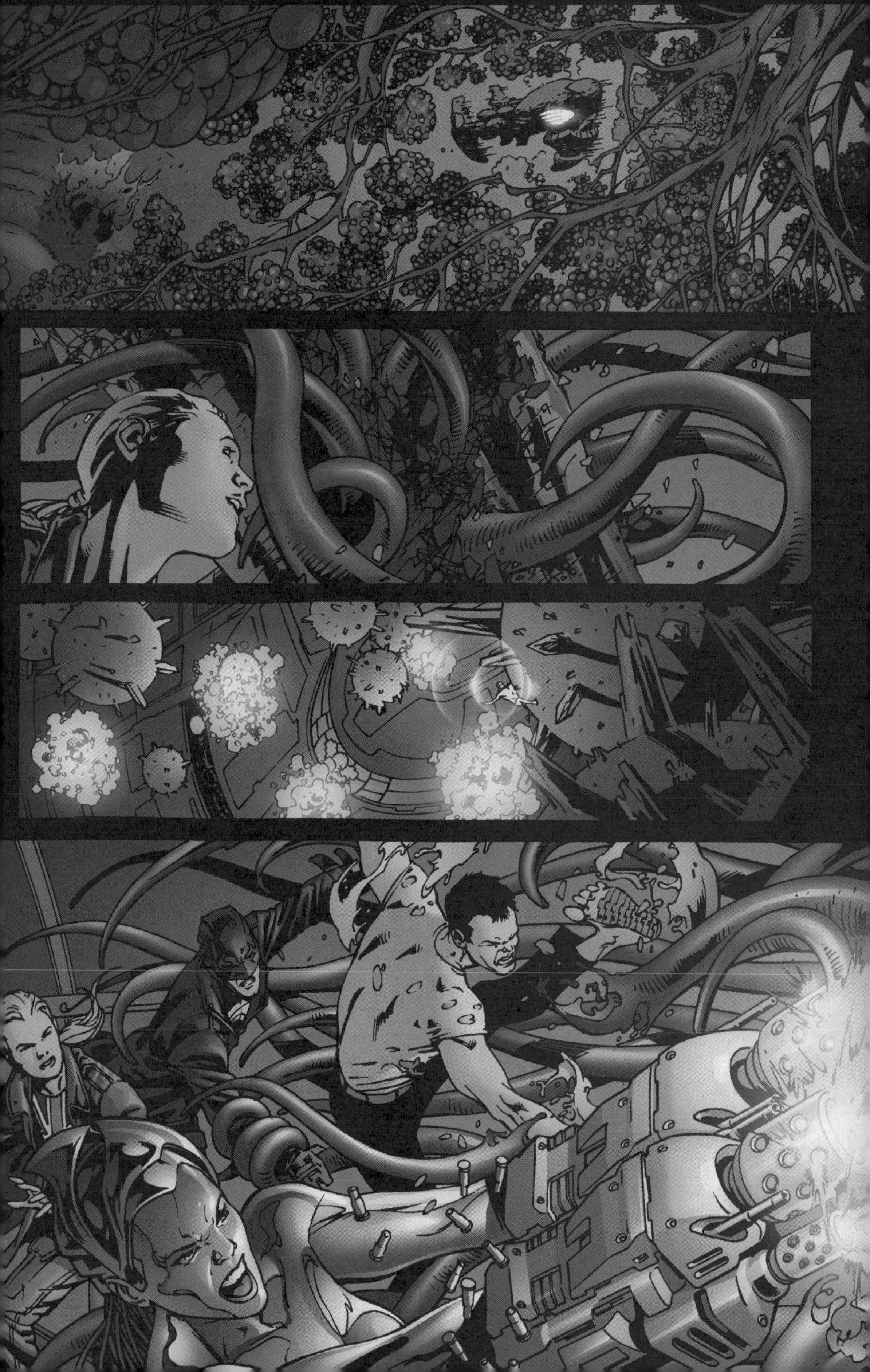

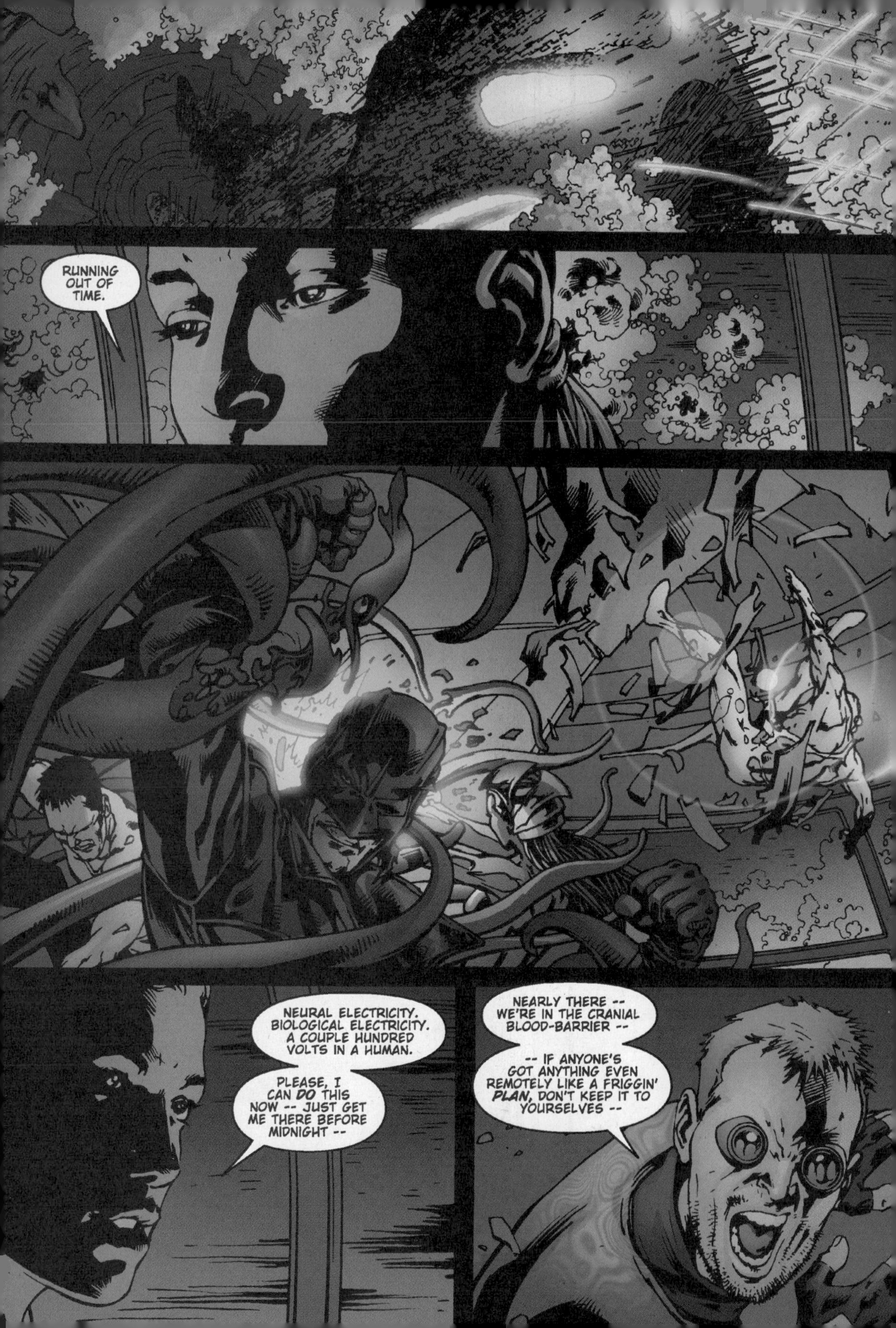
RUNNING OUT OF TIME.
NEURAL ELECTRICITY. BIOLOGICAL ELECTRICITY. A COUPLE HUNDRED VOLTS IN A HUMAN.
PLEASE, I CAN ***DO*** THIS NOW -- JUST GET ME THERE BEFORE MIDNIGHT --
NEARLY THERE -- WE'RE IN THE CRANIAL BLOOD-BARRIER --
-- IF ANYONE'S GOT ANYTHING EVEN REMOTELY LIKE A FRIGGIN' ***PLAN***, DON'T KEEP IT TO YOURSELVES --

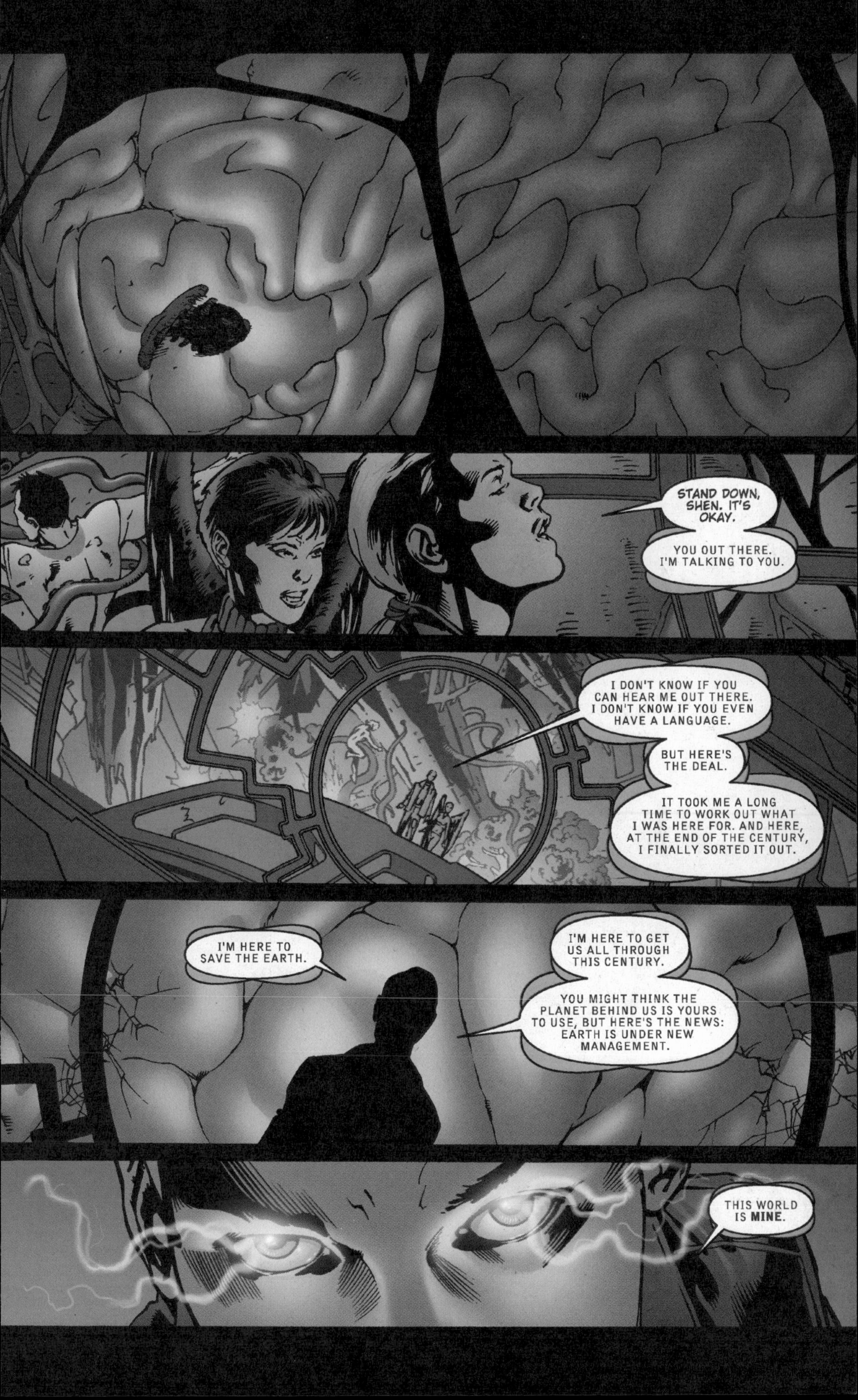
STAND DOWN, SHEN. IT'S OKAY.
YOU OUT THERE. I'M TALKING TO YOU.
I DON'T KNOW IF YOU CAN HEAR ME OUT THERE. I DON'T KNOW IF YOU EVEN HAVE A LANGUAGE.
BUT HERE'S THE DEAL.
IT TOOK ME A LONG TIME TO WORK OUT WHAT I WAS HERE FOR. AND HERE, AT THE END OF THE CENTURY, I FINALLY SORTED IT OUT.
I'M HERE TO SAVE THE EARTH.
I'M HERE TO GET US ALL THROUGH THIS CENTURY.
YOU MIGHT THINK THE PLANET BEHIND US IS YOURS TO USE, BUT HERE'S THE NEWS: EARTH IS UNDER NEW MANAGEMENT.
THIS WORLD IS **MINE**.

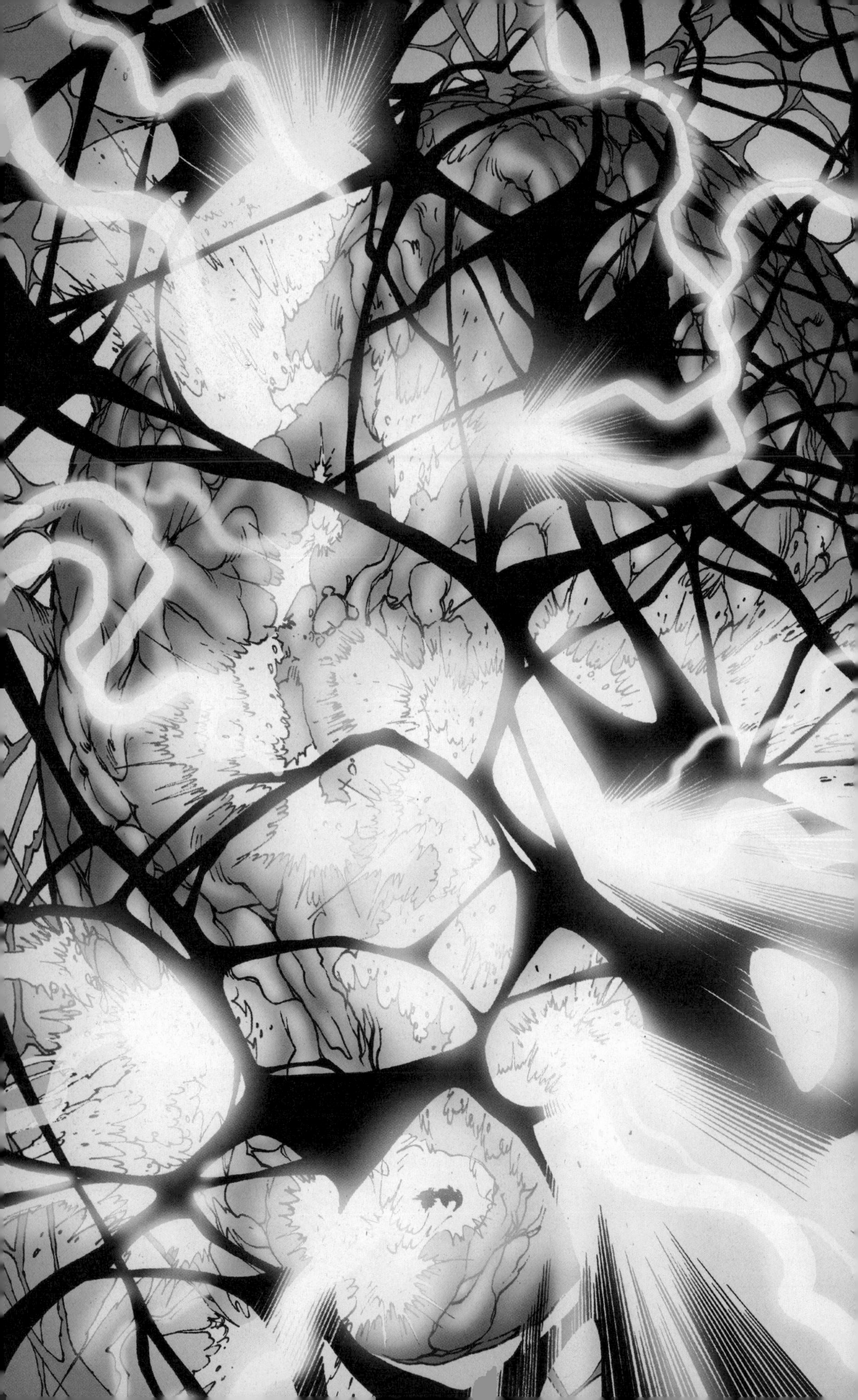

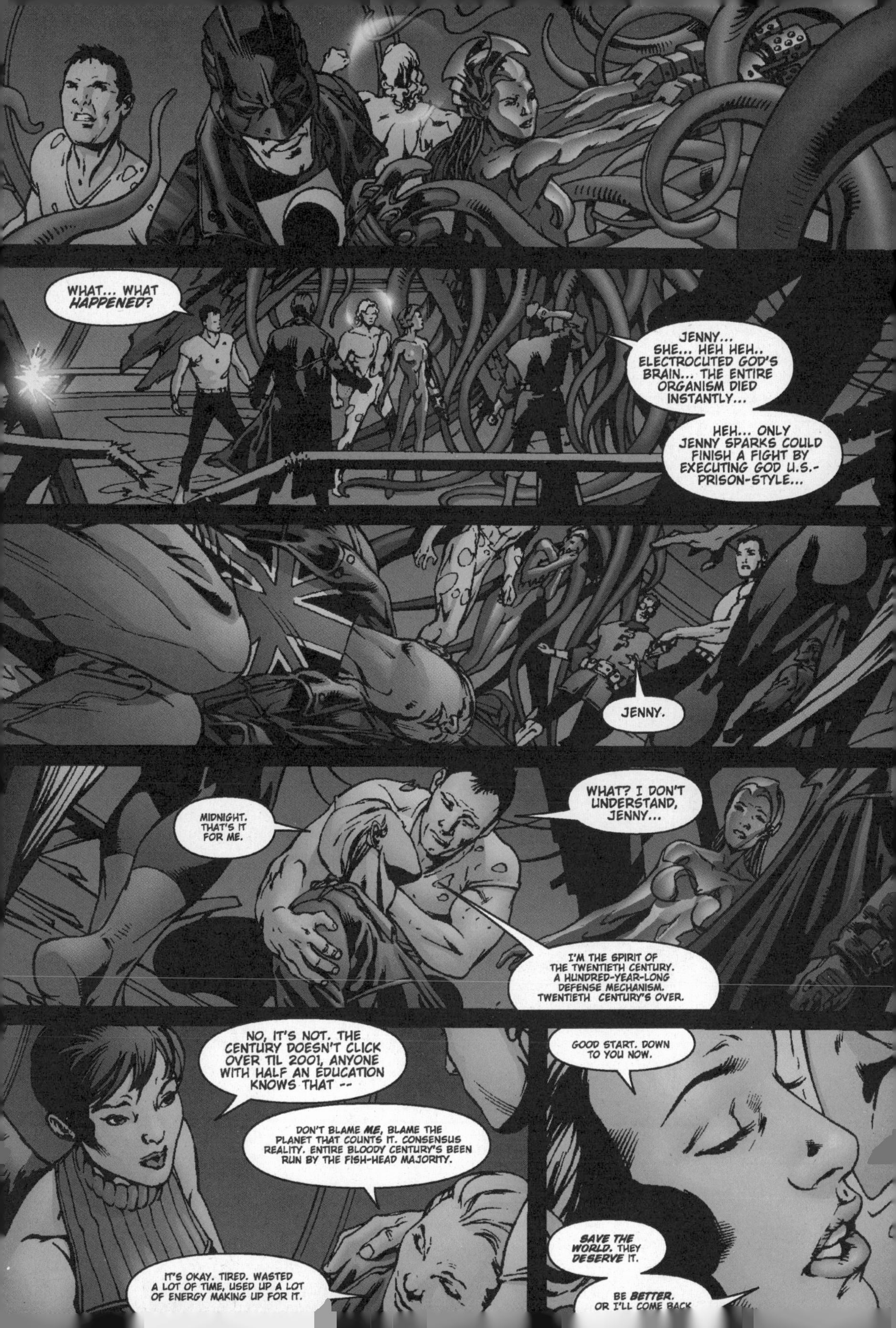
WHAT... WHAT HAPPENED?
JENNY... SHE... HEH HEH.. ELECTROCUTED GOD'S BRAIN... THE ENTIRE ORGANISM DIED INSTANTLY...
HEH... ONLY JENNY SPARKS COULD FINISH A FIGHT BY EXECUTING GOD U.S.-PRISON-STYLE...
JENNY.
MIDNIGHT. THAT'S IT FOR ME.
WHAT? I DON'T UNDERSTAND, JENNY...
I'M THE SPIRIT OF THE TWENTIETH CENTURY. A HUNDRED-YEAR-LONG DEFENSE MECHANISM. TWENTIETH CENTURY'S OVER.
NO, IT'S NOT. THE CENTURY DOESN'T CLICK OVER TIL 2001, ANYONE WITH HALF AN EDUCATION KNOWS THAT --
DON'T BLAME ME, BLAME THE PLANET THAT COUNTS IT. CONSENSUS REALITY. ENTIRE BLOODY CENTURY'S BEEN RUN BY THE FISH-HEAD MAJORITY.
IT'S OKAY. TIRED. WASTED A LOT OF TIME, USED UP A LOT OF ENERGY MAKING UP FOR IT.
GOOD START. DOWN TO YOU NOW.
SAVE THE WORLD. THEY DESERVE IT.
BE BETTER. OR I'LL COME BACK

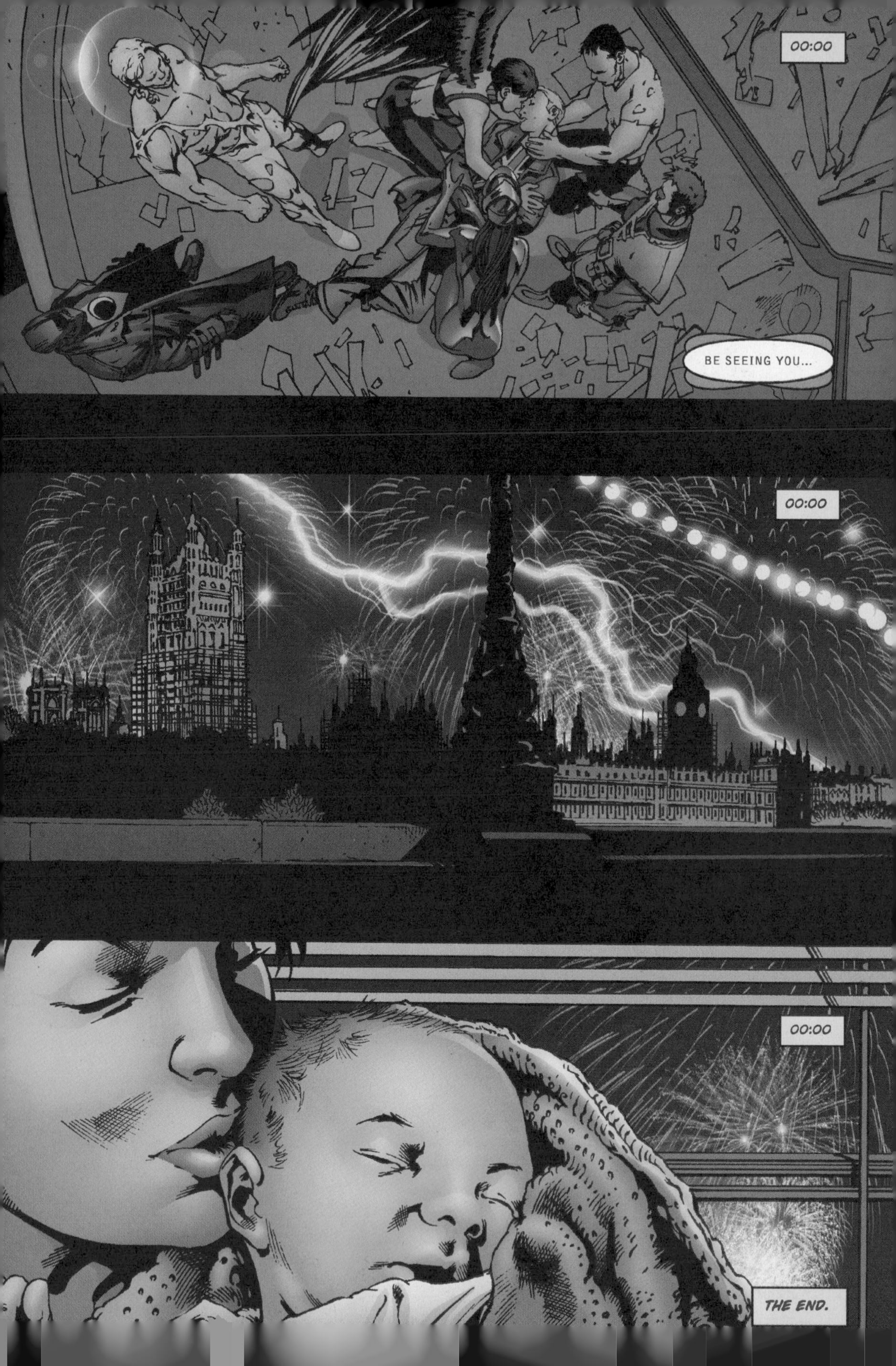
00:00
BE SEEING YOU...
00:00
00:00
THE END.

"THE NATIVITY"

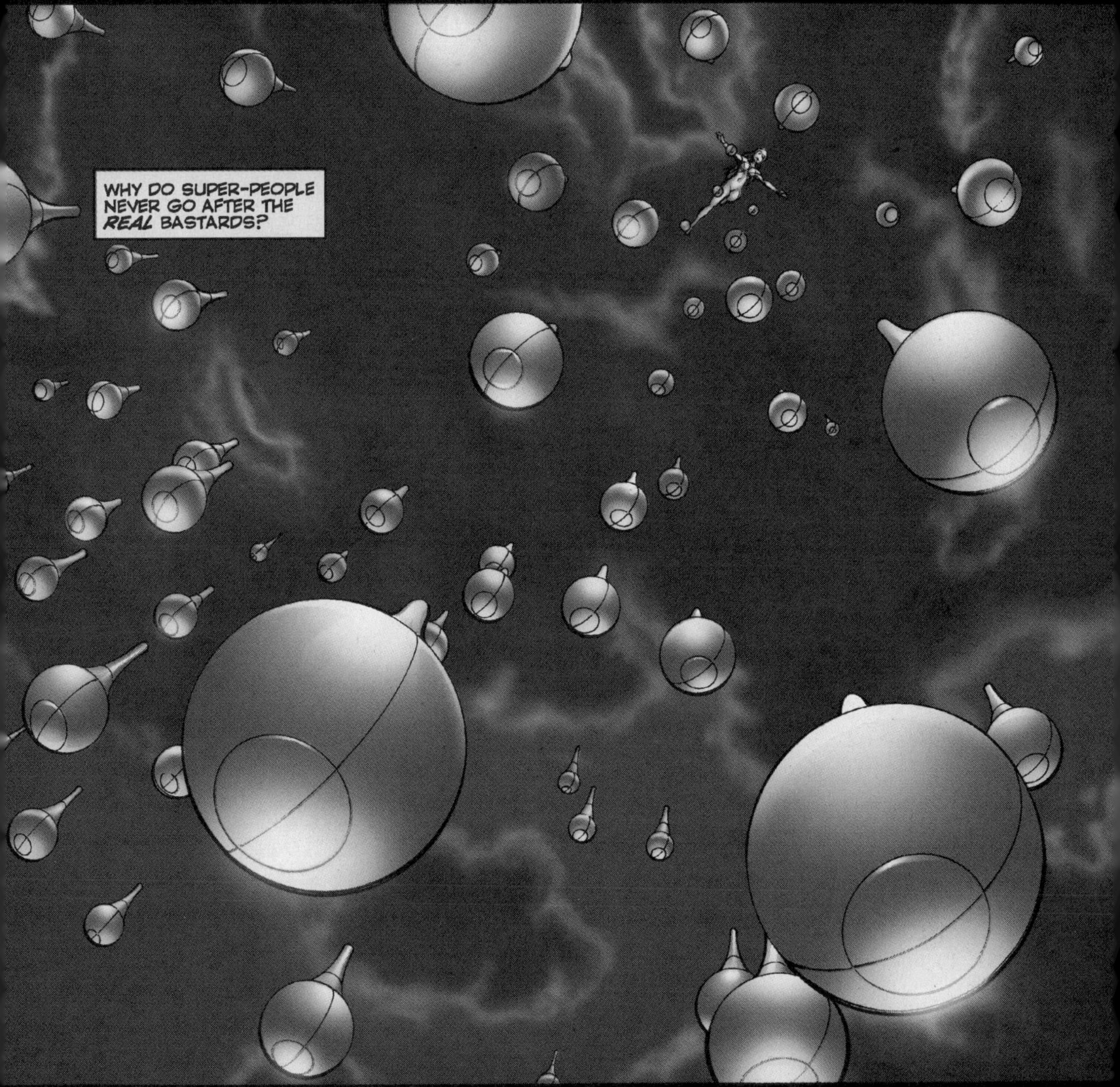
WHY DO SUPER-PEOPLE NEVER GO AFTER THE *REAL* BASTARDS?

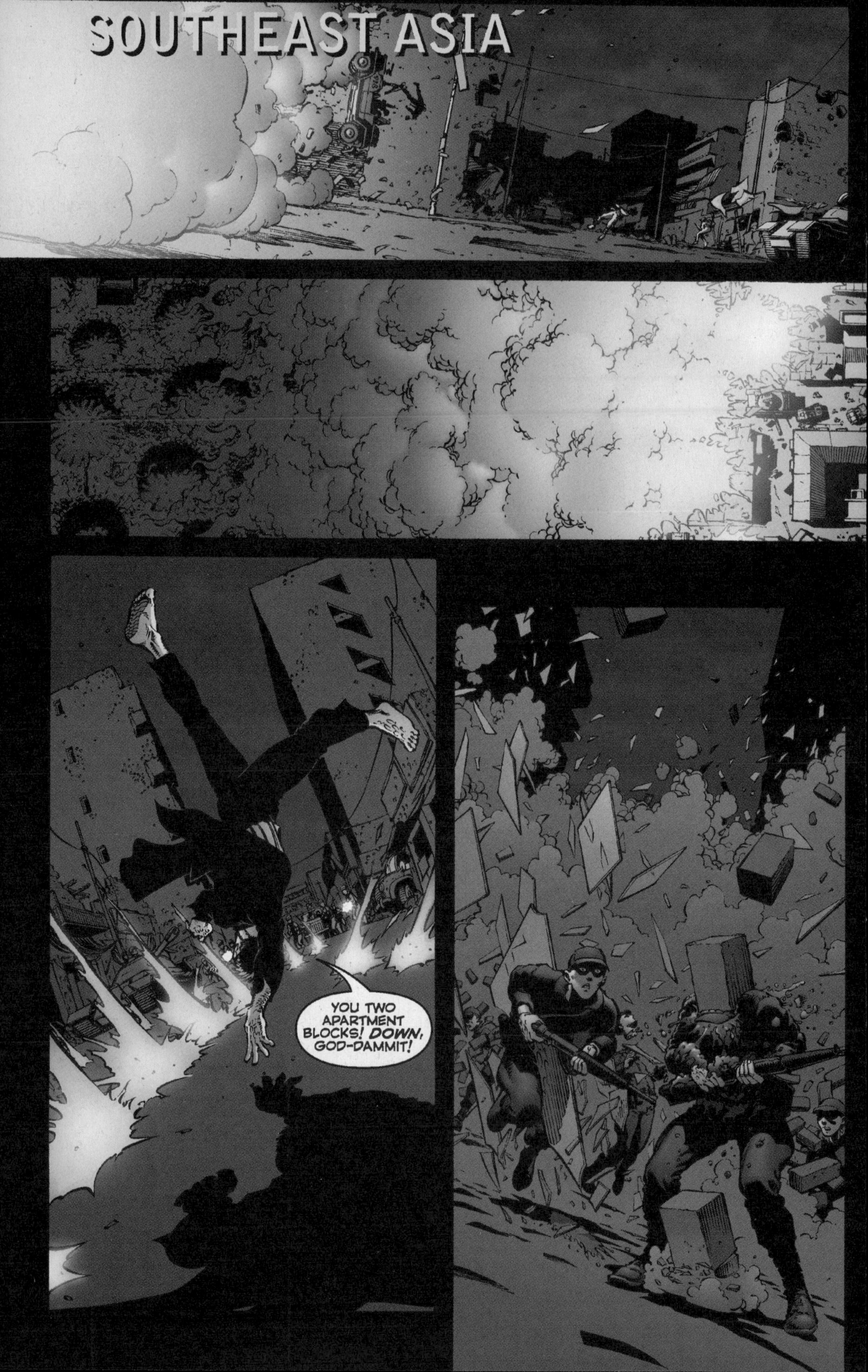
SOUTHEAST ASIA
YOU TWO APARTMENT BLOCKS! *DOWN,* GOD-DAMMIT!

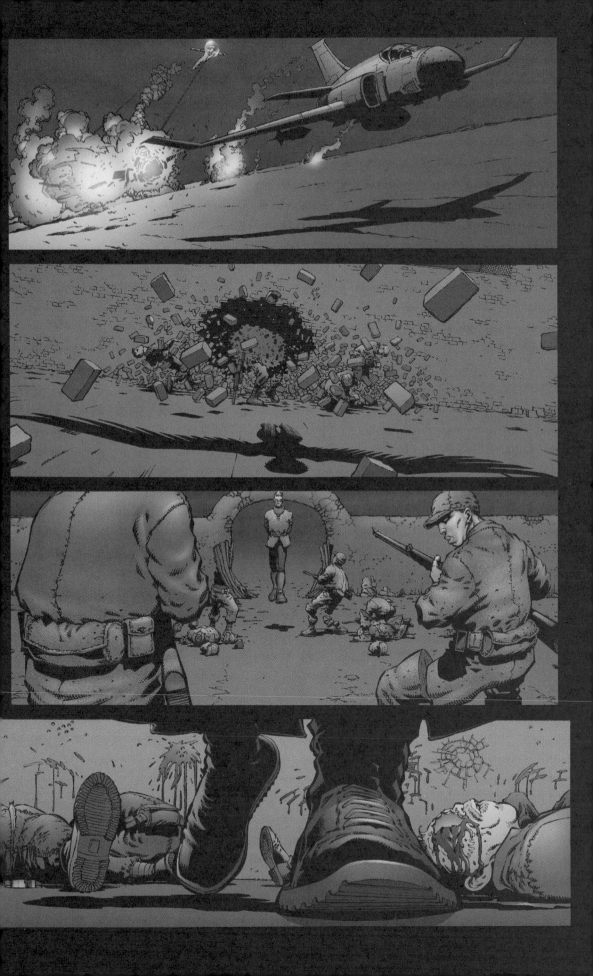

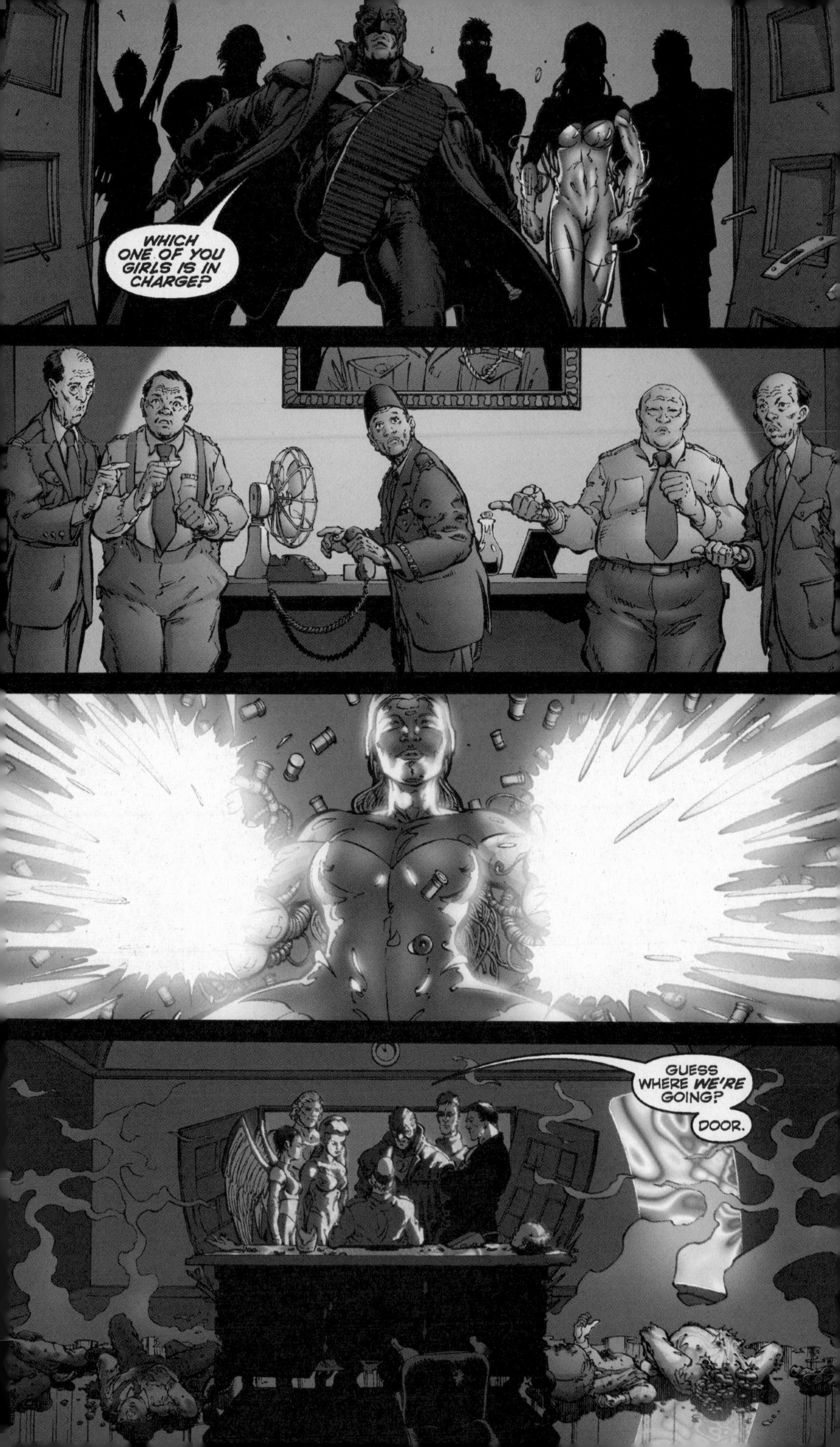
WHICH ONE OF YOU GIRLS IS IN CHARGE?
GUESS WHERE WE'RE GOING?
DOOR.

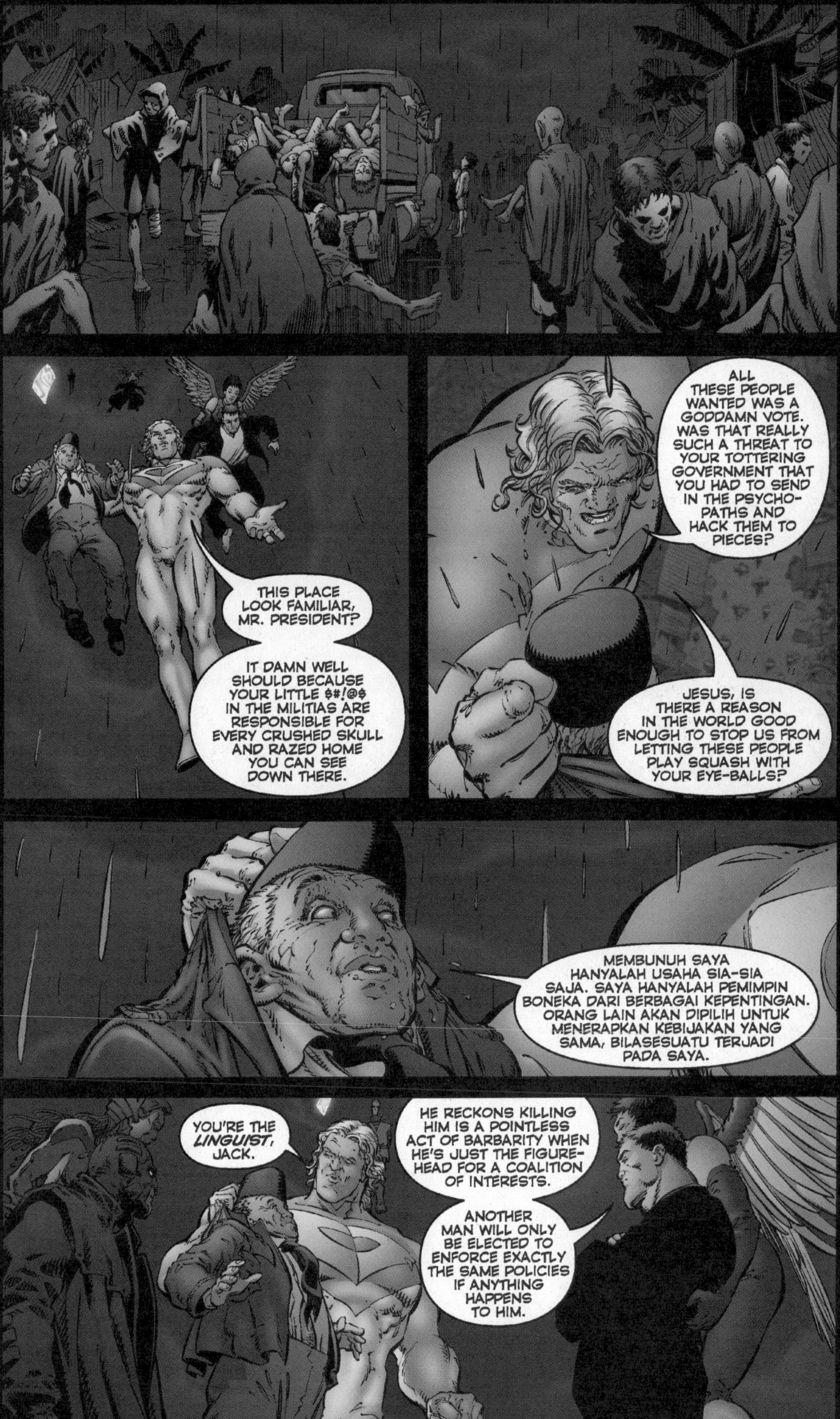
THIS PLACE LOOK FAMILIAR, MR. PRESIDENT?
IT DAMN WELL SHOULD BECAUSE YOUR LITTLE $#!@$ IN THE MILITIAS ARE RESPONSIBLE FOR EVERY CRUSHED SKULL AND RAZED HOME YOU CAN SEE DOWN THERE.
ALL THESE PEOPLE WANTED WAS A GODDAMN VOTE. WAS THAT REALLY SUCH A THREAT TO YOUR TOTTERING GOVERNMENT THAT YOU HAD TO SEND IN THE PSYCHO-PATHS AND HACK THEM TO PIECES?
JESUS, IS THERE A REASON IN THE WORLD GOOD ENOUGH TO STOP US FROM LETTING THESE PEOPLE PLAY SQUASH WITH YOUR EYE-BALLS?
MEMBUNUH SAYA HANYALAH USAHA SIA-SIA SAJA. SAYA HANYALAH PEMIMPIN BONEKA DARI BERBAGAI KEPENTINGAN. ORANG LAIN AKAN DIPILIH UNTUK MENERAPKAN KEBIJAKAN YANG SAMA, BILASESUATU TERJADI PADA SAYA.
YOU'RE THE *LINGUIST*, JACK.
HE RECKONS KILLING HIM IS A POINTLESS ACT OF BARBARITY WHEN HE'S JUST THE FIGURE-HEAD FOR A COALITION OF INTERESTS.
ANOTHER MAN WILL ONLY BE ELECTED TO ENFORCE EXACTLY THE SAME POLICIES IF ANYTHING HAPPENS TO HIM.

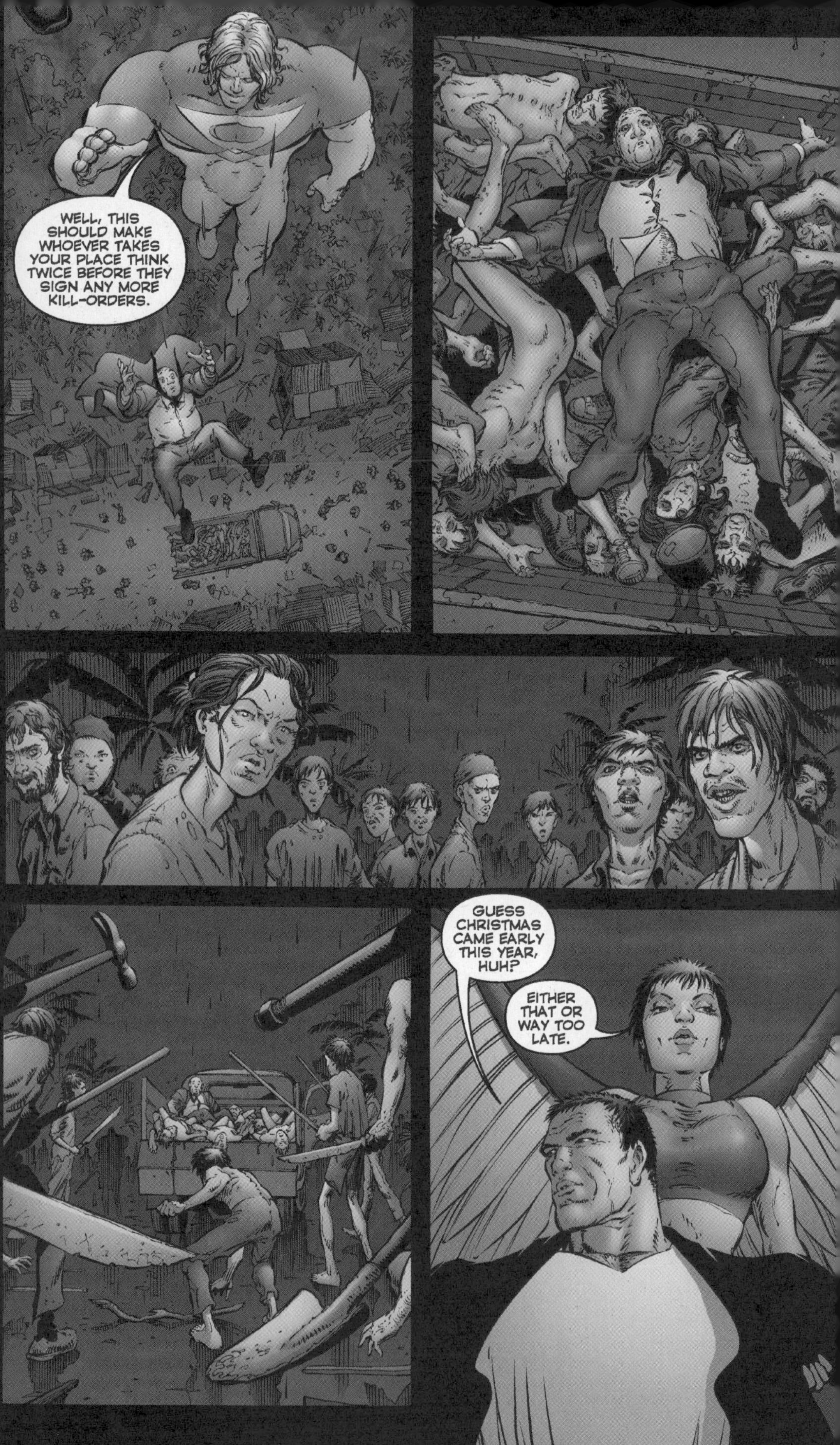
WELL, THIS SHOULD MAKE WHOEVER TAKES YOUR PLACE THINK TWICE BEFORE THEY SIGN ANY MORE KILL-ORDERS.
GUESS CHRISTMAS CAME EARLY THIS YEAR, HUH?
EITHER THAT OR WAY TOO LATE.

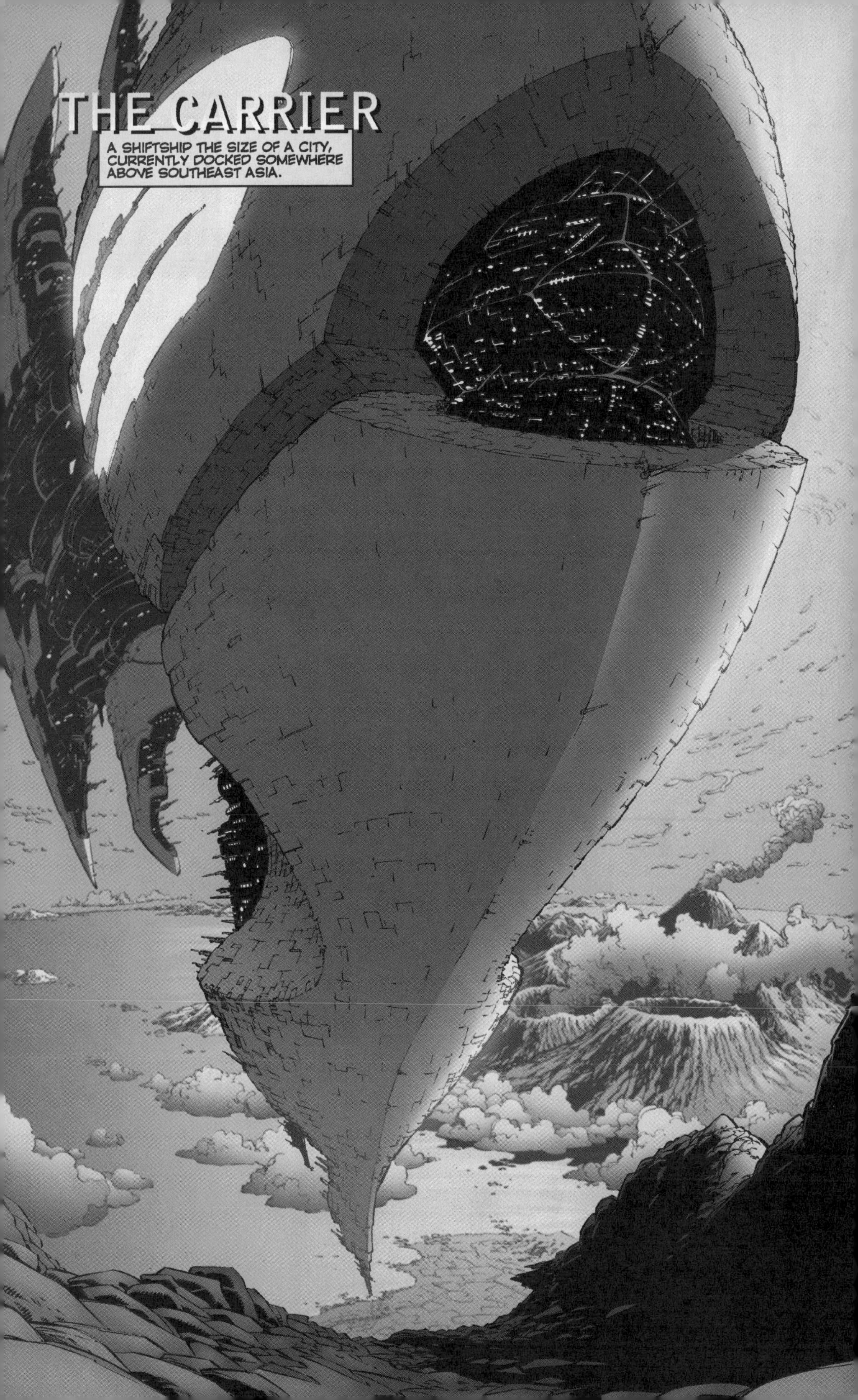
THE CARRIER
A SHIFTSHIP THE SIZE OF A CITY, CURRENTLY DOCKED SOMEWHERE ABOVE SOUTHEAST ASIA.

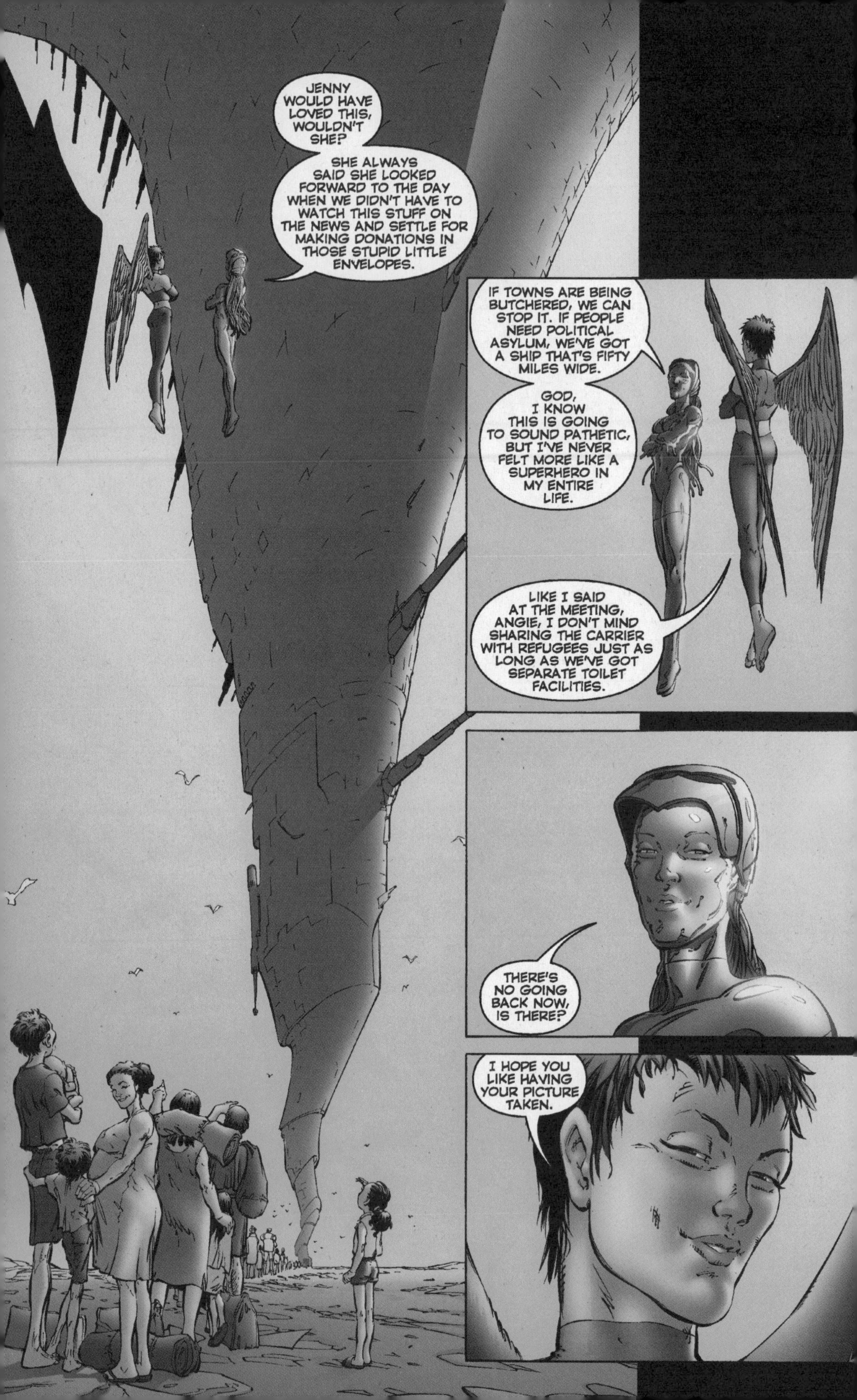
JENNY WOULD HAVE LOVED THIS, WOULDN'T SHE?
SHE ALWAYS SAID SHE LOOKED FORWARD TO THE DAY WHEN WE DIDN'T HAVE TO WATCH THIS STUFF ON THE NEWS AND SETTLE FOR MAKING DONATIONS IN THOSE STUPID LITTLE ENVELOPES.
IF TOWNS ARE BEING BUTCHERED, WE CAN STOP IT. IF PEOPLE NEED POLITICAL ASYLUM, WE'VE GOT A SHIP THAT'S FIFTY MILES WIDE.
GOD, I KNOW THIS IS GOING TO SOUND PATHETIC, BUT I'VE NEVER FELT MORE LIKE A SUPERHERO IN MY ENTIRE LIFE.
LIKE I SAID AT THE MEETING, ANGIE, I DON'T MIND SHARING THE CARRIER WITH REFUGEES JUST AS LONG AS WE'VE GOT SEPARATE TOILET FACILITIES.
THERE'S NO GOING BACK NOW, IS THERE?
I HOPE YOU LIKE HAVING YOUR PICTURE TAKEN.

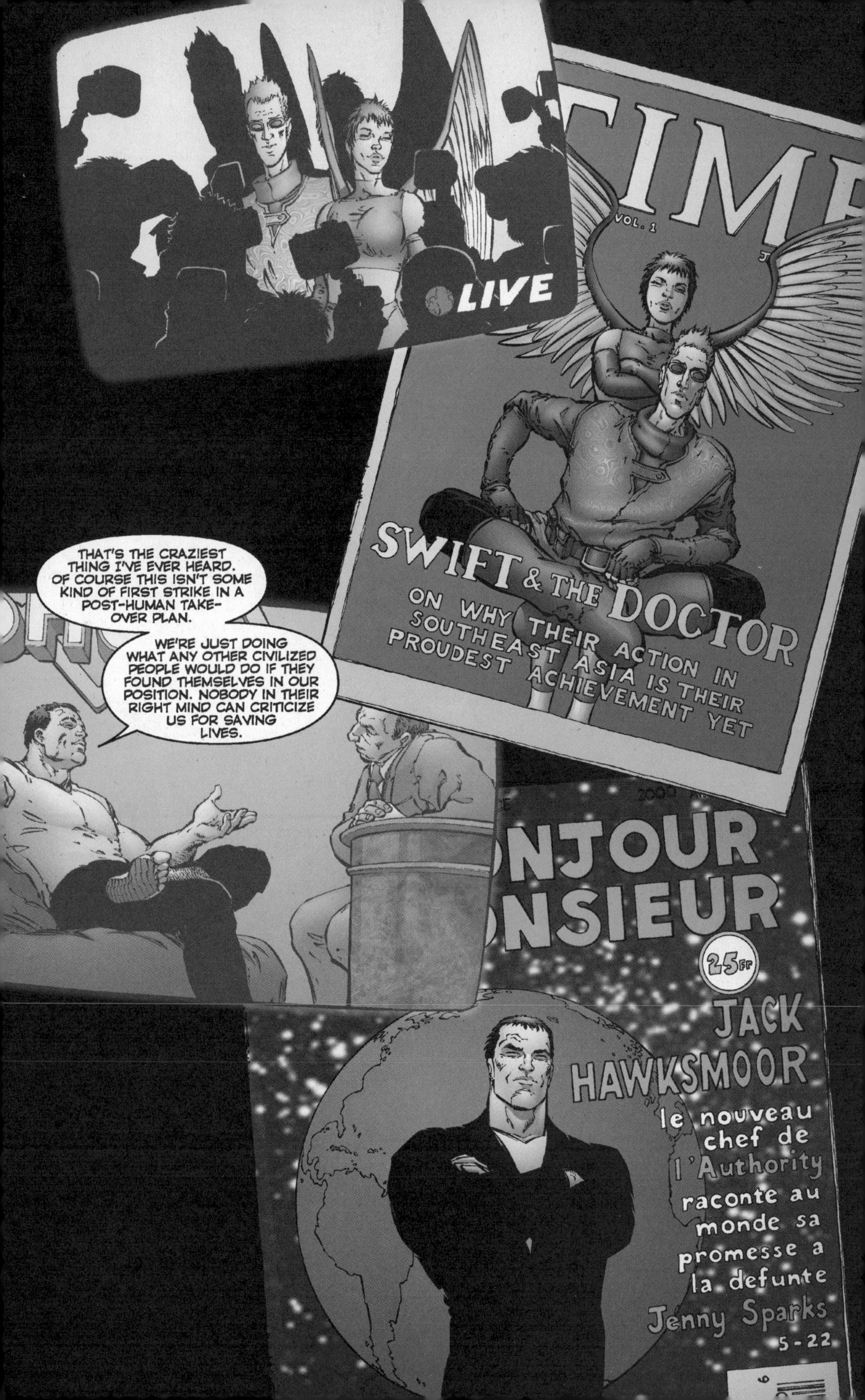

LIVE
TIME
VOL. 1
SWIFT & THE DOCTOR
ON WHY THEIR ACTION IN SOUTHEAST ASIA IS THEIR PROUDEST ACHIEVEMENT YET
THAT'S THE CRAZIEST THING I'VE EVER HEARD. OF COURSE THIS ISN'T SOME KIND OF FIRST STRIKE IN A POST-HUMAN TAKE-OVER PLAN.
WE'RE JUST DOING WHAT ANY OTHER CIVILIZED PEOPLE WOULD DO IF THEY FOUND THEMSELVES IN OUR POSITION. NOBODY IN THEIR RIGHT MIND CAN CRITICIZE US FOR SAVING LIVES.
ONJOUR
ONSIEUR
25Fr
JACK HAWKSMOOR
le nouveau chef de l'Authority raconte au monde sa promesse a la defunte Jenny Sparks
5-22

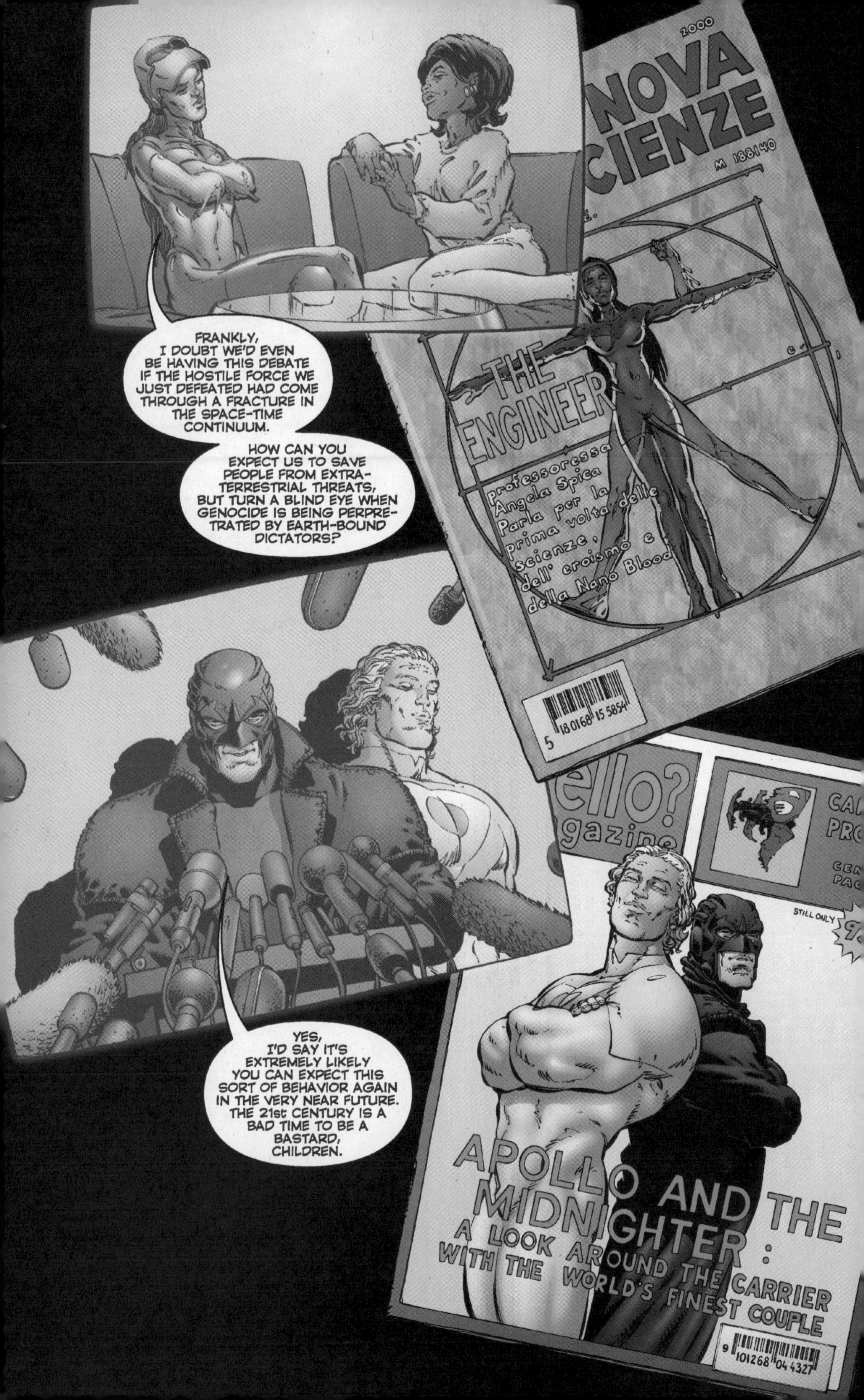

FRANKLY, I DOUBT WE'D EVEN BE HAVING THIS DEBATE IF THE HOSTILE FORCE WE JUST DEFEATED HAD COME THROUGH A FRACTURE IN THE SPACE-TIME CONTINUUM.
HOW CAN YOU EXPECT US TO SAVE PEOPLE FROM EXTRA-TERRESTRIAL THREATS, BUT TURN A BLIND EYE WHEN GENOCIDE IS BEING PERPRE-TRATED BY EARTH-BOUND DICTATORS?
2000
NOVA CIENZE
M 188140
THE ENGINEER
professoressa Angela Spica Parla per la prima volta delle scienze, dell' eroismo e della Nano Blood
YES, I'D SAY IT'S EXTREMELY LIKELY YOU CAN EXPECT THIS SORT OF BEHAVIOR AGAIN IN THE VERY NEAR FUTURE. THE 21st CENTURY IS A BAD TIME TO BE A BASTARD, CHILDREN.
ello?
gazine
STILL ONLY
APOLLO AND THE MIDNIGHTER:
A LOOK AROUND THE CARRIER WITH THE WORLD'S FINEST COUPLE

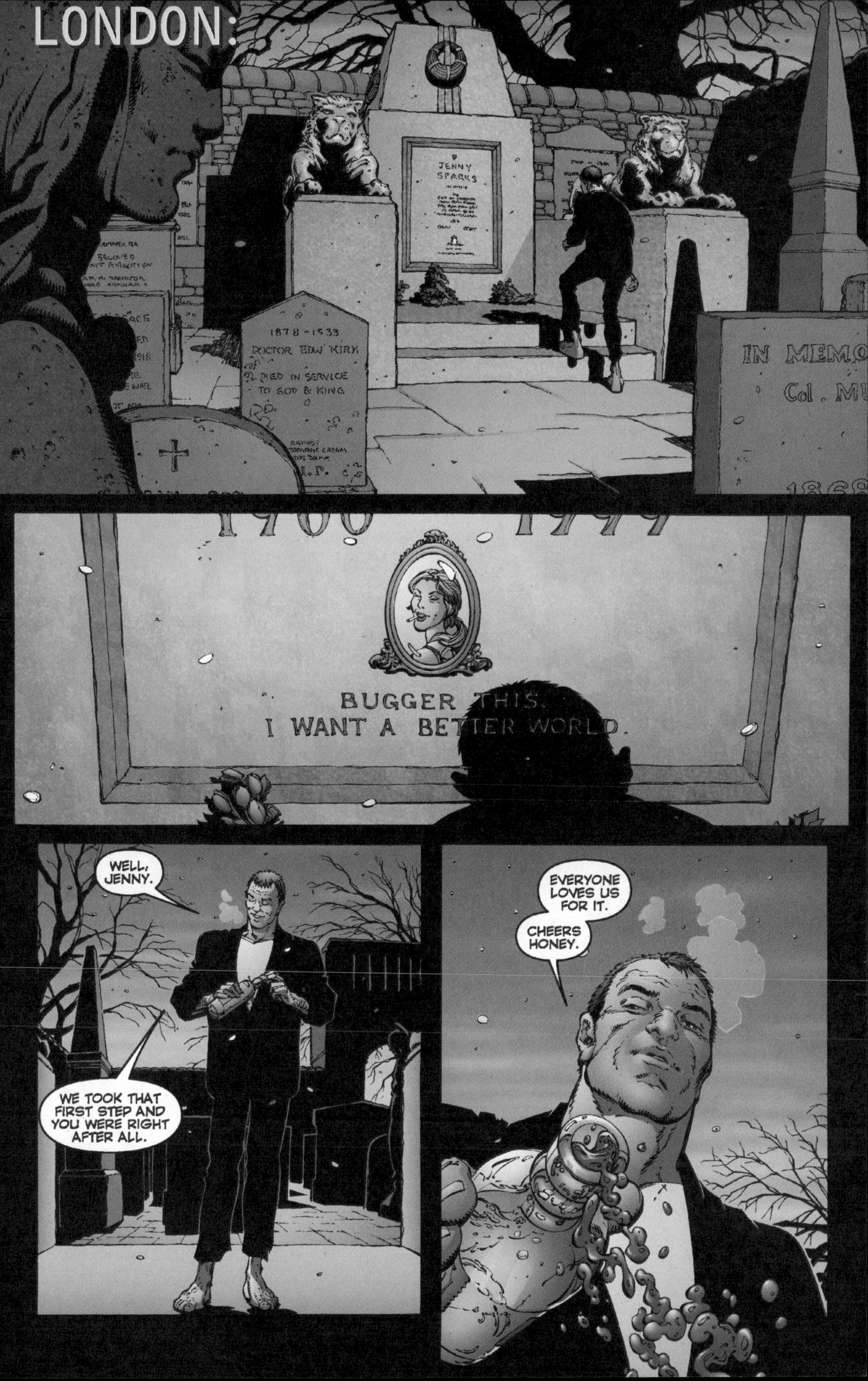

LONDON:
JENNY SPARKS
1878 - 1933
DOCTOR EDW KIRK
DIED IN SERVICE
TO GOD & KING
IN MEMO
Col. MU
BUGGER THIS.
I WANT A BETTER WORLD.
WELL, JENNY.
WE TOOK THAT FIRST STEP AND YOU WERE RIGHT AFTER ALL.
EVERYONE LOVES US FOR IT.
CHEERS HONEY.

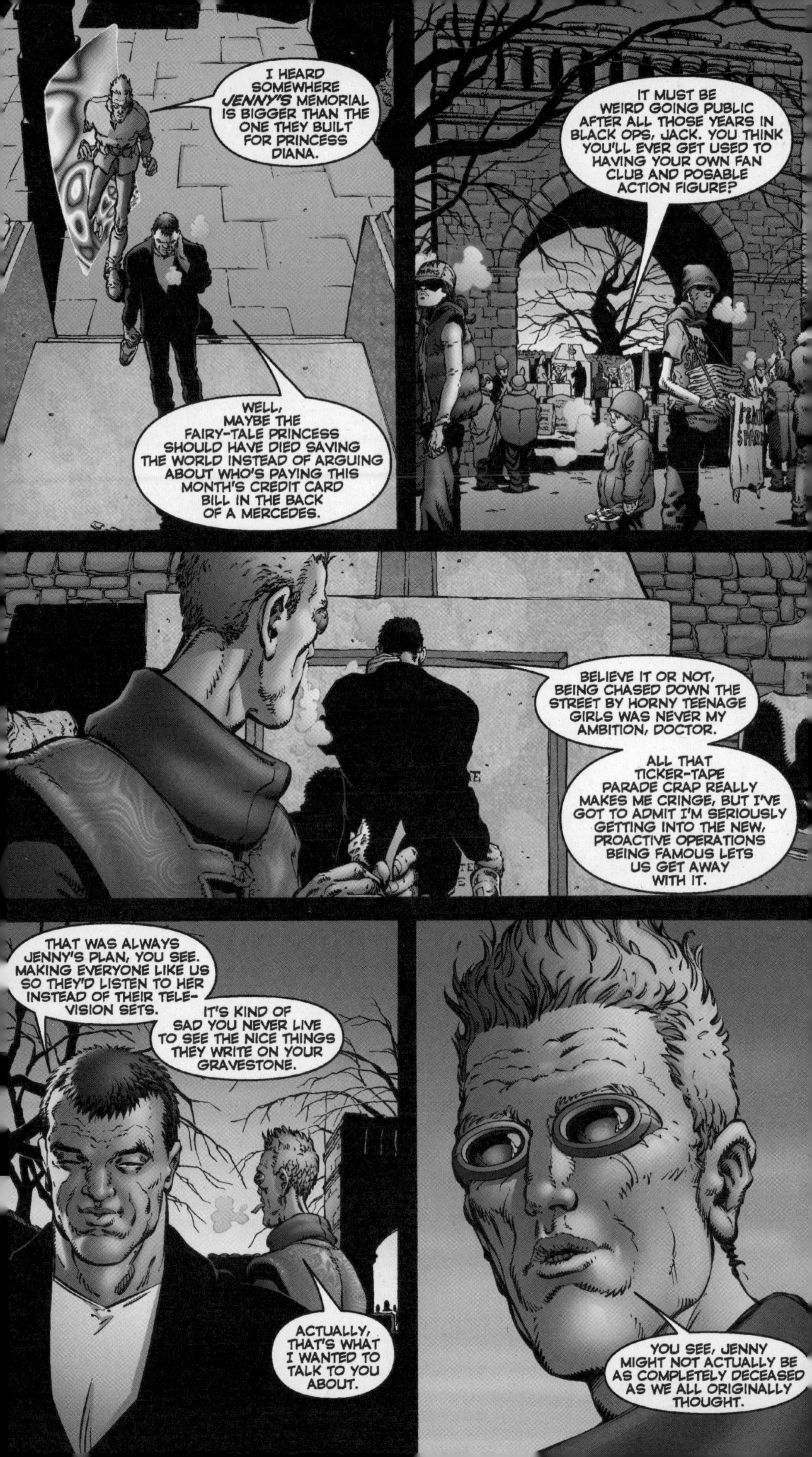
I HEARD SOMEWHERE JENNY'S MEMORIAL IS BIGGER THAN THE ONE THEY BUILT FOR PRINCESS DIANA.
WELL, MAYBE THE FAIRY-TALE PRINCESS SHOULD HAVE DIED SAVING THE WORLD INSTEAD OF ARGUING ABOUT WHO'S PAYING THIS MONTH'S CREDIT CARD BILL IN THE BACK OF A MERCEDES.
IT MUST BE WEIRD GOING PUBLIC AFTER ALL THOSE YEARS IN BLACK OPS, JACK. YOU THINK YOU'LL EVER GET USED TO HAVING YOUR OWN FAN CLUB AND POSABLE ACTION FIGURE?
BELIEVE IT OR NOT, BEING CHASED DOWN THE STREET BY HORNY TEENAGE GIRLS WAS NEVER MY AMBITION, DOCTOR.
ALL THAT TICKER-TAPE PARADE CRAP REALLY MAKES ME CRINGE, BUT I'VE GOT TO ADMIT I'M SERIOUSLY GETTING INTO THE NEW, PROACTIVE OPERATIONS BEING FAMOUS LETS US GET AWAY WITH IT.
THAT WAS ALWAYS JENNY'S PLAN, YOU SEE. MAKING EVERYONE LIKE US SO THEY'D LISTEN TO HER INSTEAD OF THEIR TELE-VISION SETS.
IT'S KIND OF SAD YOU NEVER LIVE TO SEE THE NICE THINGS THEY WRITE ON YOUR GRAVESTONE.
ACTUALLY, THAT'S WHAT I WANTED TO TALK TO YOU ABOUT.
YOU SEE, JENNY MIGHT NOT ACTUALLY BE AS COMPLETELY DECEASED AS WE ALL ORIGINALLY THOUGHT.

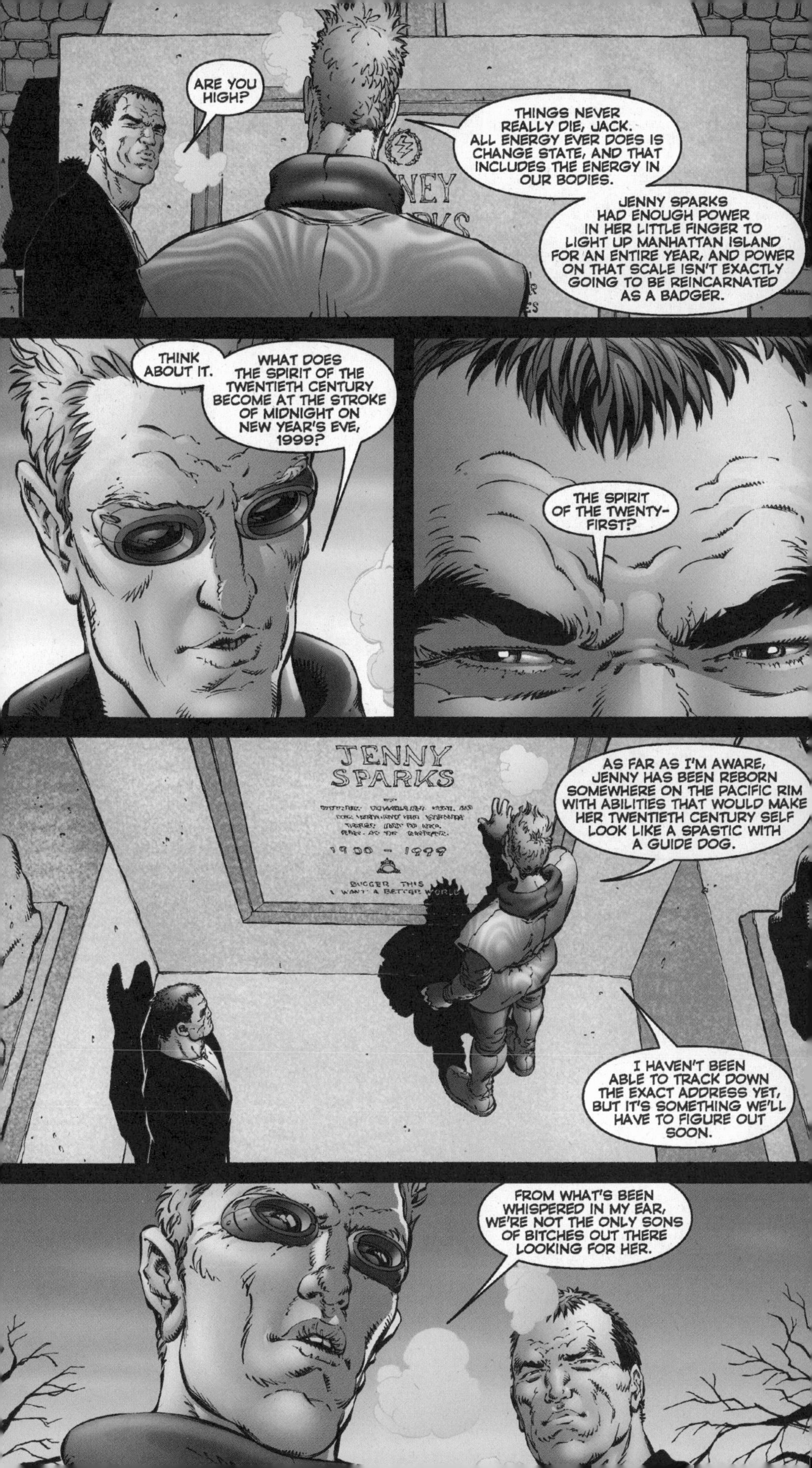
ARE YOU HIGH?
THINGS NEVER REALLY DIE, JACK. ALL ENERGY EVER DOES IS CHANGE STATE, AND THAT INCLUDES THE ENERGY IN OUR BODIES.
JENNY SPARKS HAD ENOUGH POWER IN HER LITTLE FINGER TO LIGHT UP MANHATTAN ISLAND FOR AN ENTIRE YEAR, AND POWER ON THAT SCALE ISN'T EXACTLY GOING TO BE REINCARNATED AS A BADGER.
THINK ABOUT IT.
WHAT DOES THE SPIRIT OF THE TWENTIETH CENTURY BECOME AT THE STROKE OF MIDNIGHT ON NEW YEAR'S EVE, 1999?
THE SPIRIT OF THE TWENTY-FIRST?
JENNY SPARKS
1900 - 1999
BUGGER THIS
AS FAR AS I'M AWARE, JENNY HAS BEEN REBORN SOMEWHERE ON THE PACIFIC RIM WITH ABILITIES THAT WOULD MAKE HER TWENTIETH CENTURY SELF LOOK LIKE A SPASTIC WITH A GUIDE DOG.
I HAVEN'T BEEN ABLE TO TRACK DOWN THE EXACT ADDRESS YET, BUT IT'S SOMETHING WE'LL HAVE TO FIGURE OUT SOON.
FROM WHAT'S BEEN WHISPERED IN MY EAR, WE'RE NOT THE ONLY SONS OF BITCHES OUT THERE LOOKING FOR HER.

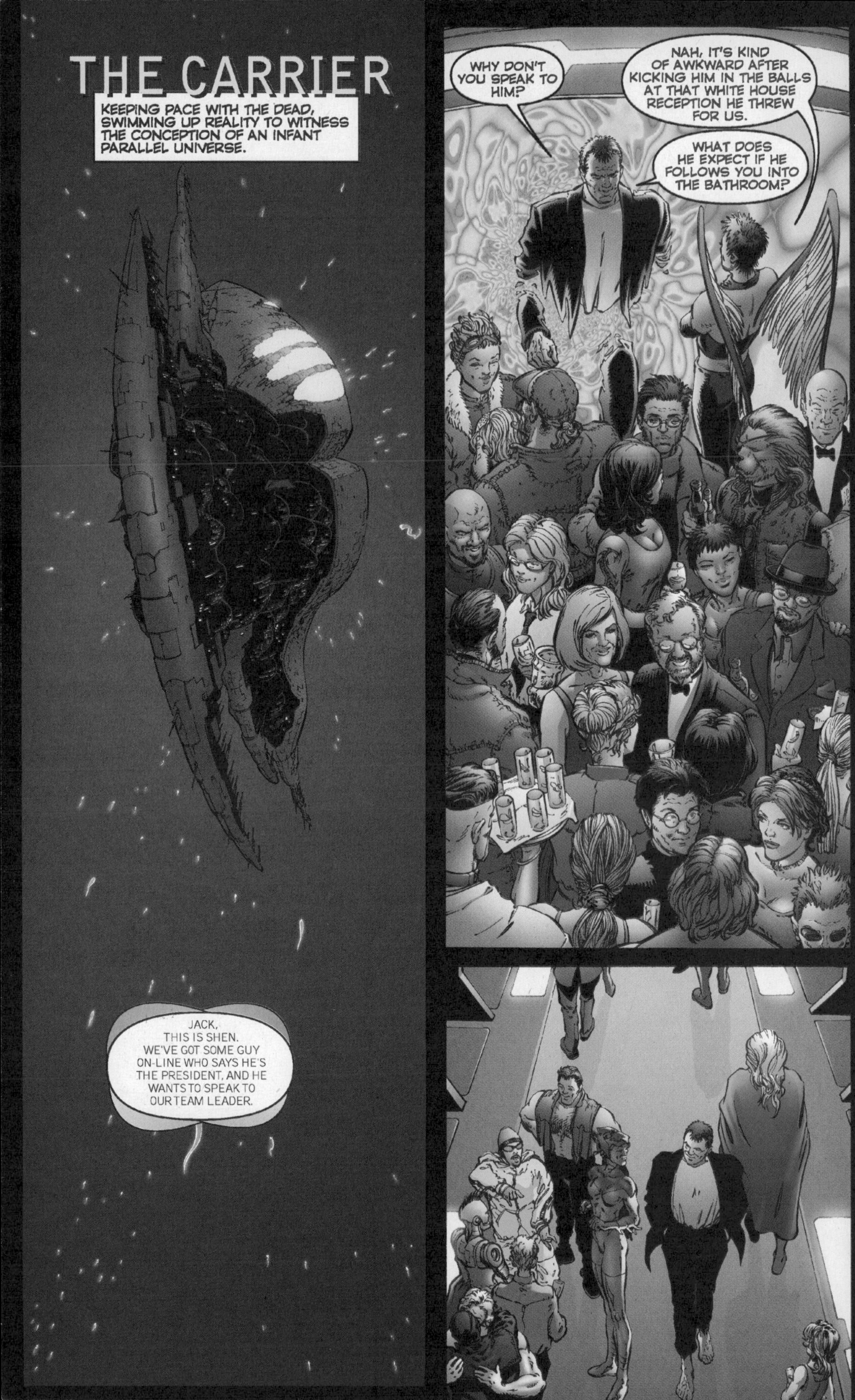
THE CARRIER
KEEPING PACE WITH THE DEAD, SWIMMING UP REALITY TO WITNESS THE CONCEPTION OF AN INFANT PARALLEL UNIVERSE.
JACK, THIS IS SHEN. WE'VE GOT SOME GUY ON-LINE WHO SAYS HE'S THE PRESIDENT, AND HE WANTS TO SPEAK TO OUR TEAM LEADER.
WHY DON'T YOU SPEAK TO HIM?
NAH, IT'S KIND OF AWKWARD AFTER KICKING HIM IN THE BALLS AT THAT WHITE HOUSE RECEPTION HE THREW FOR US.
WHAT DOES HE EXPECT IF HE FOLLOWS YOU INTO THE BATHROOM?

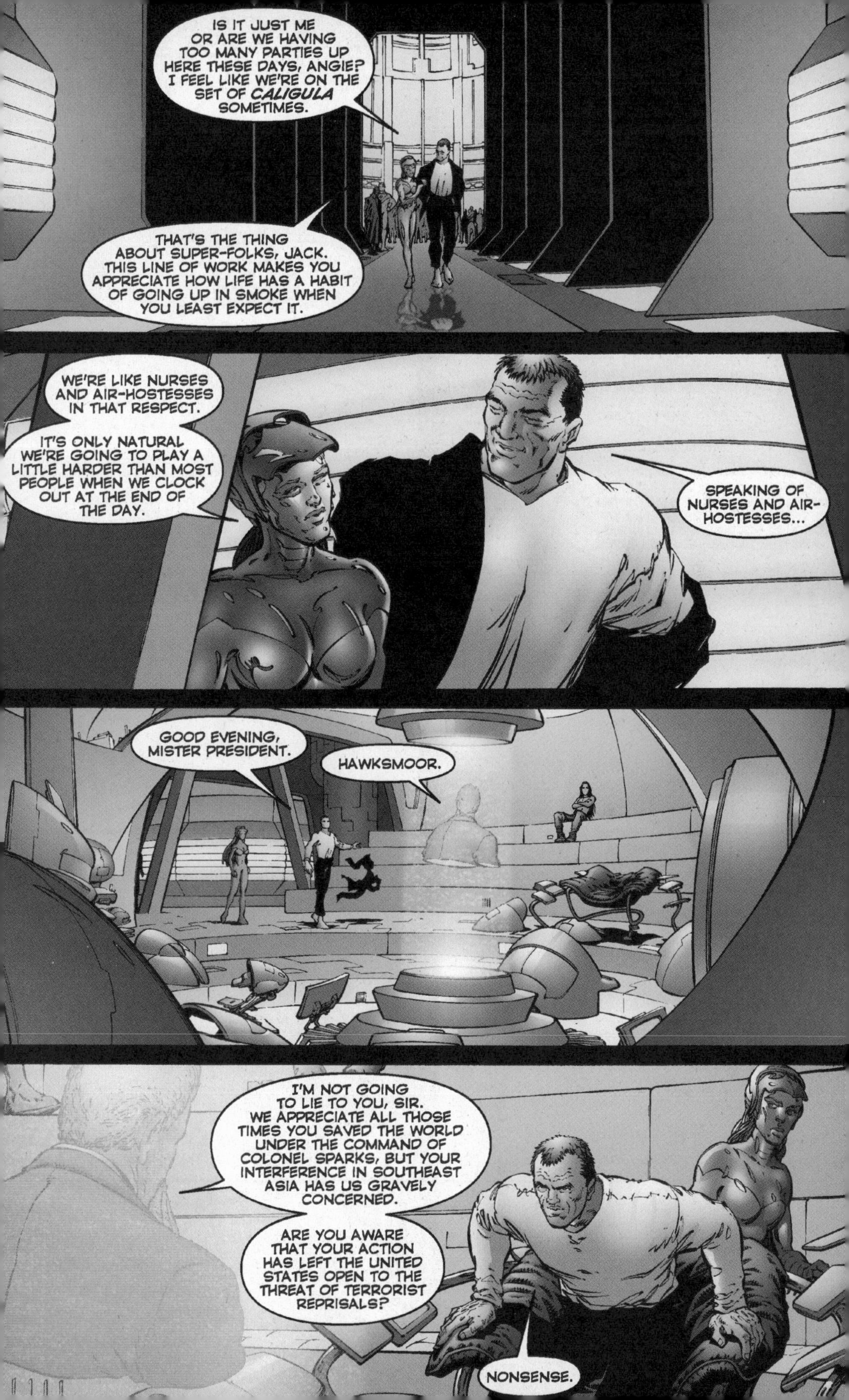
IS IT JUST ME OR ARE WE HAVING TOO MANY PARTIES UP HERE THESE DAYS, ANGIE? I FEEL LIKE WE'RE ON THE SET OF *CALIGULA* SOMETIMES.
THAT'S THE THING ABOUT SUPER-FOLKS, JACK. THIS LINE OF WORK MAKES YOU APPRECIATE HOW LIFE HAS A HABIT OF GOING UP IN SMOKE WHEN YOU LEAST EXPECT IT.
WE'RE LIKE NURSES AND AIR-HOSTESSES IN THAT RESPECT.
IT'S ONLY NATURAL WE'RE GOING TO PLAY A LITTLE HARDER THAN MOST PEOPLE WHEN WE CLOCK OUT AT THE END OF THE DAY.
SPEAKING OF NURSES AND AIR-HOSTESSES...
GOOD EVENING, MISTER PRESIDENT.
HAWKSMOOR.
I'M NOT GOING TO LIE TO YOU, SIR. WE APPRECIATE ALL THOSE TIMES YOU SAVED THE WORLD UNDER THE COMMAND OF COLONEL SPARKS, BUT YOUR INTERFERENCE IN SOUTHEAST ASIA HAS US GRAVELY CONCERNED.
ARE YOU AWARE THAT YOUR ACTION HAS LEFT THE UNITED STATES OPEN TO THE THREAT OF TERRORIST REPRISALS?
NONSENSE.

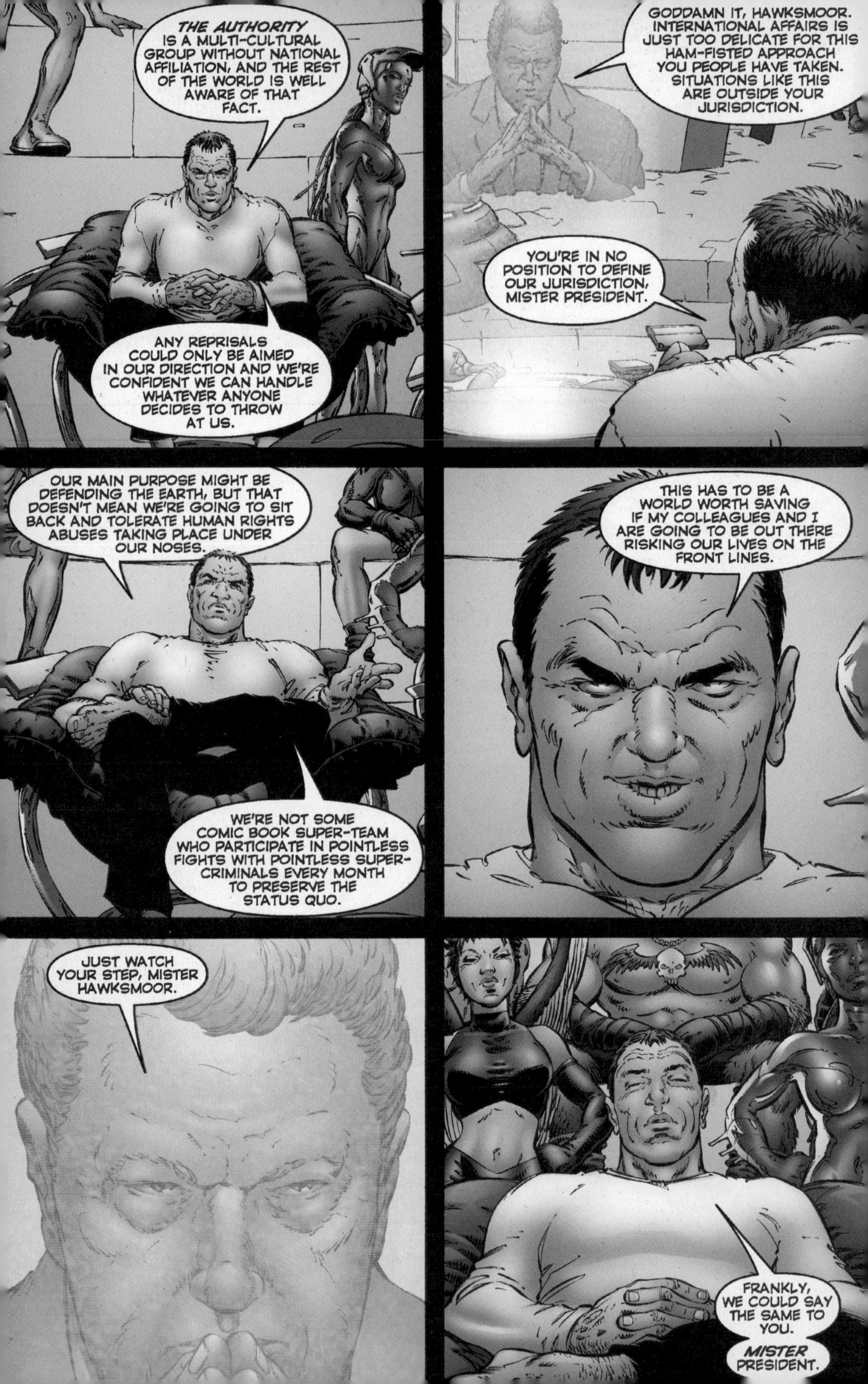
THE AUTHORITY IS A MULTI-CULTURAL GROUP WITHOUT NATIONAL AFFILIATION, AND THE REST OF THE WORLD IS WELL AWARE OF THAT FACT.
ANY REPRISALS COULD ONLY BE AIMED IN OUR DIRECTION AND WE'RE CONFIDENT WE CAN HANDLE WHATEVER ANYONE DECIDES TO THROW AT US.
GODDAMN IT, HAWKSMOOR. INTERNATIONAL AFFAIRS IS JUST TOO DELICATE FOR THIS HAM-FISTED APPROACH YOU PEOPLE HAVE TAKEN. SITUATIONS LIKE THIS ARE OUTSIDE YOUR JURISDICTION.
YOU'RE IN NO POSITION TO DEFINE OUR JURISDICTION, MISTER PRESIDENT.
OUR MAIN PURPOSE MIGHT BE DEFENDING THE EARTH, BUT THAT DOESN'T MEAN WE'RE GOING TO SIT BACK AND TOLERATE HUMAN RIGHTS ABUSES TAKING PLACE UNDER OUR NOSES.
WE'RE NOT SOME COMIC BOOK SUPER-TEAM WHO PARTICIPATE IN POINTLESS FIGHTS WITH POINTLESS SUPER-CRIMINALS EVERY MONTH TO PRESERVE THE STATUS QUO.
THIS HAS TO BE A WORLD WORTH SAVING IF MY COLLEAGUES AND I ARE GOING TO BE OUT THERE RISKING OUR LIVES ON THE FRONT LINES.
JUST WATCH YOUR STEP, MISTER HAWKSMOOR.
FRANKLY, WE COULD SAY THE SAME TO YOU.
MISTER PRESIDENT.

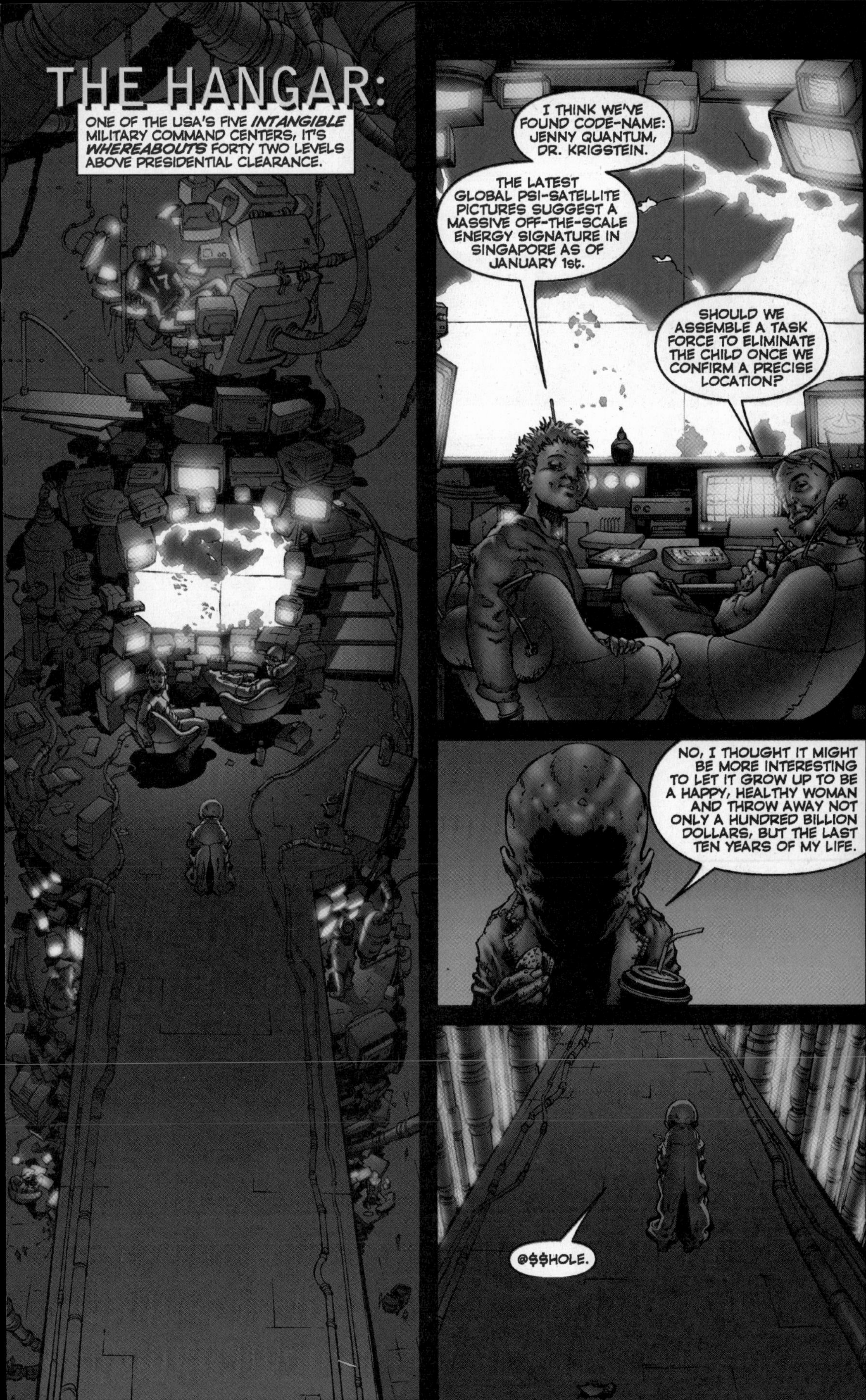
THE HANGAR:
ONE OF THE USA'S FIVE *INTANGIBLE* MILITARY COMMAND CENTERS, IT'S *WHEREABOUTS* FORTY TWO LEVELS ABOVE PRESIDENTIAL CLEARANCE.
I THINK WE'VE FOUND CODE-NAME: JENNY QUANTUM, DR. KRIGSTEIN.
THE LATEST GLOBAL PSI-SATELLITE PICTURES SUGGEST A MASSIVE OFF-THE-SCALE ENERGY SIGNATURE IN SINGAPORE AS OF JANUARY 1st.
SHOULD WE ASSEMBLE A TASK FORCE TO ELIMINATE THE CHILD ONCE WE CONFIRM A PRECISE LOCATION?
NO, I THOUGHT IT MIGHT BE MORE INTERESTING TO LET IT GROW UP TO BE A HAPPY, HEALTHY WOMAN AND THROW AWAY NOT ONLY A HUNDRED BILLION DOLLARS, BUT THE LAST TEN YEARS OF MY LIFE.
@$$HOLE.

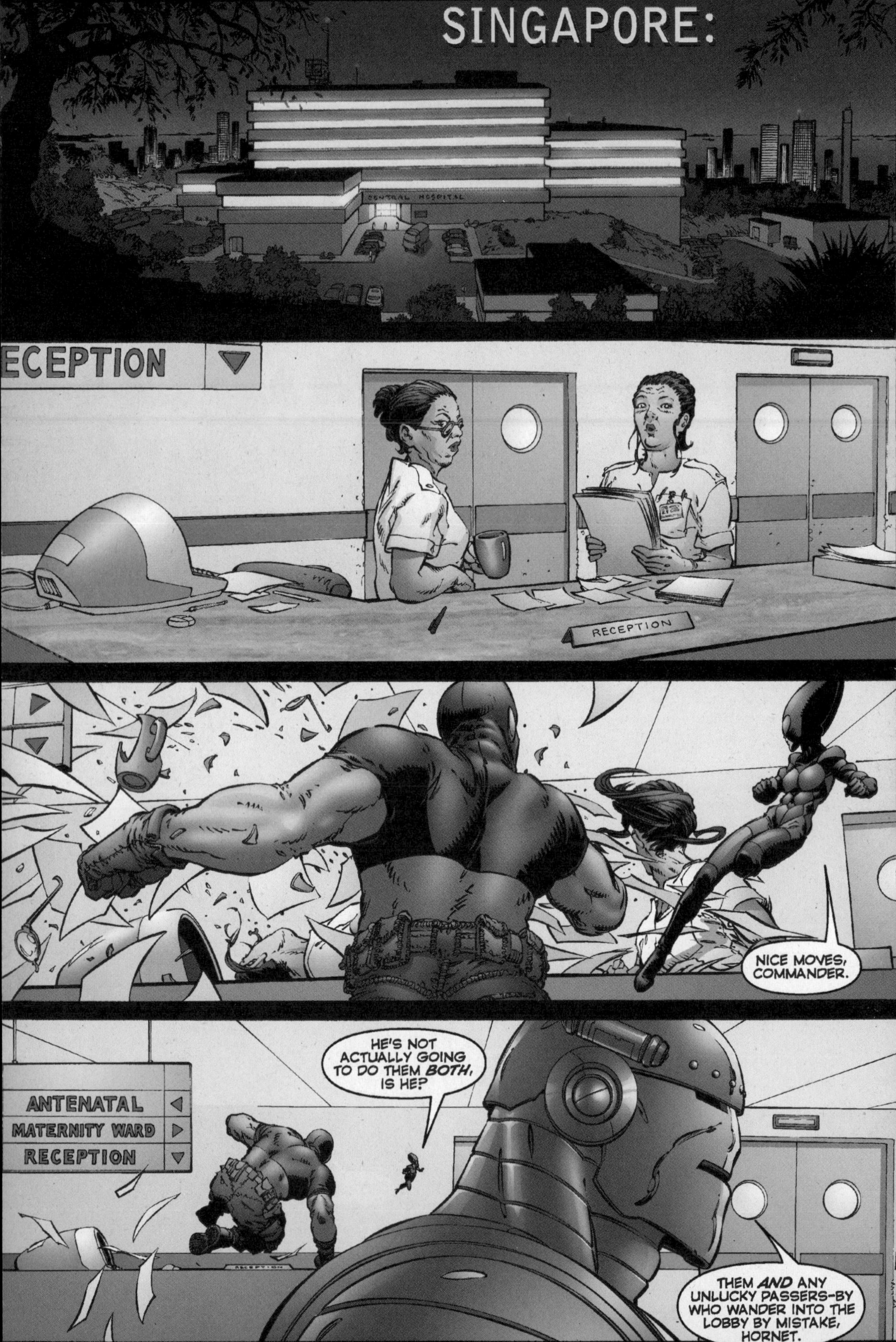
SINGAPORE:
ECEPTION
RECEPTION
NICE MOVES, COMMANDER.
HE'S NOT ACTUALLY GOING TO DO THEM *BOTH*, IS HE?
ANTENATAL
MATERNITY WARD
RECEPTION
THEM *AND* ANY UNLUCKY PASSERS-BY WHO WANDER INTO THE LOBBY BY MISTAKE, HORNET.

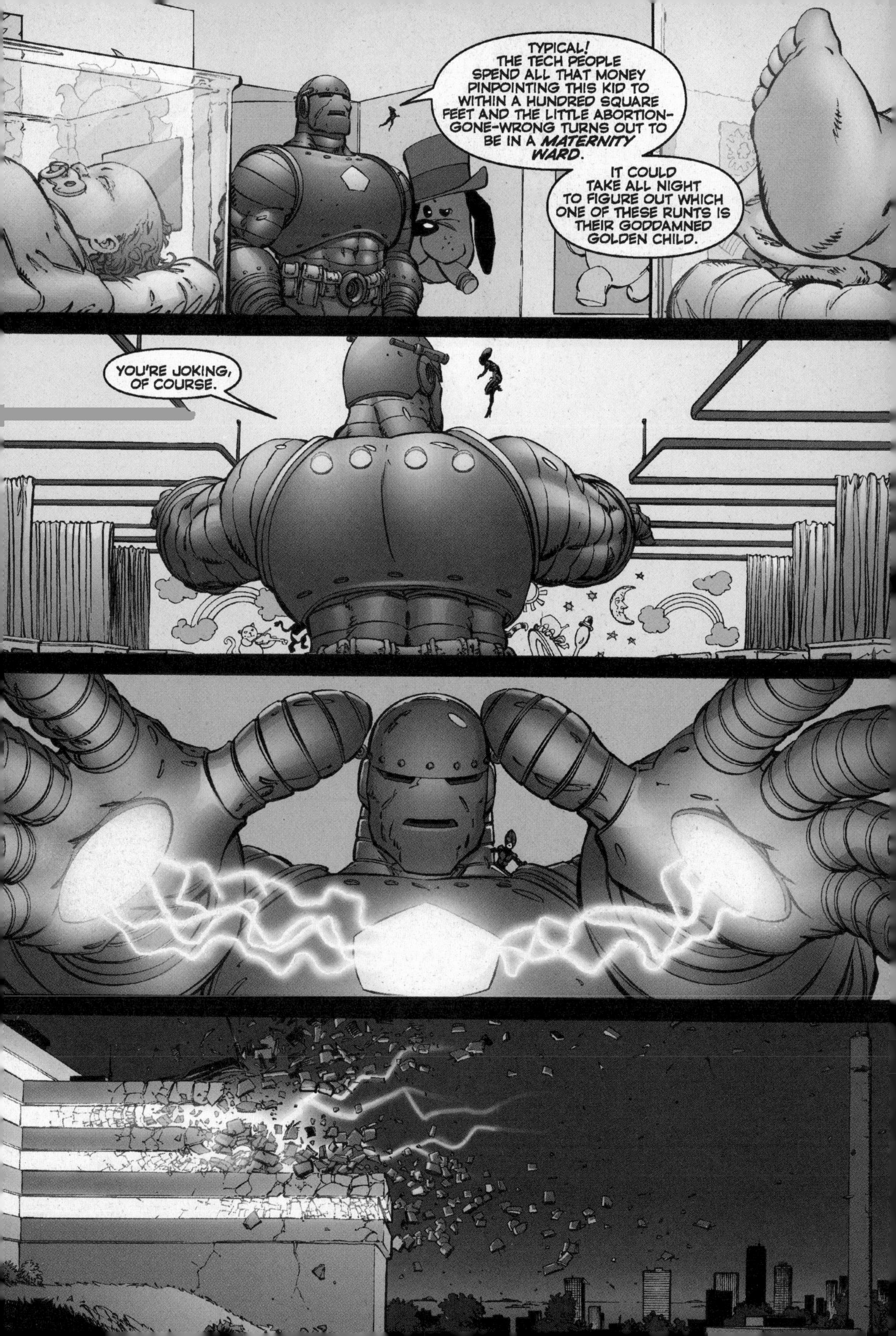
TYPICAL! THE TECH PEOPLE SPEND ALL THAT MONEY PINPOINTING THIS KID TO WITHIN A HUNDRED SQUARE FEET AND THE LITTLE ABORTION-GONE-WRONG TURNS OUT TO BE IN A *MATERNITY WARD*.
IT COULD TAKE ALL NIGHT TO FIGURE OUT WHICH ONE OF THESE RUNTS IS THEIR GODDAMNED GOLDEN CHILD.
YOU'RE JOKING, OF COURSE.

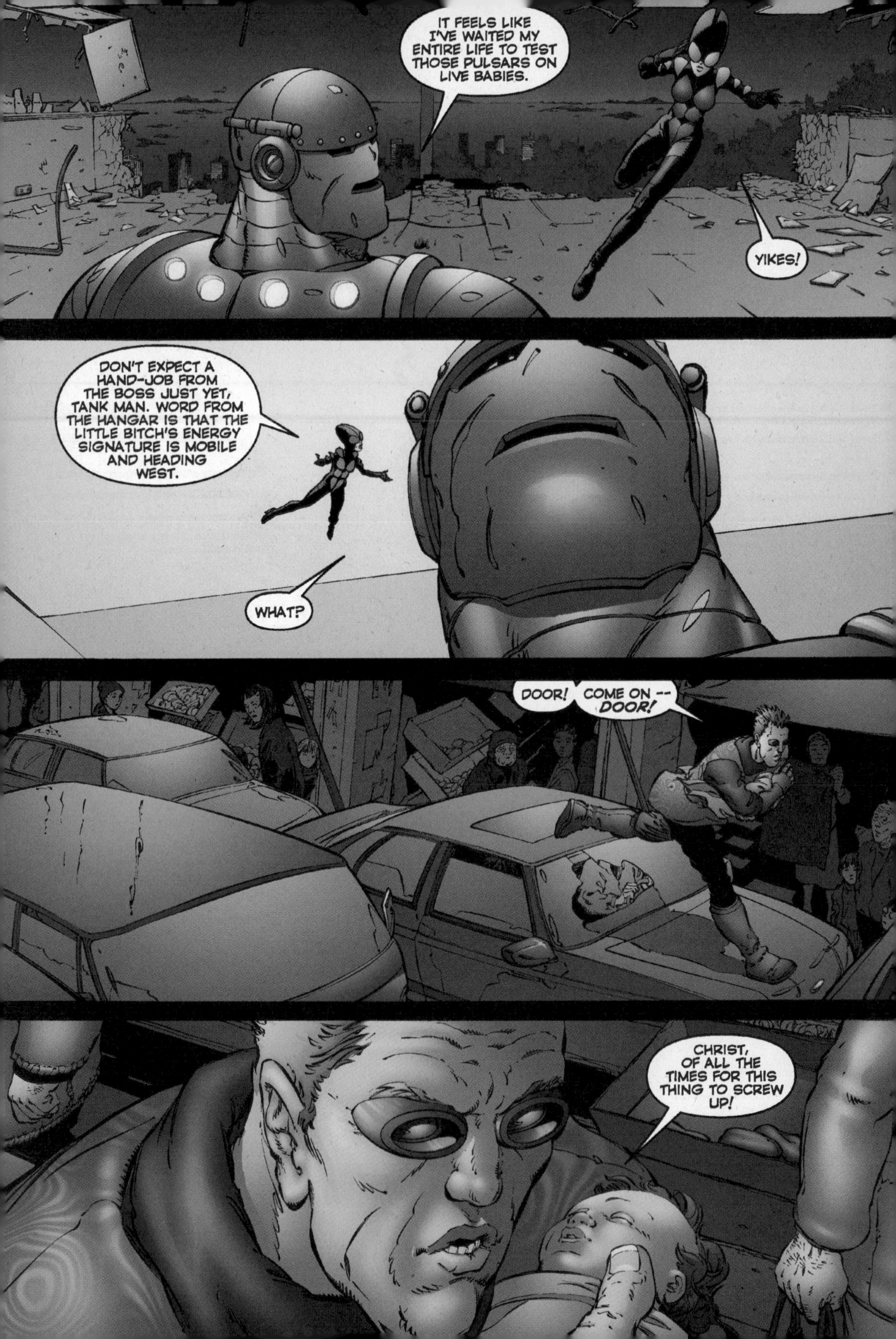
IT FEELS LIKE I'VE WAITED MY ENTIRE LIFE TO TEST THOSE PULSARS ON LIVE BABIES.
YIKES!
DON'T EXPECT A HAND-JOB FROM THE BOSS JUST YET, TANK MAN. WORD FROM THE HANGAR IS THAT THE LITTLE BITCH'S ENERGY SIGNATURE IS MOBILE AND HEADING WEST.
WHAT?
DOOR!
COME ON -- DOOR!
CHRIST, OF ALL THE TIMES FOR THIS THING TO SCREW UP!

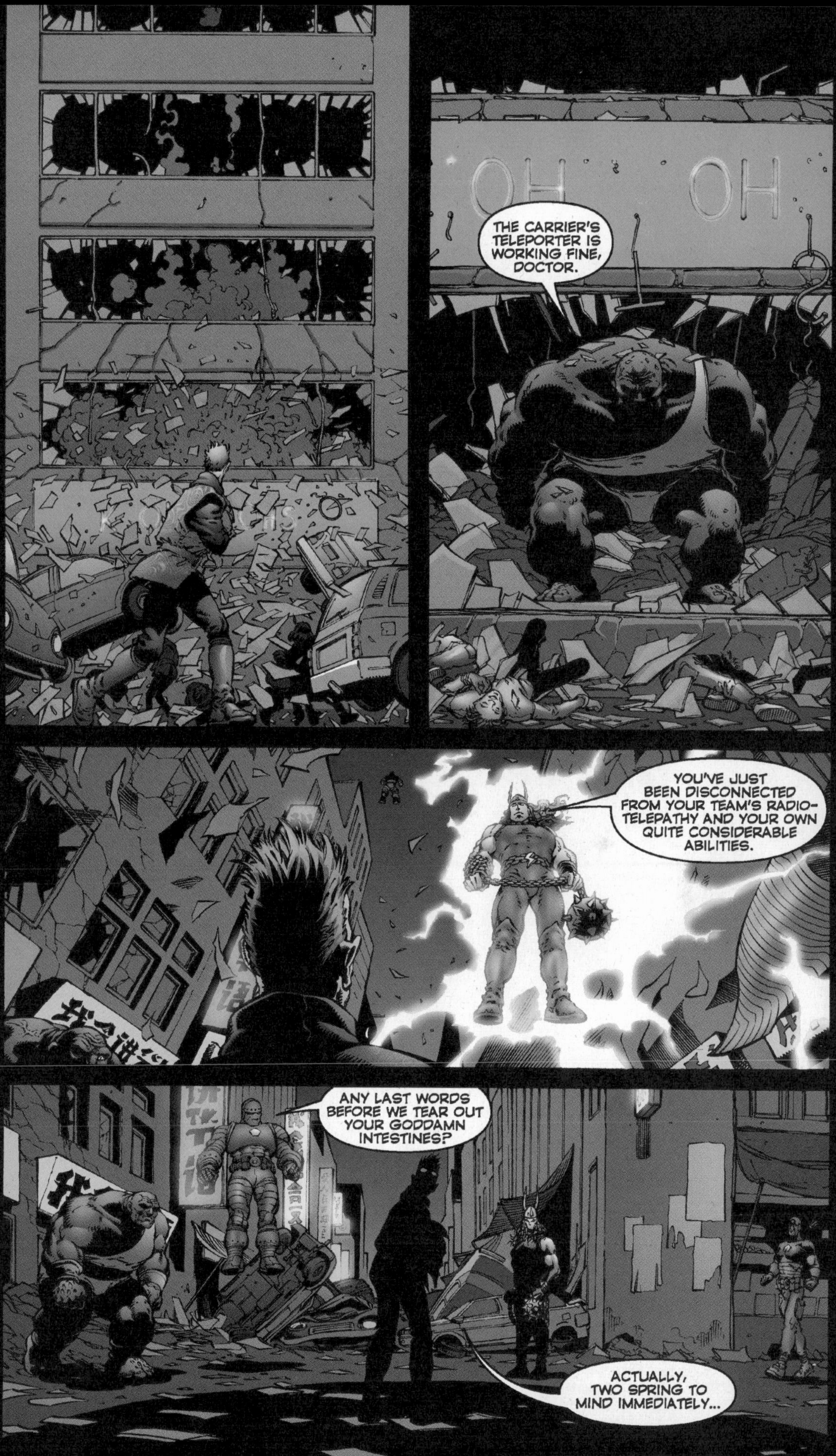
THE CARRIER'S TELEPORTER IS WORKING FINE, DOCTOR.
YOU'VE JUST BEEN DISCONNECTED FROM YOUR TEAM'S RADIO-TELEPATHY AND YOUR OWN QUITE CONSIDERABLE ABILITIES.
ANY LAST WORDS BEFORE WE TEAR OUT YOUR GODDAMN INTESTINES?
ACTUALLY, TWO SPRING TO MIND IMMEDIATELY...

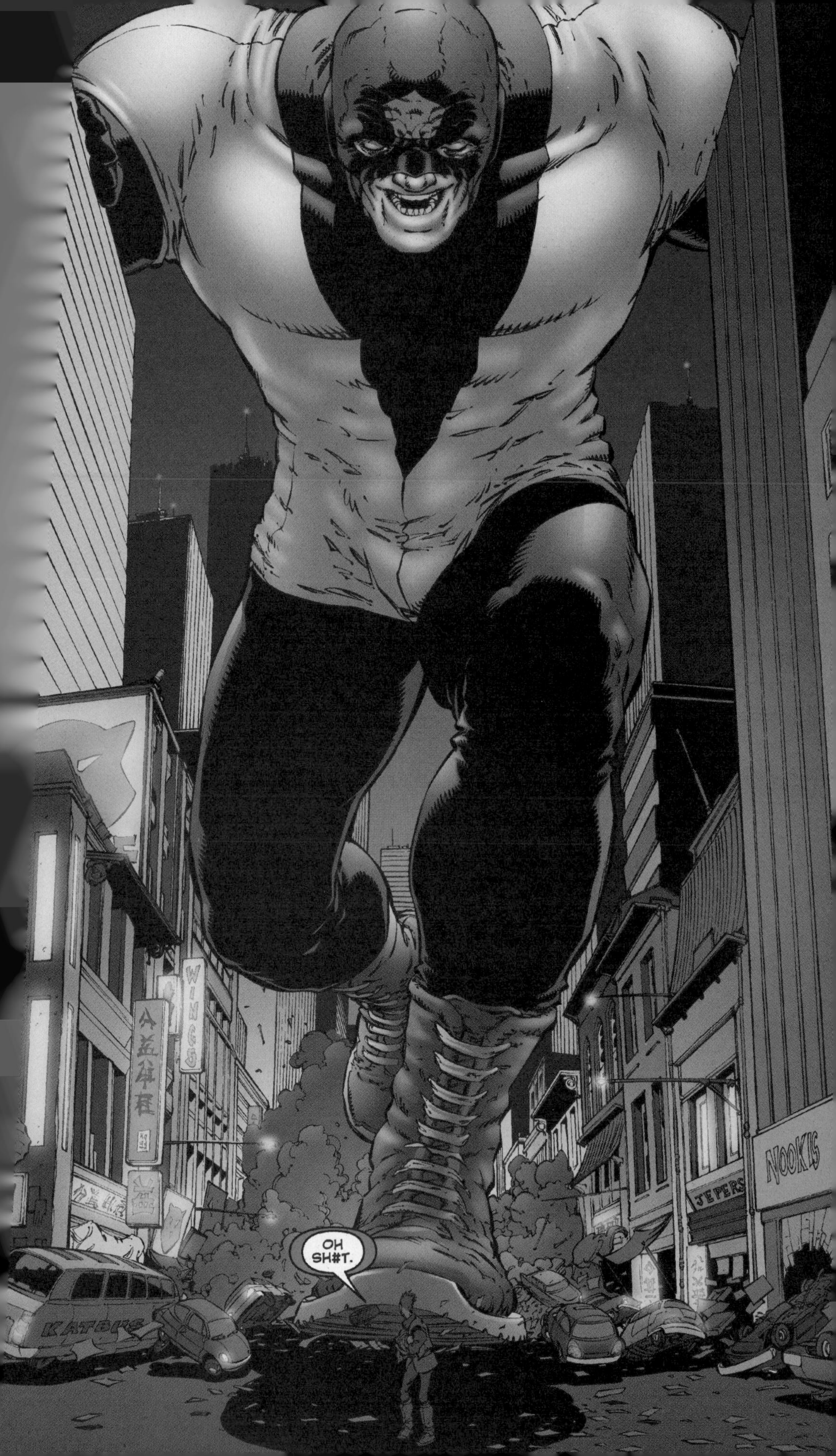
OH SH#T.

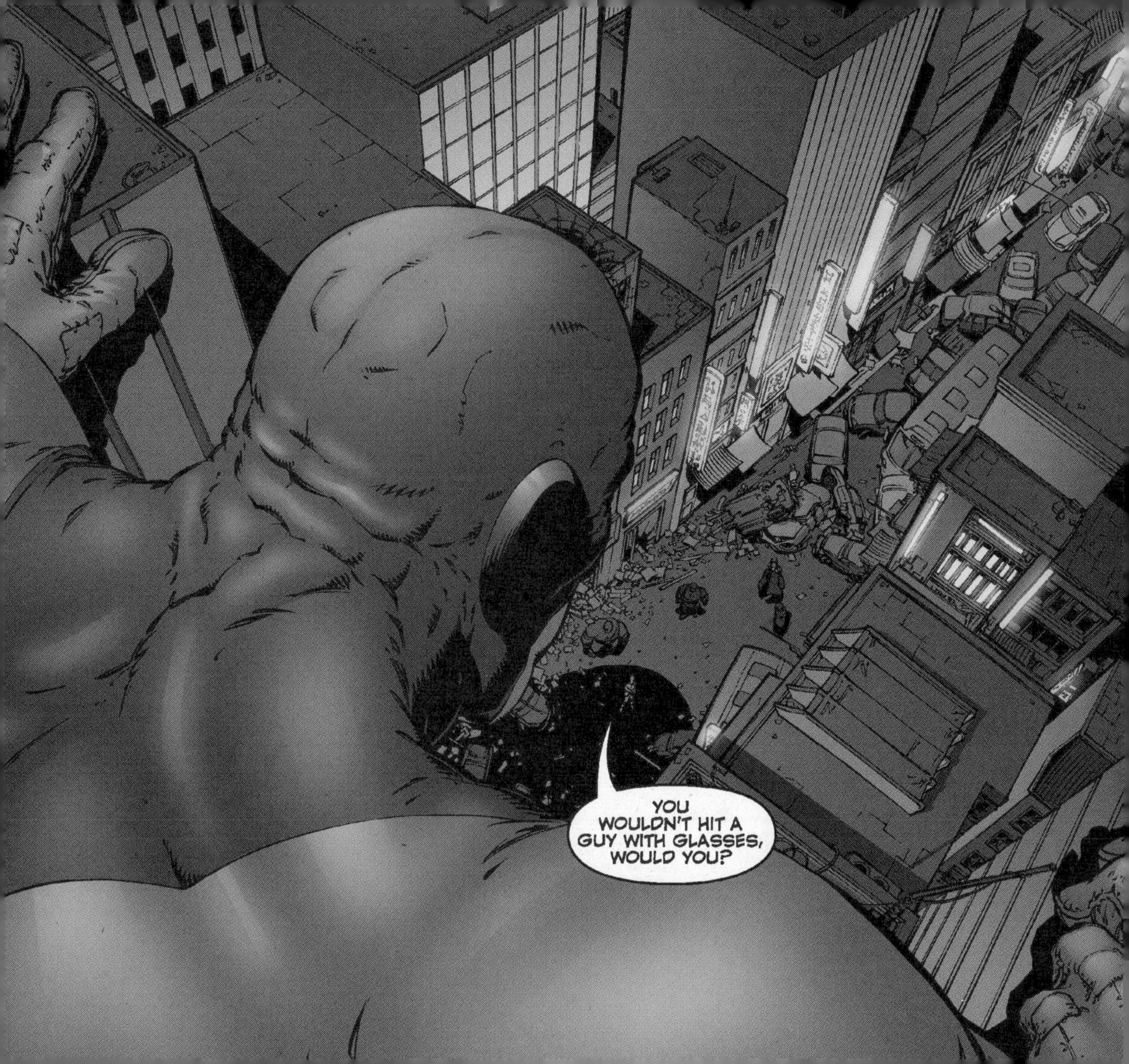
YOU WOULDN'T HIT A GUY WITH GLASSES, WOULD YOU?

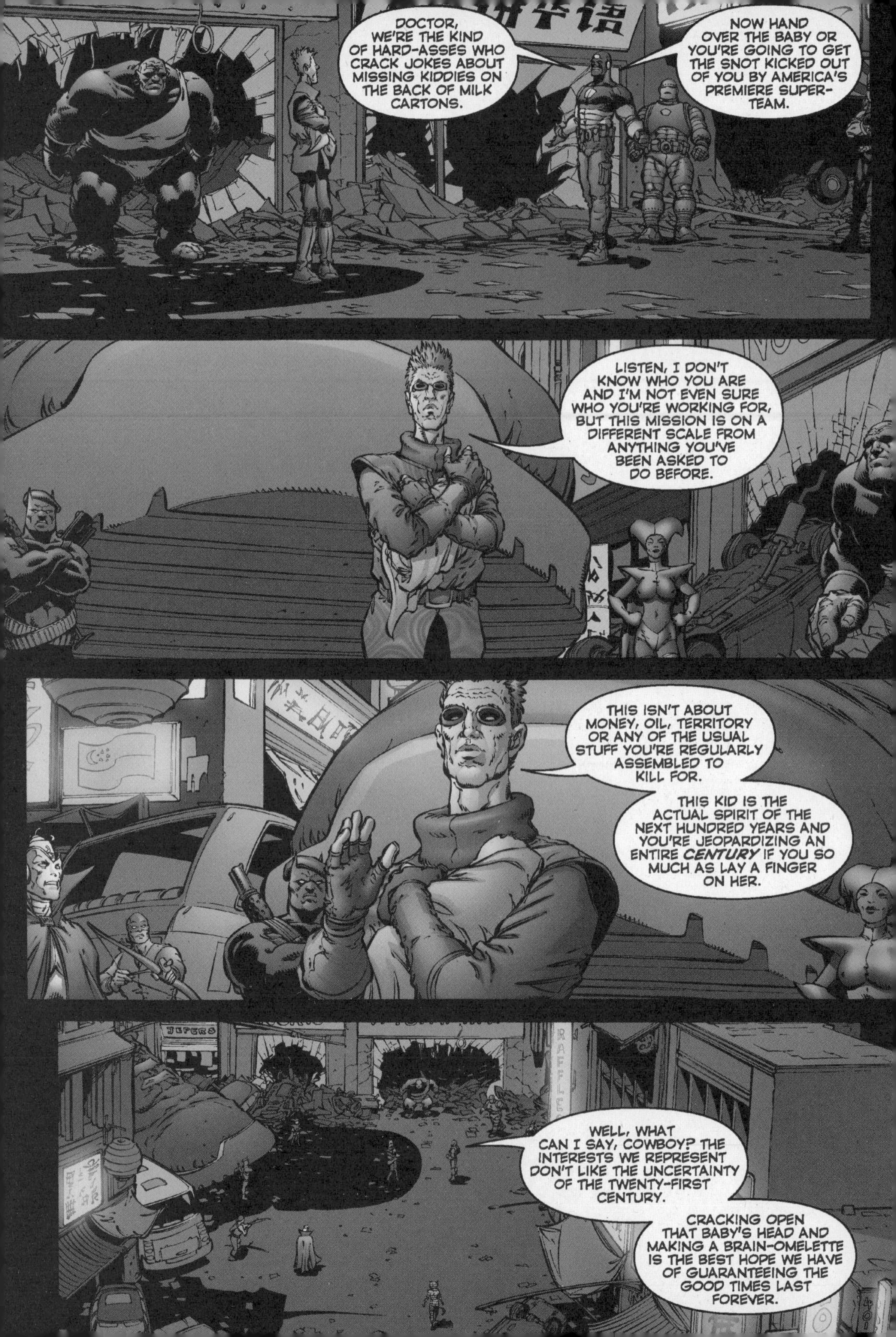
DOCTOR, WE'RE THE KIND OF HARD-ASSES WHO CRACK JOKES ABOUT MISSING KIDDIES ON THE BACK OF MILK CARTONS.
NOW HAND OVER THE BABY OR YOU'RE GOING TO GET THE SNOT KICKED OUT OF YOU BY AMERICA'S PREMIERE SUPER-TEAM.
LISTEN, I DON'T KNOW WHO YOU ARE AND I'M NOT EVEN SURE WHO YOU'RE WORKING FOR, BUT THIS MISSION IS ON A DIFFERENT SCALE FROM ANYTHING YOU'VE BEEN ASKED TO DO BEFORE.
THIS ISN'T ABOUT MONEY, OIL, TERRITORY OR ANY OF THE USUAL STUFF YOU'RE REGULARLY ASSEMBLED TO KILL FOR.
THIS KID IS THE ACTUAL SPIRIT OF THE NEXT HUNDRED YEARS AND YOU'RE JEOPARDIZING AN ENTIRE *CENTURY* IF YOU SO MUCH AS LAY A FINGER ON HER.
WELL, WHAT CAN I SAY, COWBOY? THE INTERESTS WE REPRESENT DON'T LIKE THE UNCERTAINTY OF THE TWENTY-FIRST CENTURY.
CRACKING OPEN THAT BABY'S HEAD AND MAKING A BRAIN-OMELETTE IS THE BEST HOPE WE HAVE OF GUARANTEEING THE GOOD TIMES LAST FOREVER.

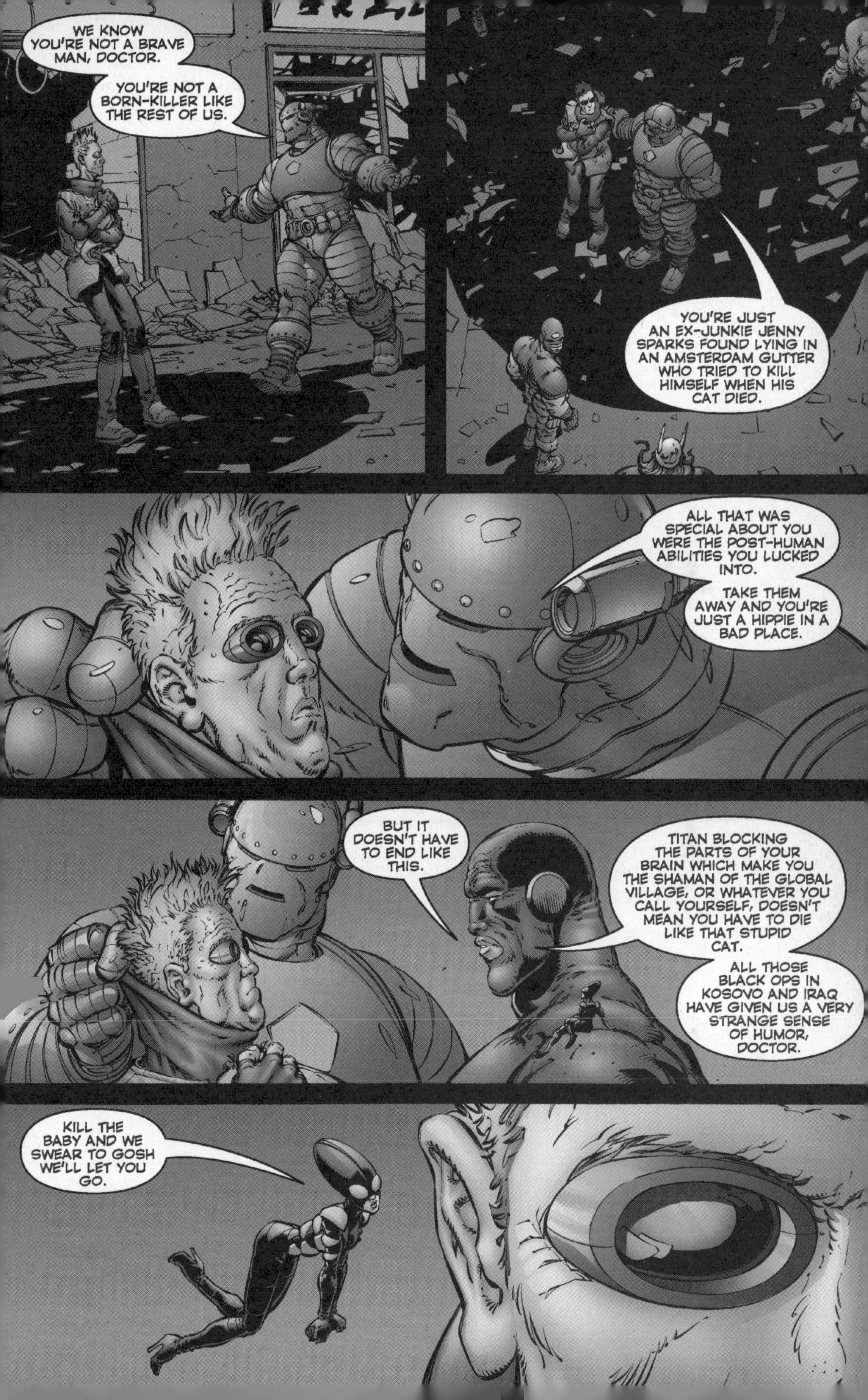
WE KNOW YOU'RE NOT A BRAVE MAN, DOCTOR.
YOU'RE NOT A BORN-KILLER LIKE THE REST OF US.
YOU'RE JUST AN EX-JUNKIE JENNY SPARKS FOUND LYING IN AN AMSTERDAM GUTTER WHO TRIED TO KILL HIMSELF WHEN HIS CAT DIED.
ALL THAT WAS SPECIAL ABOUT YOU WERE THE POST-HUMAN ABILITIES YOU LUCKED INTO.
TAKE THEM AWAY AND YOU'RE JUST A HIPPIE IN A BAD PLACE.
BUT IT DOESN'T HAVE TO END LIKE THIS.
TITAN BLOCKING THE PARTS OF YOUR BRAIN WHICH MAKE YOU THE SHAMAN OF THE GLOBAL VILLAGE, OR WHATEVER YOU CALL YOURSELF, DOESN'T MEAN YOU HAVE TO DIE LIKE THAT STUPID CAT.
ALL THOSE BLACK OPS IN KOSOVO AND IRAQ HAVE GIVEN US A VERY STRANGE SENSE OF HUMOR, DOCTOR.
KILL THE BABY AND WE SWEAR TO GOSH WE'LL LET YOU GO.

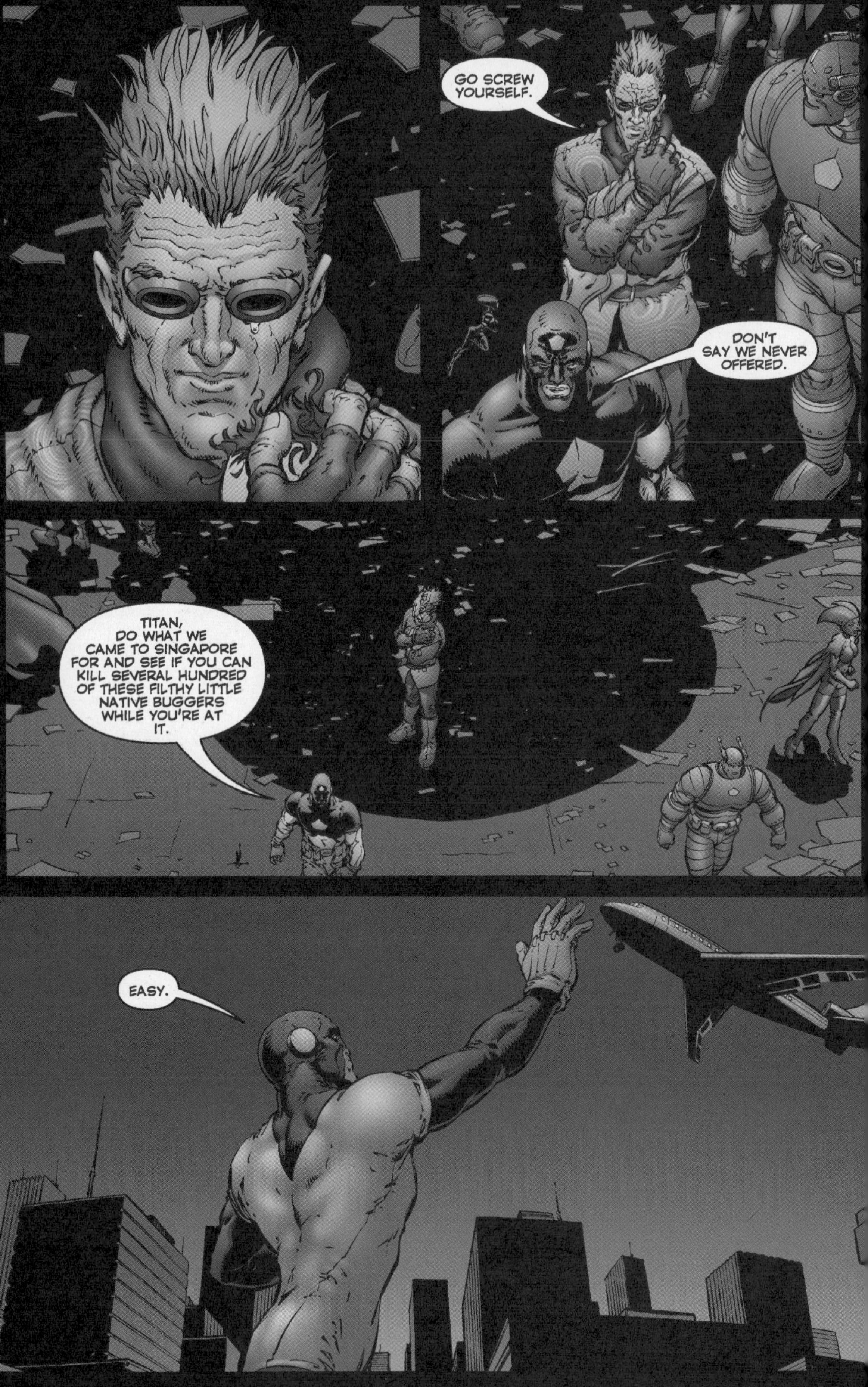
GO SCREW YOURSELF.
DON'T SAY WE NEVER OFFERED.
TITAN, DO WHAT WE CAME TO SINGAPORE FOR AND SEE IF YOU CAN KILL SEVERAL HUNDRED OF THESE FILTHY LITTLE NATIVE BUGGERS WHILE YOU'RE AT IT.
EASY.

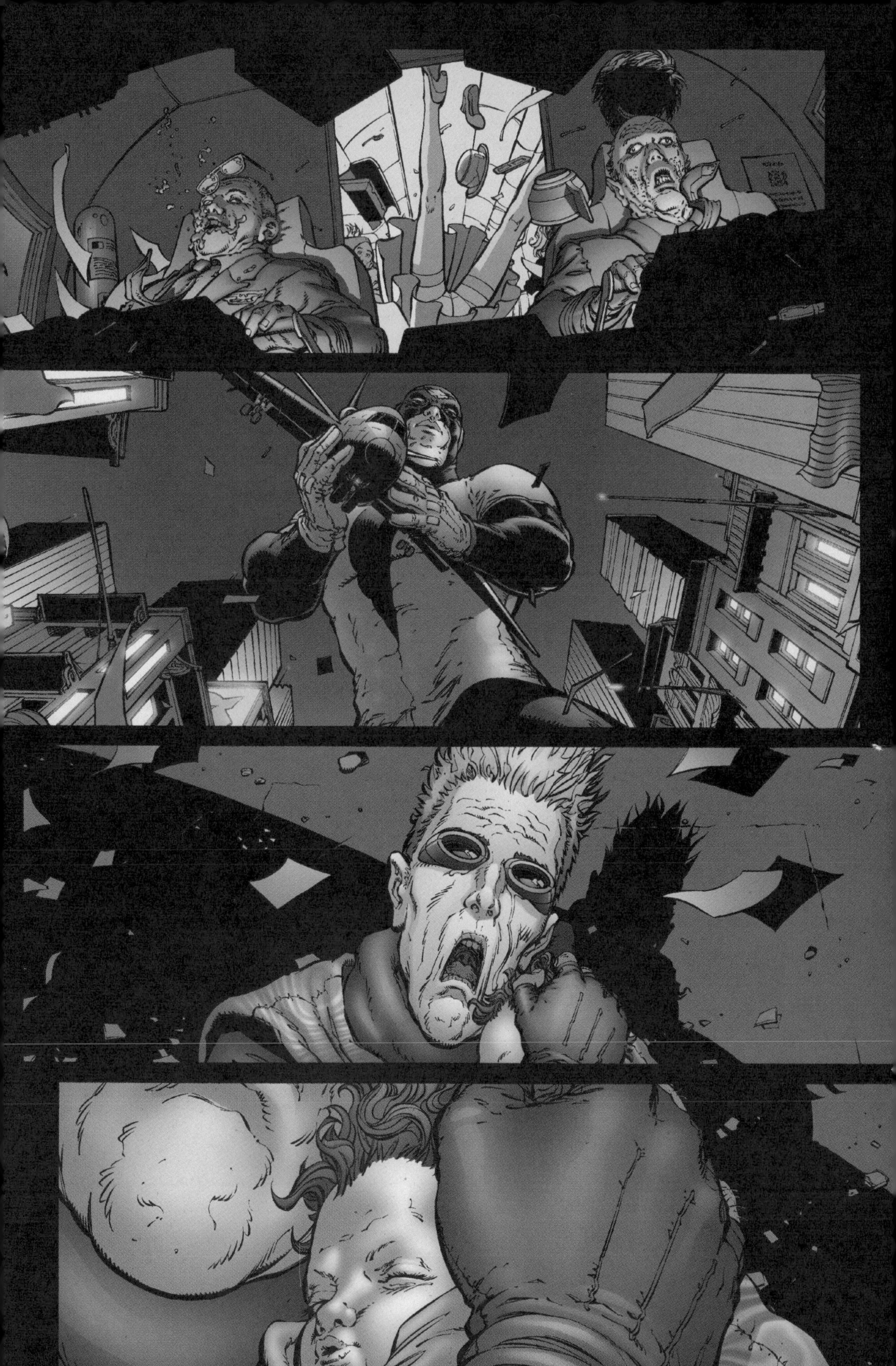

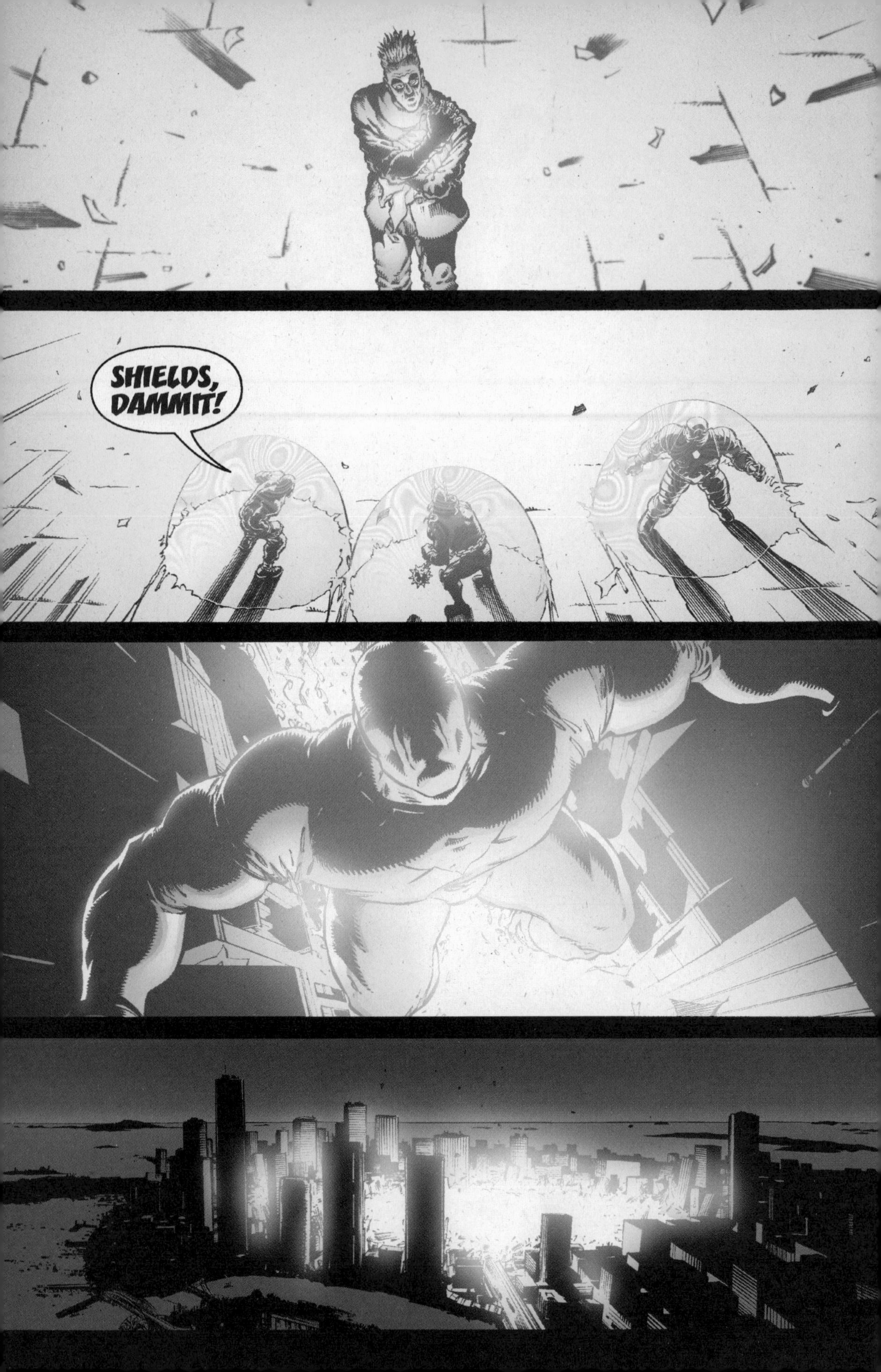
SHIELDS, DAMMIT!

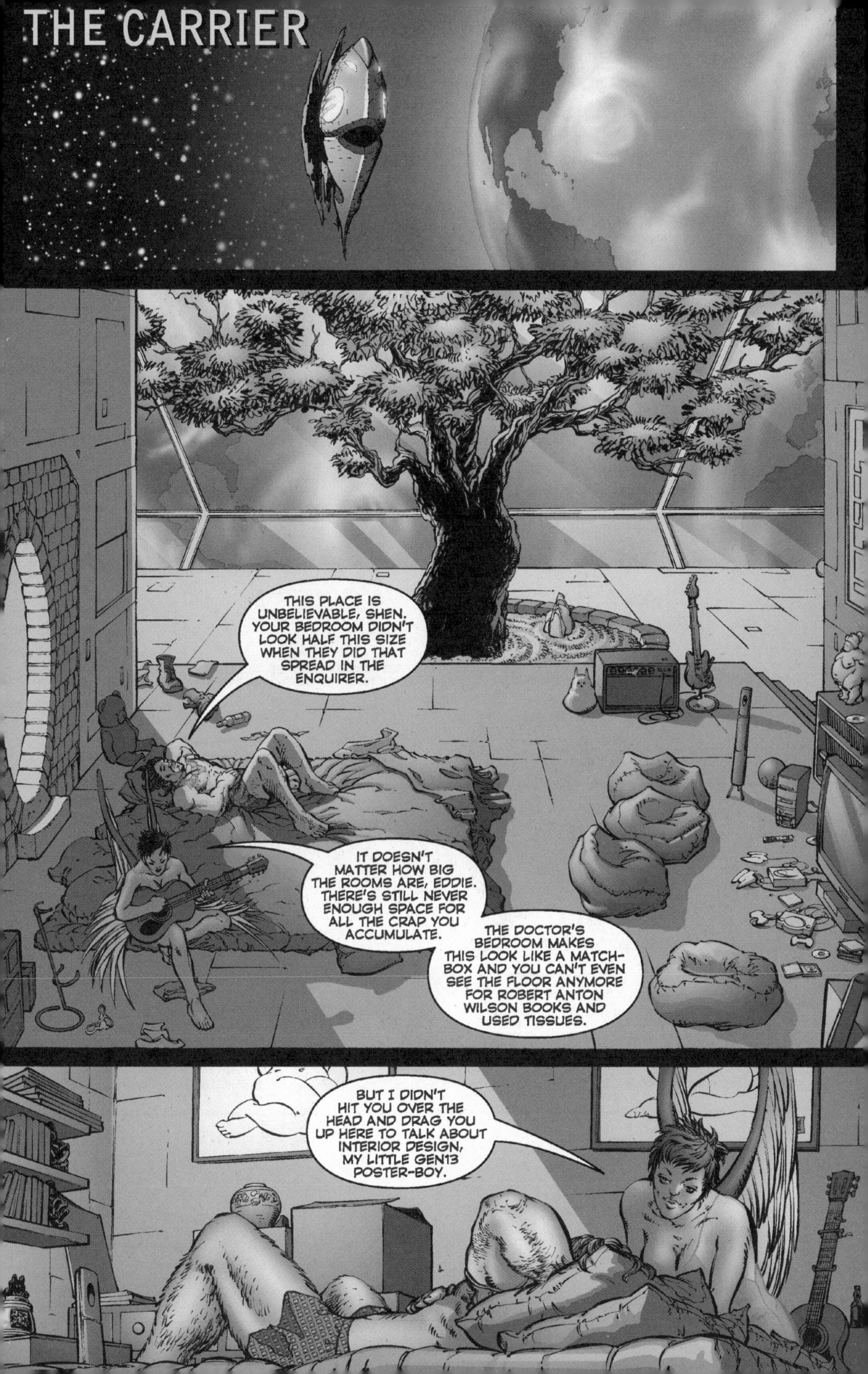
THE CARRIER
THIS PLACE IS UNBELIEVABLE, SHEN. YOUR BEDROOM DIDN'T LOOK HALF THIS SIZE WHEN THEY DID THAT SPREAD IN THE ENQUIRER.
IT DOESN'T MATTER HOW BIG THE ROOMS ARE, EDDIE. THERE'S STILL NEVER ENOUGH SPACE FOR ALL THE CRAP YOU ACCUMULATE.
THE DOCTOR'S BEDROOM MAKES THIS LOOK LIKE A MATCH-BOX AND YOU CAN'T EVEN SEE THE FLOOR ANYMORE FOR ROBERT ANTON WILSON BOOKS AND USED TISSUES.
BUT I DIDN'T HIT YOU OVER THE HEAD AND DRAG YOU UP HERE TO TALK ABOUT INTERIOR DESIGN, MY LITTLE GEN13 POSTER-BOY.

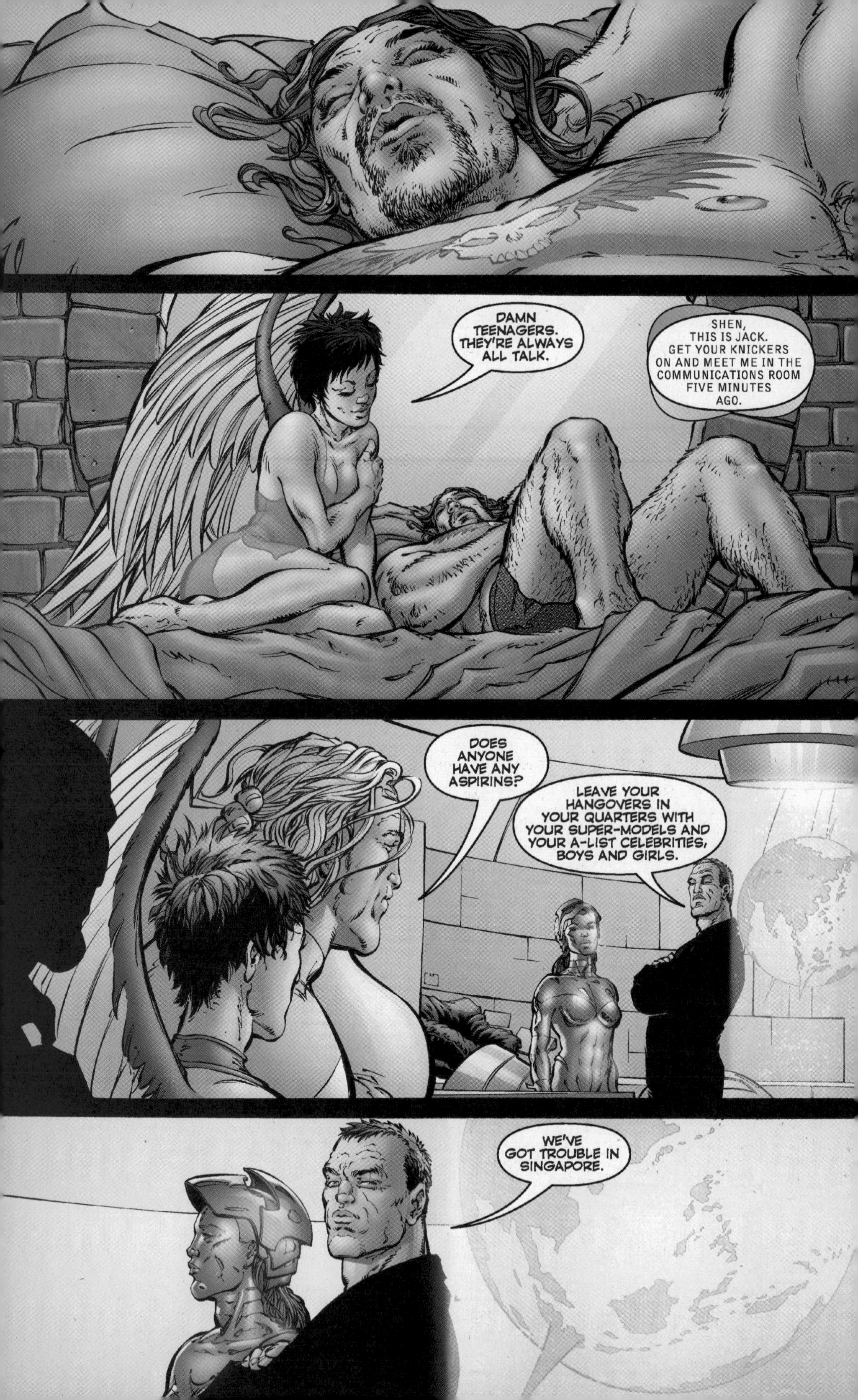
DAMN TEENAGERS. THEY'RE ALWAYS ALL TALK.
SHEN, THIS IS JACK. GET YOUR KNICKERS ON AND MEET ME IN THE COMMUNICATIONS ROOM FIVE MINUTES AGO.
DOES ANYONE HAVE ANY ASPIRINS?
LEAVE YOUR HANGOVERS IN YOUR QUARTERS WITH YOUR SUPER-MODELS AND YOUR A-LIST CELEBRITIES, BOYS AND GIRLS.
WE'VE GOT TROUBLE IN SINGAPORE.

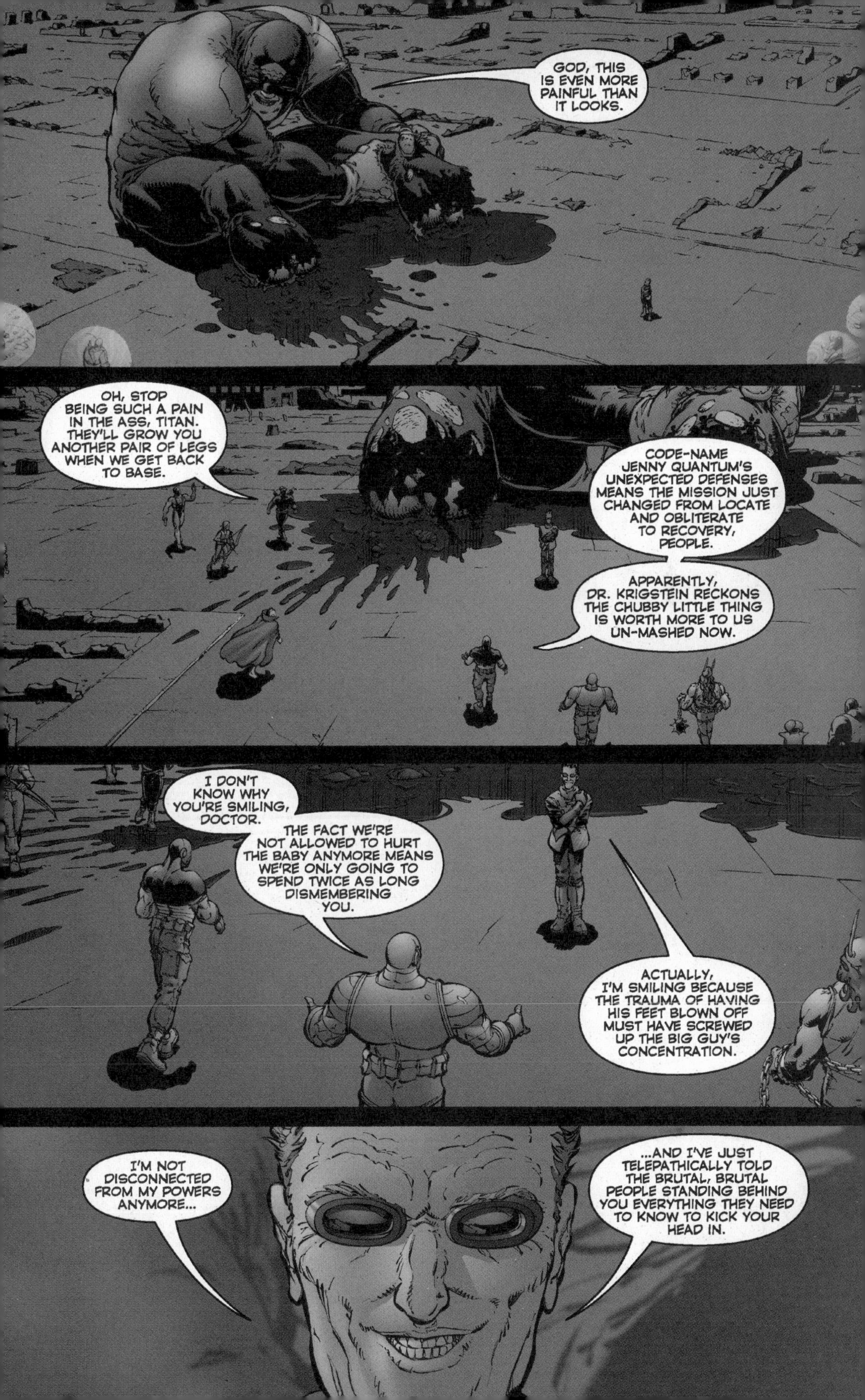
GOD, THIS IS EVEN MORE PAINFUL THAN IT LOOKS.
OH, STOP BEING SUCH A PAIN IN THE ASS, TITAN. THEY'LL GROW YOU ANOTHER PAIR OF LEGS WHEN WE GET BACK TO BASE.
CODE-NAME JENNY QUANTUM'S UNEXPECTED DEFENSES MEANS THE MISSION JUST CHANGED FROM LOCATE AND OBLITERATE TO RECOVERY, PEOPLE.
APPARENTLY, DR. KRIGSTEIN RECKONS THE CHUBBY LITTLE THING IS WORTH MORE TO US UN-MASHED NOW.
I DON'T KNOW WHY YOU'RE SMILING, DOCTOR.
THE FACT WE'RE NOT ALLOWED TO HURT THE BABY ANYMORE MEANS WE'RE ONLY GOING TO SPEND TWICE AS LONG DISMEMBERING YOU.
ACTUALLY, I'M SMILING BECAUSE THE TRAUMA OF HAVING HIS FEET BLOWN OFF MUST HAVE SCREWED UP THE BIG GUY'S CONCENTRATION.
I'M NOT DISCONNECTED FROM MY POWERS ANYMORE...
...AND I'VE JUST TELEPATHICALLY TOLD THE BRUTAL, BRUTAL PEOPLE STANDING BEHIND YOU EVERYTHING THEY NEED TO KNOW TO KICK YOUR HEAD IN.

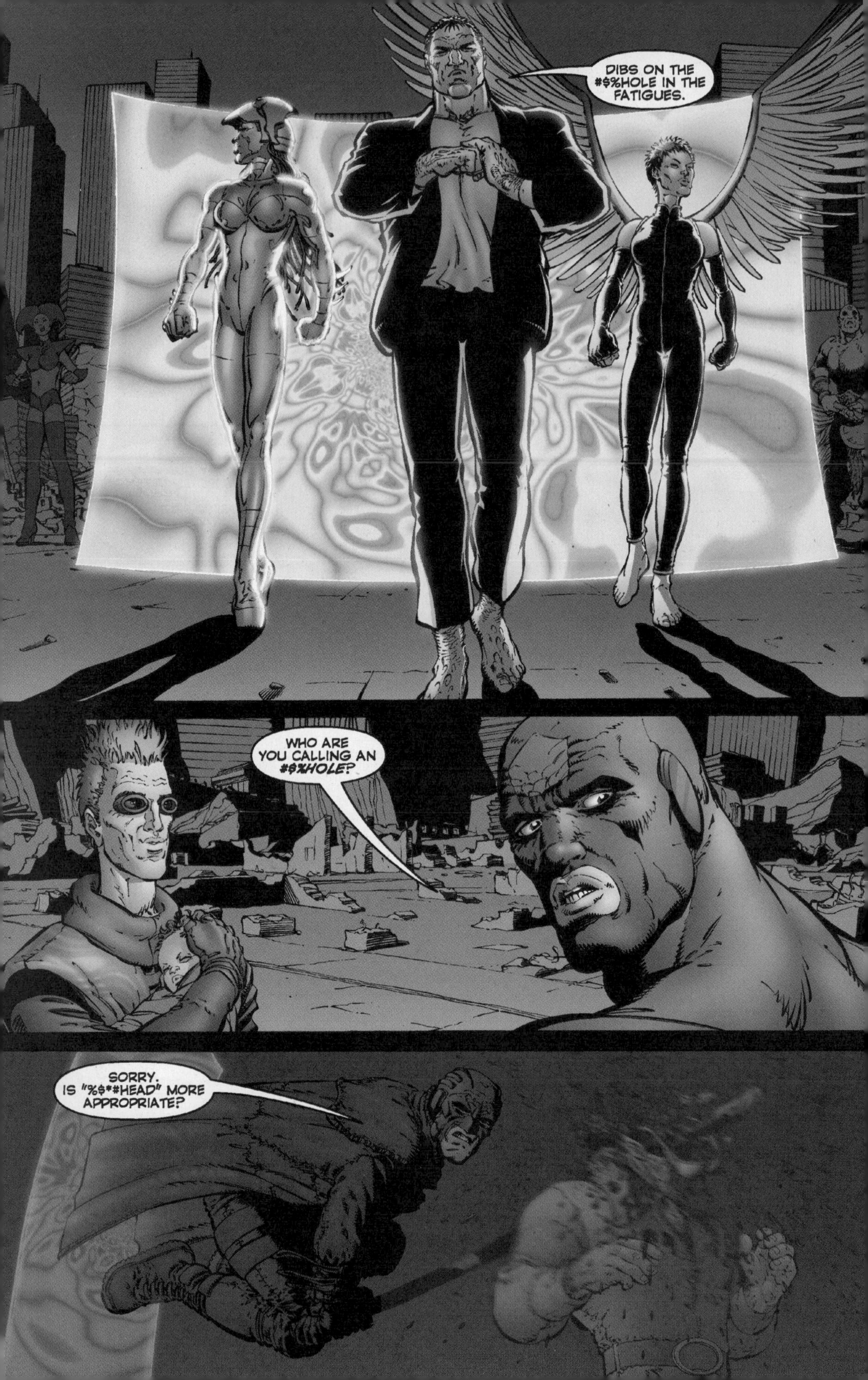
DIBS ON THE #$%HOLE IN THE FATIGUES.
WHO ARE YOU CALLING AN #$%HOLE?
SORRY. IS "%$*#HEAD" MORE APPROPRIATE?

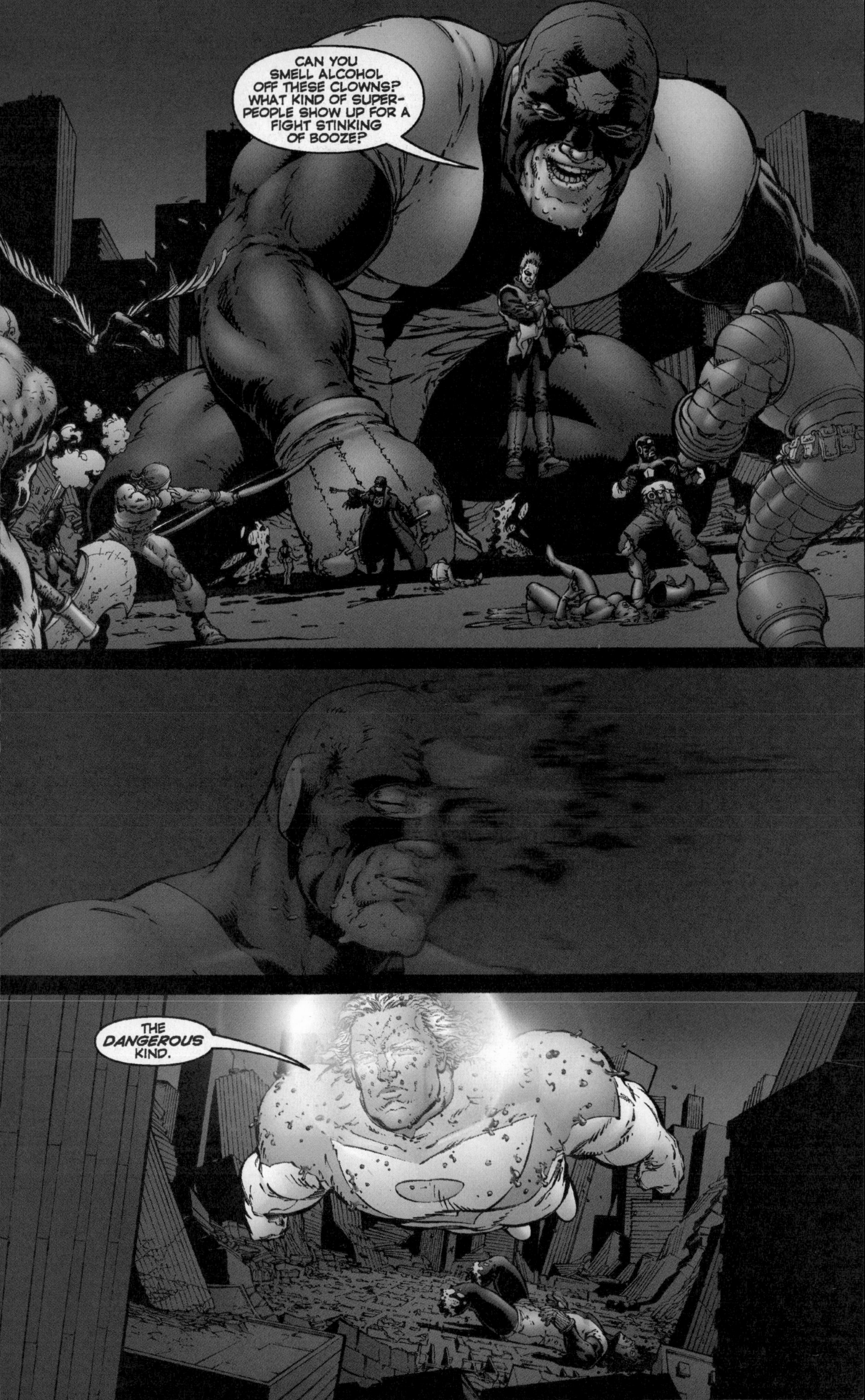
CAN YOU SMELL ALCOHOL OFF THESE CLOWNS? WHAT KIND OF SUPER-PEOPLE SHOW UP FOR A FIGHT STINKING OF BOOZE?
THE *DANGEROUS* KIND.

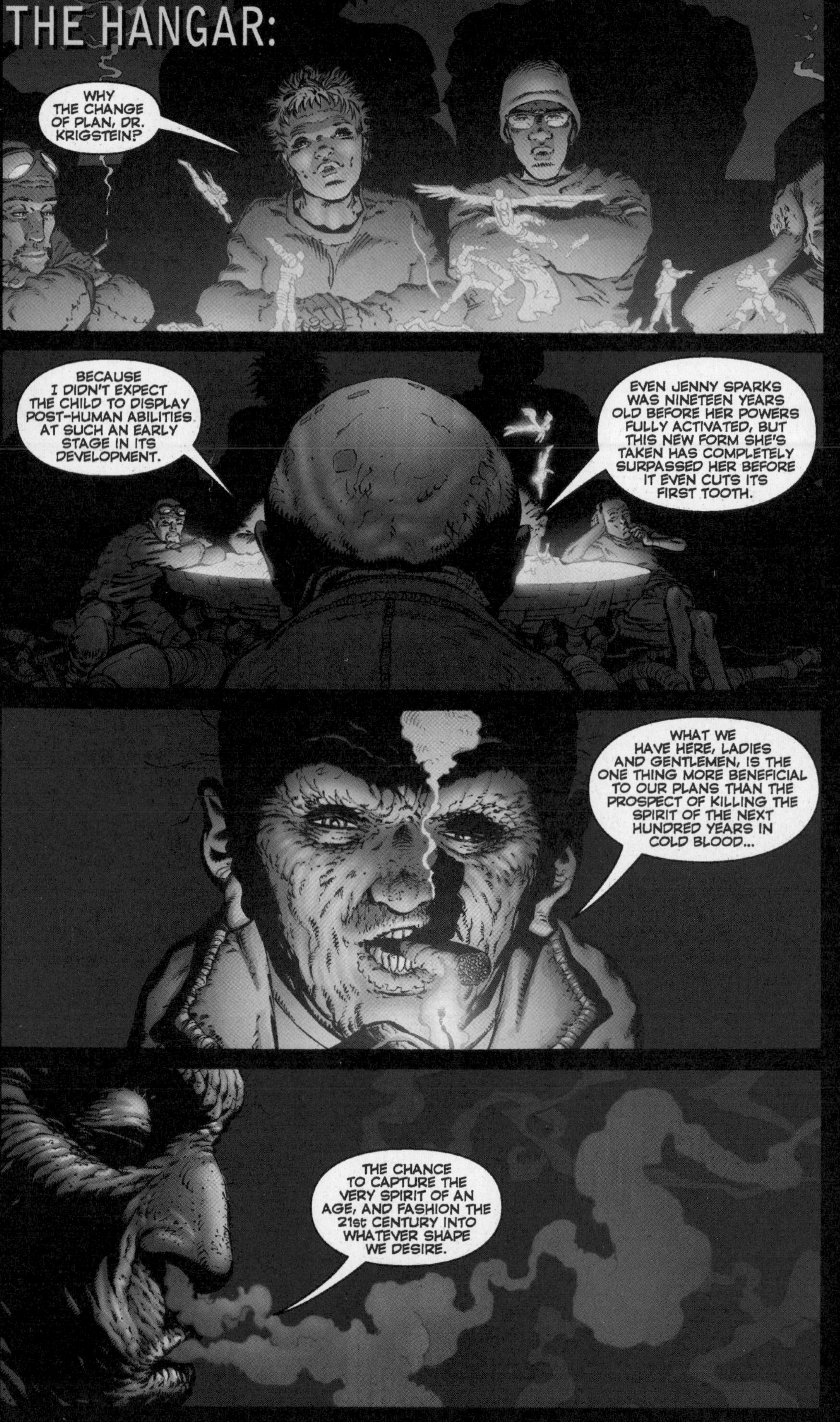
THE HANGAR:
WHY THE CHANGE OF PLAN, DR. KRIGSTEIN?
BECAUSE I DIDN'T EXPECT THE CHILD TO DISPLAY POST-HUMAN ABILITIES AT SUCH AN EARLY STAGE IN ITS DEVELOPMENT.
EVEN JENNY SPARKS WAS NINETEEN YEARS OLD BEFORE HER POWERS FULLY ACTIVATED, BUT THIS NEW FORM SHE'S TAKEN HAS COMPLETELY SURPASSED HER BEFORE IT EVEN CUTS ITS FIRST TOOTH.
WHAT WE HAVE HERE, LADIES AND GENTLEMEN, IS THE ONE THING MORE BENEFICIAL TO OUR PLANS THAN THE PROSPECT OF KILLING THE SPIRIT OF THE NEXT HUNDRED YEARS IN COLD BLOOD...
THE CHANCE TO CAPTURE THE VERY SPIRIT OF AN AGE, AND FASHION THE 21st CENTURY INTO WHATEVER SHAPE WE DESIRE.

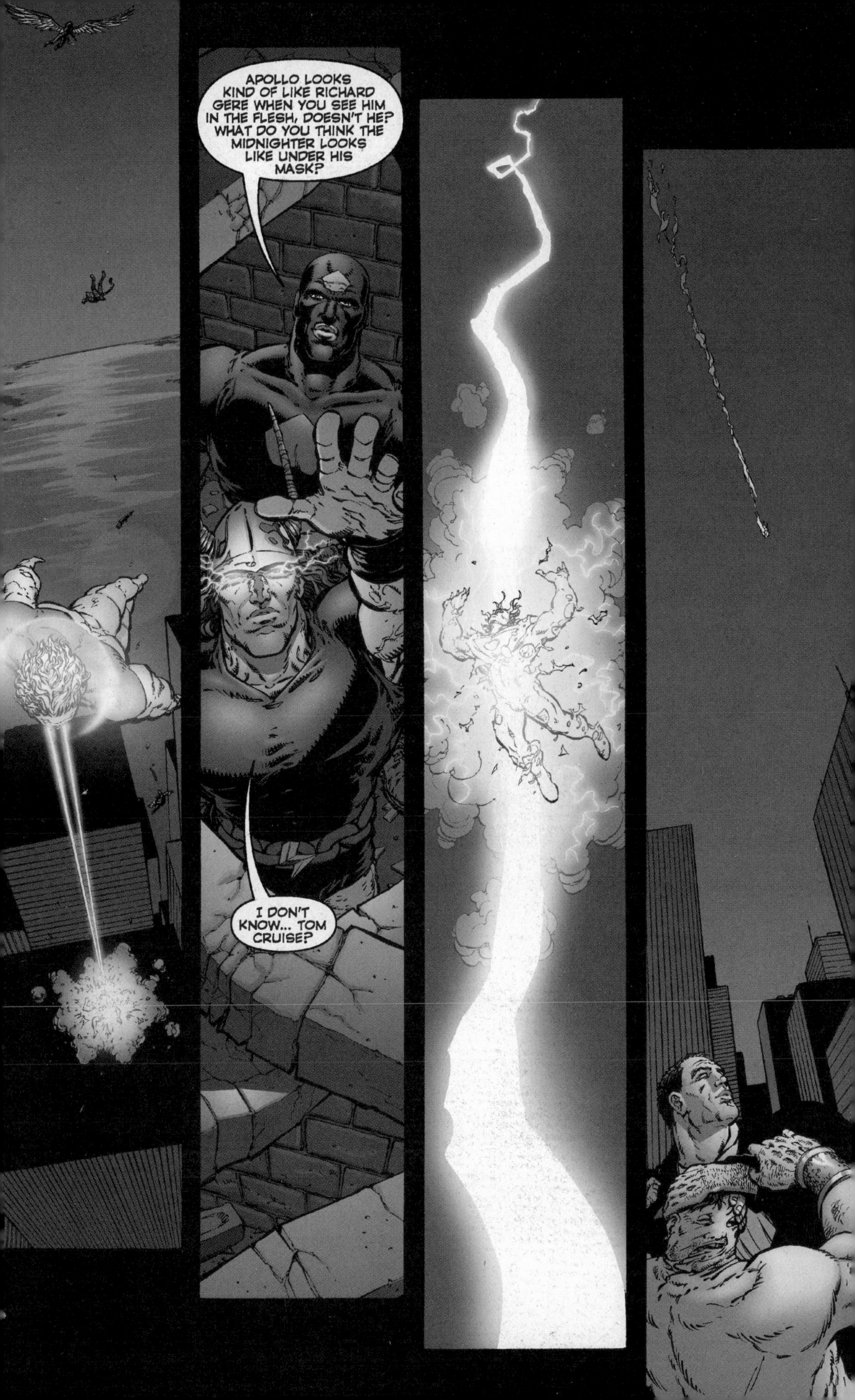
APOLLO LOOKS KIND OF LIKE RICHARD GERE WHEN YOU SEE HIM IN THE FLESH, DOESN'T HE? WHAT DO YOU THINK THE MIDNIGHTER LOOKS LIKE UNDER HIS MASK?
I DON'T KNOW... TOM CRUISE?

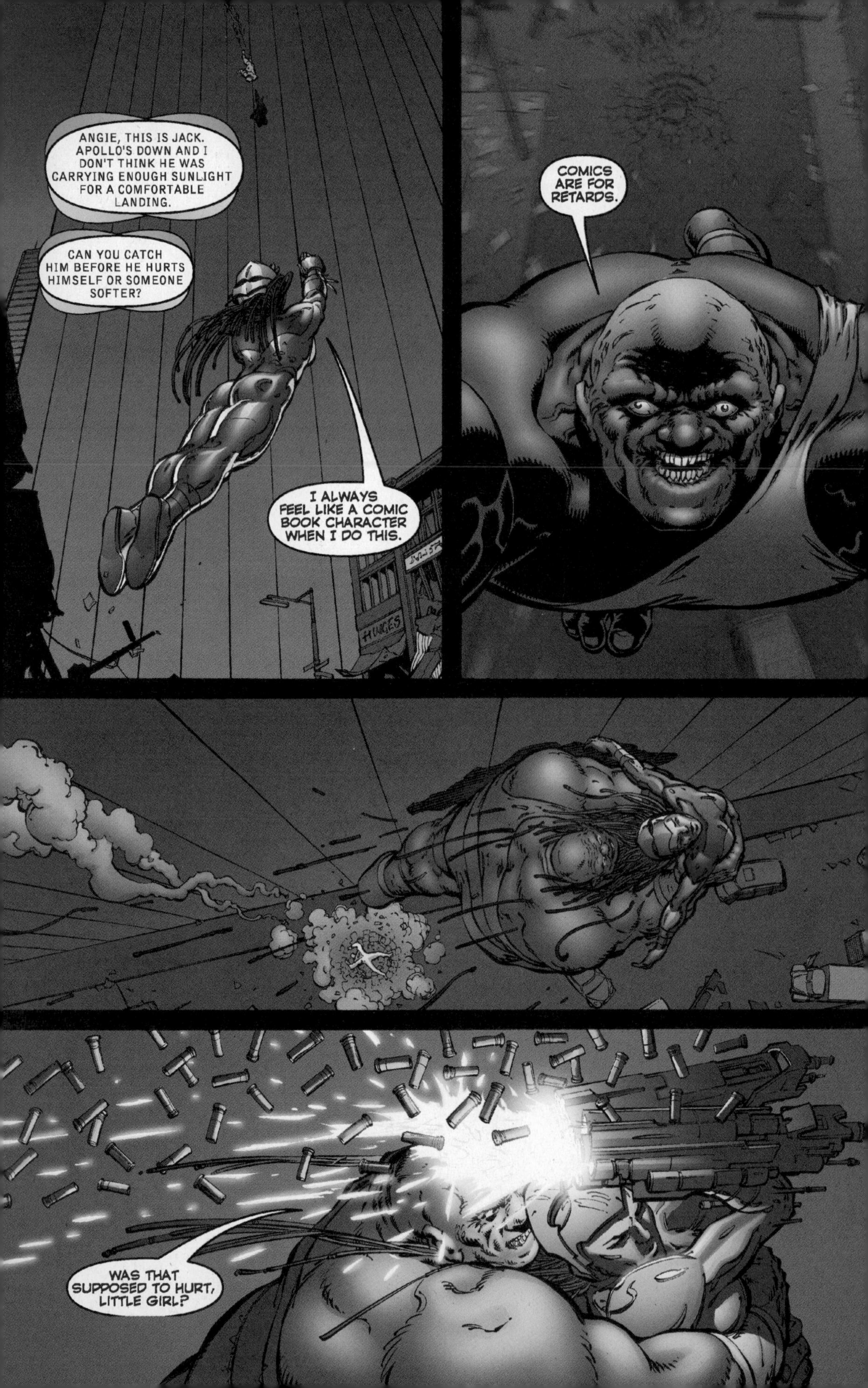
ANGIE, THIS IS JACK. APOLLO'S DOWN AND I DON'T THINK HE WAS CARRYING ENOUGH SUNLIGHT FOR A COMFORTABLE LANDING.
CAN YOU CATCH HIM BEFORE HE HURTS HIMSELF OR SOMEONE SOFTER?
I ALWAYS FEEL LIKE A COMIC BOOK CHARACTER WHEN I DO THIS.
COMICS ARE FOR RETARDS.
WAS THAT SUPPOSED TO HURT, LITTLE GIRL?

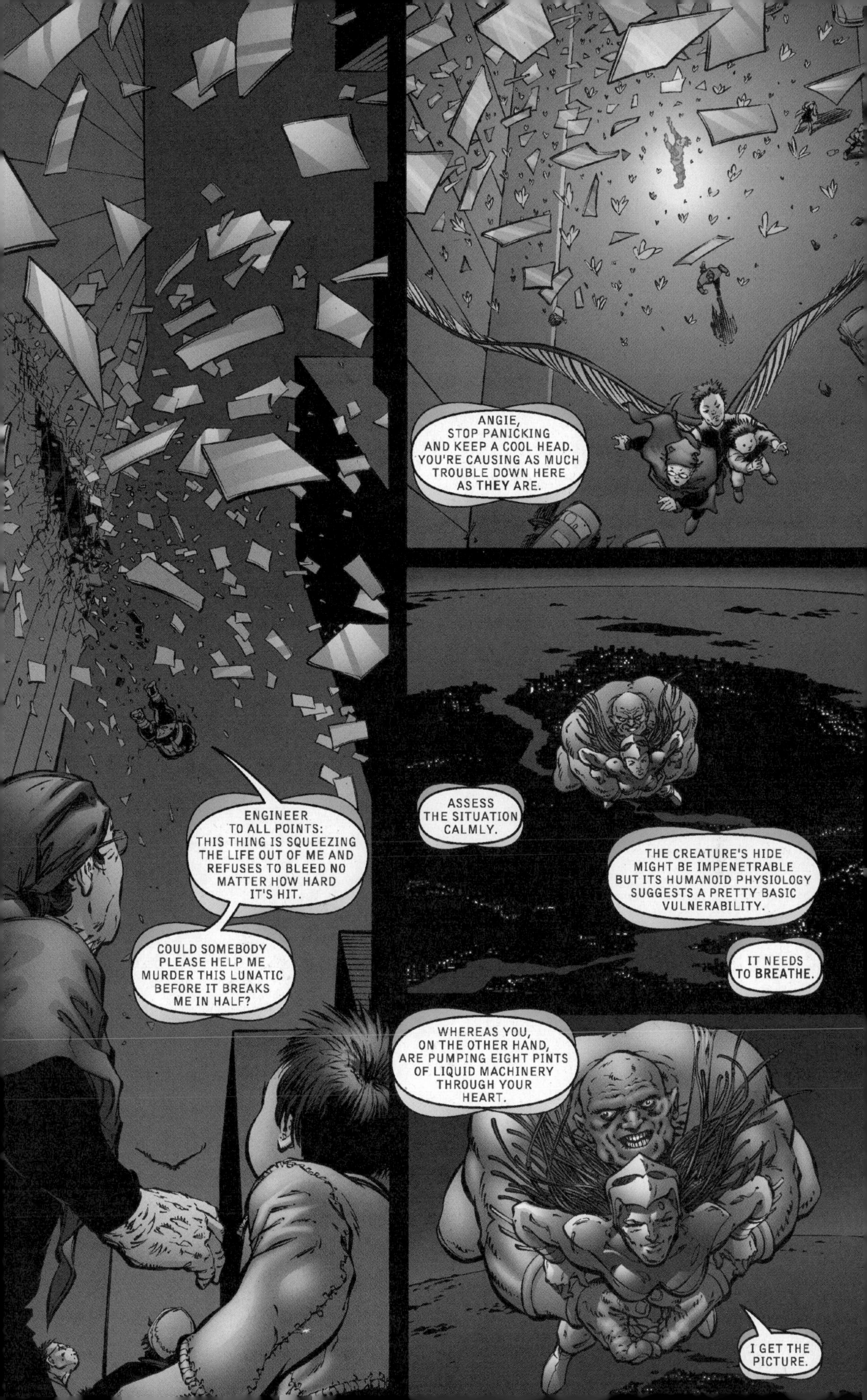
ANGIE, STOP PANICKING AND KEEP A COOL HEAD. YOU'RE CAUSING AS MUCH TROUBLE DOWN HERE AS THEY ARE.
ENGINEER TO ALL POINTS: THIS THING IS SQUEEZING THE LIFE OUT OF ME AND REFUSES TO BLEED NO MATTER HOW HARD IT'S HIT.
COULD SOMEBODY PLEASE HELP ME MURDER THIS LUNATIC BEFORE IT BREAKS ME IN HALF?
ASSESS THE SITUATION CALMLY.
THE CREATURE'S HIDE MIGHT BE IMPENETRABLE BUT ITS HUMANOID PHYSIOLOGY SUGGESTS A PRETTY BASIC VULNERABILITY.
IT NEEDS TO BREATHE.
WHEREAS YOU, ON THE OTHER HAND, ARE PUMPING EIGHT PINTS OF LIQUID MACHINERY THROUGH YOUR HEART.
I GET THE PICTURE.

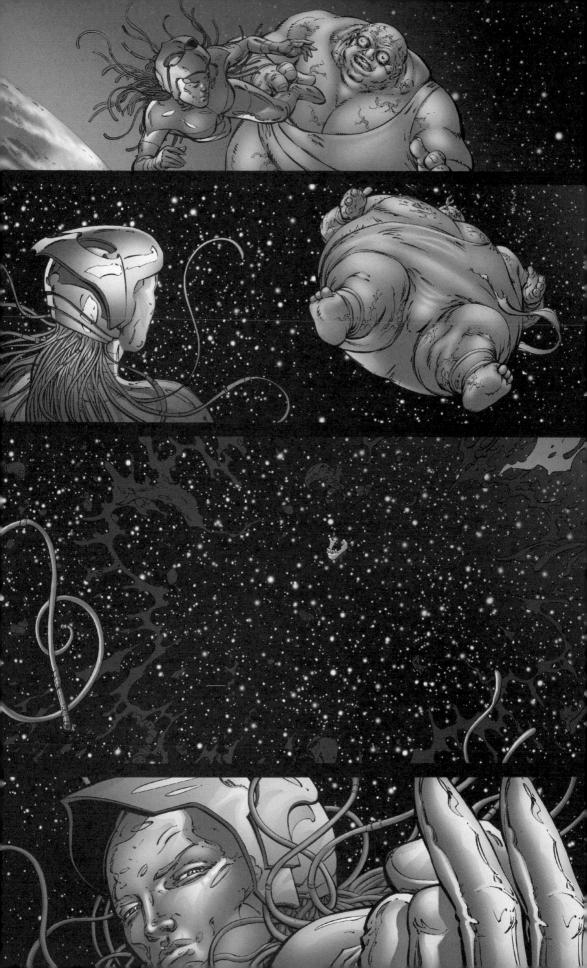

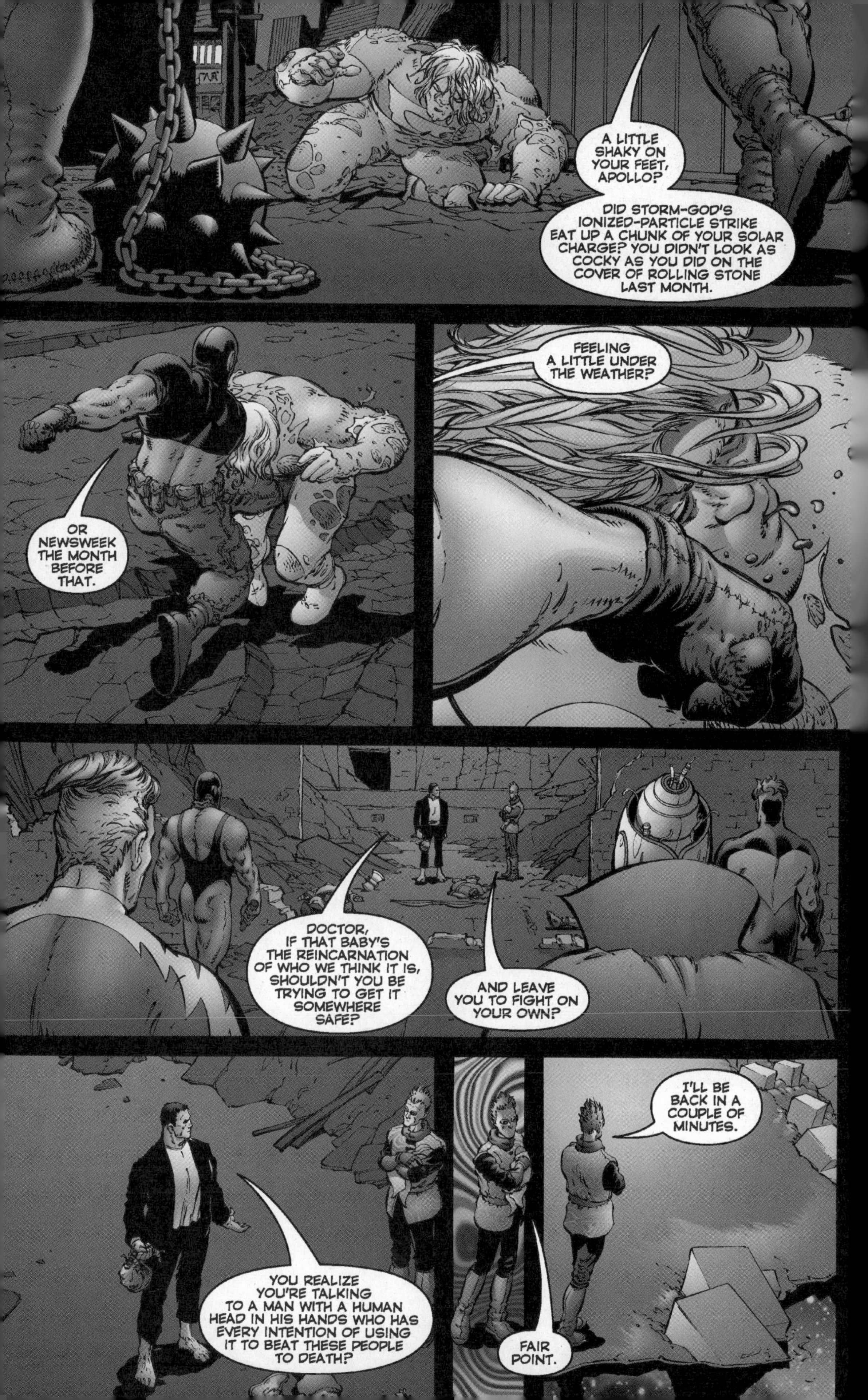
A LITTLE SHAKY ON YOUR FEET, APOLLO?
DID STORM-GOD'S IONIZED-PARTICLE STRIKE EAT UP A CHUNK OF YOUR SOLAR CHARGE? YOU DIDN'T LOOK AS COCKY AS YOU DID ON THE COVER OF ROLLING STONE LAST MONTH.
OR NEWSWEEK THE MONTH BEFORE THAT.
FEELING A LITTLE UNDER THE WEATHER?
DOCTOR, IF THAT BABY'S THE REINCARNATION OF WHO WE THINK IT IS, SHOULDN'T YOU BE TRYING TO GET IT SOMEWHERE SAFE?
AND LEAVE YOU TO FIGHT ON YOUR OWN?
YOU REALIZE YOU'RE TALKING TO A MAN WITH A HUMAN HEAD IN HIS HANDS WHO HAS EVERY INTENTION OF USING IT TO BEAT THESE PEOPLE TO DEATH?
FAIR POINT.
I'LL BE BACK IN A COUPLE OF MINUTES.

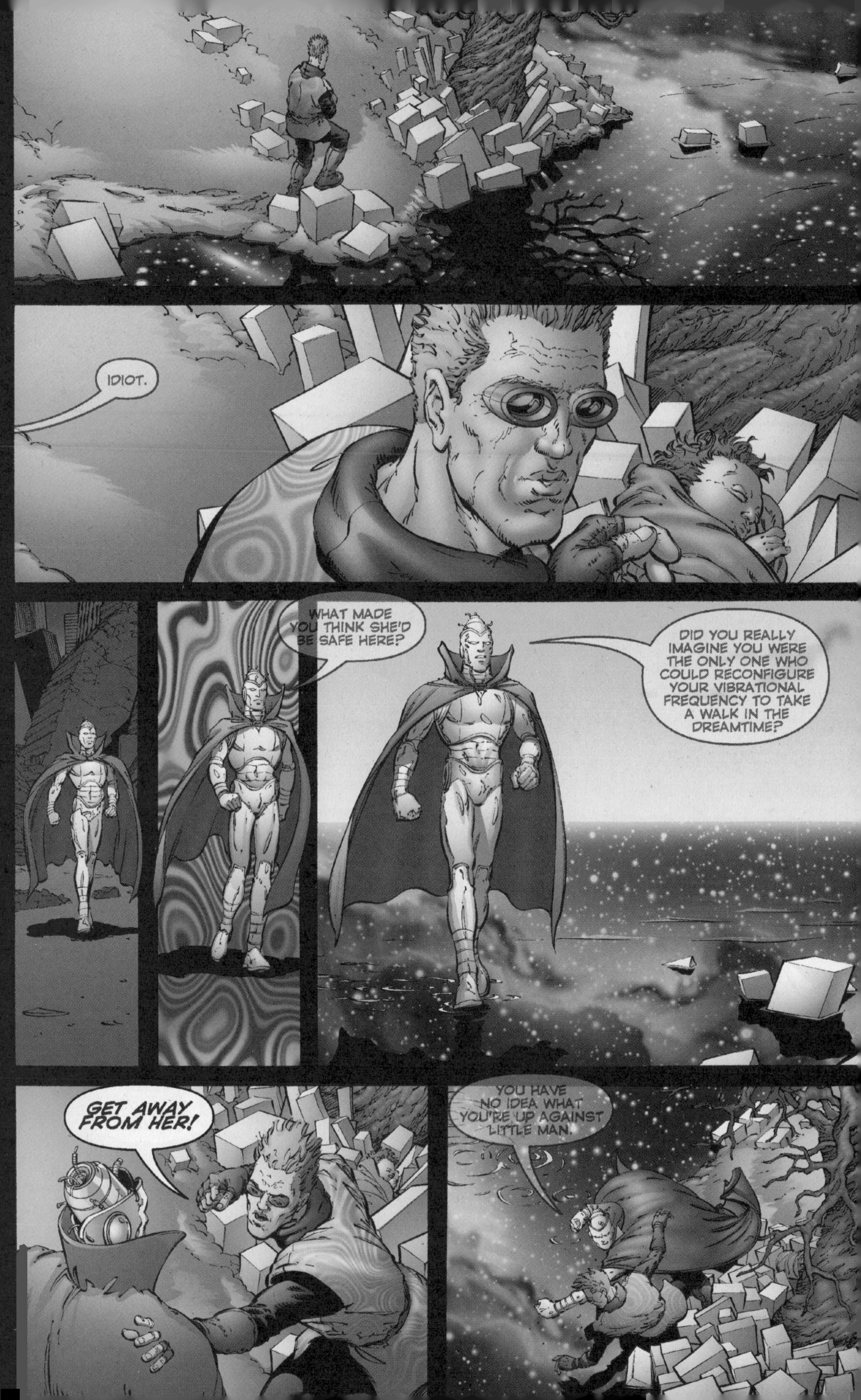
IDIOT.
WHAT MADE YOU THINK SHE'D BE SAFE HERE?
DID YOU REALLY IMAGINE YOU WERE THE ONLY ONE WHO COULD RECONFIGURE YOUR VIBRATIONAL FREQUENCY TO TAKE A WALK IN THE DREAMTIME?
GET AWAY FROM HER!
YOU HAVE NO IDEA WHAT YOU'RE UP AGAINST LITTLE MAN.

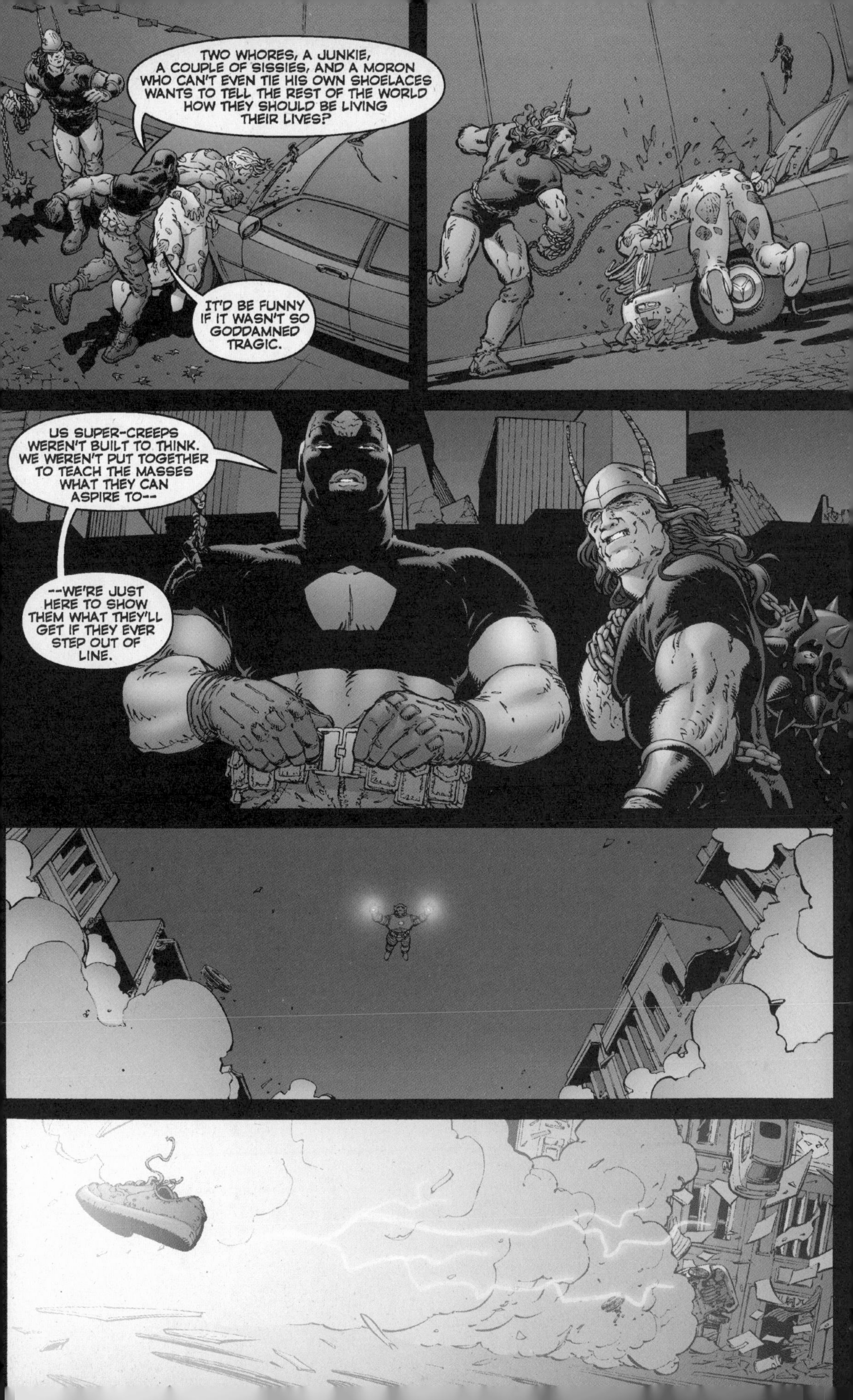
TWO WHORES, A JUNKIE, A COUPLE OF SISSIES, AND A MORON WHO CAN'T EVEN TIE HIS OWN SHOELACES WANTS TO TELL THE REST OF THE WORLD HOW THEY SHOULD BE LIVING THEIR LIVES?
IT'D BE FUNNY IF IT WASN'T SO GODDAMNED TRAGIC.
US SUPER-CREEPS WEREN'T BUILT TO THINK. WE WEREN'T PUT TOGETHER TO TEACH THE MASSES WHAT THEY CAN ASPIRE TO--
--WE'RE JUST HERE TO SHOW THEM WHAT THEY'LL GET IF THEY EVER STEP OUT OF LINE.

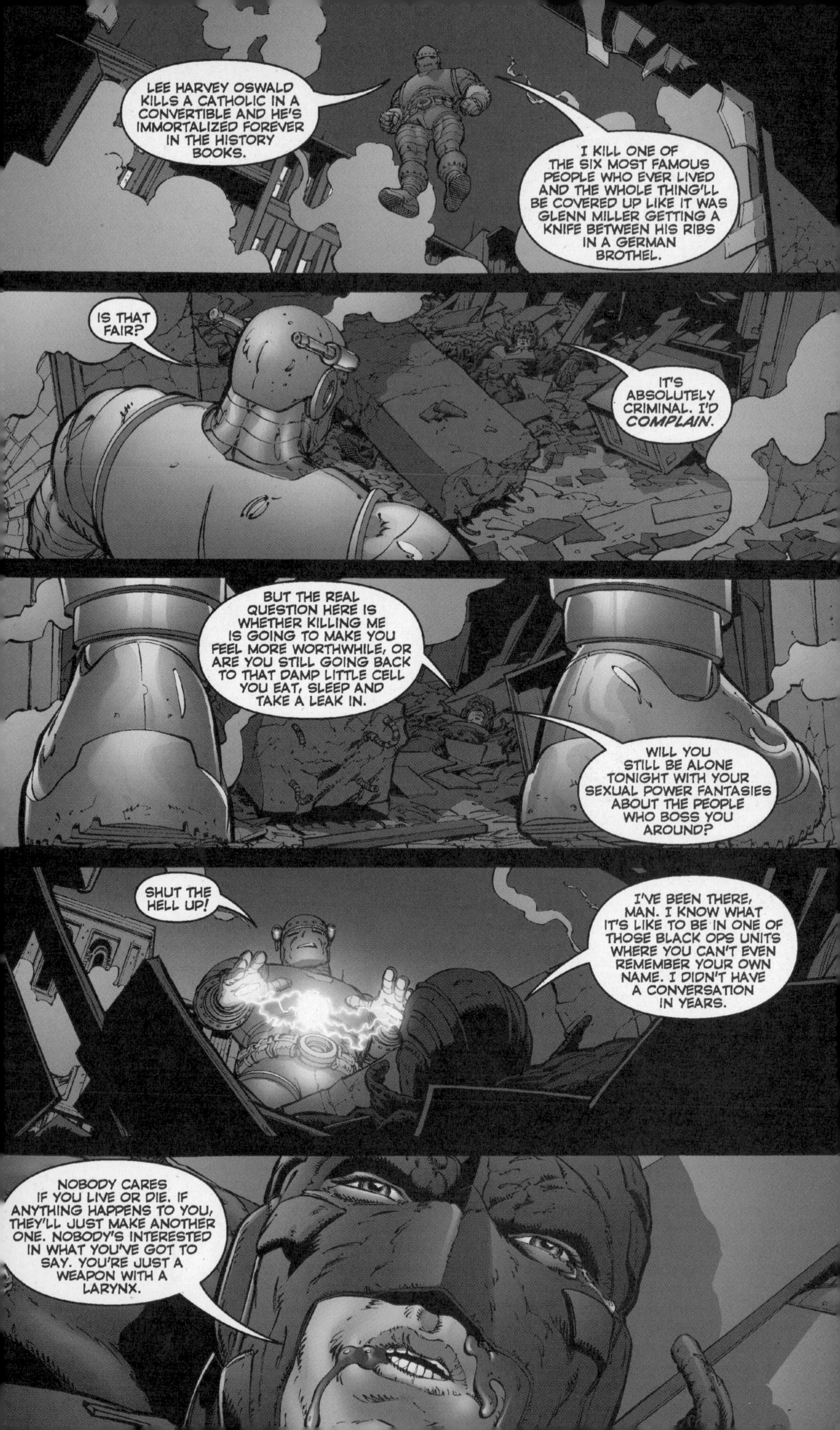
LEE HARVEY OSWALD KILLS A CATHOLIC IN A CONVERTIBLE AND HE'S IMMORTALIZED FOREVER IN THE HISTORY BOOKS.
I KILL ONE OF THE SIX MOST FAMOUS PEOPLE WHO EVER LIVED AND THE WHOLE THING'LL BE COVERED UP LIKE IT WAS GLENN MILLER GETTING A KNIFE BETWEEN HIS RIBS IN A GERMAN BROTHEL.
IS THAT FAIR?
IT'S ABSOLUTELY CRIMINAL. I'D *COMPLAIN*.
BUT THE REAL QUESTION HERE IS WHETHER KILLING ME IS GOING TO MAKE YOU FEEL MORE WORTHWHILE, OR ARE YOU STILL GOING BACK TO THAT DAMP LITTLE CELL YOU EAT, SLEEP AND TAKE A LEAK IN.
WILL YOU STILL BE ALONE TONIGHT WITH YOUR SEXUAL POWER FANTASIES ABOUT THE PEOPLE WHO BOSS YOU AROUND?
SHUT THE HELL UP!
I'VE BEEN THERE, MAN. I KNOW WHAT IT'S LIKE TO BE IN ONE OF THOSE BLACK OPS UNITS WHERE YOU CAN'T EVEN REMEMBER YOUR OWN NAME. I DIDN'T HAVE A CONVERSATION IN YEARS.
NOBODY CARES IF YOU LIVE OR DIE. IF ANYTHING HAPPENS TO YOU, THEY'LL JUST MAKE ANOTHER ONE. NOBODY'S INTERESTED IN WHAT YOU'VE GOT TO SAY. YOU'RE JUST A WEAPON WITH A LARYNX.

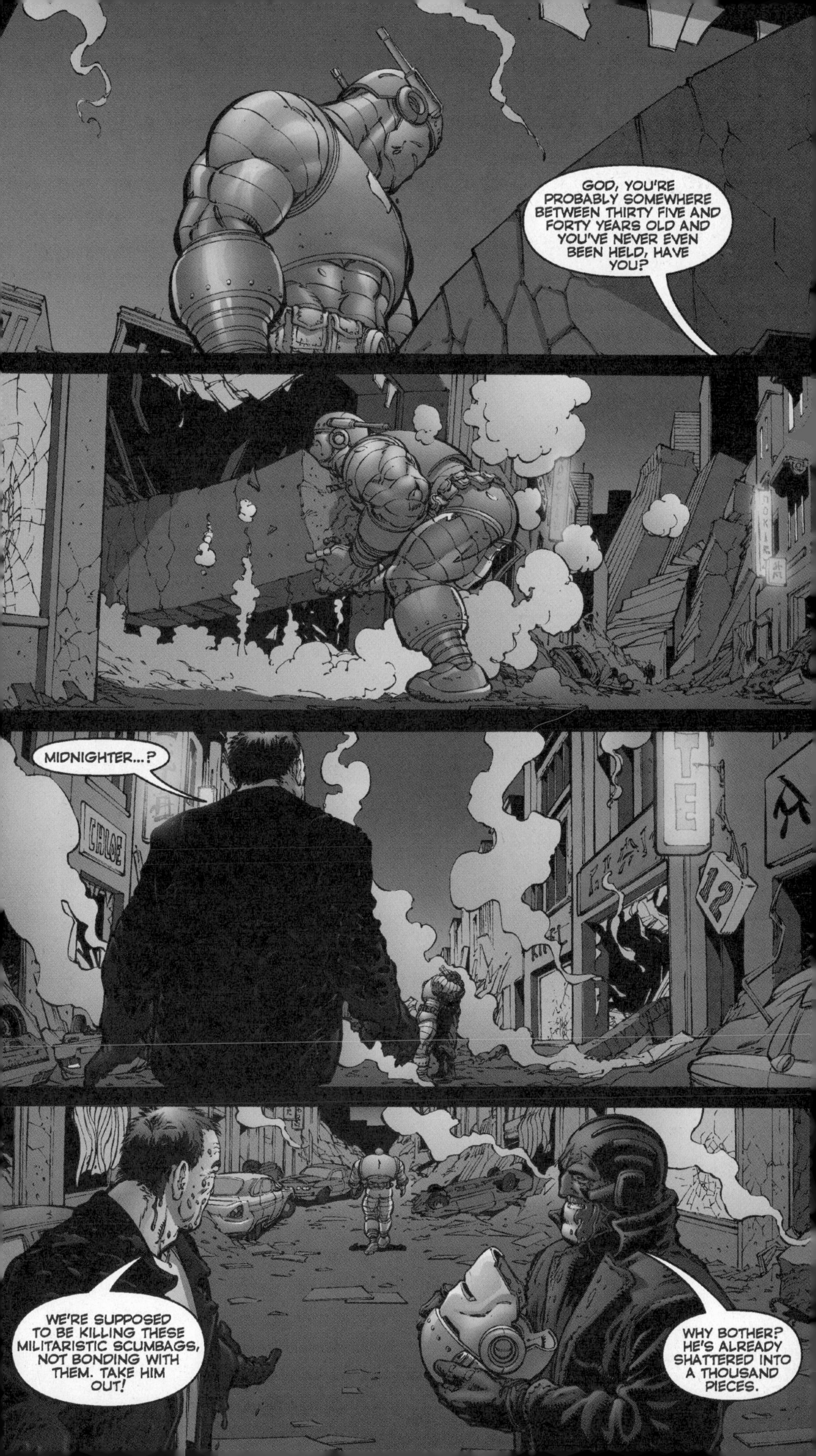
GOD, YOU'RE PROBABLY SOMEWHERE BETWEEN THIRTY FIVE AND FORTY YEARS OLD AND YOU'VE NEVER EVEN BEEN HELD, HAVE YOU?
MIDNIGHTER...?
WE'RE SUPPOSED TO BE KILLING THESE MILITARISTIC SCUMBAGS, NOT BONDING WITH THEM. TAKE HIM OUT!
WHY BOTHER? HE'S ALREADY SHATTERED INTO A THOUSAND PIECES.

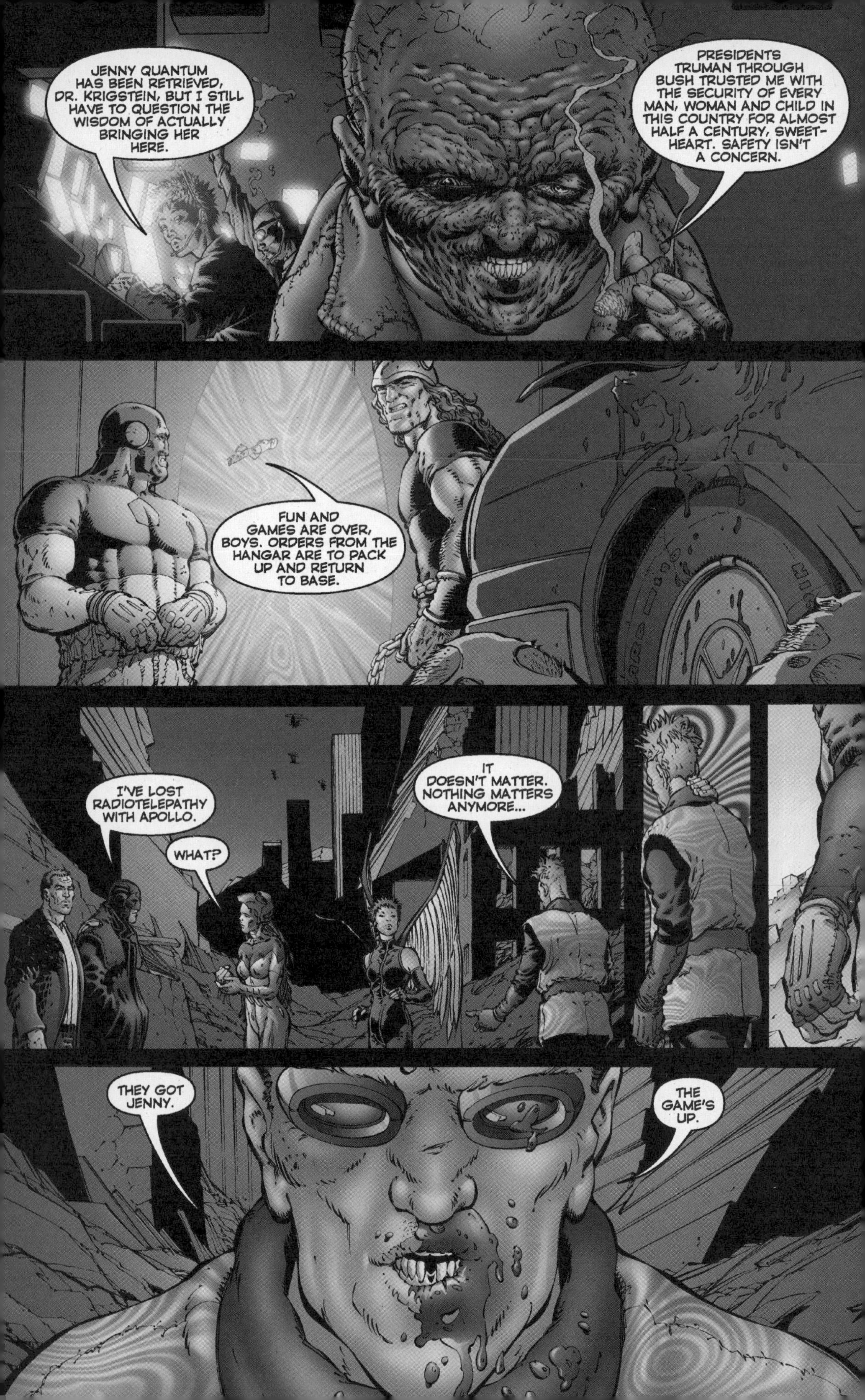

JENNY QUANTUM HAS BEEN RETRIEVED, DR. KRIGSTEIN, BUT I STILL HAVE TO QUESTION THE WISDOM OF ACTUALLY BRINGING HER HERE.
PRESIDENTS TRUMAN THROUGH BUSH TRUSTED ME WITH THE SECURITY OF EVERY MAN, WOMAN AND CHILD IN THIS COUNTRY FOR ALMOST HALF A CENTURY, SWEET-HEART. SAFETY ISN'T A CONCERN.
FUN AND GAMES ARE OVER, BOYS. ORDERS FROM THE HANGAR ARE TO PACK UP AND RETURN TO BASE.
I'VE LOST RADIOTELEPATHY WITH APOLLO.
WHAT?
IT DOESN'T MATTER. NOTHING MATTERS ANYMORE...
THEY GOT JENNY.
THE GAME'S UP.

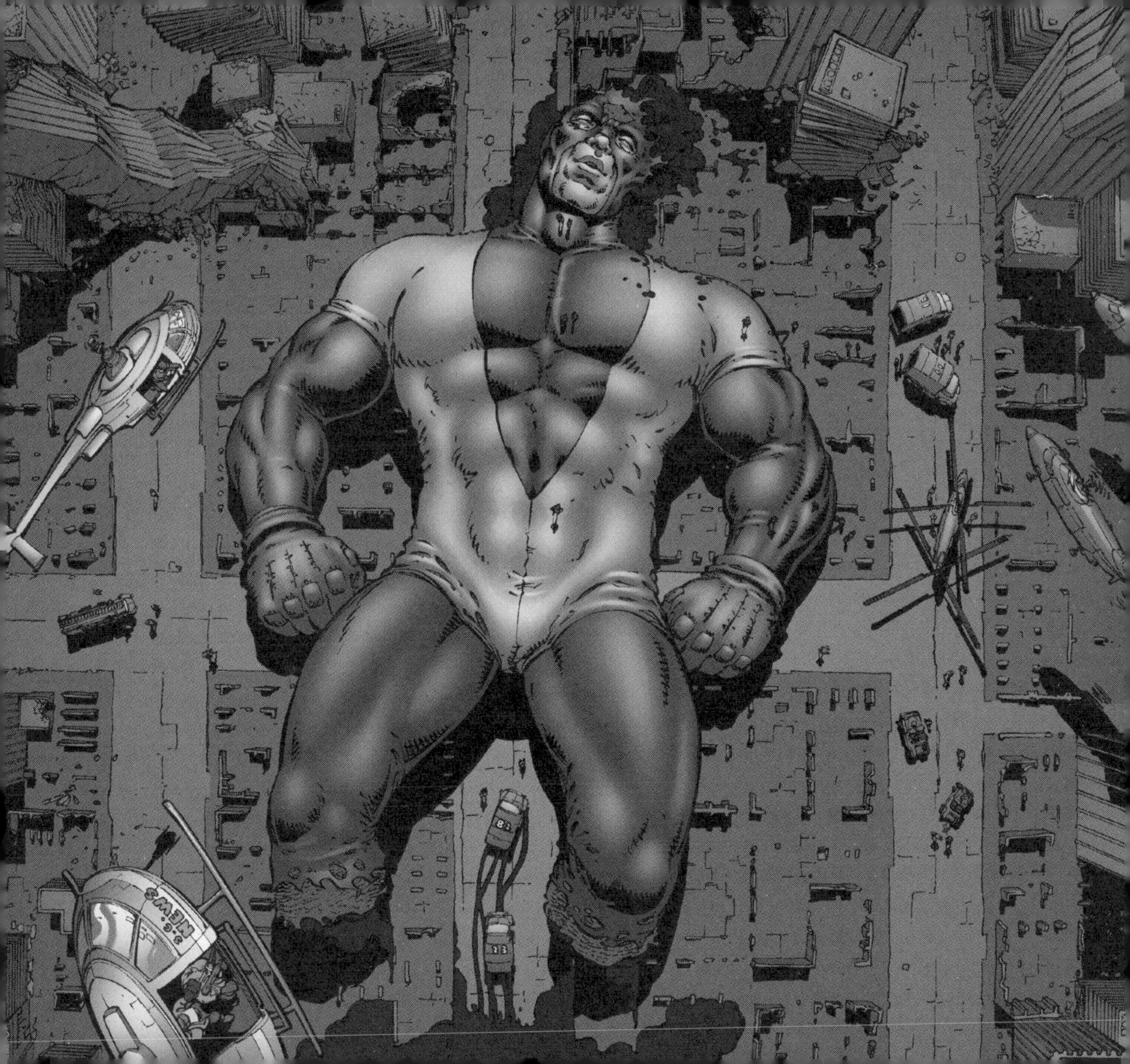

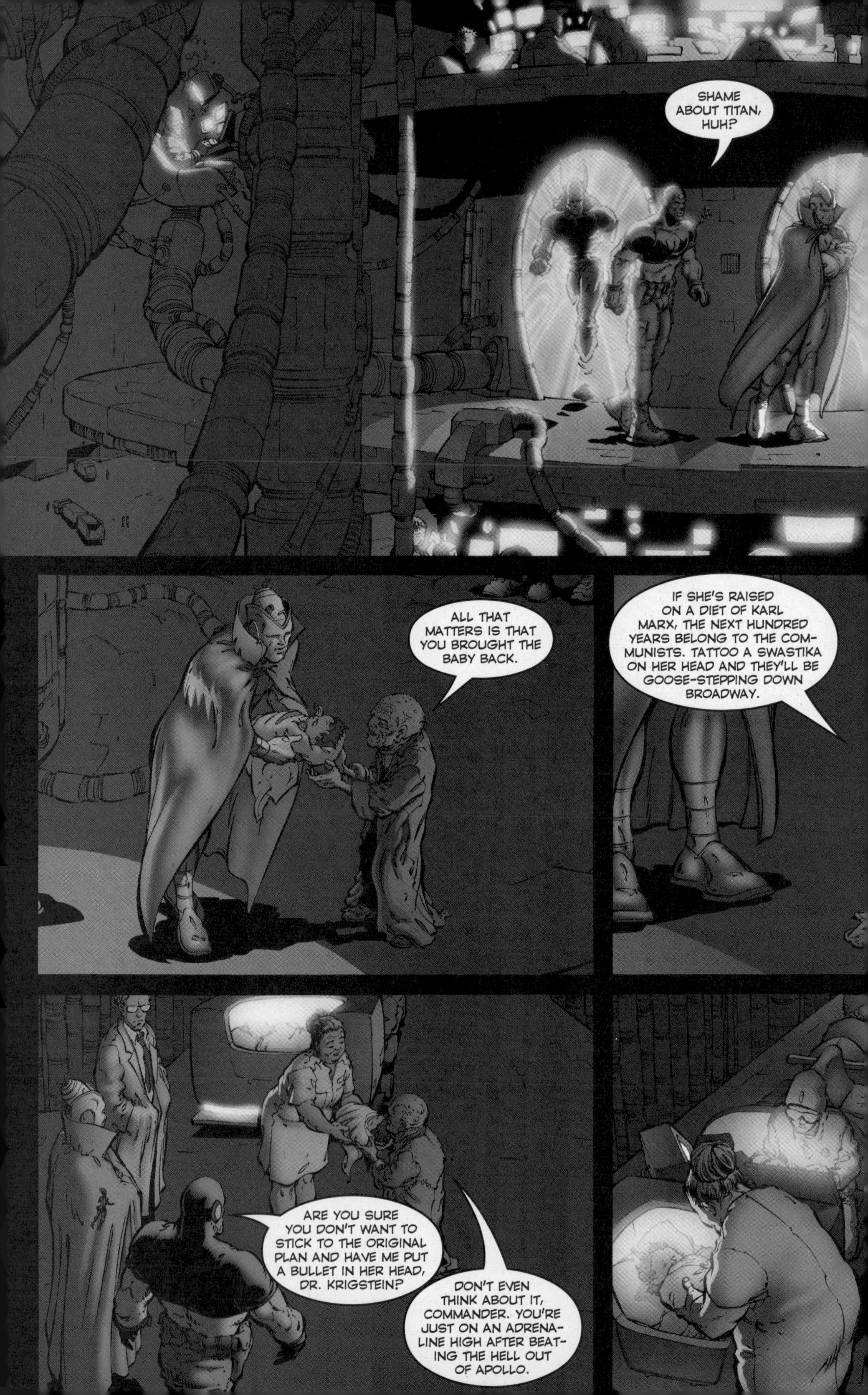
SHAME ABOUT TITAN, HUH?
ALL THAT MATTERS IS THAT YOU BROUGHT THE BABY BACK.
IF SHE'S RAISED ON A DIET OF KARL MARX, THE NEXT HUNDRED YEARS BELONG TO THE COMMUNISTS. TATTOO A SWASTIKA ON HER HEAD AND THEY'LL BE GOOSE-STEPPING DOWN BROADWAY.
ARE YOU SURE YOU DON'T WANT TO STICK TO THE ORIGINAL PLAN AND HAVE ME PUT A BULLET IN HER HEAD, DR. KRIGSTEIN?
DON'T EVEN THINK ABOUT IT, COMMANDER. YOU'RE JUST ON AN ADRENALINE HIGH AFTER BEATING THE HELL OUT OF APOLLO.

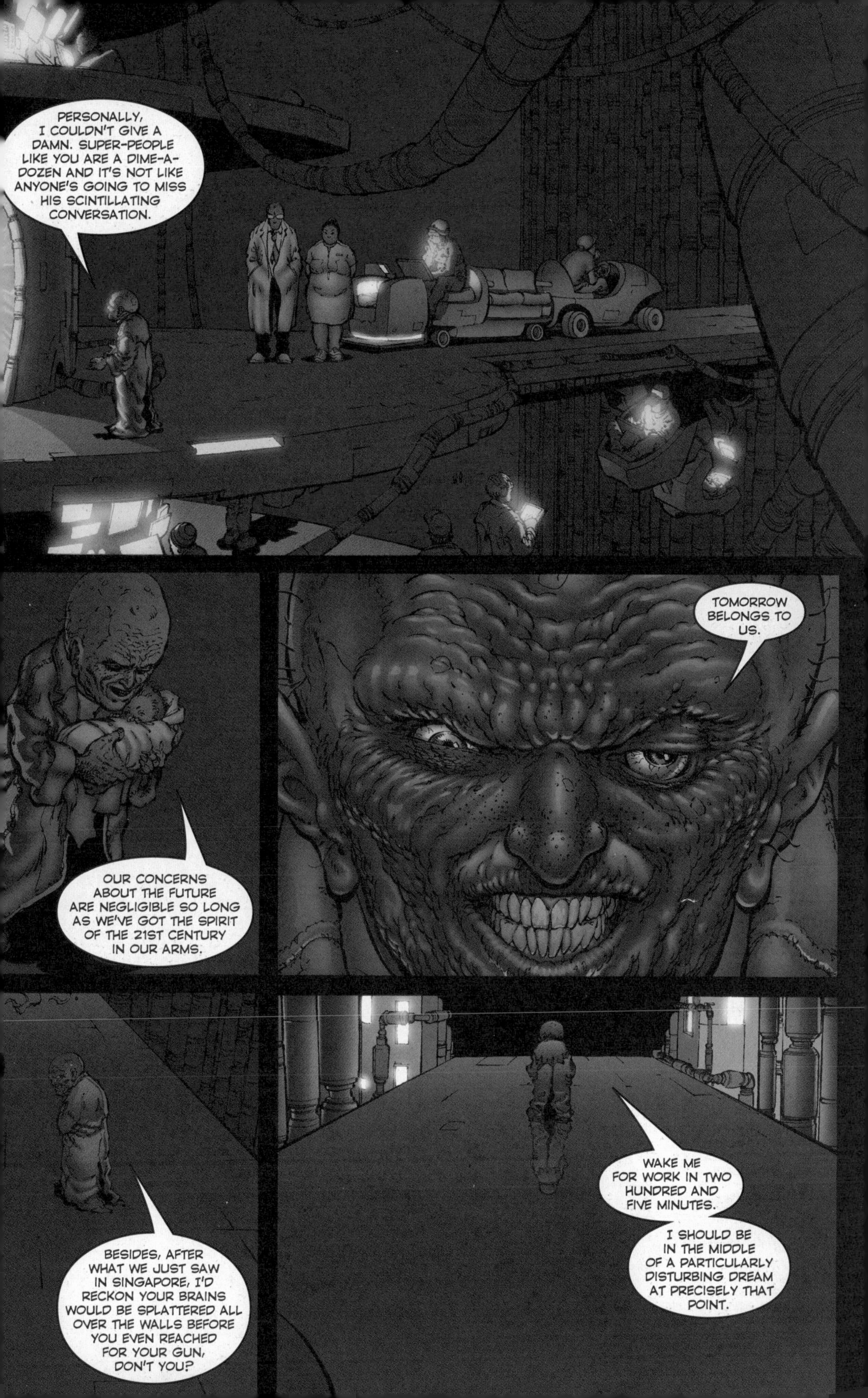
PERSONALLY, I COULDN'T GIVE A DAMN. SUPER-PEOPLE LIKE YOU ARE A DIME-A-DOZEN AND IT'S NOT LIKE ANYONE'S GOING TO MISS HIS SCINTILLATING CONVERSATION.
OUR CONCERNS ABOUT THE FUTURE ARE NEGLIGIBLE SO LONG AS WE'VE GOT THE SPIRIT OF THE 21ST CENTURY IN OUR ARMS.
TOMORROW BELONGS TO US.
BESIDES, AFTER WHAT WE JUST SAW IN SINGAPORE, I'D RECKON YOUR BRAINS WOULD BE SPLATTERED ALL OVER THE WALLS BEFORE YOU EVEN REACHED FOR YOUR GUN, DON'T YOU?
WAKE ME FOR WORK IN TWO HUNDRED AND FIVE MINUTES.
I SHOULD BE IN THE MIDDLE OF A PARTICULARLY DISTURBING DREAM AT PRECISELY THAT POINT.

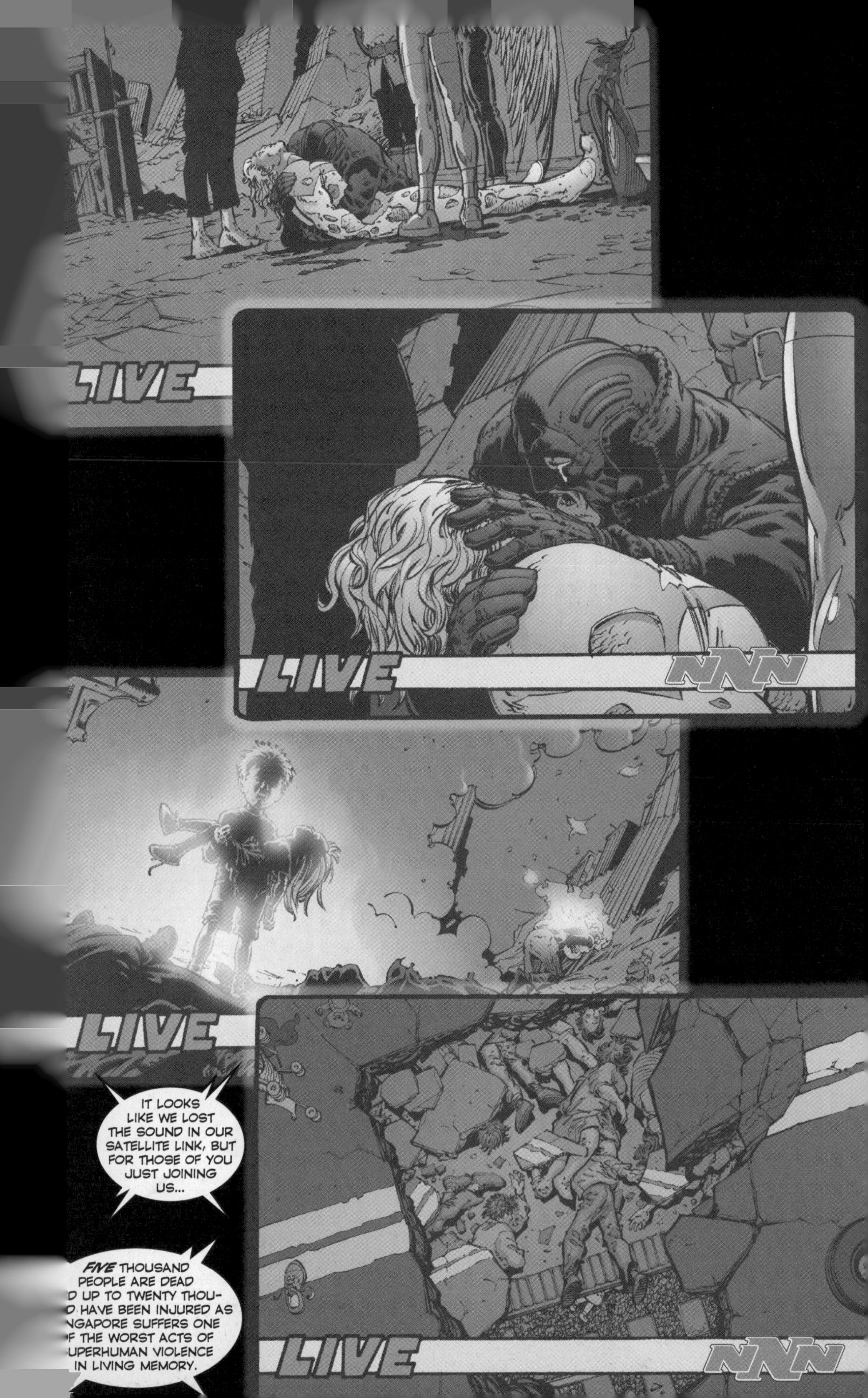
LIVE
LIVE
NNN
LIVE
IT LOOKS LIKE WE LOST THE SOUND IN OUR SATELLITE LINK, BUT FOR THOSE OF YOU JUST JOINING US...
FIVE THOUSAND PEOPLE ARE DEAD D UP TO TWENTY THOU- D HAVE BEEN INJURED AS NGAPORE SUFFERS ONE F THE WORST ACTS OF UPERHUMAN VIOLENCE IN LIVING MEMORY.
LIVE
NNN

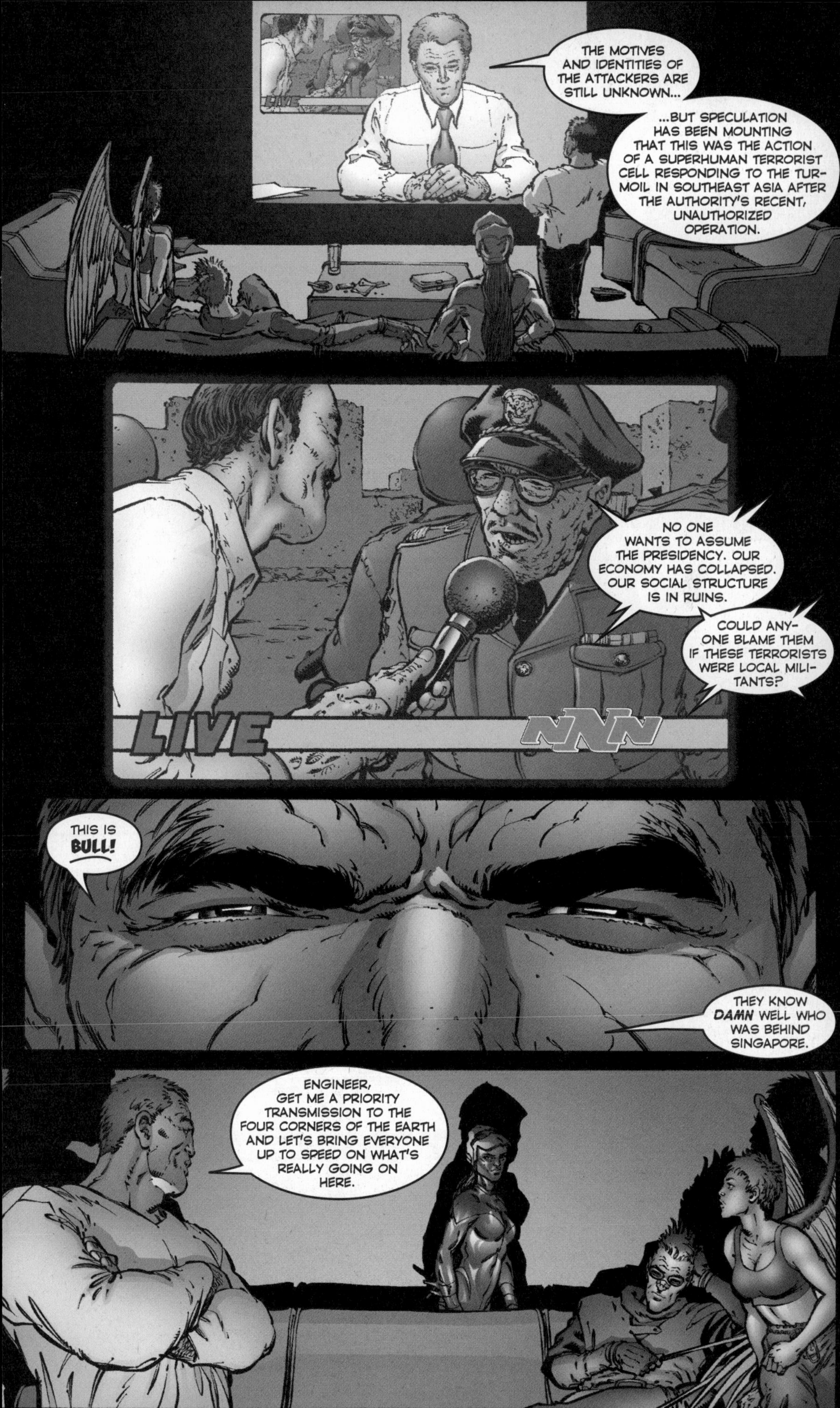
THE MOTIVES AND IDENTITIES OF THE ATTACKERS ARE STILL UNKNOWN...
...BUT SPECULATION HAS BEEN MOUNTING THAT THIS WAS THE ACTION OF A SUPERHUMAN TERRORIST CELL RESPONDING TO THE TURMOIL IN SOUTHEAST ASIA AFTER THE AUTHORITY'S RECENT, UNAUTHORIZED OPERATION.
NO ONE WANTS TO ASSUME THE PRESIDENCY. OUR ECONOMY HAS COLLAPSED. OUR SOCIAL STRUCTURE IS IN RUINS.
COULD ANYONE BLAME THEM IF THESE TERRORISTS WERE LOCAL MILITANTS?
LIVE
NNN
THIS IS **BULL!**
THEY KNOW ***DAMN*** WELL WHO WAS BEHIND SINGAPORE.
ENGINEER, GET ME A PRIORITY TRANSMISSION TO THE FOUR CORNERS OF THE EARTH AND LET'S BRING EVERYONE UP TO SPEED ON WHAT'S REALLY GOING ON HERE.

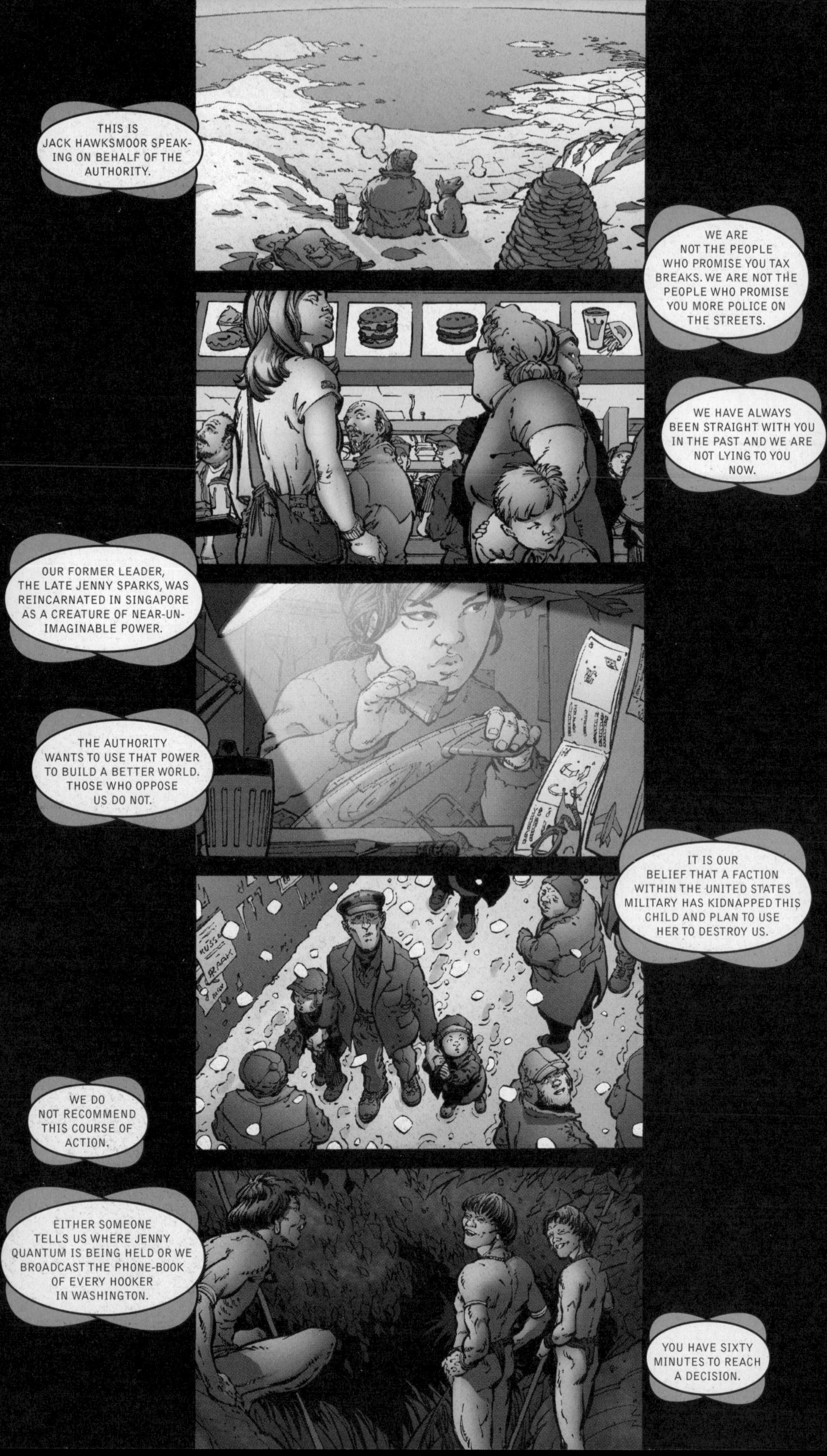
THIS IS JACK HAWKSMOOR SPEAKING ON BEHALF OF THE AUTHORITY.
WE ARE NOT THE PEOPLE WHO PROMISE YOU TAX BREAKS. WE ARE NOT THE PEOPLE WHO PROMISE YOU MORE POLICE ON THE STREETS.
WE HAVE ALWAYS BEEN STRAIGHT WITH YOU IN THE PAST AND WE ARE NOT LYING TO YOU NOW.
OUR FORMER LEADER, THE LATE JENNY SPARKS, WAS REINCARNATED IN SINGAPORE AS A CREATURE OF NEAR-UNIMAGINABLE POWER.
THE AUTHORITY WANTS TO USE THAT POWER TO BUILD A BETTER WORLD. THOSE WHO OPPOSE US DO NOT.
IT IS OUR BELIEF THAT A FACTION WITHIN THE UNITED STATES MILITARY HAS KIDNAPPED THIS CHILD AND PLAN TO USE HER TO DESTROY US.
WE DO NOT RECOMMEND THIS COURSE OF ACTION.
EITHER SOMEONE TELLS US WHERE JENNY QUANTUM IS BEING HELD OR WE BROADCAST THE PHONE-BOOK OF EVERY HOOKER IN WASHINGTON.
YOU HAVE SIXTY MINUTES TO REACH A DECISION.

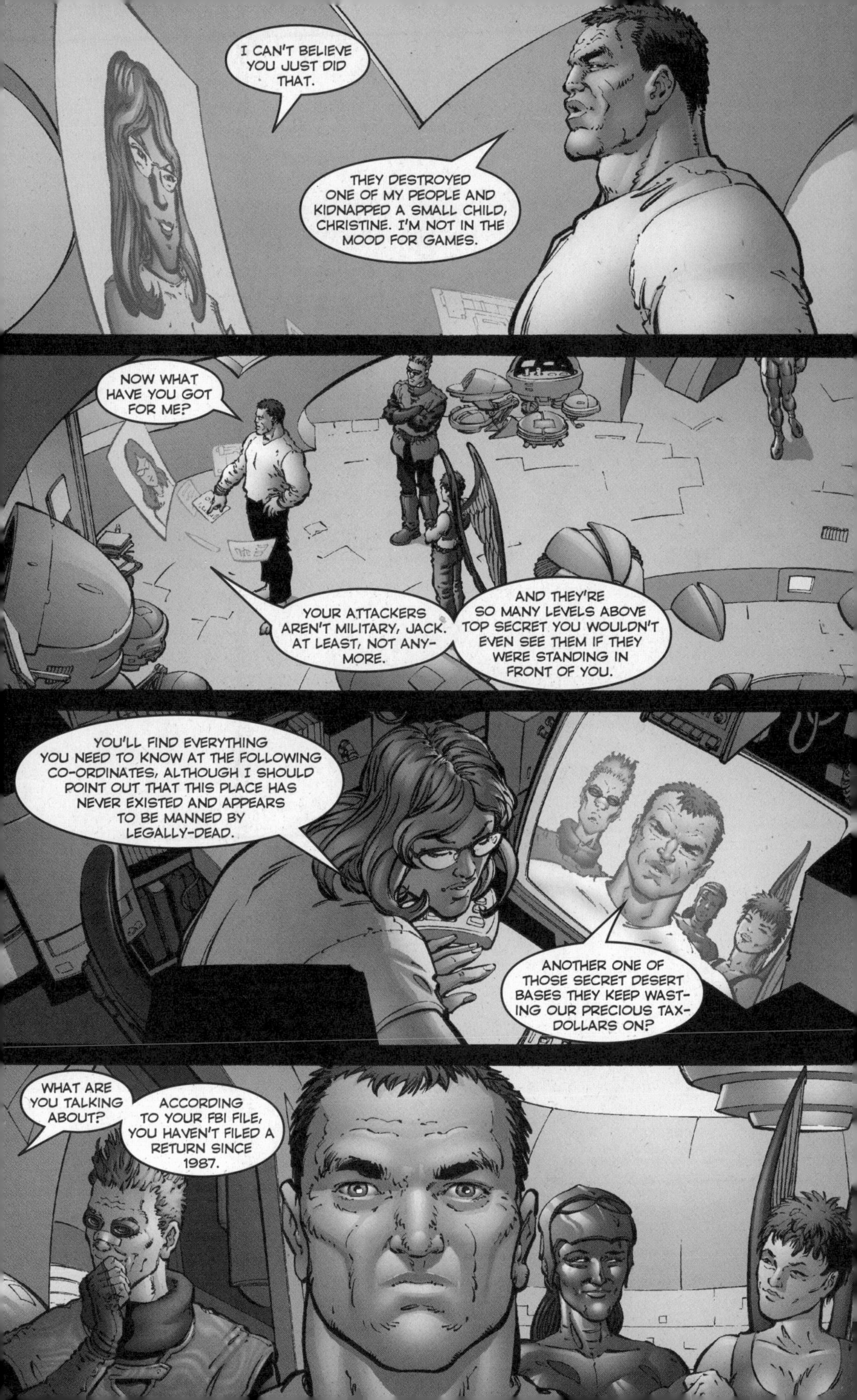
I CAN'T BELIEVE YOU JUST DID THAT.
THEY DESTROYED ONE OF MY PEOPLE AND KIDNAPPED A SMALL CHILD, CHRISTINE. I'M NOT IN THE MOOD FOR GAMES.
NOW WHAT HAVE YOU GOT FOR ME?
YOUR ATTACKERS AREN'T MILITARY, JACK. AT LEAST, NOT ANY-MORE.
AND THEY'RE SO MANY LEVELS ABOVE TOP SECRET YOU WOULDN'T EVEN SEE THEM IF THEY WERE STANDING IN FRONT OF YOU.
YOU'LL FIND EVERYTHING YOU NEED TO KNOW AT THE FOLLOWING CO-ORDINATES, ALTHOUGH I SHOULD POINT OUT THAT THIS PLACE HAS NEVER EXISTED AND APPEARS TO BE MANNED BY LEGALLY-DEAD.
ANOTHER ONE OF THOSE SECRET DESERT BASES THEY KEEP WAST-ING OUR PRECIOUS TAX-DOLLARS ON?
WHAT ARE YOU TALKING ABOUT?
ACCORDING TO YOUR FBI FILE, YOU HAVEN'T FILED A RETURN SINCE 1987.

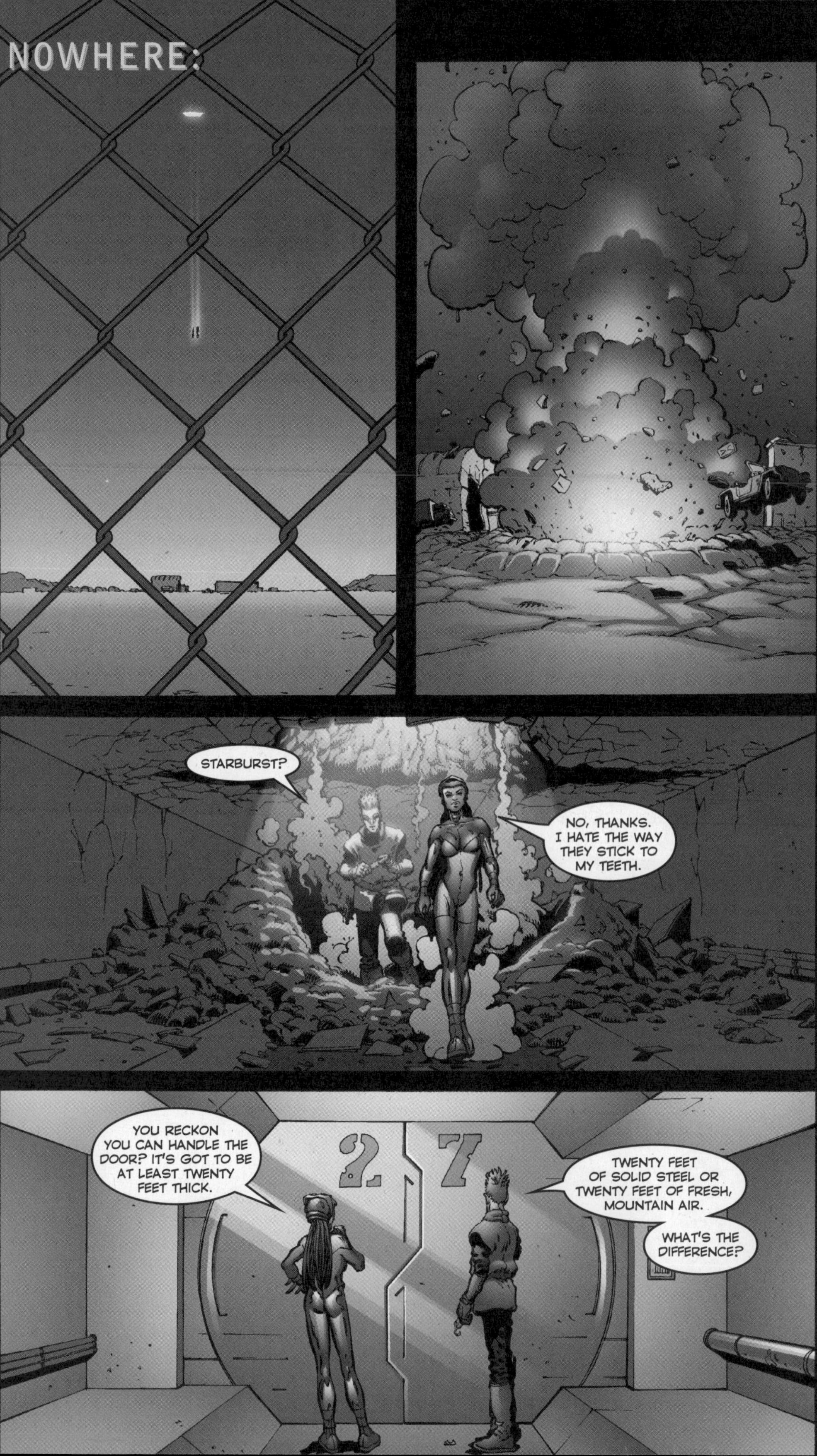
NOWHERE:
STARBURST?
NO, THANKS. I HATE THE WAY THEY STICK TO MY TEETH.
YOU RECKON YOU CAN HANDLE THE DOOR? IT'S GOT TO BE AT LEAST TWENTY FEET THICK.
2 7
TWENTY FEET OF SOLID STEEL OR TWENTY FEET OF FRESH, MOUNTAIN AIR.
WHAT'S THE DIFFERENCE?

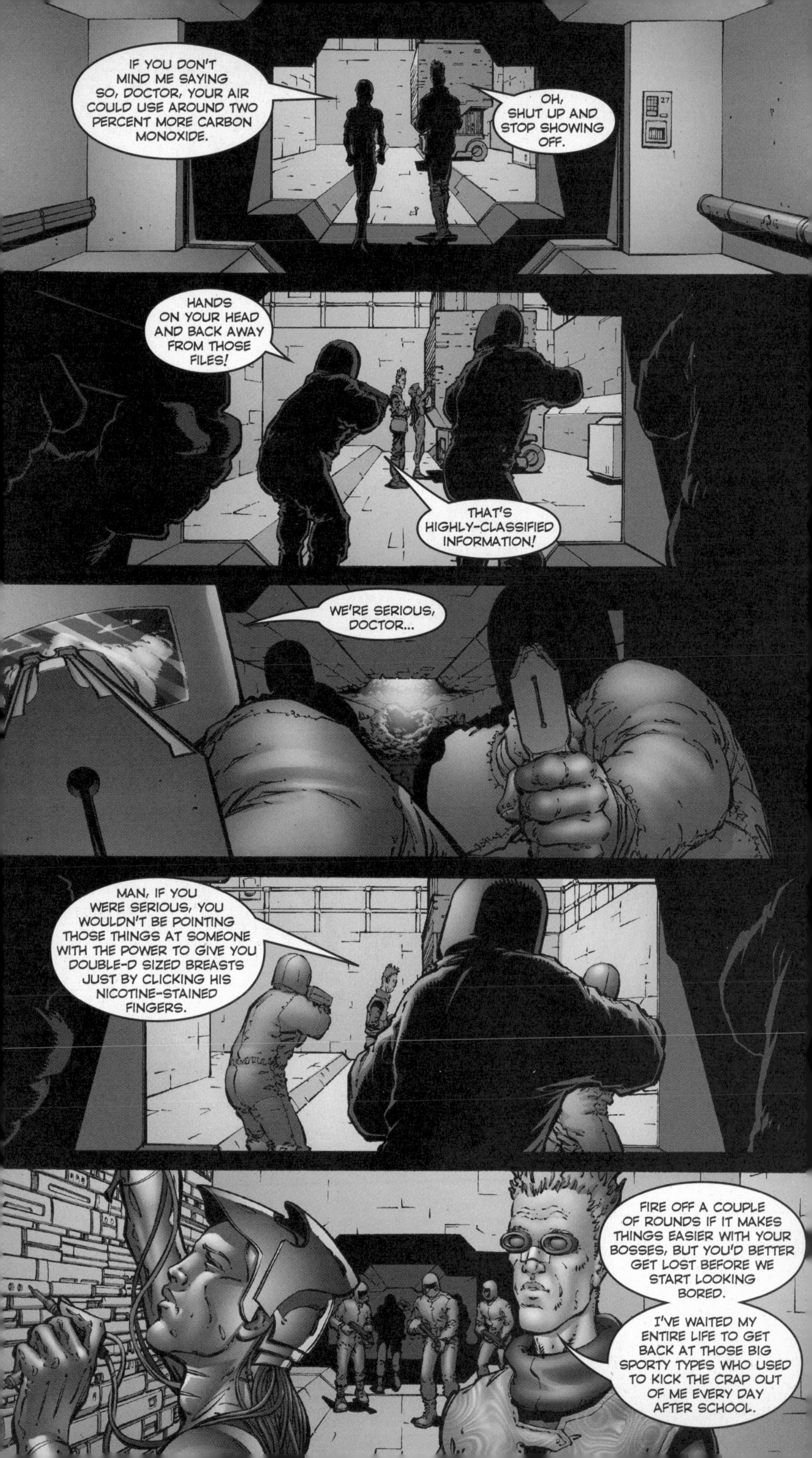
IF YOU DON'T MIND ME SAYING SO, DOCTOR, YOUR AIR COULD USE AROUND TWO PERCENT MORE CARBON MONOXIDE.
OH, SHUT UP AND STOP SHOWING OFF.
HANDS ON YOUR HEAD AND BACK AWAY FROM THOSE FILES!
THAT'S HIGHLY-CLASSIFIED INFORMATION!
WE'RE SERIOUS, DOCTOR...
MAN, IF YOU WERE SERIOUS, YOU WOULDN'T BE POINTING THOSE THINGS AT SOMEONE WITH THE POWER TO GIVE YOU DOUBLE-D SIZED BREASTS JUST BY CLICKING HIS NICOTINE-STAINED FINGERS.
FIRE OFF A COUPLE OF ROUNDS IF IT MAKES THINGS EASIER WITH YOUR BOSSES, BUT YOU'D BETTER GET LOST BEFORE WE START LOOKING BORED.
I'VE WAITED MY ENTIRE LIFE TO GET BACK AT THOSE BIG SPORTY TYPES WHO USED TO KICK THE CRAP OUT OF ME EVERY DAY AFTER SCHOOL.

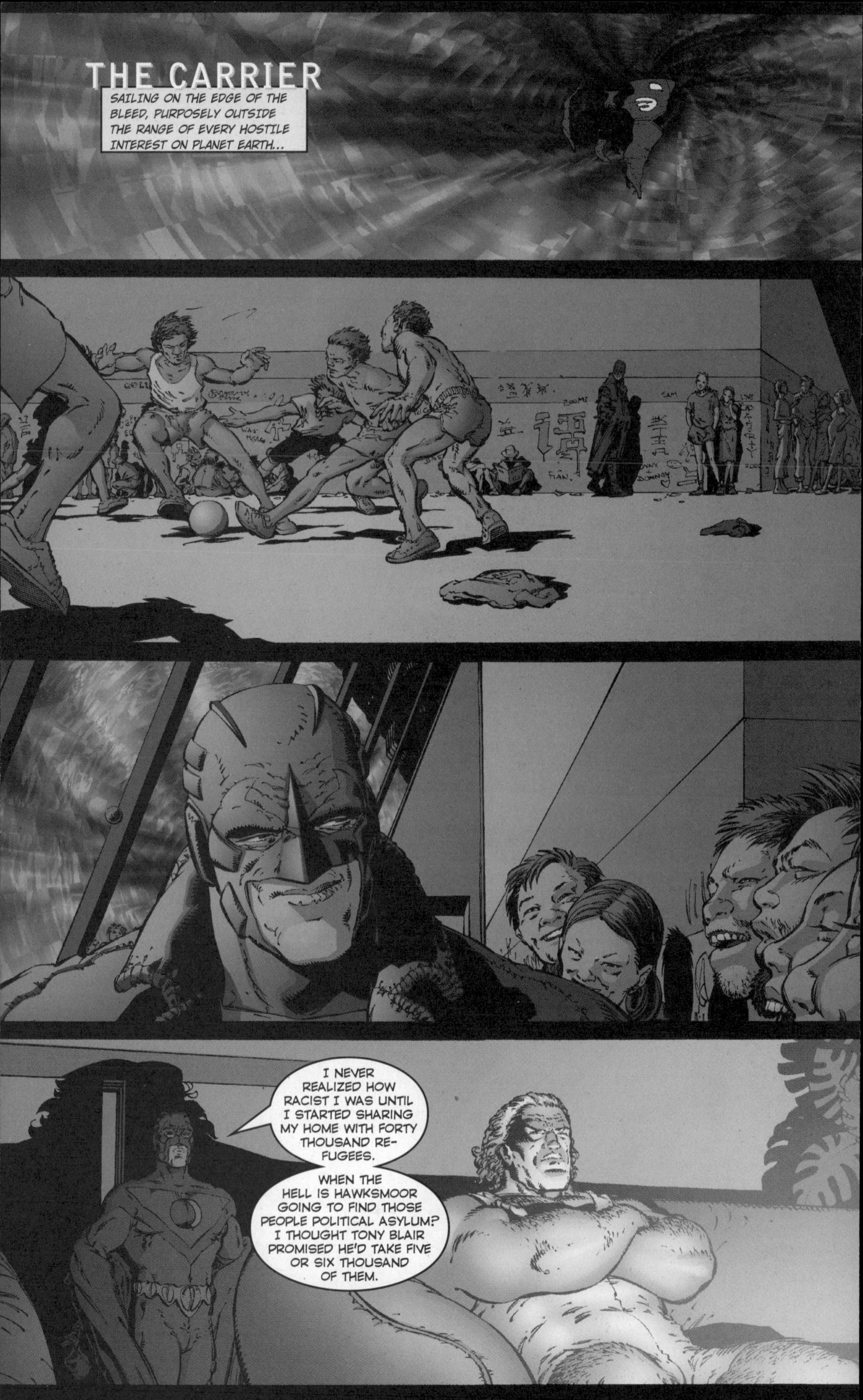
THE CARRIER
SAILING ON THE EDGE OF THE BLEED, PURPOSELY OUTSIDE THE RANGE OF EVERY HOSTILE INTEREST ON PLANET EARTH...
I NEVER REALIZED HOW RACIST I WAS UNTIL I STARTED SHARING MY HOME WITH FORTY THOUSAND RE-FUGEES.
WHEN THE HELL IS HAWKSMOOR GOING TO FIND THOSE PEOPLE POLITICAL ASYLUM? I THOUGHT TONY BLAIR PROMISED HE'D TAKE FIVE OR SIX THOUSAND OF THEM.

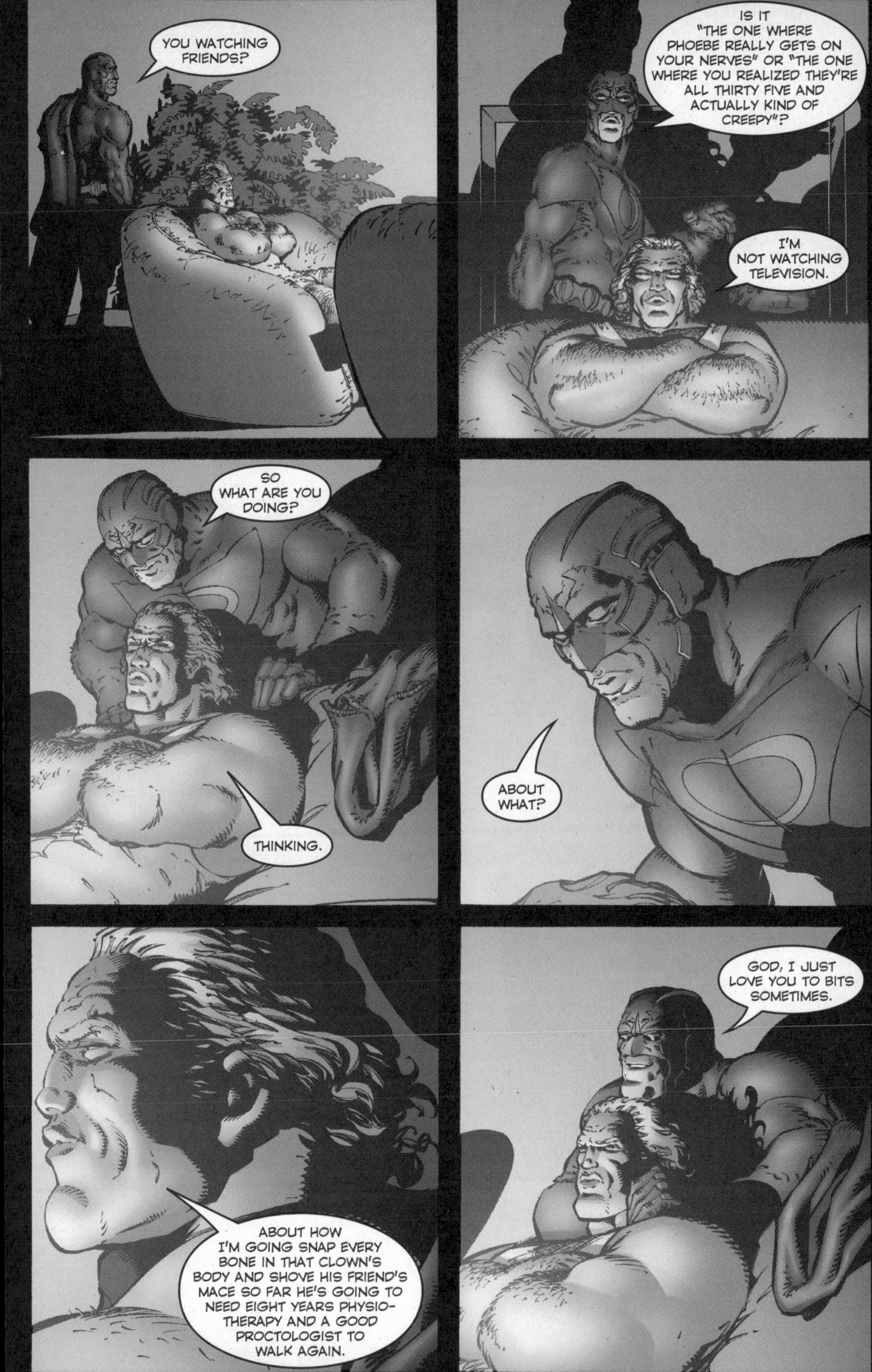
YOU WATCHING FRIENDS?
IS IT "THE ONE WHERE PHOEBE REALLY GETS ON YOUR NERVES" OR "THE ONE WHERE YOU REALIZED THEY'RE ALL THIRTY FIVE AND ACTUALLY KIND OF CREEPY"?
I'M NOT WATCHING TELEVISION.
SO WHAT ARE YOU DOING?
THINKING.
ABOUT WHAT?
ABOUT HOW I'M GOING SNAP EVERY BONE IN THAT CLOWN'S BODY AND SHOVE HIS FRIEND'S MACE SO FAR HE'S GOING TO NEED EIGHT YEARS PHYSIO-THERAPY AND A GOOD PROCTOLOGIST TO WALK AGAIN.
GOD, I JUST LOVE YOU TO BITS SOMETIMES.

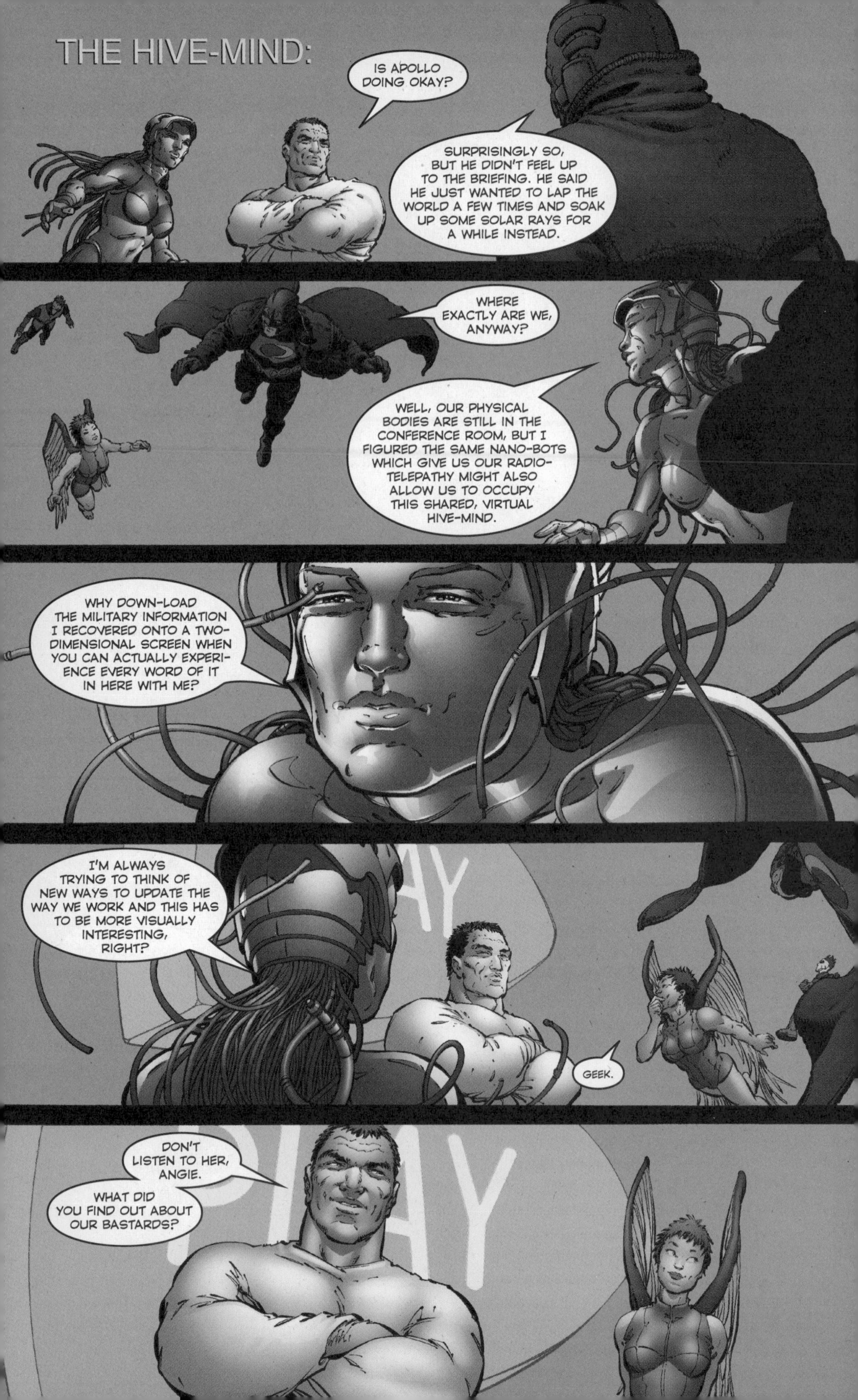
THE HIVE-MIND:
IS APOLLO DOING OKAY?
SURPRISINGLY SO, BUT HE DIDN'T FEEL UP TO THE BRIEFING. HE SAID HE JUST WANTED TO LAP THE WORLD A FEW TIMES AND SOAK UP SOME SOLAR RAYS FOR A WHILE INSTEAD.
WHERE EXACTLY ARE WE, ANYWAY?
WELL, OUR PHYSICAL BODIES ARE STILL IN THE CONFERENCE ROOM, BUT I FIGURED THE SAME NANO-BOTS WHICH GIVE US OUR RADIO-TELEPATHY MIGHT ALSO ALLOW US TO OCCUPY THIS SHARED, VIRTUAL HIVE-MIND.
WHY DOWN-LOAD THE MILITARY INFORMATION I RECOVERED ONTO A TWO-DIMENSIONAL SCREEN WHEN YOU CAN ACTUALLY EXPERIENCE EVERY WORD OF IT IN HERE WITH ME?
I'M ALWAYS TRYING TO THINK OF NEW WAYS TO UPDATE THE WAY WE WORK AND THIS HAS TO BE MORE VISUALLY INTERESTING, RIGHT?
GEEK.
DON'T LISTEN TO HER, ANGIE.
WHAT DID YOU FIND OUT ABOUT OUR BASTARDS?

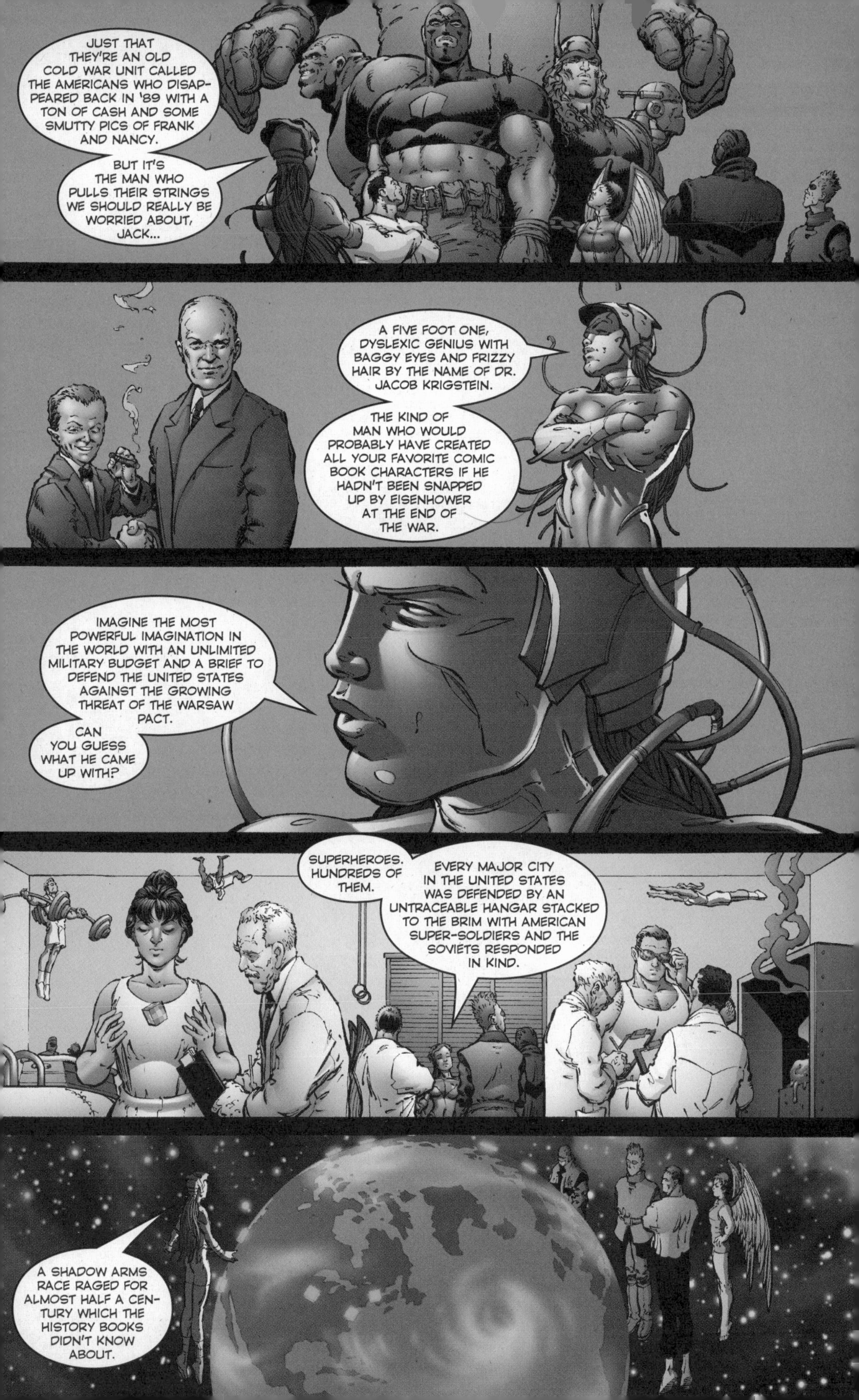
JUST THAT THEY'RE AN OLD COLD WAR UNIT CALLED THE AMERICANS WHO DISAP-PEARED BACK IN '89 WITH A TON OF CASH AND SOME SMUTTY PICS OF FRANK AND NANCY.
BUT IT'S THE MAN WHO PULLS THEIR STRINGS WE SHOULD REALLY BE WORRIED ABOUT, JACK...
A FIVE FOOT ONE, DYSLEXIC GENIUS WITH BAGGY EYES AND FRIZZY HAIR BY THE NAME OF DR. JACOB KRIGSTEIN.
THE KIND OF MAN WHO WOULD PROBABLY HAVE CREATED ALL YOUR FAVORITE COMIC BOOK CHARACTERS IF HE HADN'T BEEN SNAPPED UP BY EISENHOWER AT THE END OF THE WAR.
IMAGINE THE MOST POWERFUL IMAGINATION IN THE WORLD WITH AN UNLIMITED MILITARY BUDGET AND A BRIEF TO DEFEND THE UNITED STATES AGAINST THE GROWING THREAT OF THE WARSAW PACT.
CAN YOU GUESS WHAT HE CAME UP WITH?
SUPERHEROES. HUNDREDS OF THEM.
EVERY MAJOR CITY IN THE UNITED STATES WAS DEFENDED BY AN UNTRACEABLE HANGAR STACKED TO THE BRIM WITH AMERICAN SUPER-SOLDIERS AND THE SOVIETS RESPONDED IN KIND.
A SHADOW ARMS RACE RAGED FOR ALMOST HALF A CEN-TURY WHICH THE HISTORY BOOKS DIDN'T KNOW ABOUT.

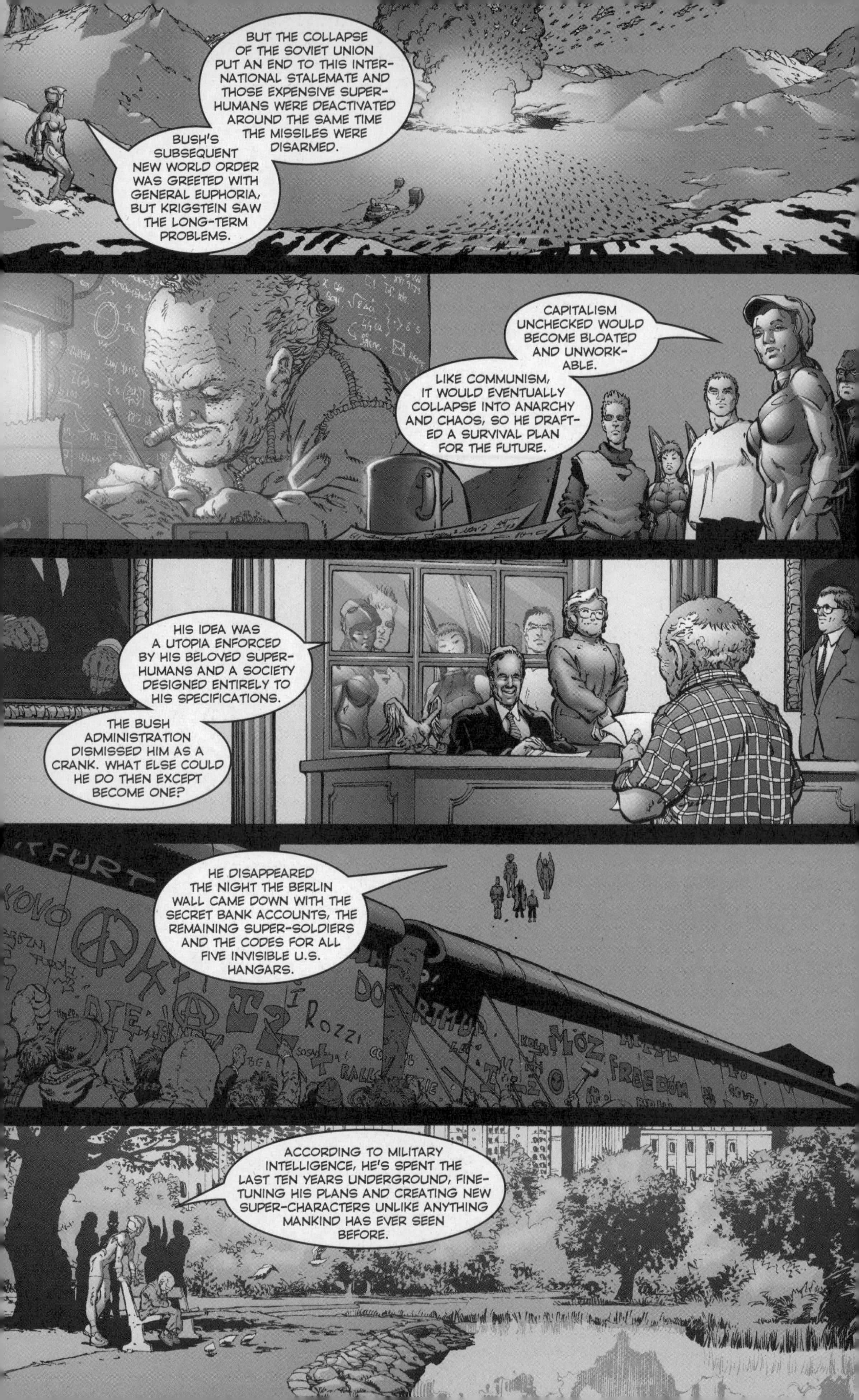
BUT THE COLLAPSE OF THE SOVIET UNION PUT AN END TO THIS INTERNATIONAL STALEMATE AND THOSE EXPENSIVE SUPER-HUMANS WERE DEACTIVATED AROUND THE SAME TIME THE MISSILES WERE DISARMED.
BUSH'S SUBSEQUENT NEW WORLD ORDER WAS GREETED WITH GENERAL EUPHORIA, BUT KRIGSTEIN SAW THE LONG-TERM PROBLEMS.
CAPITALISM UNCHECKED WOULD BECOME BLOATED AND UNWORKABLE.
LIKE COMMUNISM, IT WOULD EVENTUALLY COLLAPSE INTO ANARCHY AND CHAOS, SO HE DRAFTED A SURVIVAL PLAN FOR THE FUTURE.
HIS IDEA WAS A UTOPIA ENFORCED BY HIS BELOVED SUPER-HUMANS AND A SOCIETY DESIGNED ENTIRELY TO HIS SPECIFICATIONS.
THE BUSH ADMINISTRATION DISMISSED HIM AS A CRANK. WHAT ELSE COULD HE DO THEN EXCEPT BECOME ONE?
HE DISAPPEARED THE NIGHT THE BERLIN WALL CAME DOWN WITH THE SECRET BANK ACCOUNTS, THE REMAINING SUPER-SOLDIERS AND THE CODES FOR ALL FIVE INVISIBLE U.S. HANGARS.
ACCORDING TO MILITARY INTELLIGENCE, HE'S SPENT THE LAST TEN YEARS UNDERGROUND, FINE-TUNING HIS PLANS AND CREATING NEW SUPER-CHARACTERS UNLIKE ANYTHING MANKIND HAS EVER SEEN BEFORE.

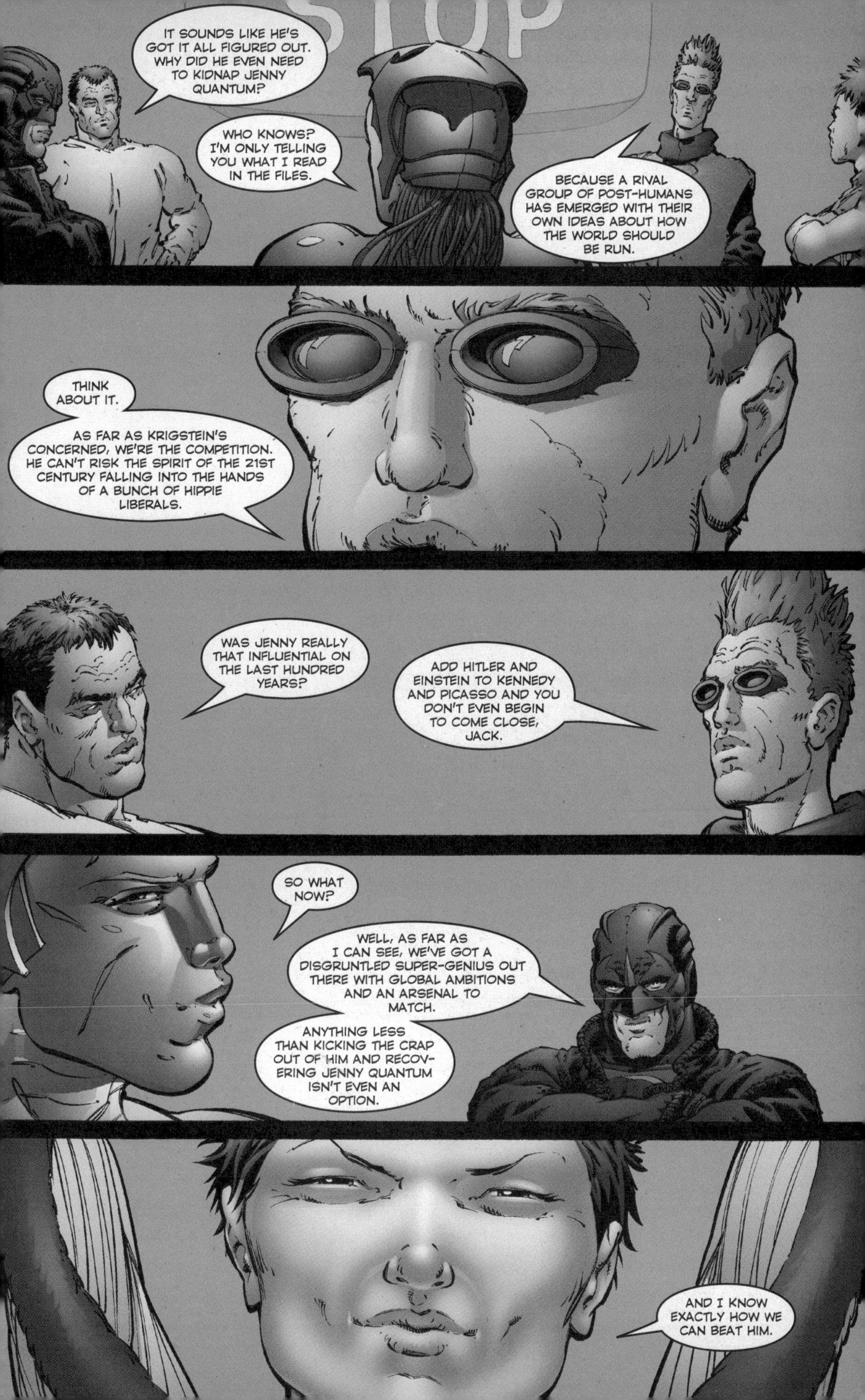

STOP
IT SOUNDS LIKE HE'S GOT IT ALL FIGURED OUT. WHY DID HE EVEN NEED TO KIDNAP JENNY QUANTUM?
WHO KNOWS? I'M ONLY TELLING YOU WHAT I READ IN THE FILES.
BECAUSE A RIVAL GROUP OF POST-HUMANS HAS EMERGED WITH THEIR OWN IDEAS ABOUT HOW THE WORLD SHOULD BE RUN.
THINK ABOUT IT.
AS FAR AS KRIGSTEIN'S CONCERNED, WE'RE THE COMPETITION. HE CAN'T RISK THE SPIRIT OF THE 21ST CENTURY FALLING INTO THE HANDS OF A BUNCH OF HIPPIE LIBERALS.
WAS JENNY REALLY THAT INFLUENTIAL ON THE LAST HUNDRED YEARS?
ADD HITLER AND EINSTEIN TO KENNEDY AND PICASSO AND YOU DON'T EVEN BEGIN TO COME CLOSE, JACK.
SO WHAT NOW?
WELL, AS FAR AS I CAN SEE, WE'VE GOT A DISGRUNTLED SUPER-GENIUS OUT THERE WITH GLOBAL AMBITIONS AND AN ARSENAL TO MATCH.
ANYTHING LESS THAN KICKING THE CRAP OUT OF HIM AND RECOVERING JENNY QUANTUM ISN'T EVEN AN OPTION.
AND I KNOW EXACTLY HOW WE CAN BEAT HIM.

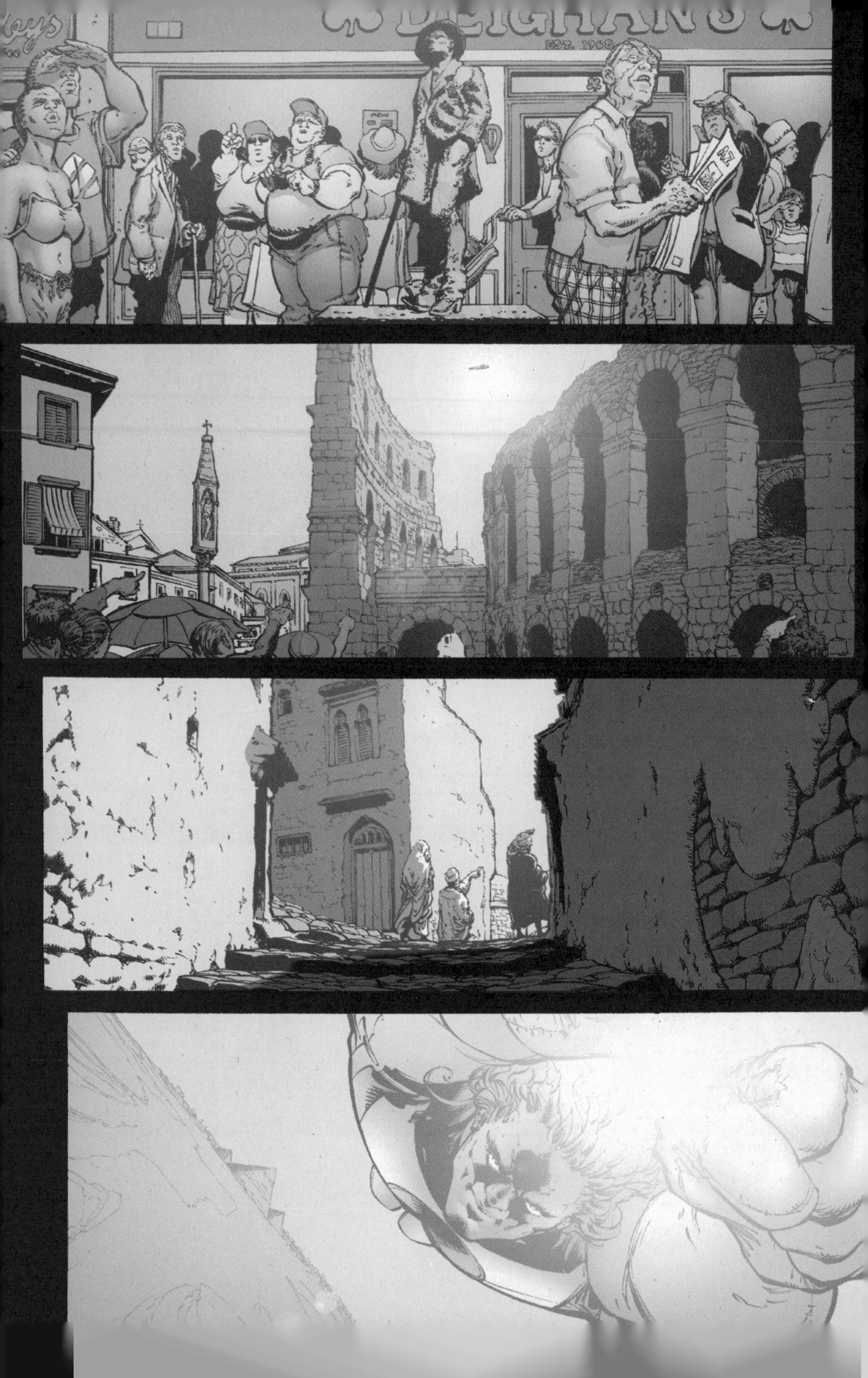
EST. 1968

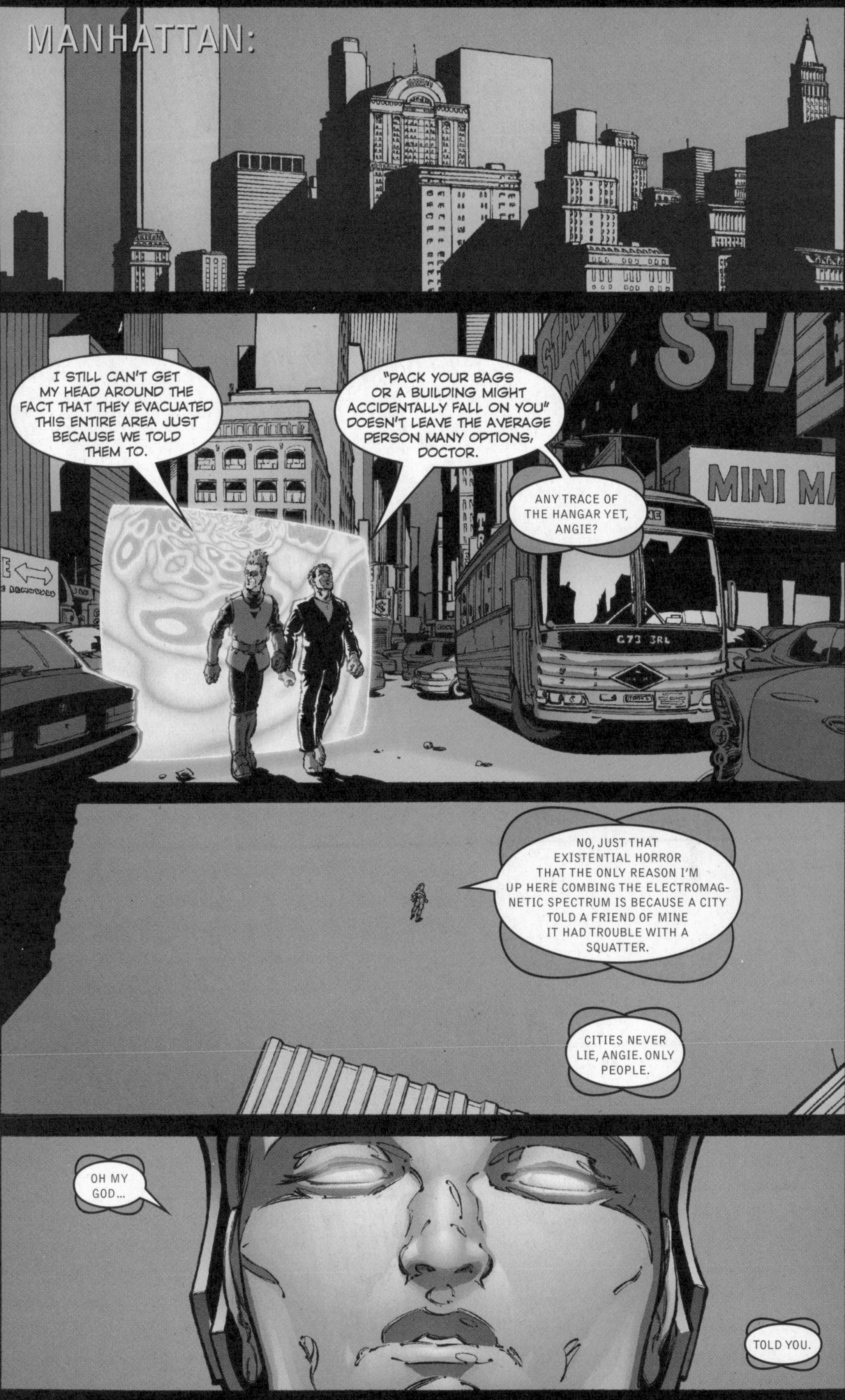
MANHATTAN:
I STILL CAN'T GET MY HEAD AROUND THE FACT THAT THEY EVACUATED THIS ENTIRE AREA JUST BECAUSE WE TOLD THEM TO.
"PACK YOUR BAGS OR A BUILDING MIGHT ACCIDENTALLY FALL ON YOU" DOESN'T LEAVE THE AVERAGE PERSON MANY OPTIONS, DOCTOR.
ANY TRACE OF THE HANGAR YET, ANGIE?
MINI MA
NO, JUST THAT EXISTENTIAL HORROR THAT THE ONLY REASON I'M UP HERE COMBING THE ELECTROMAG-NETIC SPECTRUM IS BECAUSE A CITY TOLD A FRIEND OF MINE IT HAD TROUBLE WITH A SQUATTER.
CITIES NEVER LIE, ANGIE. ONLY PEOPLE.
OH MY GOD...
TOLD YOU.

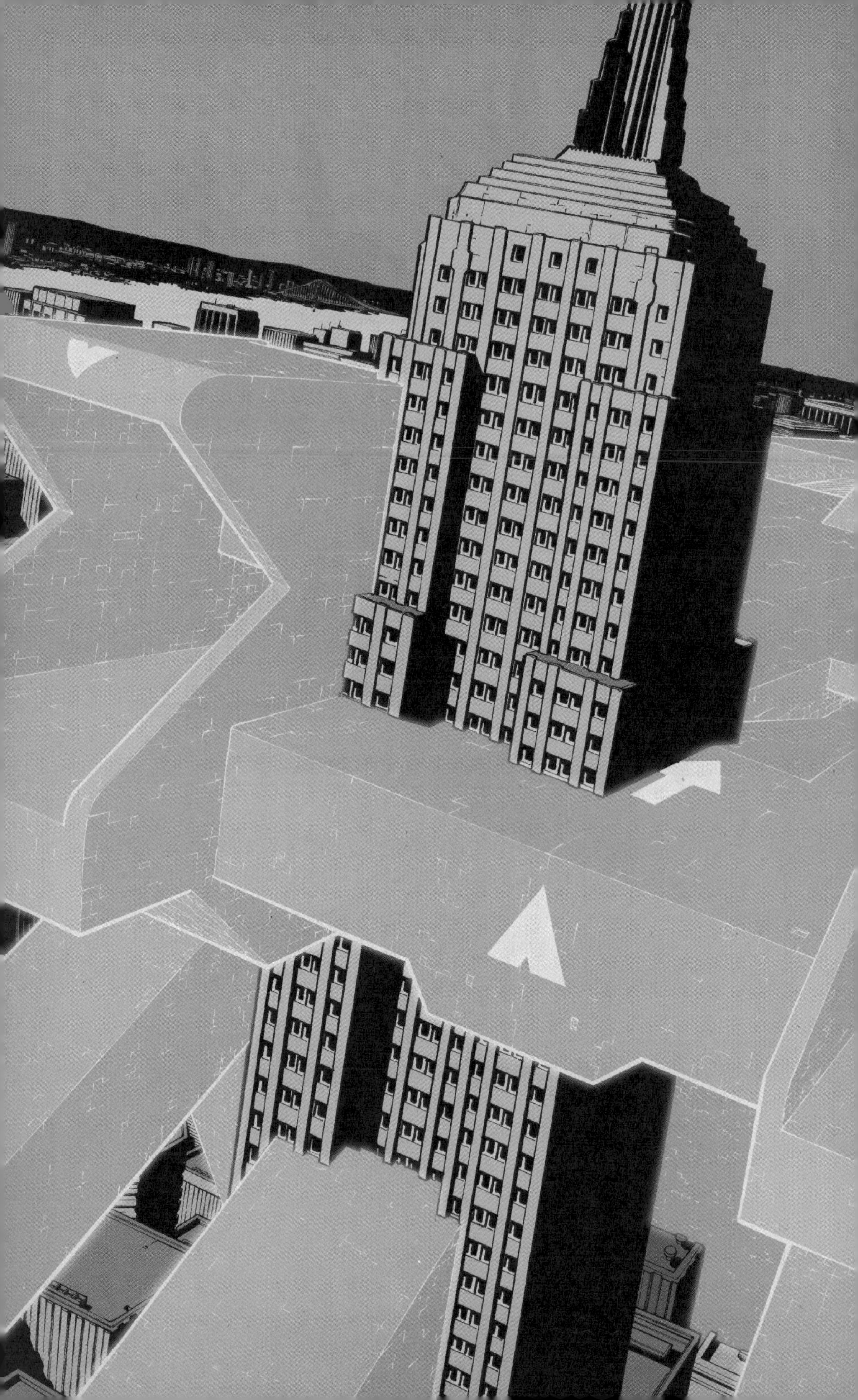

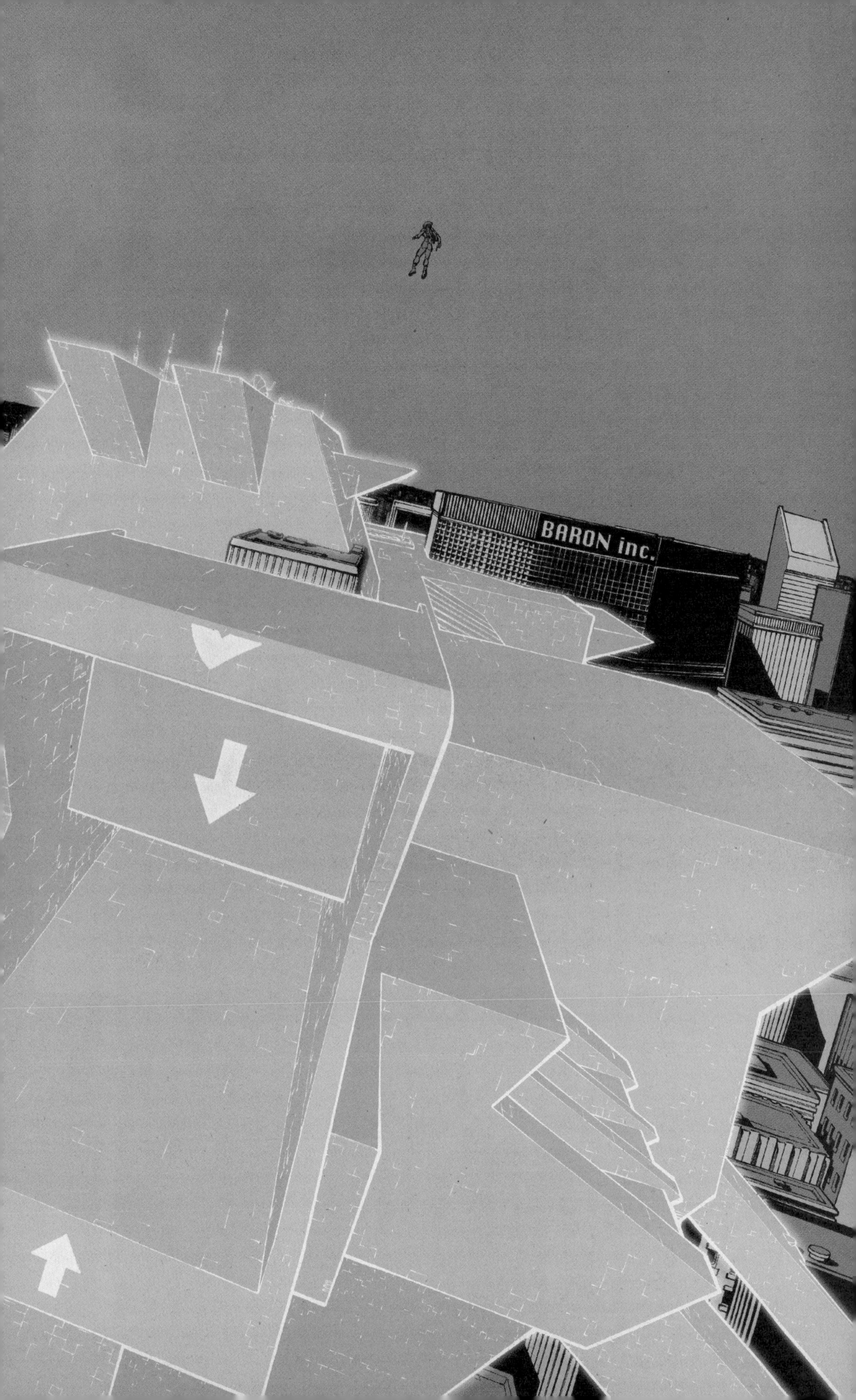
BARON inc.

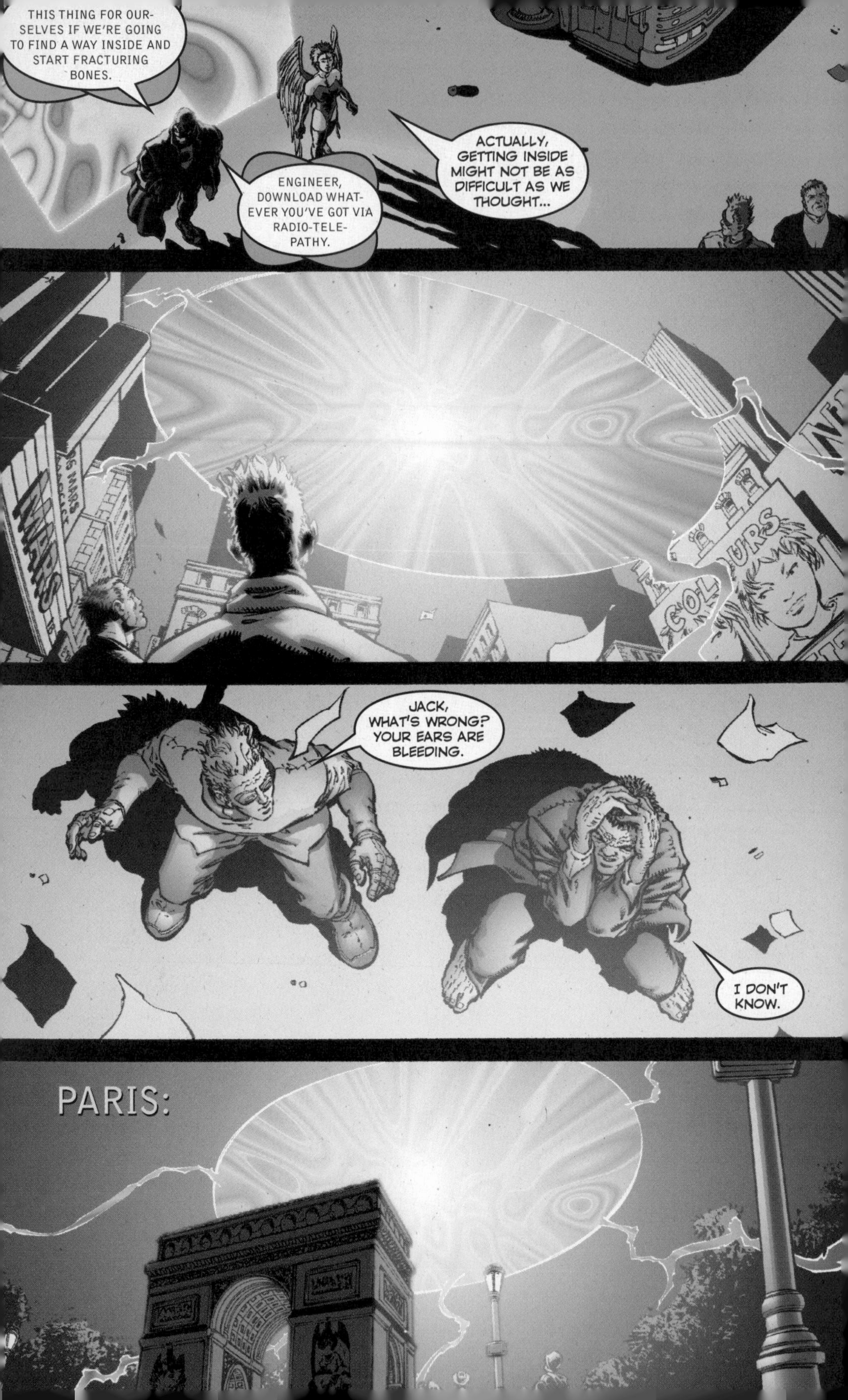
THIS THING FOR OURSELVES IF WE'RE GOING TO FIND A WAY INSIDE AND START FRACTURING BONES.
ENGINEER, DOWNLOAD WHATEVER YOU'VE GOT VIA RADIO-TELEPATHY.
ACTUALLY, GETTING INSIDE MIGHT NOT BE AS DIFFICULT AS WE THOUGHT...
MARS
COLOURS
JACK, WHAT'S WRONG? YOUR EARS ARE BLEEDING.
I DON'T KNOW.
PARIS:

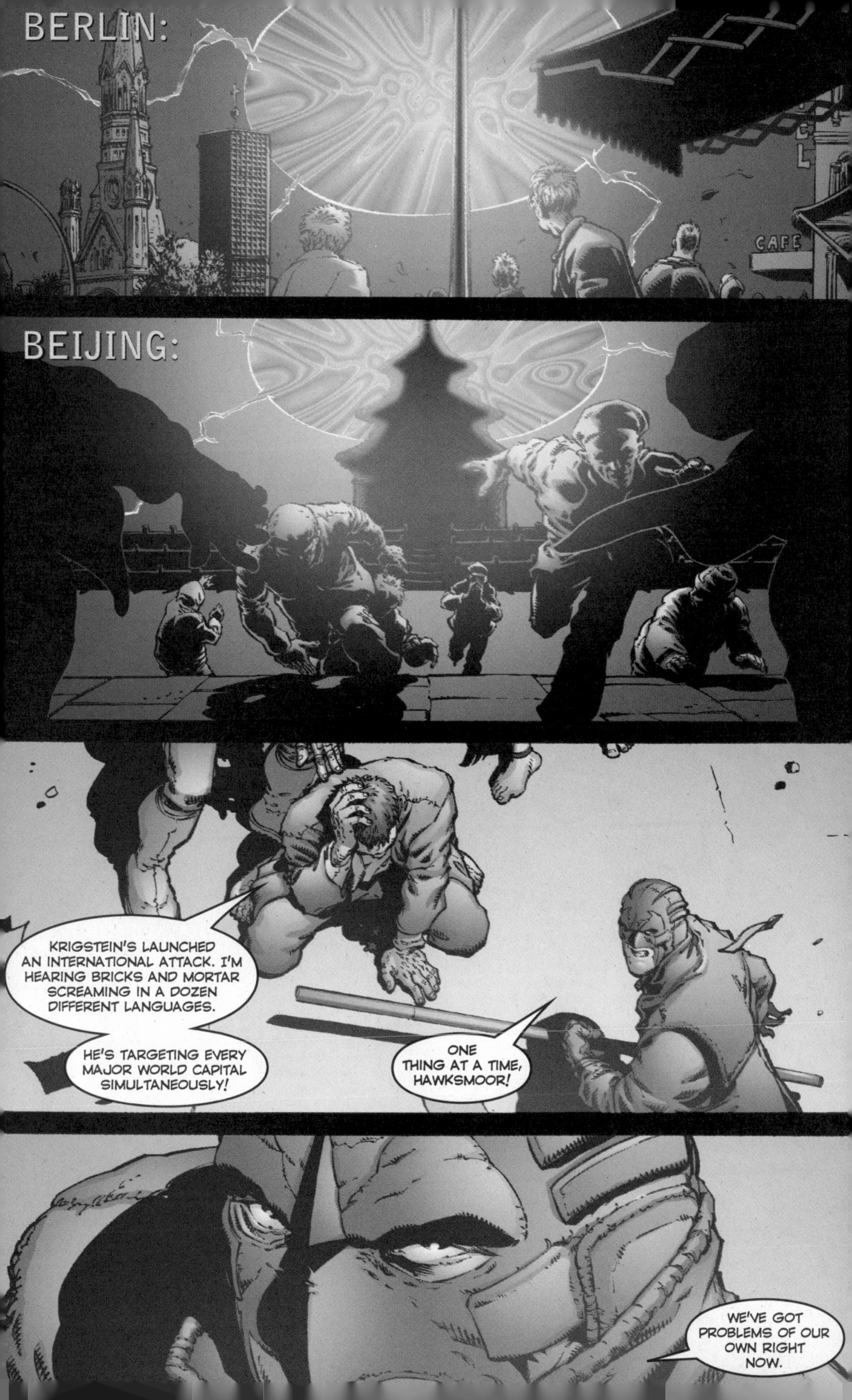
BERLIN:
CAFE
BEIJING:
KRIGSTEIN'S LAUNCHED AN INTERNATIONAL ATTACK. I'M HEARING BRICKS AND MORTAR SCREAMING IN A DOZEN DIFFERENT LANGUAGES.
HE'S TARGETING EVERY MAJOR WORLD CAPITAL SIMULTANEOUSLY!
ONE THING AT A TIME, HAWKSMOOR!
WE'VE GOT PROBLEMS OF OUR OWN RIGHT NOW.

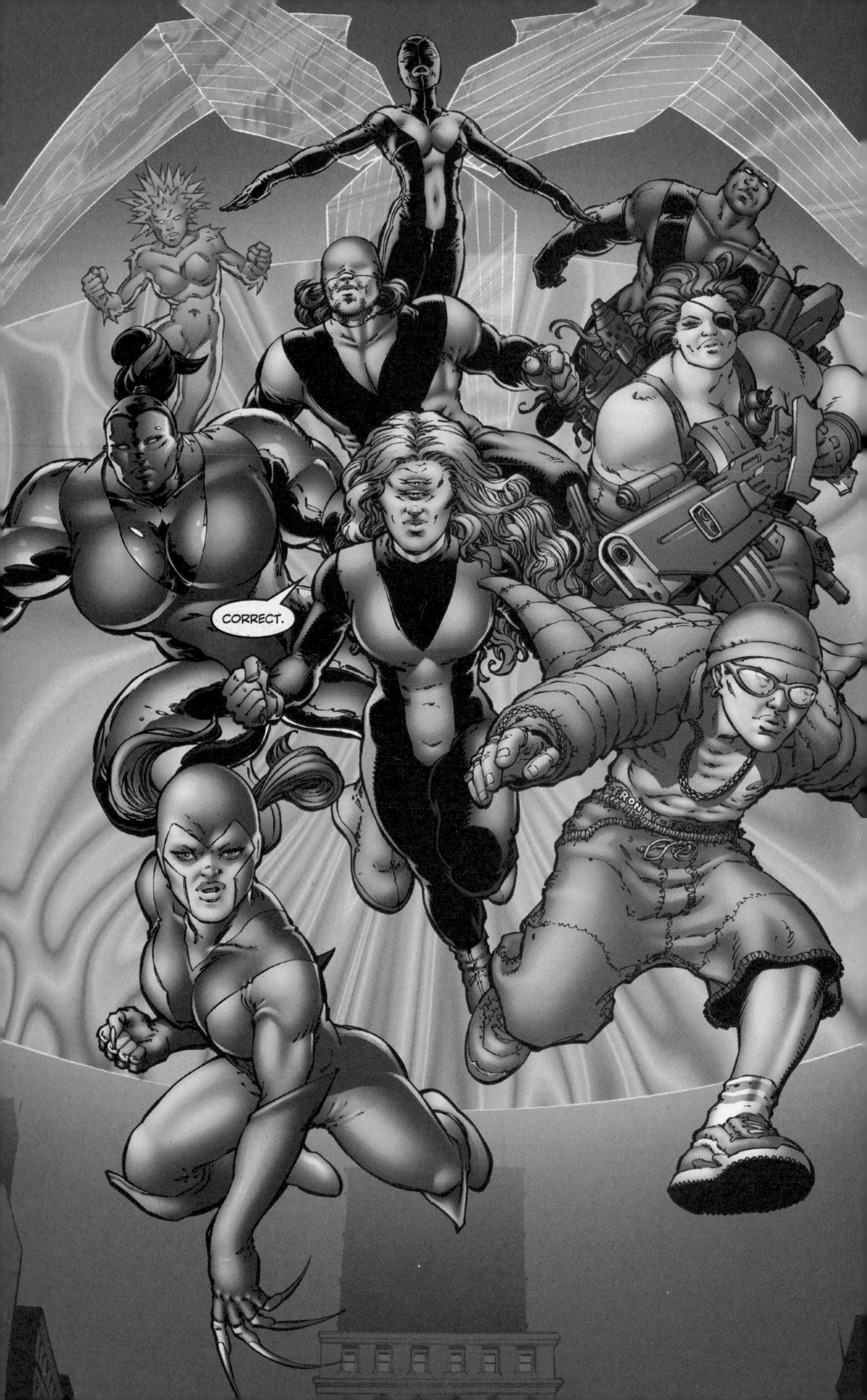
CORRECT.
FRONT-FRONT

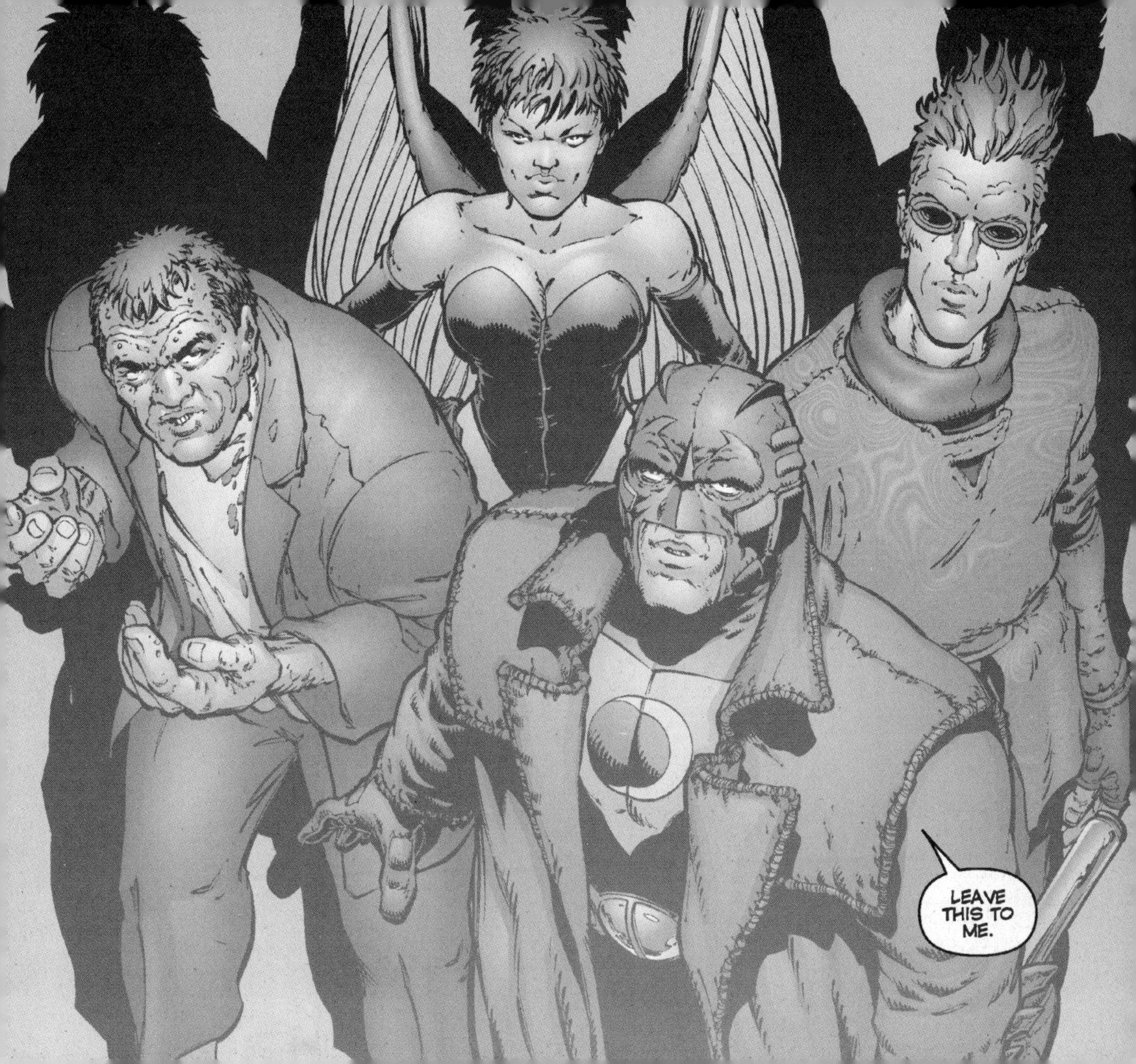
LEAVE THIS TO ME.

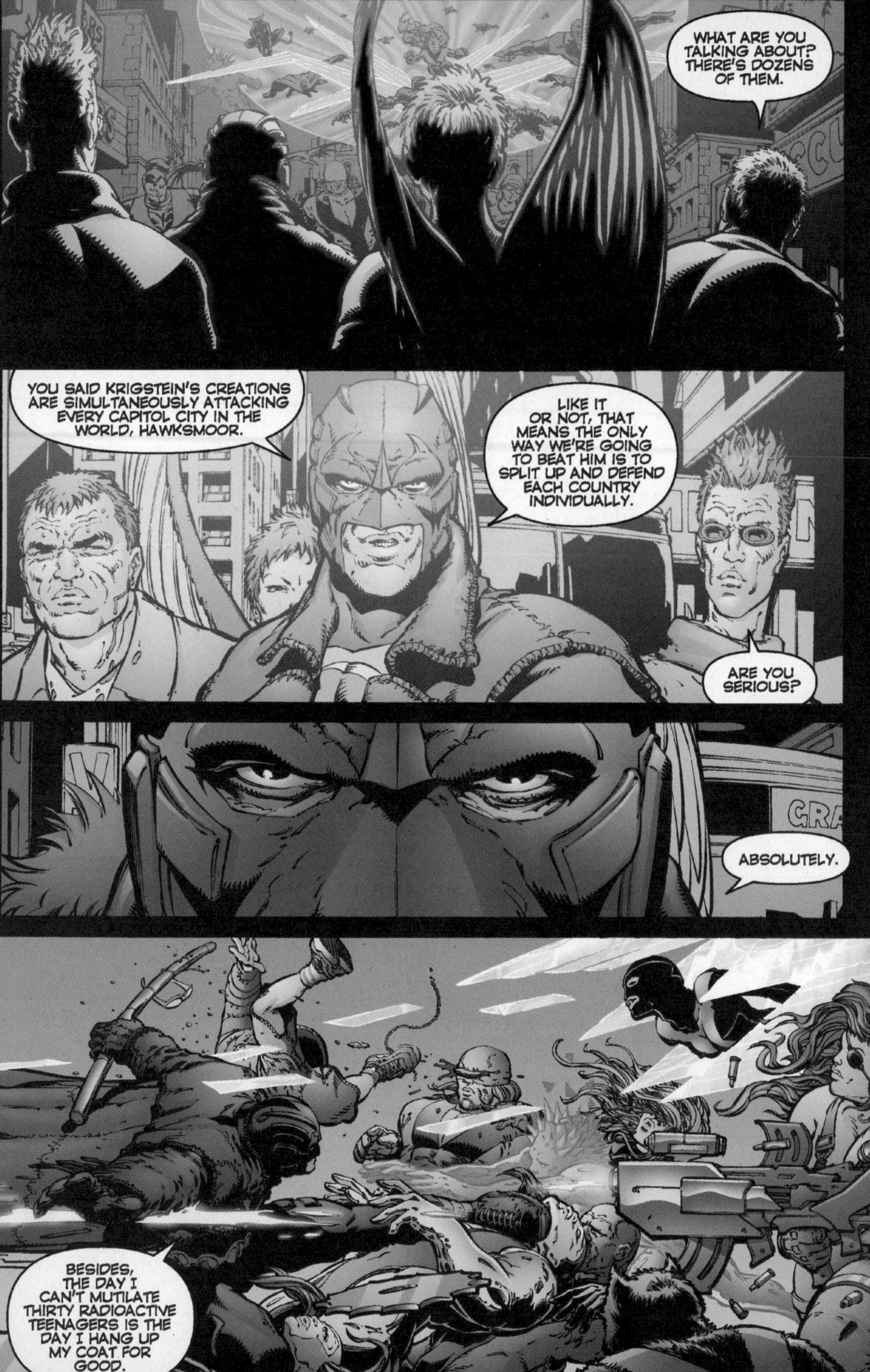
WHAT ARE YOU TALKING ABOUT? THERE'S DOZENS OF THEM.
YOU SAID KRIGSTEIN'S CREATIONS ARE SIMULTANEOUSLY ATTACKING EVERY CAPITOL CITY IN THE WORLD, HAWKSMOOR.
LIKE IT OR NOT, THAT MEANS THE ONLY WAY WE'RE GOING TO BEAT HIM IS TO SPLIT UP AND DEFEND EACH COUNTRY INDIVIDUALLY.
ARE YOU SERIOUS?
ABSOLUTELY.
BESIDES, THE DAY I CAN'T MUTILATE THIRTY RADIOACTIVE TEENAGERS IS THE DAY I HANG UP MY COAT FOR GOOD.

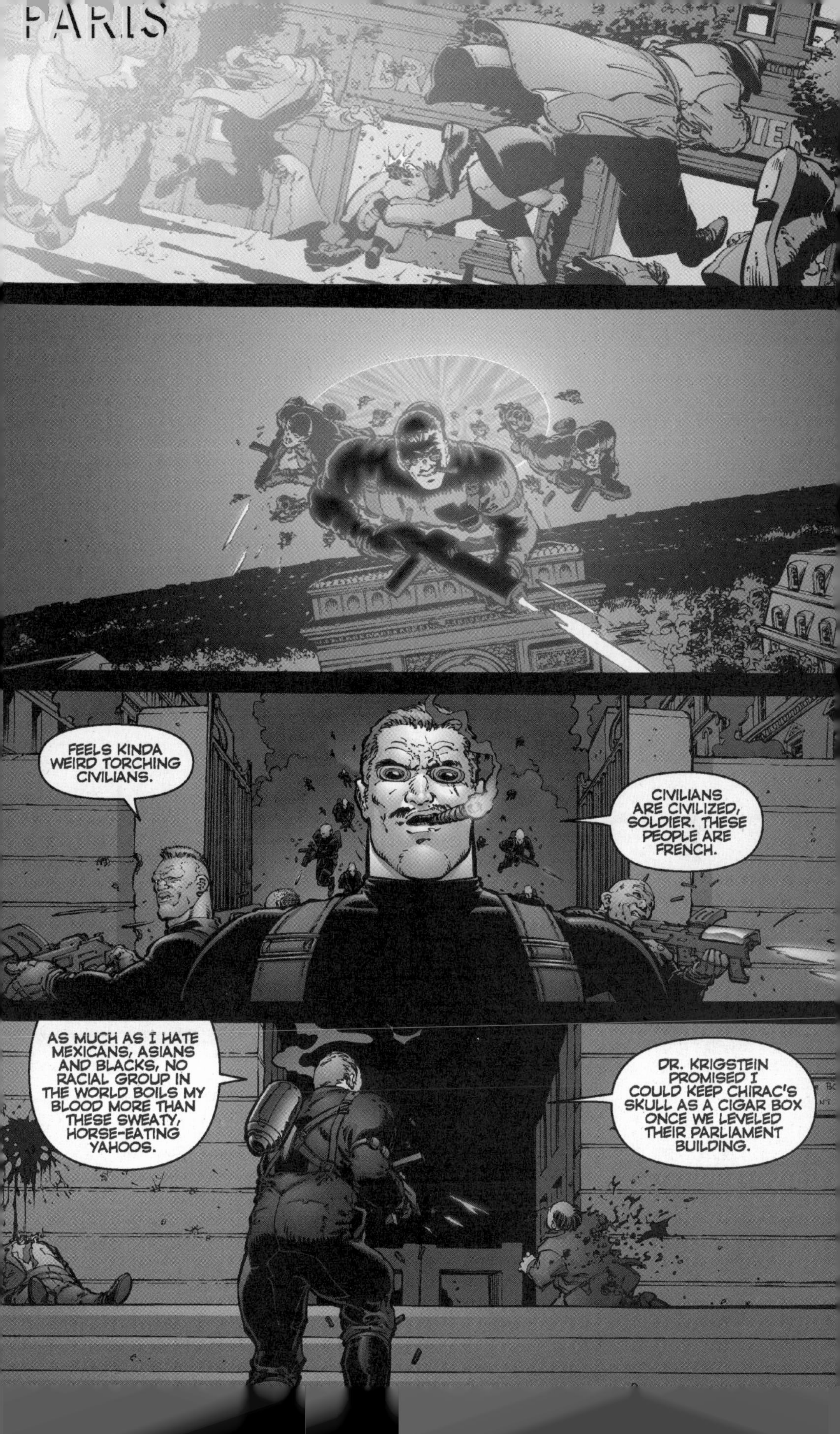
PARIS
FEELS KINDA WEIRD TORCHING CIVILIANS.
CIVILIANS ARE CIVILIZED, SOLDIER. THESE PEOPLE ARE FRENCH.
AS MUCH AS I HATE MEXICANS, ASIANS AND BLACKS, NO RACIAL GROUP IN THE WORLD BOILS MY BLOOD MORE THAN THESE SWEATY, HORSE-EATING YAHOOS.
DR. KRIGSTEIN PROMISED I COULD KEEP CHIRAC'S SKULL AS A CIGAR BOX ONCE WE LEVELED THEIR PARLIAMENT BUILDING.

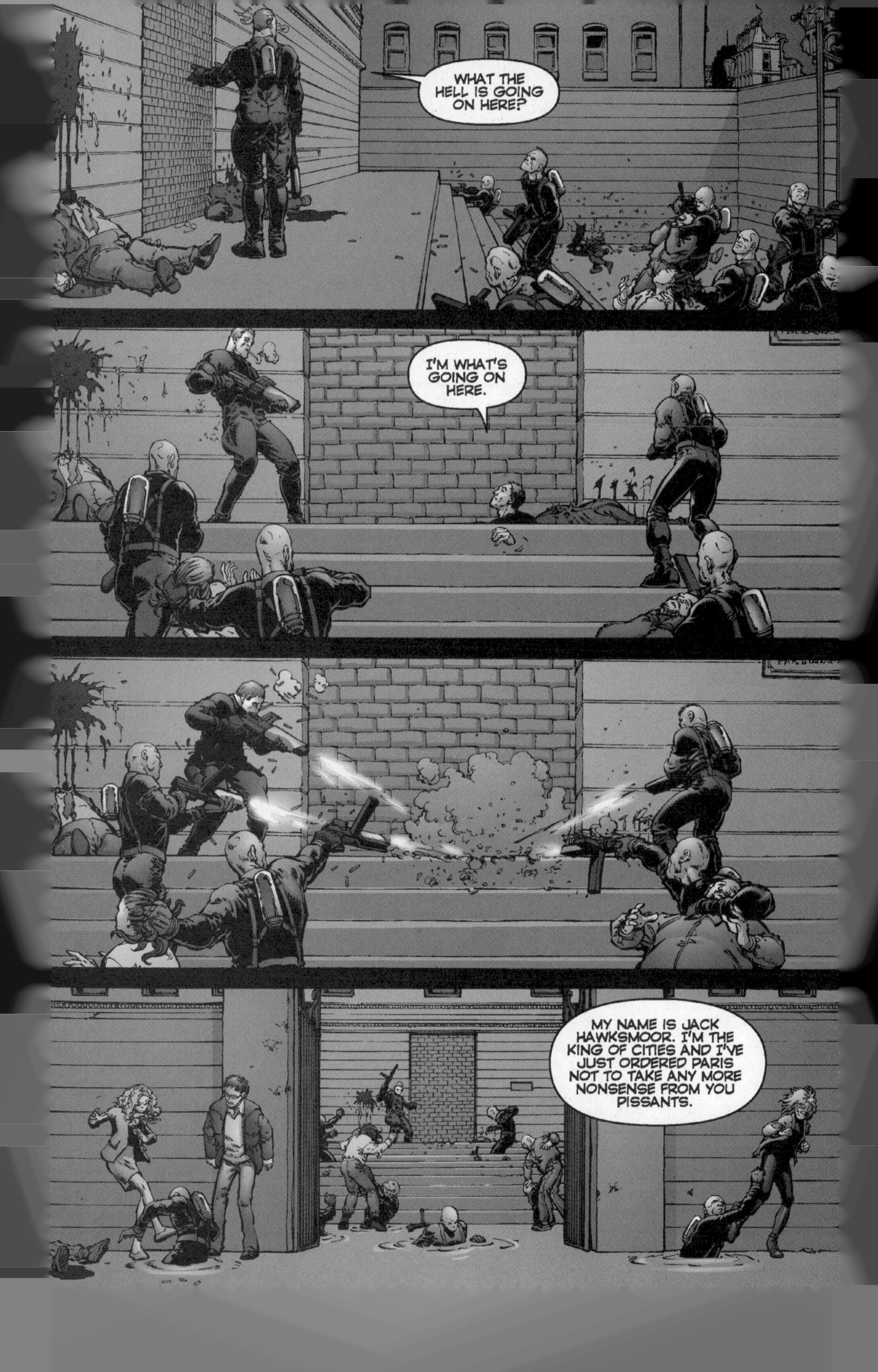
WHAT THE HELL IS GOING ON HERE?
I'M WHAT'S GOING ON HERE.
MY NAME IS JACK HAWKSMOOR. I'M THE KING OF CITIES AND I'VE JUST ORDERED PARIS NOT TO TAKE ANY MORE NONSENSE FROM YOU PISSANTS.

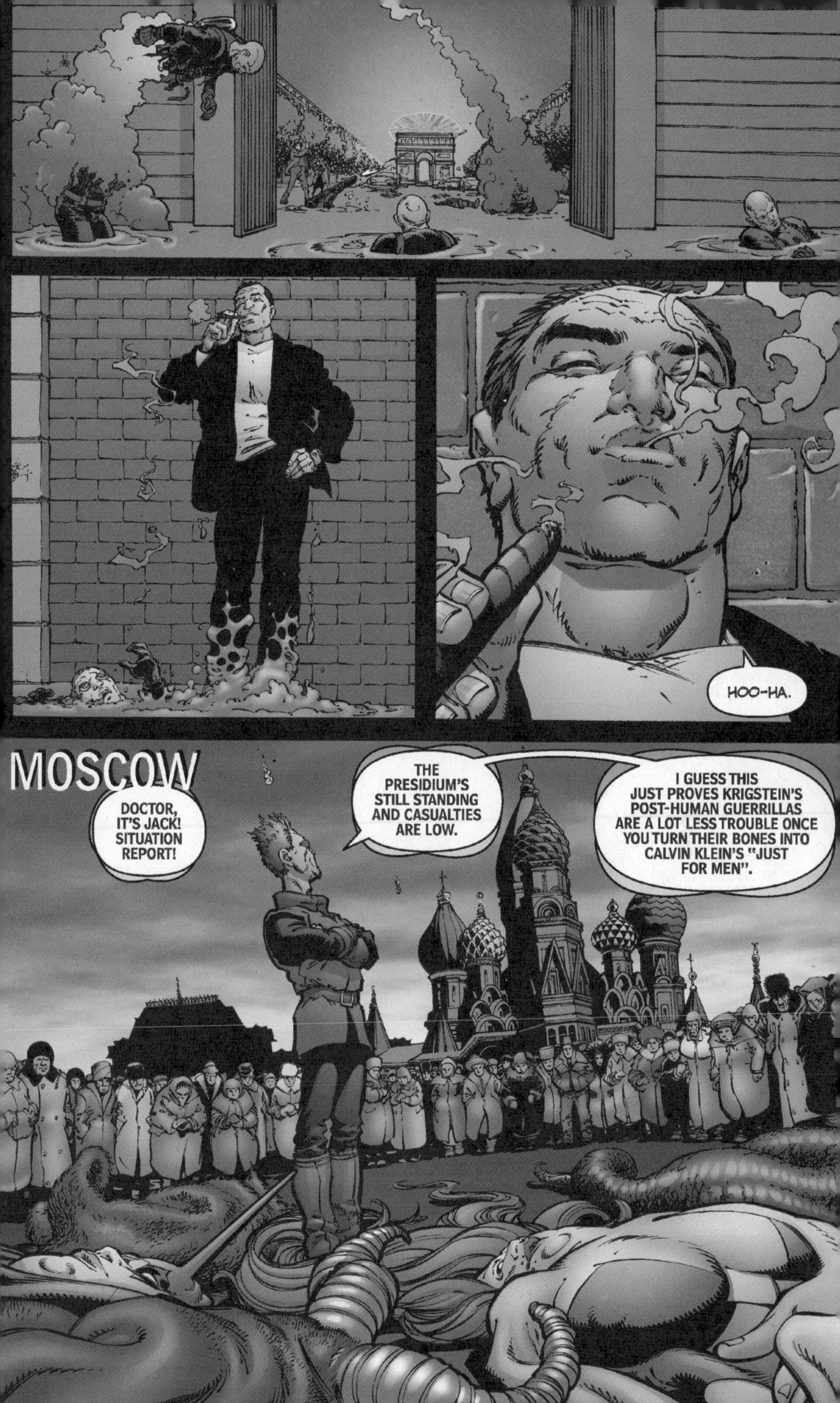
HOO-HA.
MOSCOW
DOCTOR, IT'S JACK! SITUATION REPORT!
THE PRESIDIUM'S STILL STANDING AND CASUALTIES ARE LOW.
I GUESS THIS JUST PROVES KRIGSTEIN'S POST-HUMAN GUERRILLAS ARE A LOT LESS TROUBLE ONCE YOU TURN THEIR BONES INTO CALVIN KLEIN'S "JUST FOR MEN".

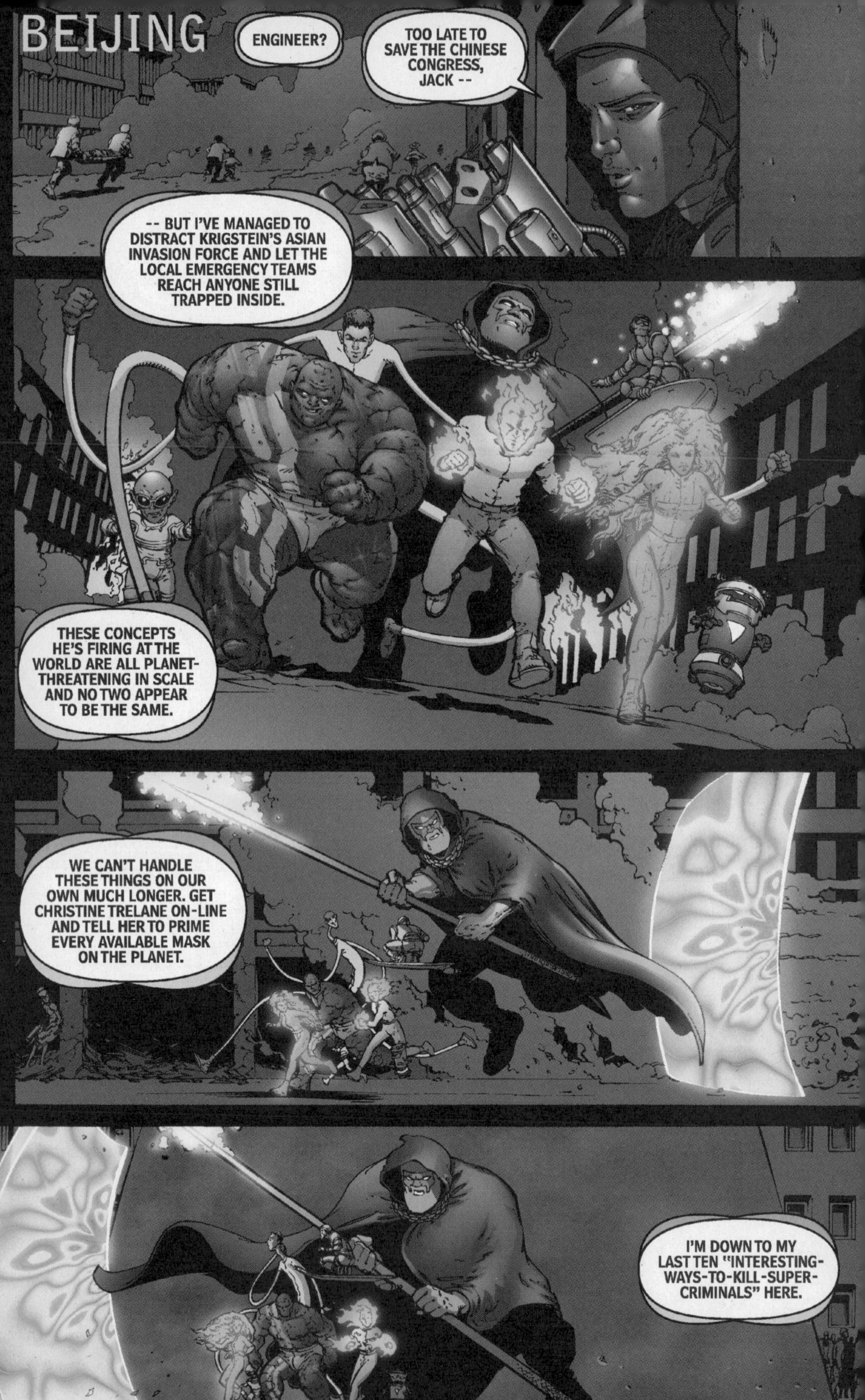
BEIJING
ENGINEER?
TOO LATE TO SAVE THE CHINESE CONGRESS, JACK --
-- BUT I'VE MANAGED TO DISTRACT KRIGSTEIN'S ASIAN INVASION FORCE AND LET THE LOCAL EMERGENCY TEAMS REACH ANYONE STILL TRAPPED INSIDE.
THESE CONCEPTS HE'S FIRING AT THE WORLD ARE ALL PLANET-THREATENING IN SCALE AND NO TWO APPEAR TO BE THE SAME.
WE CAN'T HANDLE THESE THINGS ON OUR OWN MUCH LONGER. GET CHRISTINE TRELANE ON-LINE AND TELL HER TO PRIME EVERY AVAILABLE MASK ON THE PLANET.
I'M DOWN TO MY LAST TEN "INTERESTING-WAYS-TO-KILL-SUPER-CRIMINALS" HERE.

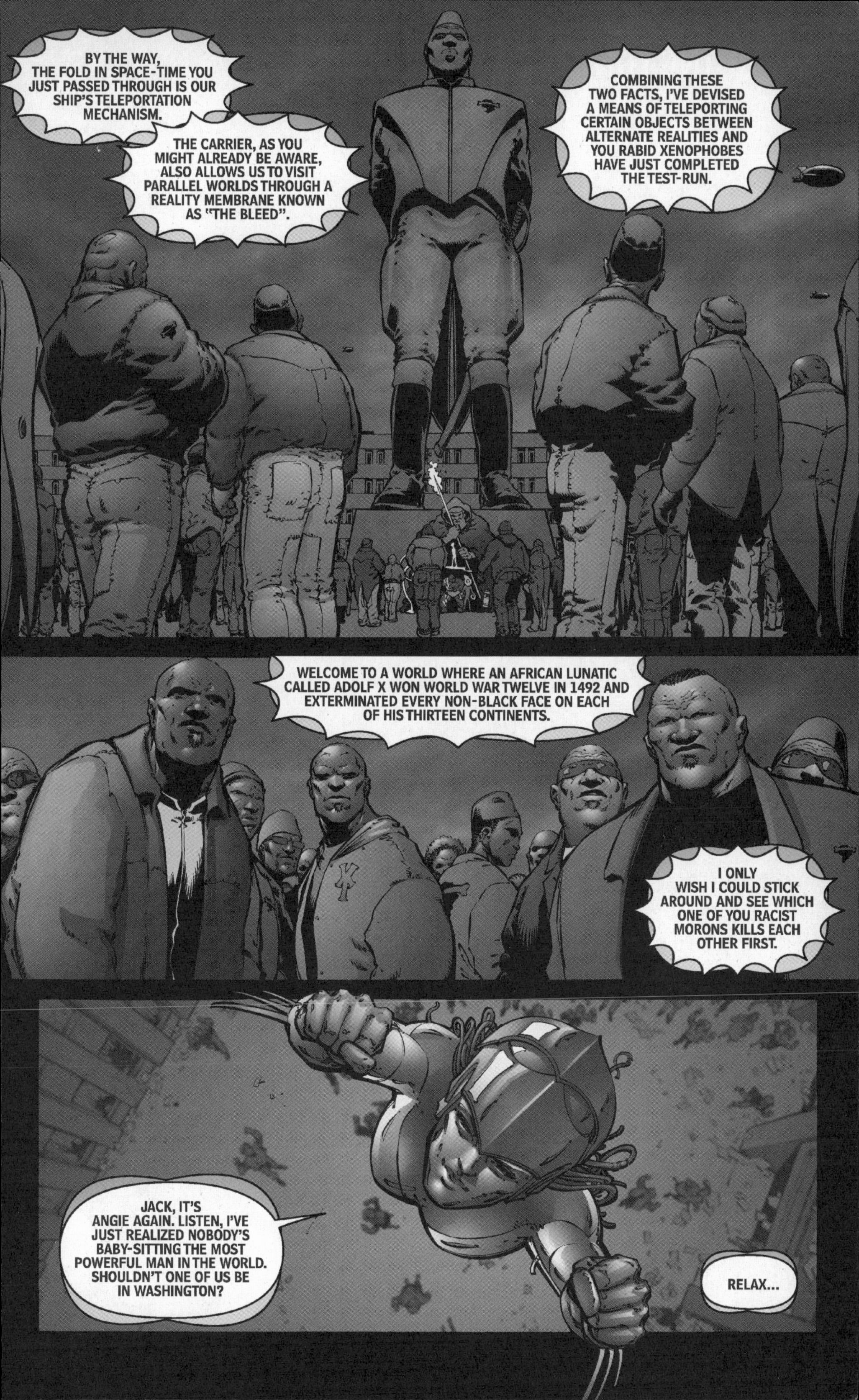
BY THE WAY, THE FOLD IN SPACE-TIME YOU JUST PASSED THROUGH IS OUR SHIP'S TELEPORTATION MECHANISM.
THE CARRIER, AS YOU MIGHT ALREADY BE AWARE, ALSO ALLOWS US TO VISIT PARALLEL WORLDS THROUGH A REALITY MEMBRANE KNOWN AS "THE BLEED".
COMBINING THESE TWO FACTS, I'VE DEVISED A MEANS OF TELEPORTING CERTAIN OBJECTS BETWEEN ALTERNATE REALITIES AND YOU RABID XENOPHOBES HAVE JUST COMPLETED THE TEST-RUN.
WELCOME TO A WORLD WHERE AN AFRICAN LUNATIC CALLED ADOLF X WON WORLD WAR TWELVE IN 1492 AND EXTERMINATED EVERY NON-BLACK FACE ON EACH OF HIS THIRTEEN CONTINENTS.
I ONLY WISH I COULD STICK AROUND AND SEE WHICH ONE OF YOU RACIST MORONS KILLS EACH OTHER FIRST.
JACK, IT'S ANGIE AGAIN. LISTEN, I'VE JUST REALIZED NOBODY'S BABY-SITTING THE MOST POWERFUL MAN IN THE WORLD. SHOULDN'T ONE OF US BE IN WASHINGTON?
RELAX...

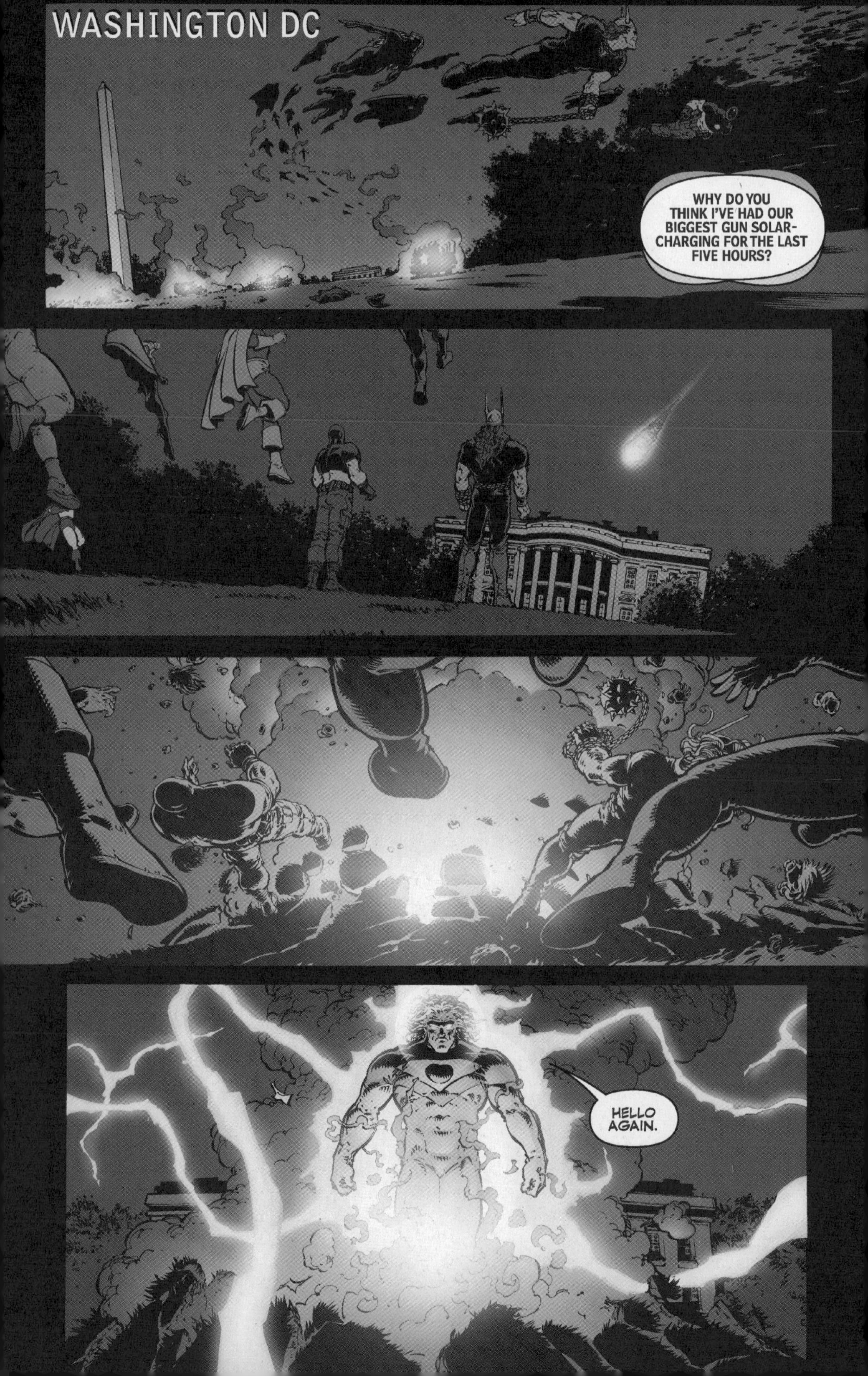
WASHINGTON DC
WHY DO YOU THINK I'VE HAD OUR BIGGEST GUN SOLAR-CHARGING FOR THE LAST FIVE HOURS?
HELLO AGAIN.

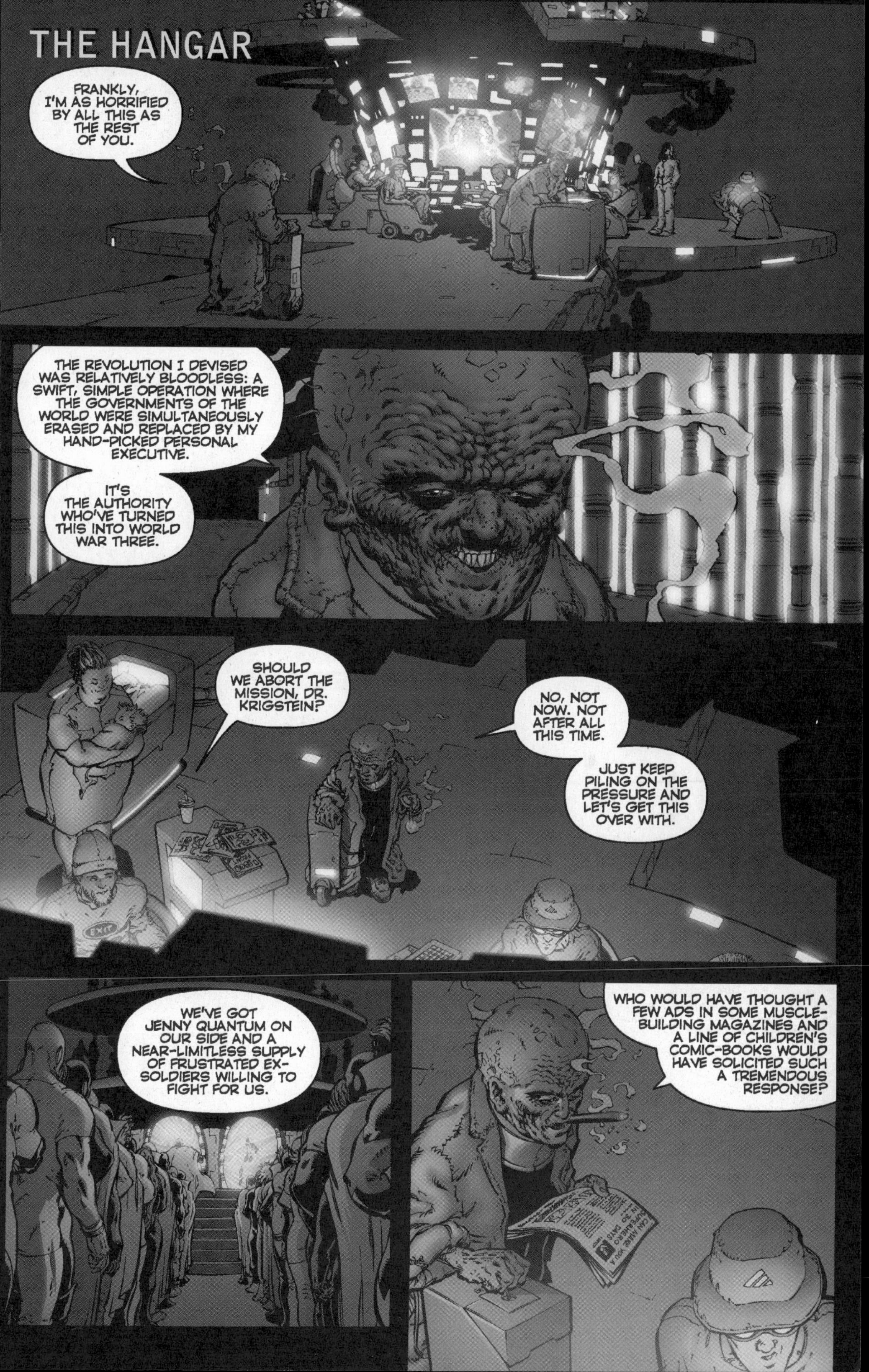
THE HANGAR
FRANKLY, I'M AS HORRIFIED BY ALL THIS AS THE REST OF YOU.
THE REVOLUTION I DEVISED WAS RELATIVELY BLOODLESS: A SWIFT, SIMPLE OPERATION WHERE THE GOVERNMENTS OF THE WORLD WERE SIMULTANEOUSLY ERASED AND REPLACED BY MY HAND-PICKED PERSONAL EXECUTIVE.
IT'S THE AUTHORITY WHO'VE TURNED THIS INTO WORLD WAR THREE.
SHOULD WE ABORT THE MISSION, DR. KRIGSTEIN?
NO, NOT NOW. NOT AFTER ALL THIS TIME.
JUST KEEP PILING ON THE PRESSURE AND LET'S GET THIS OVER WITH.
WE'VE GOT JENNY QUANTUM ON OUR SIDE AND A NEAR-LIMITLESS SUPPLY OF FRUSTRATED EX-SOLDIERS WILLING TO FIGHT FOR US.
WHO WOULD HAVE THOUGHT A FEW ADS IN SOME MUSCLE-BUILDING MAGAZINES AND A LINE OF CHILDREN'S COMIC-BOOKS WOULD HAVE SOLICITED SUCH A TREMENDOUS RESPONSE?

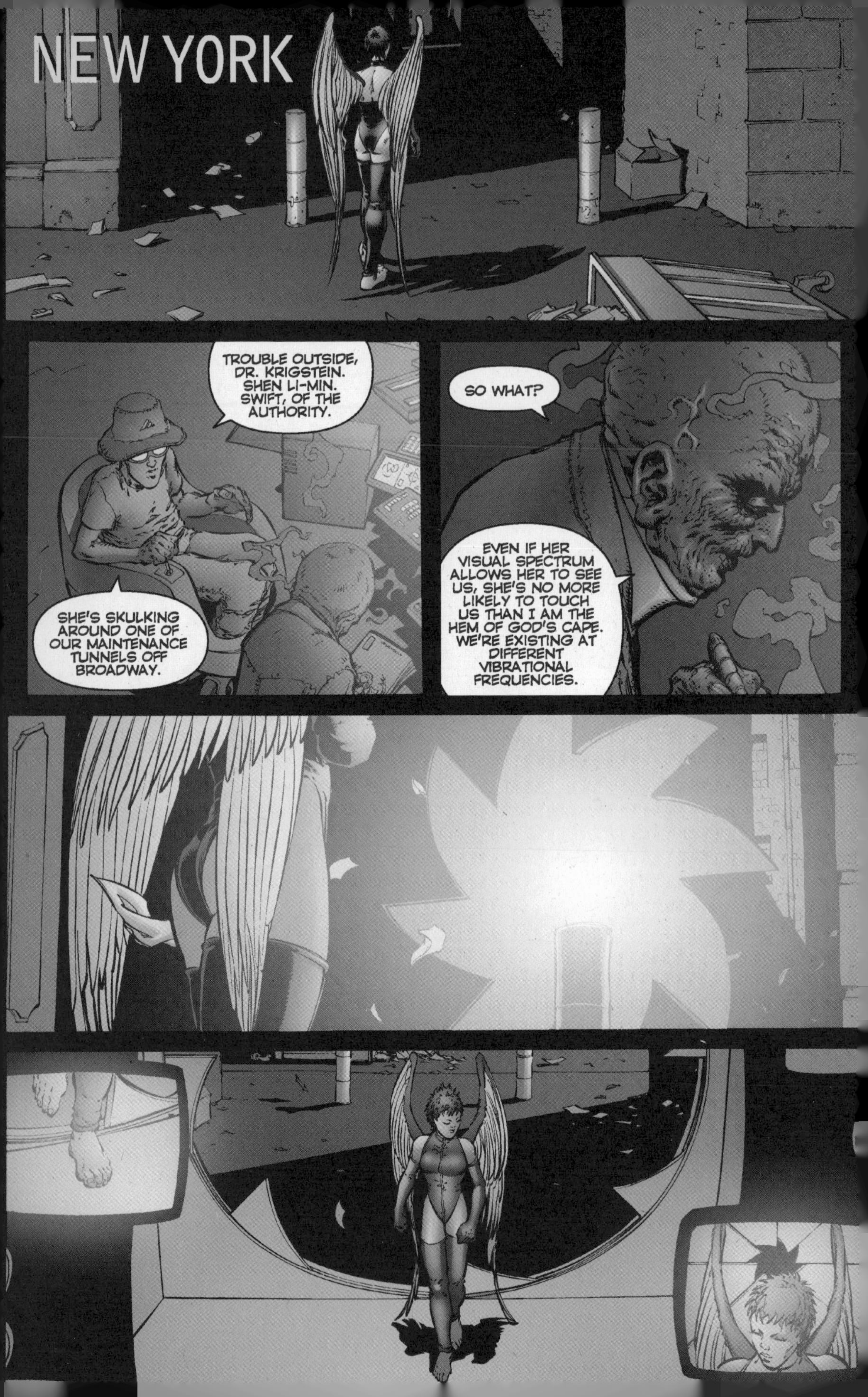
NEW YORK
TROUBLE OUTSIDE, DR. KRIGSTEIN. SHEN LI-MIN. SWIFT, OF THE AUTHORITY.
SHE'S SKULKING AROUND ONE OF OUR MAINTENANCE TUNNELS OFF BROADWAY.
SO WHAT?
EVEN IF HER VISUAL SPECTRUM ALLOWS HER TO SEE US, SHE'S NO MORE LIKELY TO TOUCH US THAN I AM THE HEM OF GOD'S CAPE. WE'RE EXISTING AT DIFFERENT VIBRATIONAL FREQUENCIES.

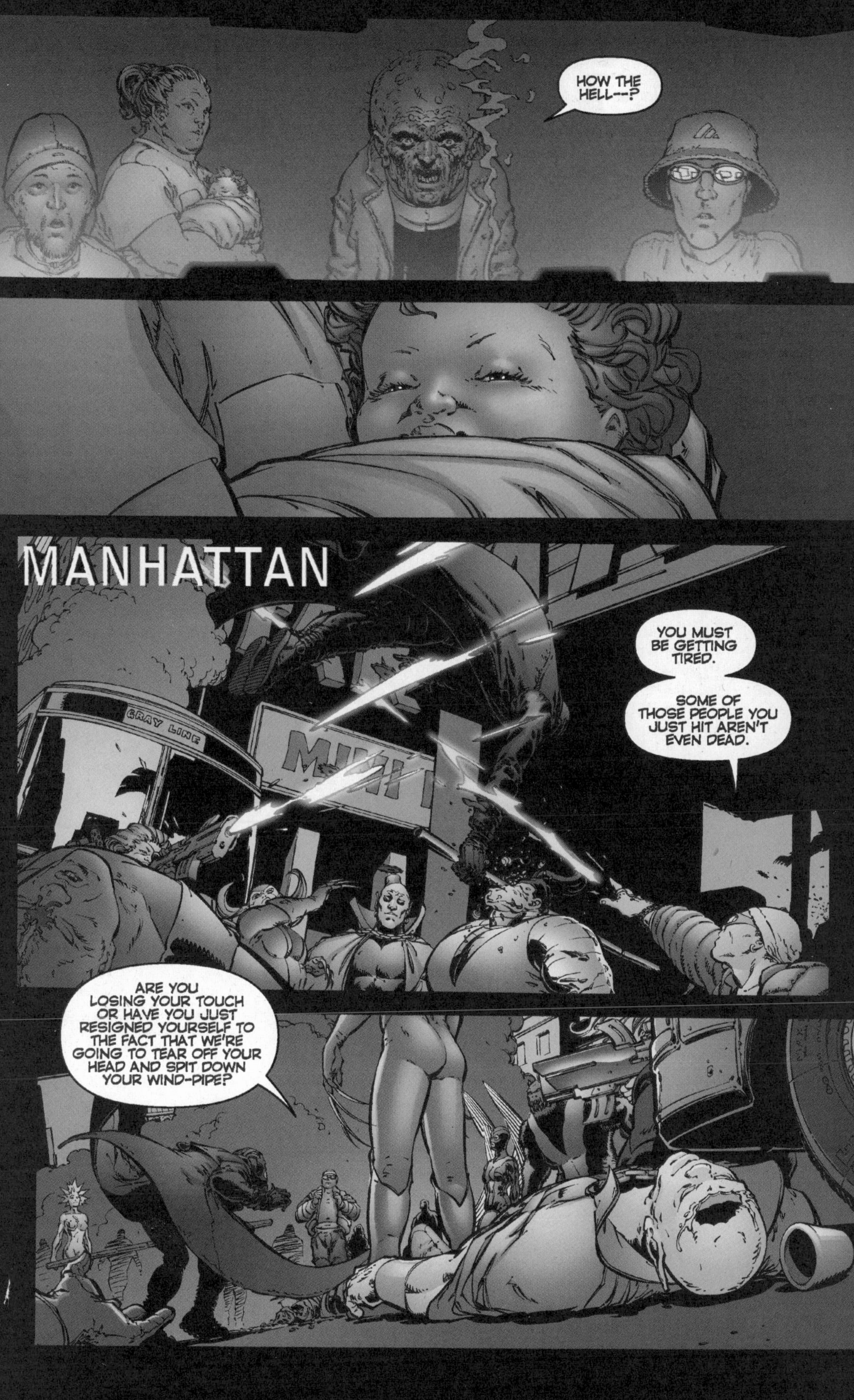
HOW THE HELL--?
MANHATTAN
YOU MUST BE GETTING TIRED.
SOME OF THOSE PEOPLE YOU JUST HIT AREN'T EVEN DEAD.
ARE YOU LOSING YOUR TOUCH OR HAVE YOU JUST RESIGNED YOURSELF TO THE FACT THAT WE'RE GOING TO TEAR OFF YOUR HEAD AND SPIT DOWN YOUR WIND-PIPE?

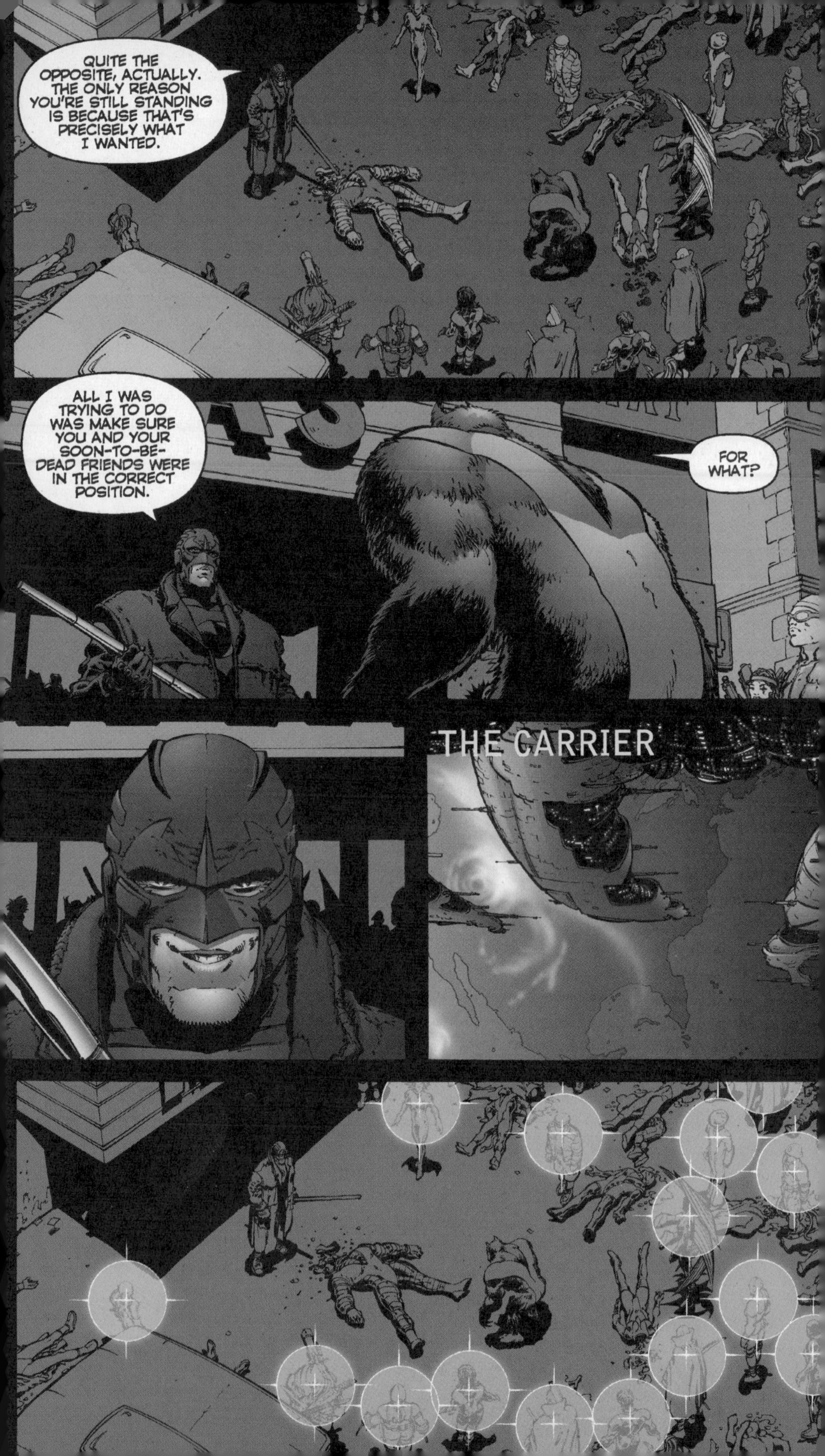
QUITE THE OPPOSITE, ACTUALLY. THE ONLY REASON YOU'RE STILL STANDING IS BECAUSE THAT'S PRECISELY WHAT I WANTED.
ALL I WAS TRYING TO DO WAS MAKE SURE YOU AND YOUR SOON-TO-BE-DEAD FRIENDS WERE IN THE CORRECT POSITION.
FOR WHAT?
THE CARRIER

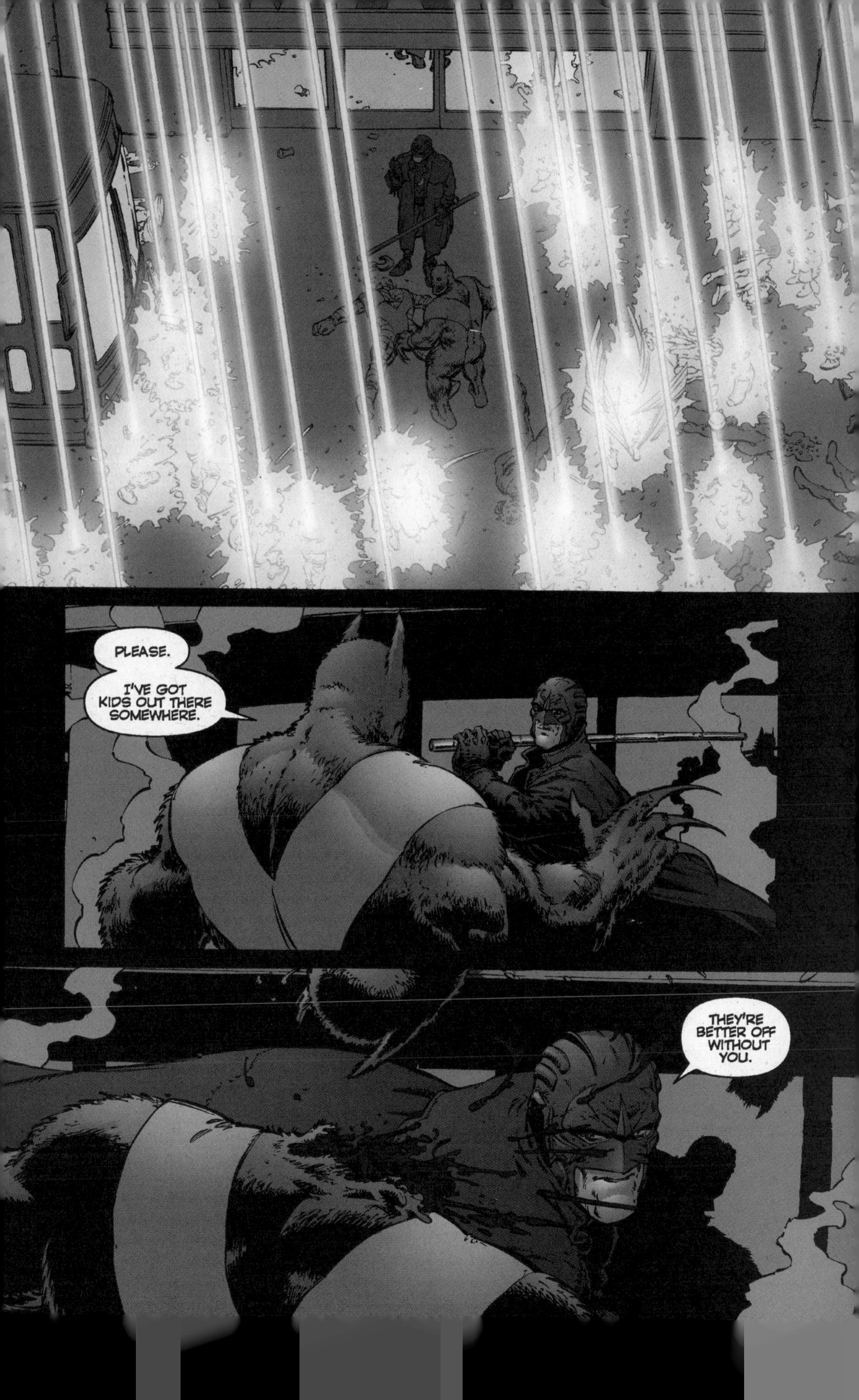
PLEASE.
I'VE GOT KIDS OUT THERE SOMEWHERE.
THEY'RE BETTER OFF WITHOUT YOU.

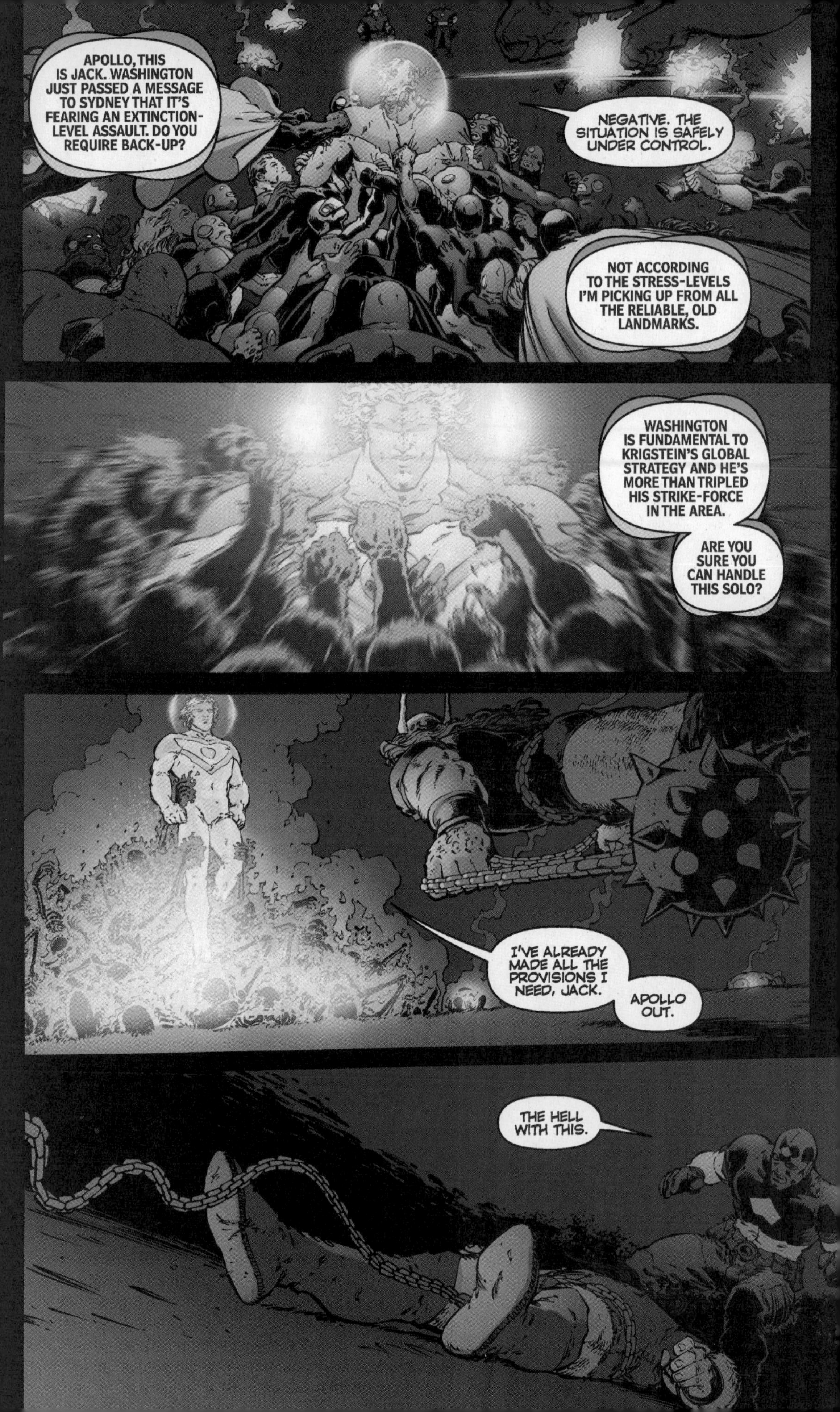
APOLLO, THIS IS JACK. WASHINGTON JUST PASSED A MESSAGE TO SYDNEY THAT IT'S FEARING AN EXTINCTION-LEVEL ASSAULT. DO YOU REQUIRE BACK-UP?
NEGATIVE. THE SITUATION IS SAFELY UNDER CONTROL.
NOT ACCORDING TO THE STRESS-LEVELS I'M PICKING UP FROM ALL THE RELIABLE, OLD LANDMARKS.
WASHINGTON IS FUNDAMENTAL TO KRIGSTEIN'S GLOBAL STRATEGY AND HE'S MORE THAN TRIPLED HIS STRIKE-FORCE IN THE AREA.
ARE YOU SURE YOU CAN HANDLE THIS SOLO?
I'VE ALREADY MADE ALL THE PROVISIONS I NEED, JACK.
APOLLO OUT.
THE HELL WITH THIS.

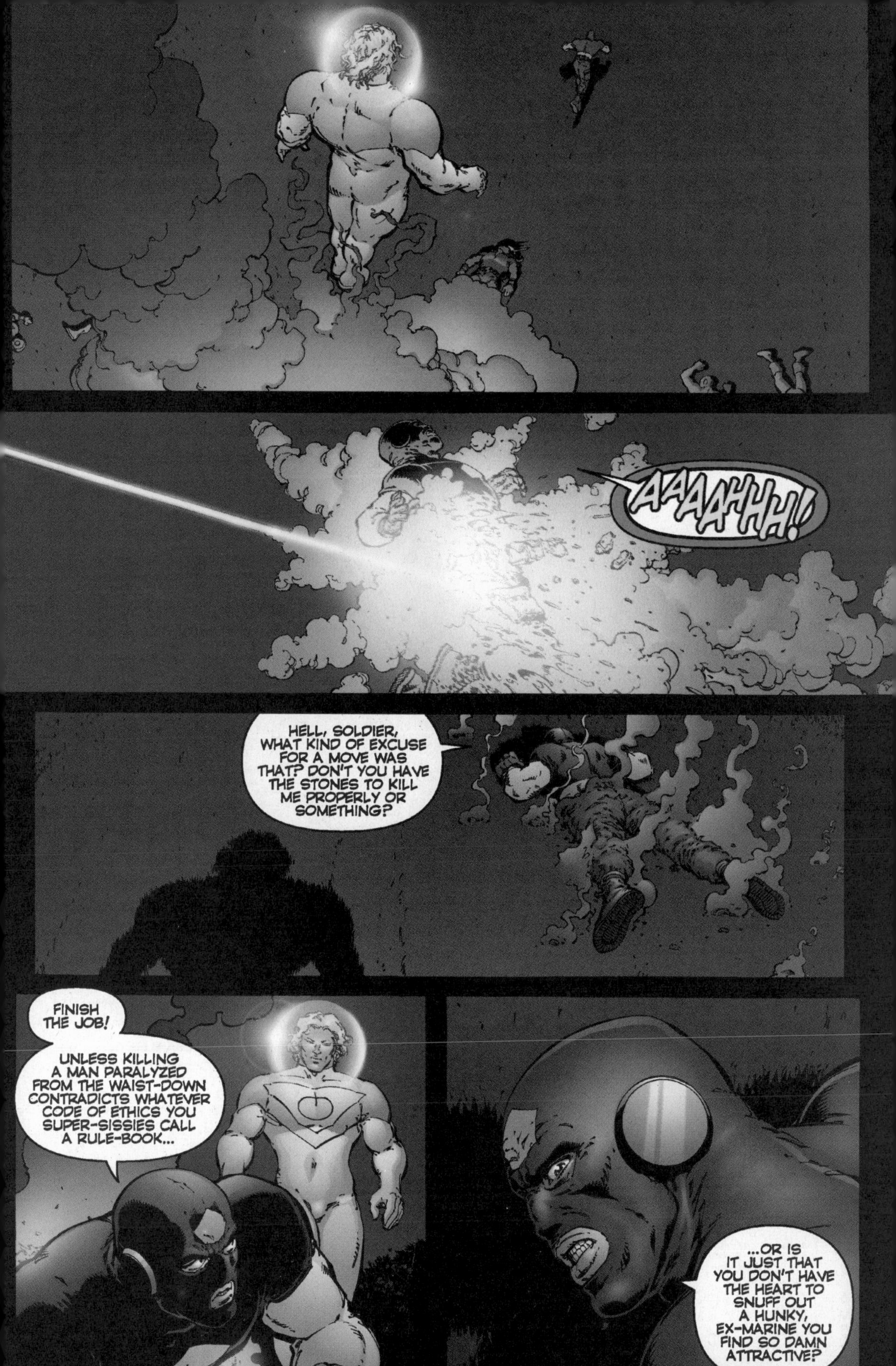
AAAAHHH!
HELL, SOLDIER, WHAT KIND OF EXCUSE FOR A MOVE WAS THAT? DON'T YOU HAVE THE STONES TO KILL ME PROPERLY OR SOMETHING?
FINISH THE JOB!
UNLESS KILLING A MAN PARALYZED FROM THE WAIST-DOWN CONTRADICTS WHATEVER CODE OF ETHICS YOU SUPER-SISSIES CALL A RULE-BOOK...
...OR IS IT JUST THAT YOU DON'T HAVE THE HEART TO SNUFF OUT A HUNKY, EX-MARINE YOU FIND SO DAMN ATTRACTIVE?

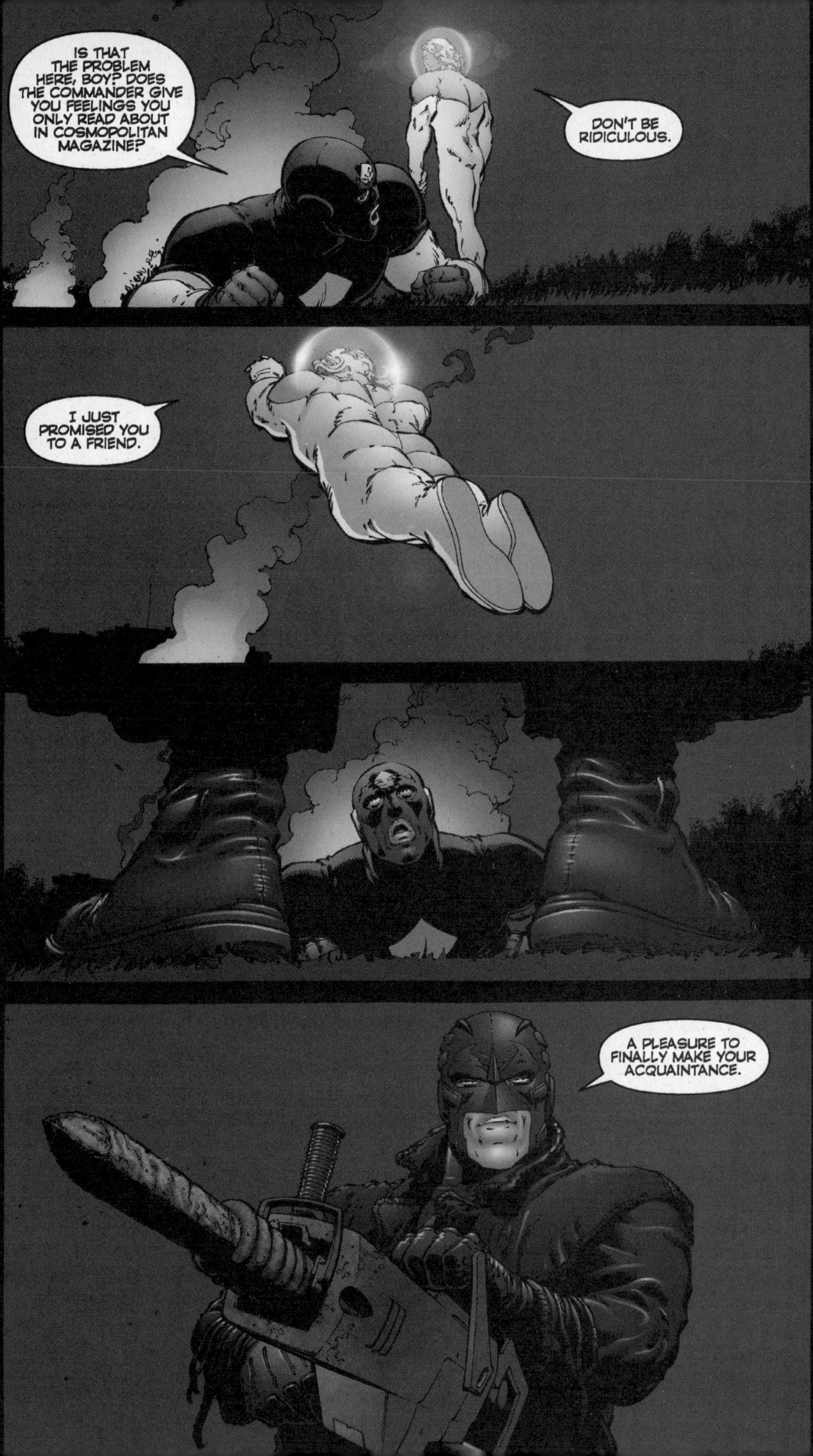
IS THAT THE PROBLEM HERE, BOY? DOES THE COMMANDER GIVE YOU FEELINGS YOU ONLY READ ABOUT IN COSMOPOLITAN MAGAZINE?
DON'T BE RIDICULOUS.
I JUST PROMISED YOU TO A FRIEND.
A PLEASURE TO FINALLY MAKE YOUR ACQUAINTANCE.

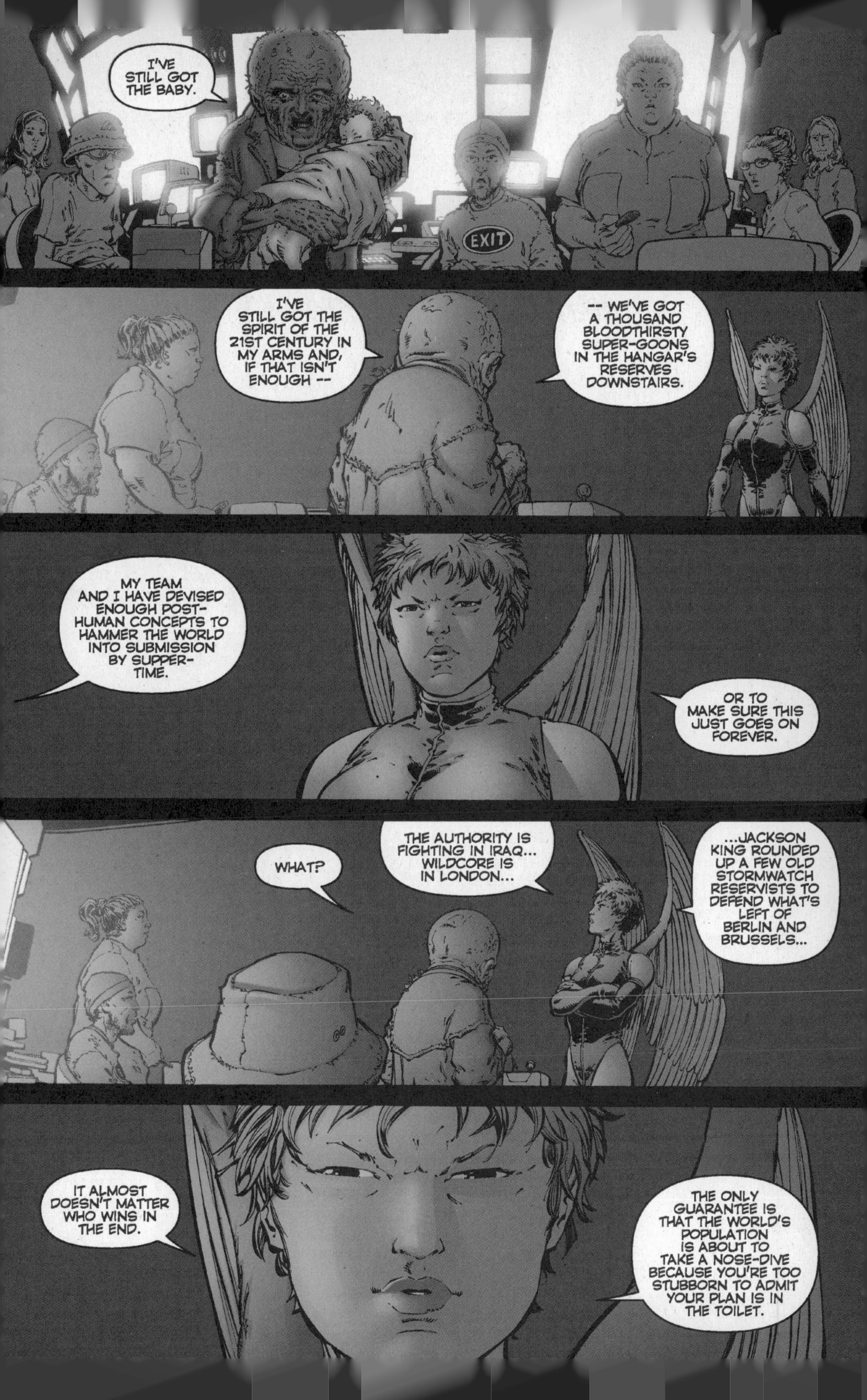
I'VE STILL GOT THE BABY.
I'VE STILL GOT THE SPIRIT OF THE 21ST CENTURY IN MY ARMS AND, IF THAT ISN'T ENOUGH --
-- WE'VE GOT A THOUSAND BLOODTHIRSTY SUPER-GOONS IN THE HANGAR'S RESERVES DOWNSTAIRS.
MY TEAM AND I HAVE DEVISED ENOUGH POST-HUMAN CONCEPTS TO HAMMER THE WORLD INTO SUBMISSION BY SUPPER-TIME.
OR TO MAKE SURE THIS JUST GOES ON FOREVER.
WHAT?
THE AUTHORITY IS FIGHTING IN IRAQ... WILDCORE IS IN LONDON...
...JACKSON KING ROUNDED UP A FEW OLD STORMWATCH RESERVISTS TO DEFEND WHAT'S LEFT OF BERLIN AND BRUSSELS...
IT ALMOST DOESN'T MATTER WHO WINS IN THE END.
THE ONLY GUARANTEE IS THAT THE WORLD'S POPULATION IS ABOUT TO TAKE A NOSE-DIVE BECAUSE YOU'RE TOO STUBBORN TO ADMIT YOUR PLAN IS IN THE TOILET.

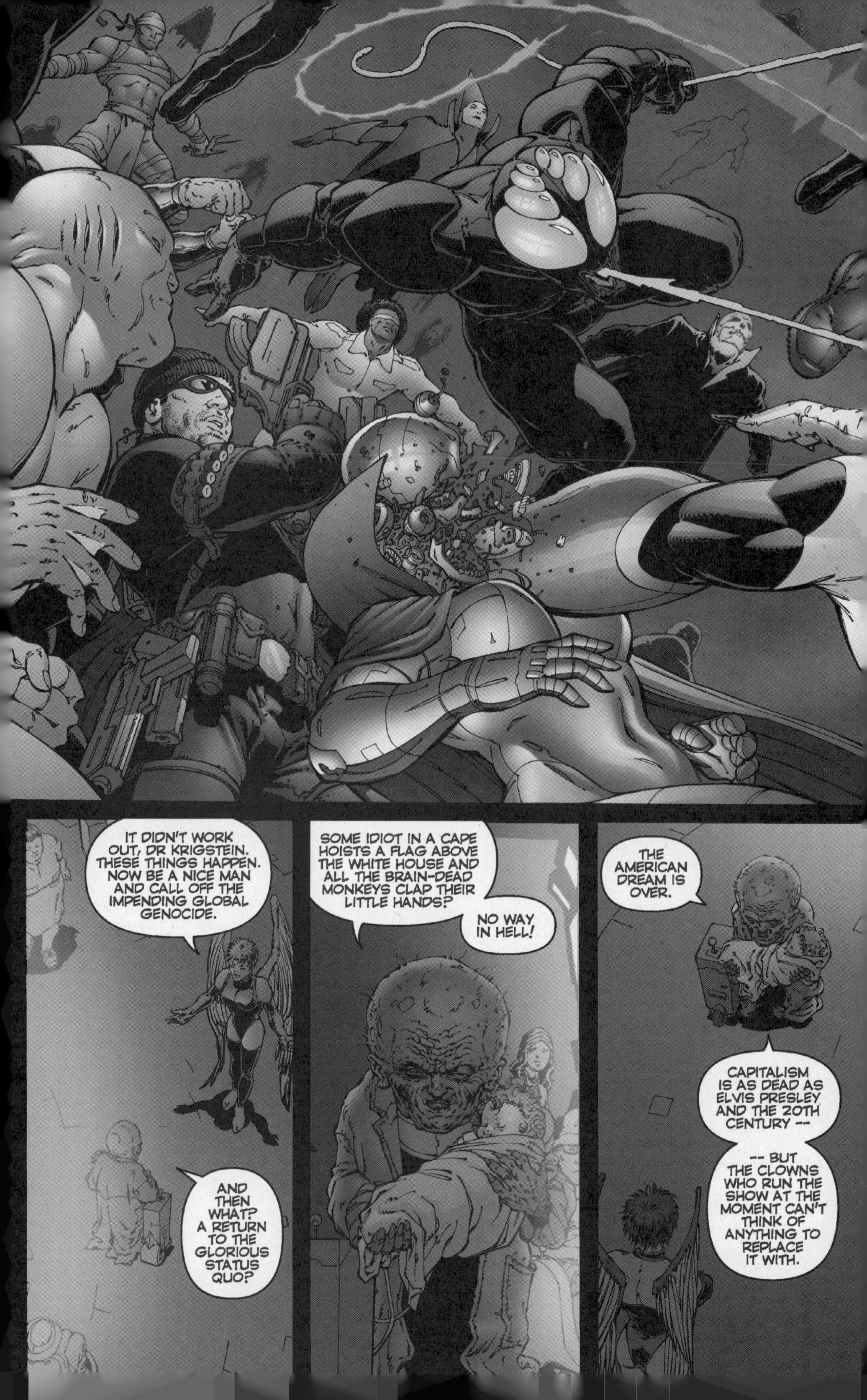
IT DIDN'T WORK OUT, DR KRIGSTEIN. THESE THINGS HAPPEN. NOW BE A NICE MAN AND CALL OFF THE IMPENDING GLOBAL GENOCIDE.
AND THEN WHAT? A RETURN TO THE GLORIOUS STATUS QUO?
SOME IDIOT IN A CAPE HOISTS A FLAG ABOVE THE WHITE HOUSE AND ALL THE BRAIN-DEAD MONKEYS CLAP THEIR LITTLE HANDS?
NO WAY IN HELL!
THE AMERICAN DREAM IS OVER.
CAPITALISM IS AS DEAD AS ELVIS PRESLEY AND THE 20TH CENTURY --
-- BUT THE CLOWNS WHO RUN THE SHOW AT THE MOMENT CAN'T THINK OF ANYTHING TO REPLACE IT WITH.

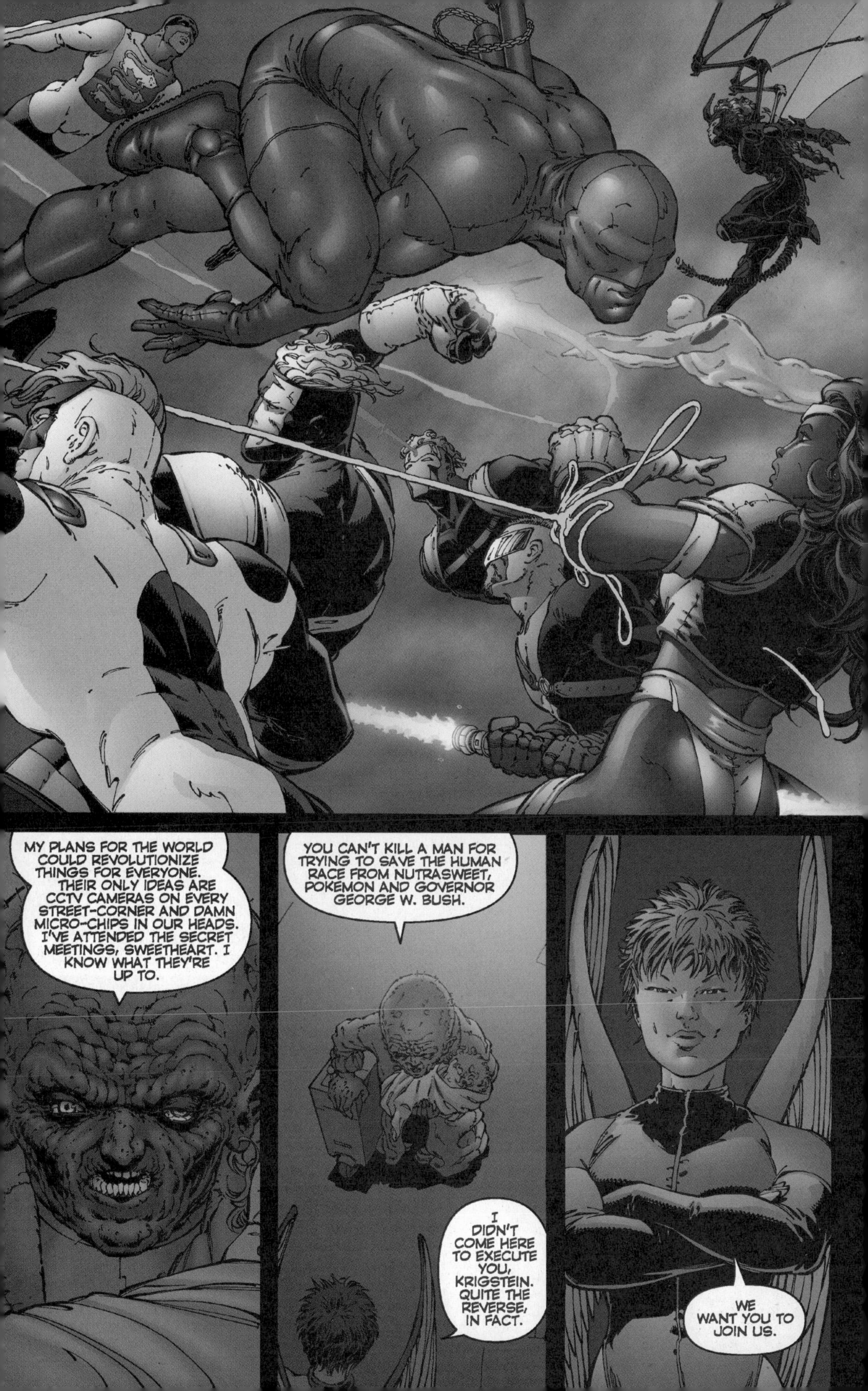
MY PLANS FOR THE WORLD COULD REVOLUTIONIZE THINGS FOR EVERYONE. THEIR ONLY IDEAS ARE CCTV CAMERAS ON EVERY STREET-CORNER AND DAMN MICRO-CHIPS IN OUR HEADS. I'VE ATTENDED THE SECRET MEETINGS, SWEETHEART. I KNOW WHAT THEY'RE UP TO.
YOU CAN'T KILL A MAN FOR TRYING TO SAVE THE HUMAN RACE FROM NUTRASWEET, POKEMON AND GOVERNOR GEORGE W. BUSH.
I DIDN'T COME HERE TO EXECUTE YOU, KRIGSTEIN. QUITE THE REVERSE, IN FACT.
WE WANT YOU TO JOIN US.

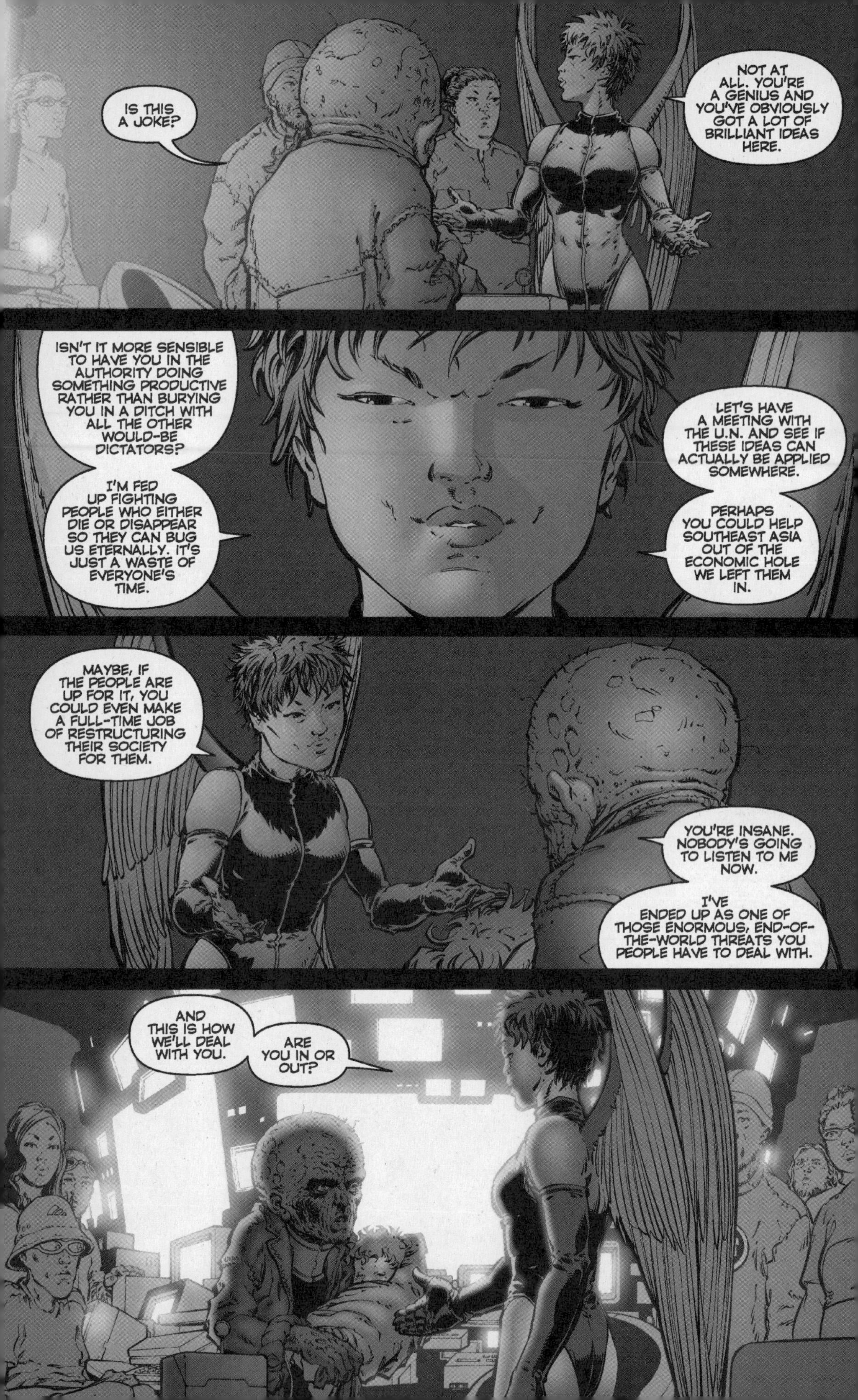
IS THIS A JOKE?
NOT AT ALL. YOU'RE A GENIUS AND YOU'VE OBVIOUSLY GOT A LOT OF BRILLIANT IDEAS HERE.
ISN'T IT MORE SENSIBLE TO HAVE YOU IN THE AUTHORITY DOING SOMETHING PRODUCTIVE RATHER THAN BURYING YOU IN A DITCH WITH ALL THE OTHER WOULD-BE DICTATORS?
I'M FED UP FIGHTING PEOPLE WHO EITHER DIE OR DISAPPEAR SO THEY CAN BUG US ETERNALLY. IT'S JUST A WASTE OF EVERYONE'S TIME.
LET'S HAVE A MEETING WITH THE U.N. AND SEE IF THESE IDEAS CAN ACTUALLY BE APPLIED SOMEWHERE.
PERHAPS YOU COULD HELP SOUTHEAST ASIA OUT OF THE ECONOMIC HOLE WE LEFT THEM IN.
MAYBE, IF THE PEOPLE ARE UP FOR IT, YOU COULD EVEN MAKE A FULL-TIME JOB OF RESTRUCTURING THEIR SOCIETY FOR THEM.
YOU'RE INSANE. NOBODY'S GOING TO LISTEN TO ME NOW.
I'VE ENDED UP AS ONE OF THOSE ENORMOUS, END-OF-THE-WORLD THREATS YOU PEOPLE HAVE TO DEAL WITH.
AND THIS IS HOW WE'LL DEAL WITH YOU.
ARE YOU IN OR OUT?

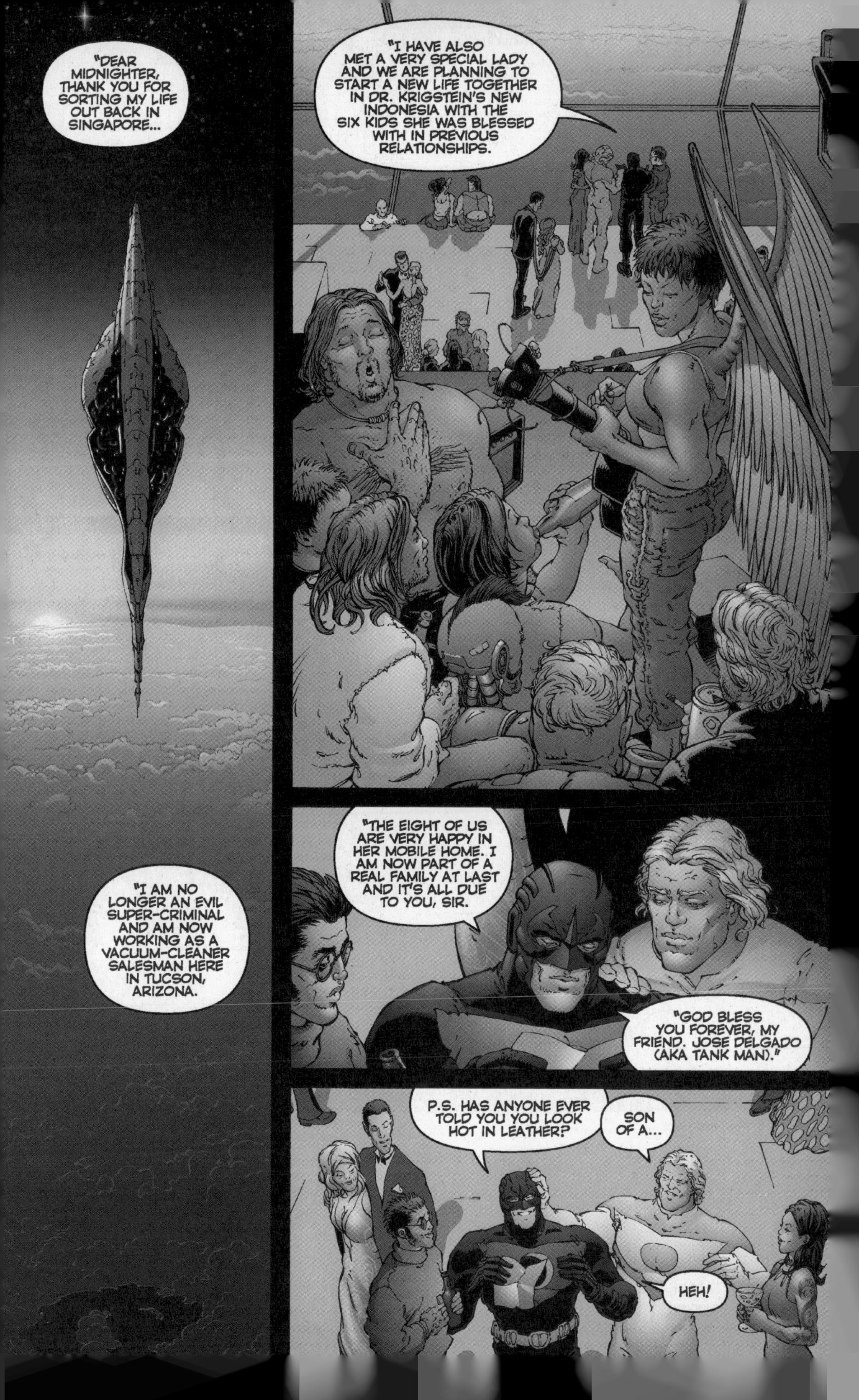
"DEAR MIDNIGHTER, THANK YOU FOR SORTING MY LIFE OUT BACK IN SINGAPORE...
"I HAVE ALSO MET A VERY SPECIAL LADY AND WE ARE PLANNING TO START A NEW LIFE TOGETHER IN DR. KRIGSTEIN'S NEW INDONESIA WITH THE SIX KIDS SHE WAS BLESSED WITH IN PREVIOUS RELATIONSHIPS.
"I AM NO LONGER AN EVIL SUPER-CRIMINAL AND AM NOW WORKING AS A VACUUM-CLEANER SALESMAN HERE IN TUCSON, ARIZONA.
"THE EIGHT OF US ARE VERY HAPPY IN HER MOBILE HOME. I AM NOW PART OF A REAL FAMILY AT LAST AND IT'S ALL DUE TO YOU, SIR.
"GOD BLESS YOU FOREVER, MY FRIEND. JOSE DELGADO (AKA TANK MAN)."
P.S. HAS ANYONE EVER TOLD YOU YOU LOOK HOT IN LEATHER?
SON OF A...
HEH!

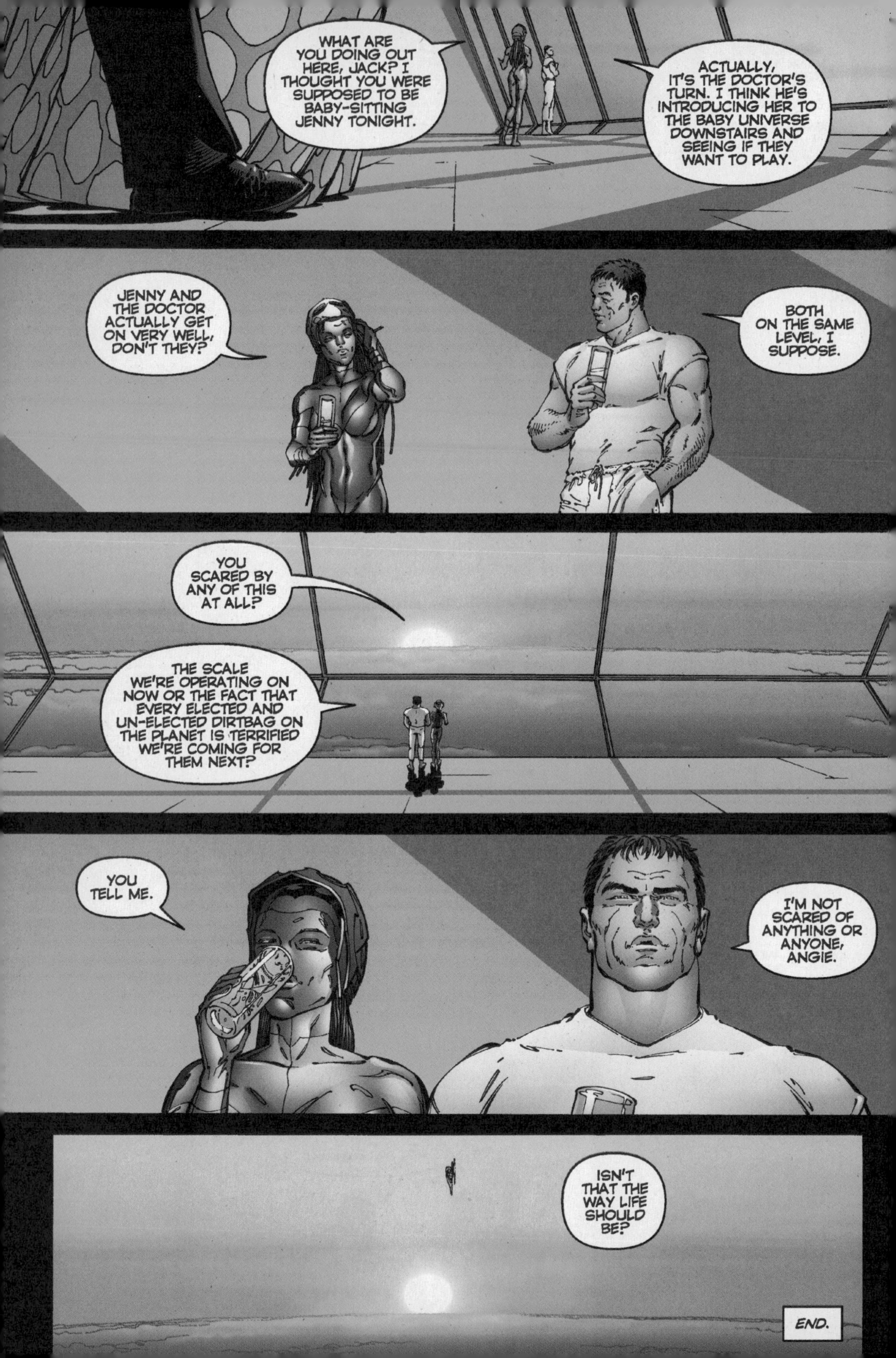
WHAT ARE YOU DOING OUT HERE, JACK? I THOUGHT YOU WERE SUPPOSED TO BE BABY-SITTING JENNY TONIGHT.
ACTUALLY, IT'S THE DOCTOR'S TURN. I THINK HE'S INTRODUCING HER TO THE BABY UNIVERSE DOWNSTAIRS AND SEEING IF THEY WANT TO PLAY.
JENNY AND THE DOCTOR ACTUALLY GET ON VERY WELL, DON'T THEY?
BOTH ON THE SAME LEVEL, I SUPPOSE.
YOU SCARED BY ANY OF THIS AT ALL?
THE SCALE WE'RE OPERATING ON NOW OR THE FACT THAT EVERY ELECTED AND UN-ELECTED DIRTBAG ON THE PLANET IS TERRIFIED WE'RE COMING FOR THEM NEXT?
YOU TELL ME.
I'M NOT SCARED OF ANYTHING OR ANYONE, ANGIE.
ISN'T THAT THE WAY LIFE SHOULD BE?
END.

GALLERY

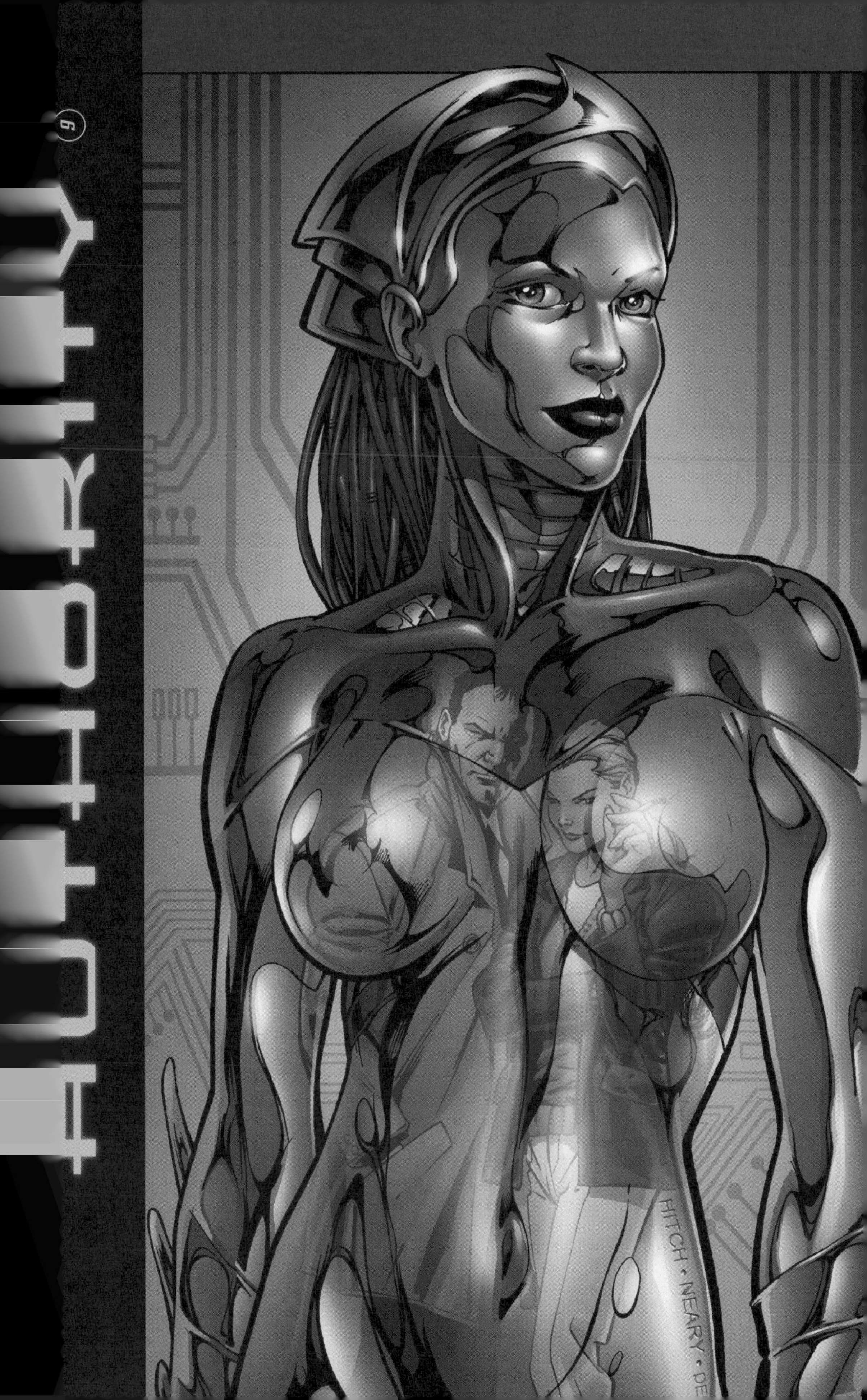
9
HITCH • NEARY • DE

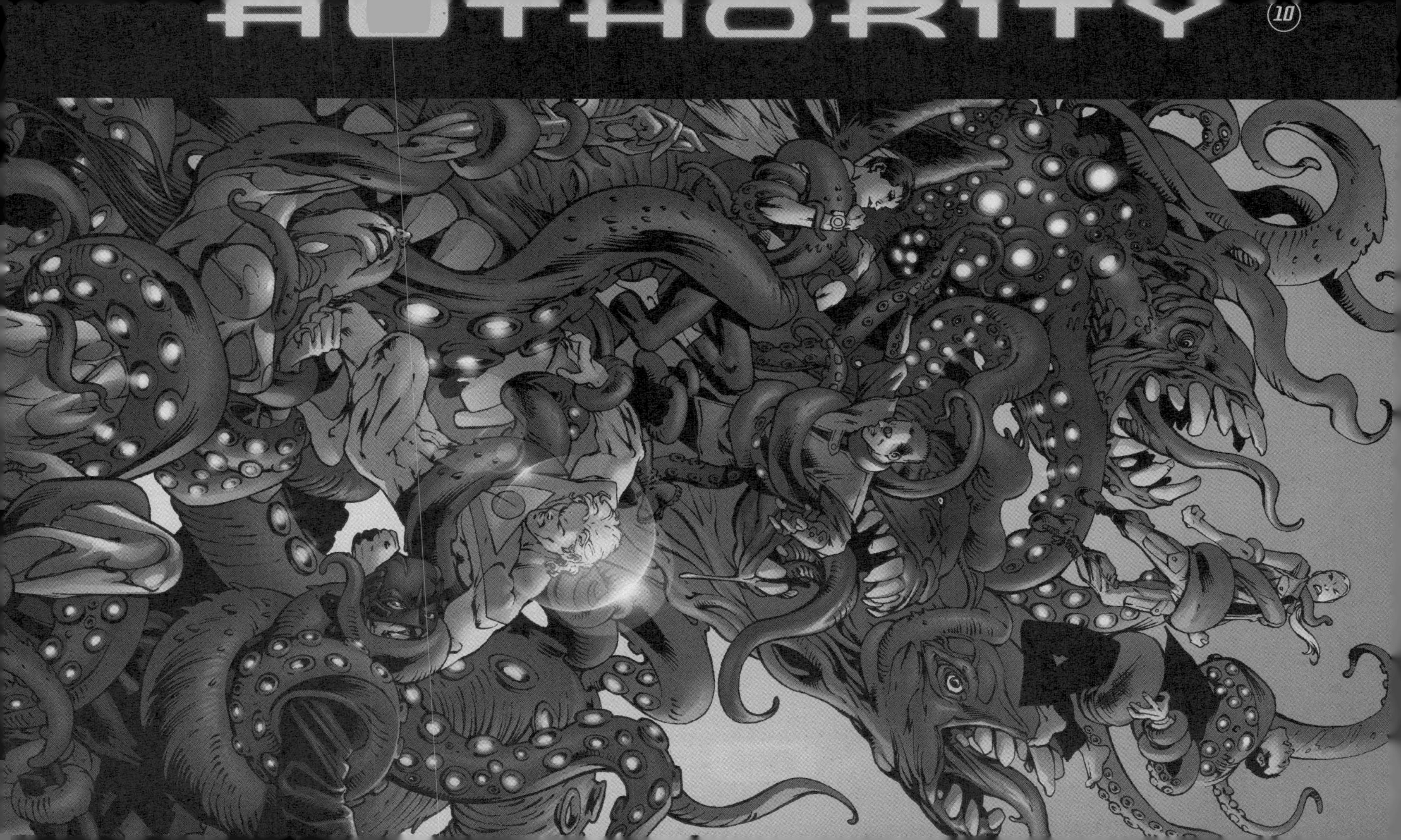
AUTHORITY
10

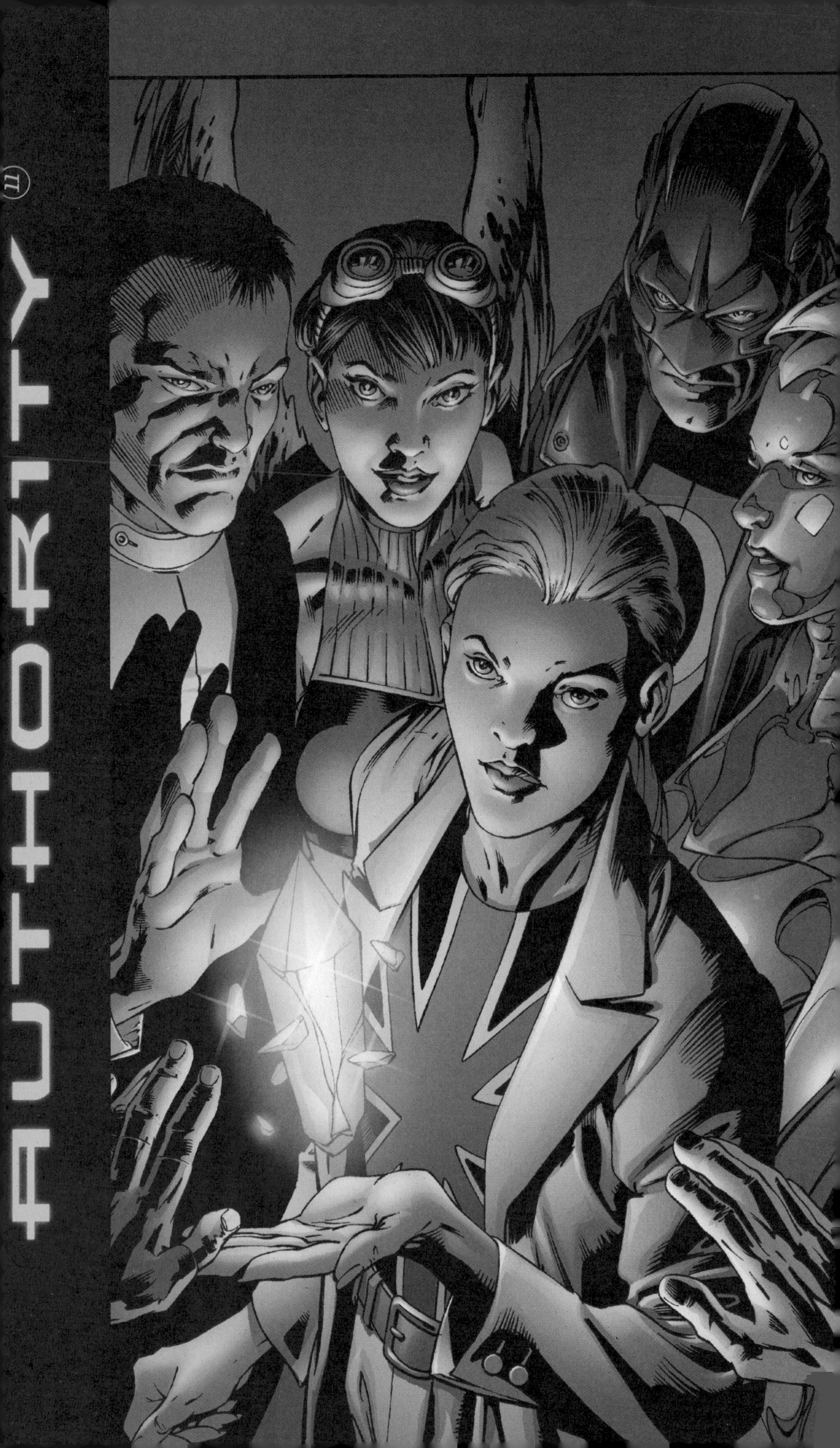
AUTHORITY
11

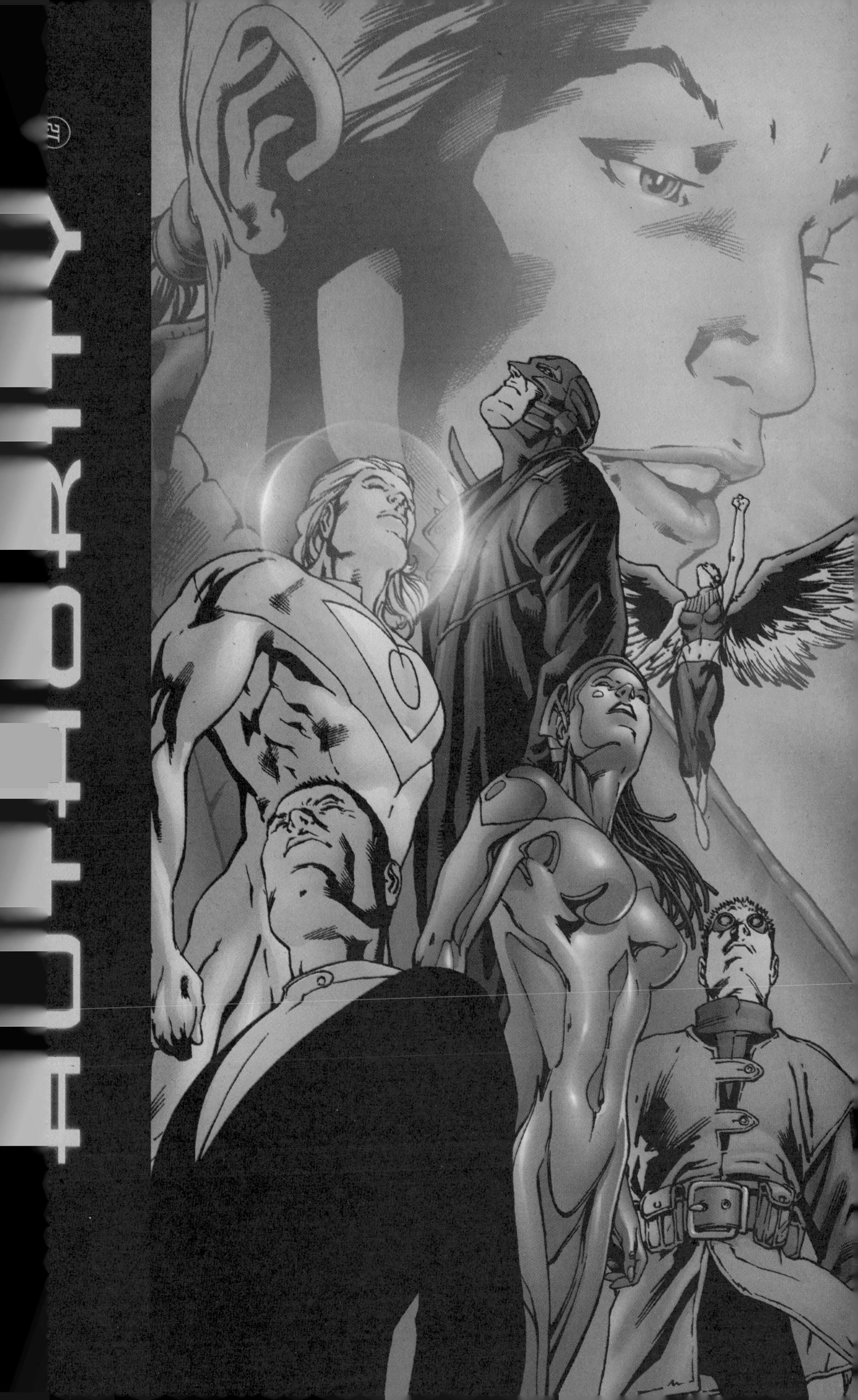
AUTHORITY

AUTHORITY 13

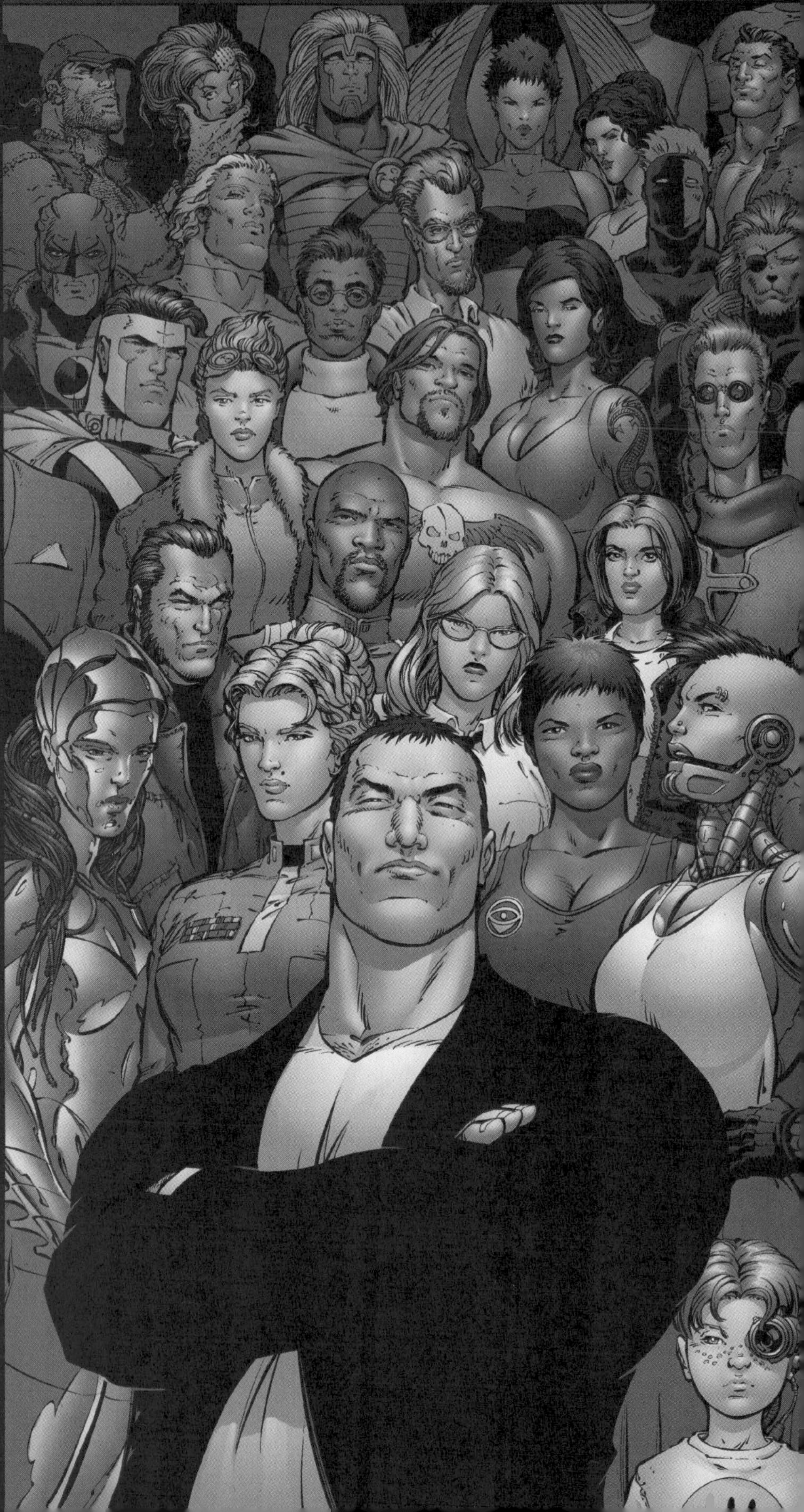

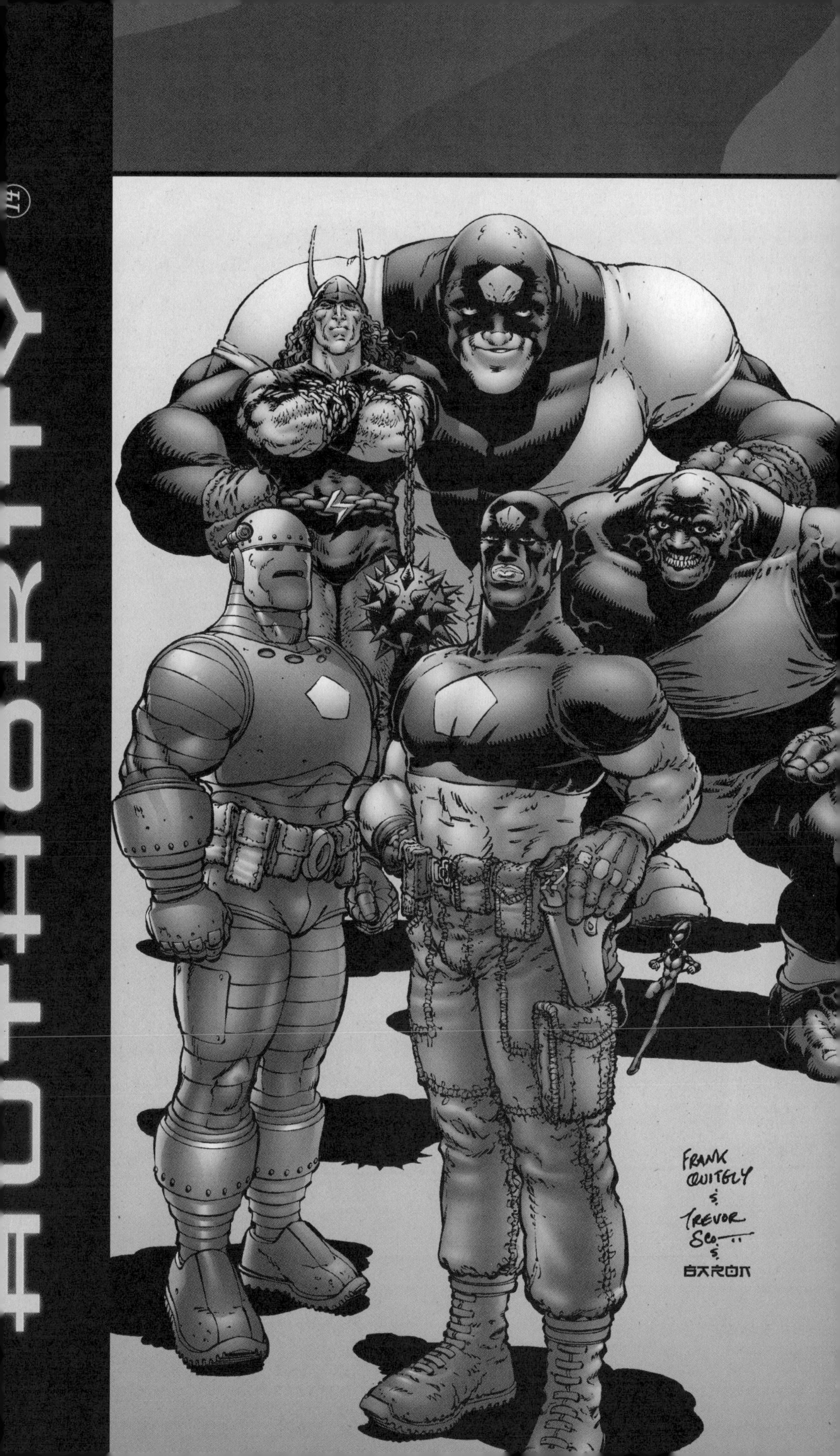
AUTHORITY
FRANK QUITELY
TREVOR
BARON

AUTHORITY 15

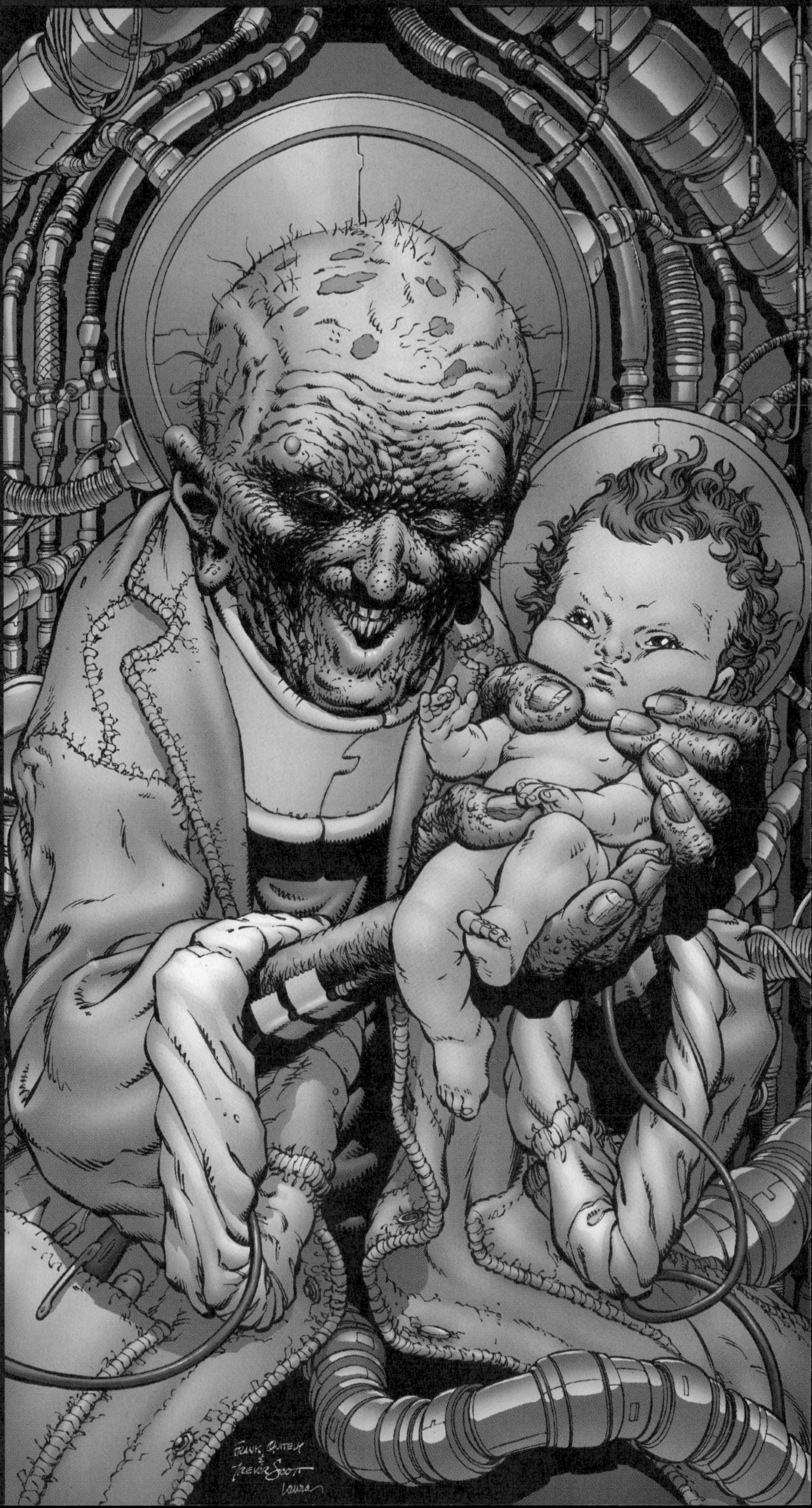

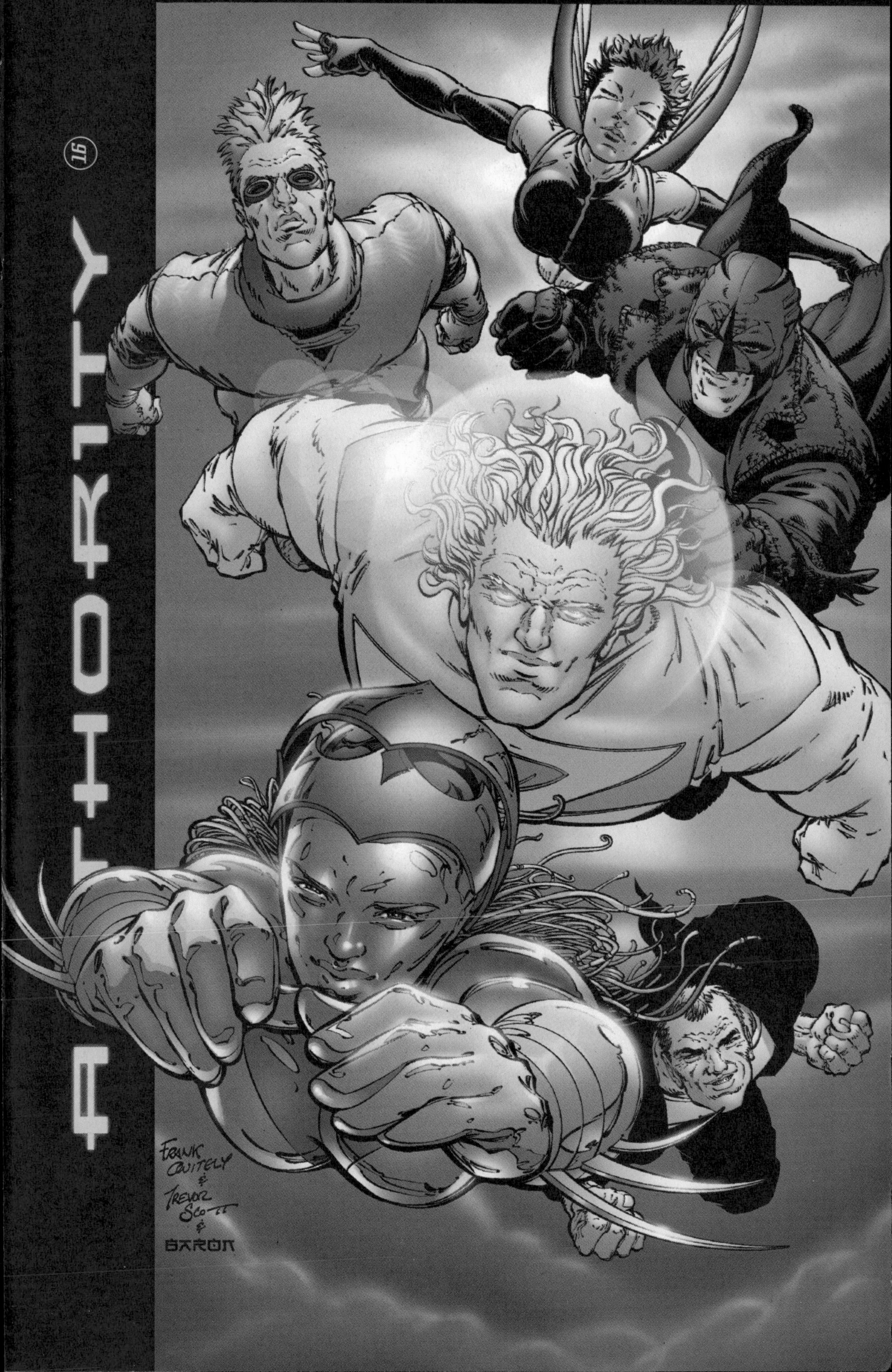
AUTHORITY
16
FRANK QUITELY
&
TREVOR SCOTT
&
BARON

JENETTE KAHN, President & Editor-in-Chief ▪ PAUL LEVITZ, Executive VP & Publisher ▪ JIM LEE, Editorial Director - WildStorm ▪
JOHN NEE, VP & General Manager - WildStorm ▪ SCOTT DUNBIER, Group Editor ▪ RICHARD BRUNING, VP - Creative Director ▪
PATRICK CALDON, Senior VP - Finance and Operations ▪ DOROTHY CROUCH, VP - Licensed Publishing ▪ TERRI CUNNINGHAM, VP - Managing Editor ▪
JOEL EHRLICH, Senior VP - Advertising & Promotions ▪ ALISON GILL, Executive Director - Manufacturing ▪ LILLIAN LASERSON, VP & General Counsel ▪
CHERYL RUBIN, VP - Licensing & Merchandising ▪ BOB WAYNE, VP - Direct Sales